THE GREAT SPORTS QUESTION & ANSWER BOOK

Written by
Michael J. Pellowski

Illustrated by
Steven Duquette

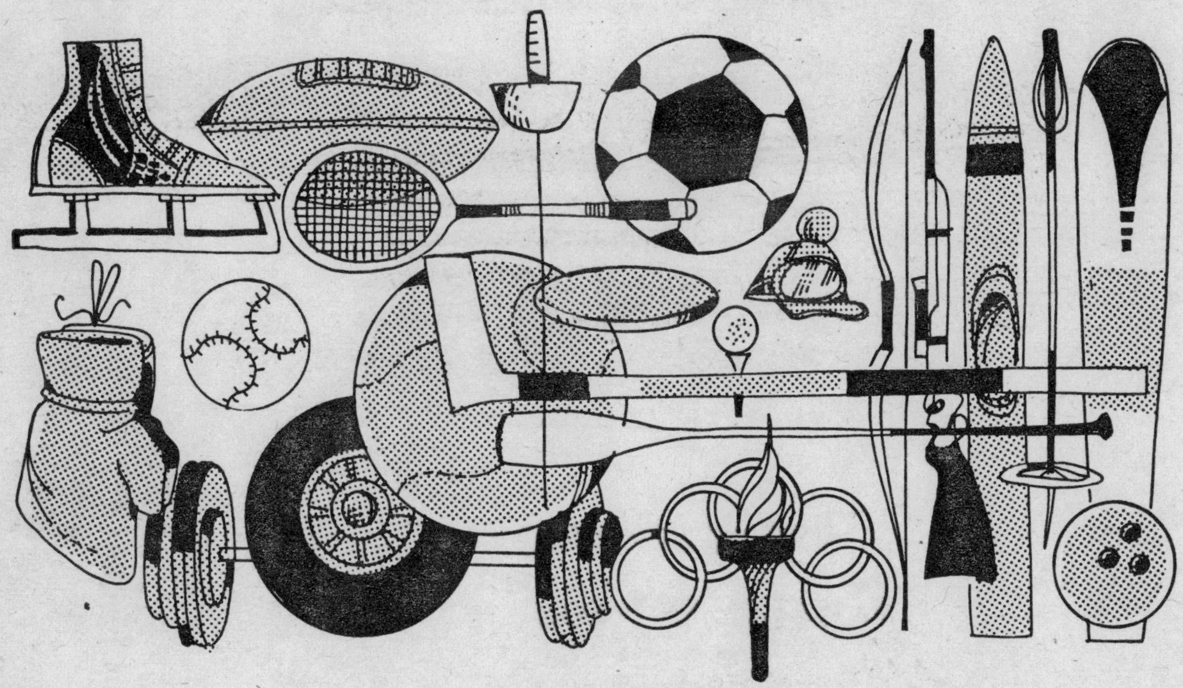

Edited by
Malvina G. Vogel

PLAYMORE, INC. Publishers
Under arrangement with I. WALDMAN AND SON, INC.
New York, New York

MOBY BOOKS is a trademark of
I. Waldman & Son, Inc.
18 East 41st Street, New York, New York 10017

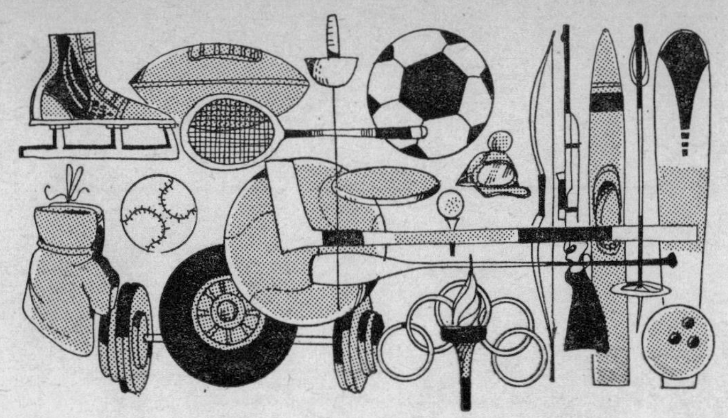

CONTENTS

82
58
25

FOOTBALL

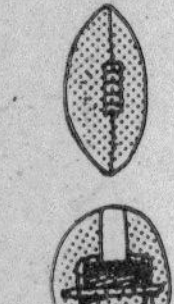

Which is the oldest of these Bowl games — the Sugar Bowl, the Rose Bowl, the Orange Bowl, or the Cotton Bowl?

Pasadena, California, had its first Rose Bowl in 1902, and it wasn't until thirty-one years later, in 1933, that Miami, Florida's, Orange Bowl was played. The first Sugar Bowl contest was held in 1935 in New Orleans, Louisiana, and Dallas, Texas', Cotton Bowl had its first game in 1937.

In what year was the Heisman Trophy awarded for the first time?

The first time the Downtown Athletic Club of New York awarded the Heisman Trophy was in 1935. The winner was Jay Berwanger, a back for the University of Chicago.

Only four professional football teams have won the Super Bowl more than once. Can you name those four teams?

If you said the Green Bay Packers, the Pittsburgh Steelers, the Miami Dolphins, and the Dallas Cowboys, you were correct. They all won the Super Bowl twice — Green Bay in the 1966-67 and 1967-68 seasons, Pittsburgh in the 1974-75 and 1975-76 seasons, Miami in the 1972-73 and 1973-74 seasons, and Dallas in the 1971-72 and 1977-78 seasons.

How many teams were members of the NFL in 1977?

In 1977, there were 14 teams in the American Football Conference and 14 teams in the National Football Conference, for a total of 28 teams in the National Football League.

Which man holds the NFL lifetime record for the most passes caught? Is it Drew Pearson, Kyle Rote, or Charlie Taylor?

Charlie Taylor of the Washington Redskins made 649 catches between 1964 and 1977, making him the record holder.

True or false? The Washington Redskins have never played in the Super Bowl.

False. The Redskins played in Super Bowl VII in 1973 and lost to the Miami Dolphins, 14 to 7.

Who was the first football player from Navy to win the Heisman Trophy?

Joe Bellino, a back for the U.S. Naval Academy, became the first Heisman Trophy winner for Navy in 1960.

When is the Orange Bowl game played?

The Orange Bowl game is always played on January 1, New Year's Day, in Miami, Florida.

Which college football team won the National Championship in 1973?

Unbeaten and untied Alabama was declared the National Champion in 1973.

Where is pro football's Hall of Fame located?

The National Professional Football Hall of Fame is in Canton, Ohio, the home city of one of football's first pro teams. Established in 1962, the Hall of Fame honors outstanding pro players. Its museum displays equipment worn by famous players and used in famous games.

True or false? No Heisman Trophy winner has ever been inducted into the pro football Hall of Fame.

True. As of 1978, not one Heisman Trophy winner has been voted into the National Profesional Football Hall of Fame.

The Oakland Raiders won Super Bowl XI in 1977. Who did they beat?

The Raiders beat the Minnesota Vikings by the score of 32 to 14.

True or false? The 1971 Heisman Trophy winner, Pat Sullivan, played quarterback for Texas Christian University.

False. Pat Sullivan quarterbacked the Auburn team that year.

Defensive lineman Ed Jones of the Dallas Cowboys has an interesting nickname. Can you guess it?

Because of his size, Ed has been nicknamed "Too Tall" Jones. He is 6'8" tall and weighs 265 pounds.

Which NFL team holds the record for scoring the most points in a single game? Is it the Washington Redskins, the Dallas Cowboys, or the Detroit Lions?

The answer is the Washington Redskins. On November 27, 1966, the Redskins established the record when they beat the New York Giants by the phenomenal score of 72 to 41. The combined score of 113 points is also the NFL record for the most points scored by two teams in one game.

How high is the crossbar on a football goal post? Is it 10, 12, or 15 feet above the ground?

The crossbar on a football goal post in 10 feet above the ground.

Only two NFL teams have ever won 18 games in a row. The Chicago Bears did it twice, once in the 1933-34 season and again in 1941-42. Can you name the other team to win 18 consecutive games?

The Miami Dolphins put together a streak of 18 consecutive victories in 1972-73 — 17 in regular season play and 1 in a playoff game.

FOOTBALL

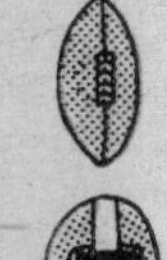

True or false? In 1960, the Dallas Cowboys entered the NFL and hired Tom Landry as their head coach.

True. Tom Landry became head coach of the Dallas team when the Cowboys entered the National Football League in 1960.

What is the nickname of Ohio State's football team? Is it the Buffaloes, the Wolverines, or the Buckeyes?

The Ohio State team is the Buckeyes.

Who was the first tight end to lead the National Football Conference in receiving? Was it Bob Tucker, Charlie Sanders, or Mike Ditka?

Bob Tucker, playing for the New York Giants, snared 59 passes in 1971 to lead the NFC in receiving.

Princeton University, then called the College of New Jersey, was one of the two teams to play in the first intercollegiate football game. Who played against Princeton? Was it Yale, Notre Dame, or Rutgers?

Princeton's opponent in the first intercollegiate football game was neighboring Rutgers. The game, played in New Brunswick, New Jersey, on Saturday, November 6, 1869, saw Rutgers defeat Princeton by the score of 6 goals to 4.

Only seven of these teams belong to the Atlantic Coast Conference. Which one does not? Clemson? Duke? Maryland? North Carolina? North Carolina State? Notre Dame? Virginia? Wake Forest?

If you guessed Notre Dame, you're correct. The Fighting Irish are one of the independent teams that include Air Force, Army, Georgia Tech, Miami (Fla.), Navy, Penn State, Pittsburgh, Syracuse, and Tulane.

The University of Pittsburgh won the Sugar Bowl in 1977. Who did they defeat? Was it Houston, Georgia, or Maryland?

In 1977, number-1-ranked Pittsburgh beat number-4-ranked Georgia in the Sugar Bowl.

There are 12 players on a Canadian pro football team. True or false?

True. U.S. football teams have 11 players, but in Canada, football teams have 12 players, with the 12th man usually lining up in the backfield.

Can you name the pro football team that plays its home games in Arrowhead Stadium?

The Kansas City Chiefs play in Arrowhead Stadium, which is part of the vast Harry S. Truman Sports Complex that also includes Royals' Stadium, the home of American League baseball's Kansas City Royals.

The 1973 winner of the Heisman Trophy played for a powerful Eastern football team. Who was he?

Running back John Cappelletti of Penn State won the Heisman Trophy in 1973.

How many times did Cleveland Browns' fullback Jim Brown lead the NFL in rushing?

Jim Brown led the NFL in rushing eight times: from 1957 to 1961 and from 1963 to 1965. His lifetime total is 12,312 yards gained.

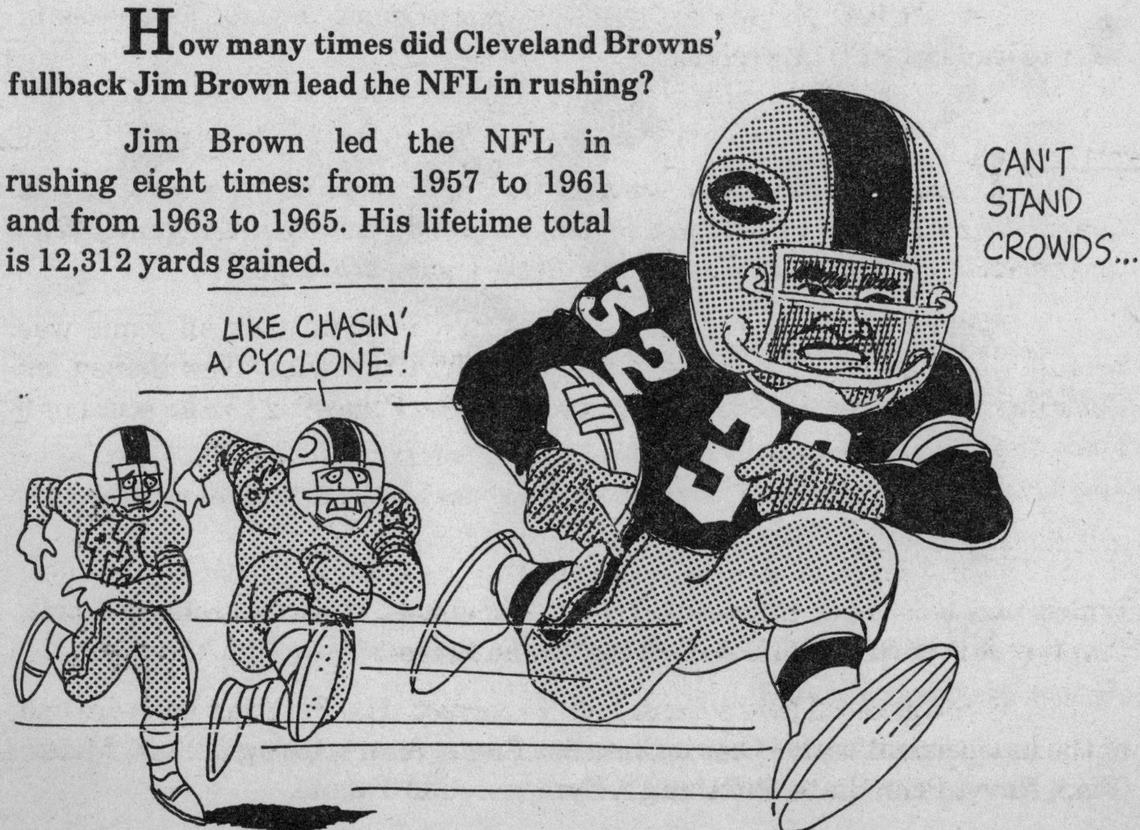

Is the location of the goal posts different in non-professional football than it is in professional football?

Yes. In high school and college football, the goal posts are located ten yards *behind* the goal line. In professional football, they are *on* the goal line.

Green Bay Packer quarterback Bart Starr once threw 294 consecutive passes without an interception. True or false?

True. During the 1964-1965 season, Bart Starr threw 294 passes in a row without being intercepted and established an NFL record.

When was the first professional football league organized in the United States?

Eleven teams formed the American Professional Football Association in 1920, but two years later, the association was reorganized and renamed the National Football League.

Who is the all-time leading lifetime scorer? Is it Don Maynard, Lou Groza, or George Blanda?

George Blanda is the all-time leading scorer, racking up 2,002 points from 1949 to 1975 in the NFL and AFL.

Which two college football teams played in the first Rose Bowl game?

In 1902, Michigan played against Stanford in the oldest of the Bowl classics. The Michigan Wolverines beat the Stanford Indians, 49 to 0.

Name the NFL teams located in the following cities: (1) Cincinnati, (2) Denver, (3) Houston, (4) Philadelphia, and (5) Kansas City.

The teams are: (1) the Cincinnati Bengals, (2) the Denver Broncos, (3) the Houston Oilers, (4) the Philadelphia Eagles, and (5) the Kansas City Chiefs.

Left halfback Jim Crowley, fullback Elmer Layden, quarterback Harry Stuhldreher, and right halfback Don Miller formed an outstanding backfield for Notre Dame from 1922 to 1924. What was the nickname of that famous backfield?

Crowley, Layden, Stuhldreher, and Miller were nicknamed "The Four Horsemen of Notre Dame."

True or false? Bob Hayes, former Dallas Cowboy and NFL star, won an Olympic gold medal before becoming a professional football player.

True. Bob Hayes ran the anchor leg of the 400-meter relay in the 1964 Olympics and won a gold medal.

In 1970, the Miami Dolphins had two running backs who were nicknamed "Butch Cassidy and the Sundance Kid." Can you name those running backs?

Because of their flamboyant activities both on and off the football field, fullback Larry Csonka and halfback Jim Kiick were the Miami running backs fondly named after the famous movie duo.

When the New York Jets won their Super Bowl crown in 1969, who was their head coach?

Weeb Ewbank was the Jets' head coach in 1968-69.

John McKay, the first man to coach the Tampa Bay Buccaneers, was formerly the head coach of which intercollegiate football power?

John McKay was formerly the coach of the University of Southern California.

Bronko Nagurski, one of the greatest fullbacks to ever play in the pro football ranks, started his career as a tackle in college. True or false?

True. Bronko Nagurski, a great all-around football player, earned All-American honors in 1929 playing tackle for the University of Minnesota. But it was because of his skill as a fullback for the NFL's Chicago Bears from 1930 to 1937 that he was voted into the Pro Football Hall of Fame in 1943.

Which two colleges played the first Canadian-American football game?

Canada's McGill University met Harvard in a two-game series in 1874, one game being played under rugby rules and the other, under soccer rules.

Is a safety man an offensive or defensive player?

A safety man is a defensive halfback who covers the middle sections of the field.

Which player calls the signals in the defensive huddle?

Except in very unusual cases, the middle linebacker calls the defensive signals.

When the referee makes the official signal pictured, what does it mean?

It means that there has been interference with a forward pass or a fair catch. The usual result is a 15-yard penalty and an automatic first down.

FOOTBALL

Richard "Night Train" Lane holds the NFL record for the most pass interceptions made in a season. How many passes did he intercept to set the record?

Richard Lane, playing for the Los Angeles Rams, intercepted 14 passes in 1952 to establish the NFL record which still stands today.

True or false? Gale Sayers and Bart Starr were inducted into pro football's Hall of Fame in 1977.

True. Gale Sayers, the Chicago Bears' halfback, and Bart Starr, the Green Bay Packers' quarterback, were inducted into the pro Hall of Fame in 1977, along with Frank Gifford, Forrest Gregg, and Bill Willis.

Who was the winner of the 1977 Fiesta Bowl?

If you guessed Penn State, you're right. Penn State beat Arizona State by the score of 42 to 30 in the Tempe, Arizona, annual Fiesta Bowl.

In 1951, a back from Princeton won the Heisman Trophy. Can you name him?

Dick Kazmaier of Princeton won the coveted trophy in 1951.

True or false? The Pittsburgh Steelers play their home football games in Three Rivers Stadium.

True. Three Rivers Stadium, so named because of its location at the juncture of the Allegheny, Monogahela, and Ohio Rivers, is the home field of the Pittsburgh Steelers. The NFL team shares the stadium with the Pittsburgh Pirates of baseball's National League.

When two pro football teams are tied at the end of regulation time in a championship game, they must play an additional *sudden-death* period to determine the winner. What is a sudden-death period?

A *sudden-death* period is the overtime during which the first team to score after the kickoff is the winner of the game.

Which NFL team's defensive unit is nicknamed "The Purple People Eaters"?

The defensive squad of the Minnesota Vikings, looking ferocious and gigantic in their purple jerseys, were labeled "The Purple People Eaters" after the song of the same name.

The New York Jets were the first American Conference team in the NFL to win the Super Bowl. Who did they beat to become Super Bowl Champions?

The underdog Jets beat the favored Baltimore Colts, 16 to 7, to win Super Bowl III in 1969.

Which pro football player has caught the most touchdown passes? Is it Frank Gifford, Don Hutson, or Charlie Taylor?

The answer is Don Hutson. As a Green Bay Packer, Hutson caught a total of 99 TD passes between 1935 and 1945.

How many times did Sammy Baugh, the great Washington Redskins' quarterback, lead the NFL in passing?

Slingin' Sammy Baugh led the league in passing in 1937, 1940, 1943, 1945, 1947, and 1949 — a total of six times.

Ernie Davis was the first black football player to win the Heisman Trophy. For which college did Davis play?

Ernie Davis was a back for Syracuse when he was voted the outstanding college player in the country in 1961.

If a player crosses the line of scrimmage before the ball is snapped, *offside* is called, and his team is given a 10-yard penalty. True or false?

False. A team is penalized 5 yards for being offside.

True or false? Benny Friedman was voted into the National Professional Football Hall of Fame as a halfback.

False. Although Benny Friedman *is* enshrined in the National Football Hall of Fame, he wasn't a halfback. He was an All-American quarterback for the University of Michigan and continued quarterbacking in professional football for the Cleveland Browns, the Detroit Lions, and the New York Giants.

The Dallas Cowboys beat the Miami Dolphins by the score of 24 to 3 in the 1972 Super Bowl. Where was Super Bowl VI played?

Super Bowl VI was played in New Orleans, Louisiana, on January 16, 1972.

Frank Nester, Charley Gogolak, and Vince Fusco all share a major college record. What is that record?

Gogolak of Princeton, Nestor of West Virginia, and Fusco of Duke each kicked six field goals in one game — a major college record.

Frank Gifford, the TV sports announcer, was once a great NFL player. Which team did he play for?

Frank Gifford was an offensive and defensive back for the New York Giants from 1952 to 1960 and from 1962 to 1964.

...AFTER MOVING PAST THE OPPOSITION'S SECONDARY, THIS IS FRANK GIFFORD ON HIS WAY TO THE GOAL LINE FOR THE VICTORIOUS GIANTS.

FOOTBALL

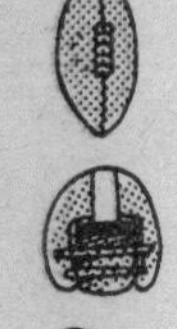

William "Pudge" Heffelfinger, Yale's great All-American lineman in 1889, 1890, and 1891 and a member of the all-time All-American team, was a center. True or false?

False. Heffelfinger was an All-American guard and one of the first pulling guards to run interference on end sweeps.

Do you know which division and conference the Detroit Lions are in?

If you guessed that the Detroit Lions are in the Central Division of the National Football Conference, you're absolutely right. They share the Central Division with the Chicago Bears, the Green Bay Packers, the Minnesota Vikings, and The Tampa Bay Buccaneers.

The Outland Trophy is awarded annually to the outstanding lineman in college football. Who won the Outland Trophy in 1976?

Defensive end Ross Browner of Notre Dame won the Outland Trophy in 1976. Dr. John Outland, a college All-American in the 1890s, was the inspiration for this trophy.

True or false? The first football helmets were made out of leather and did not have face masks.

Absolutely true. Today's helmets are made of a polycarbonate alloy shell, packed with foam. Face masks are a standard part of the helmet.

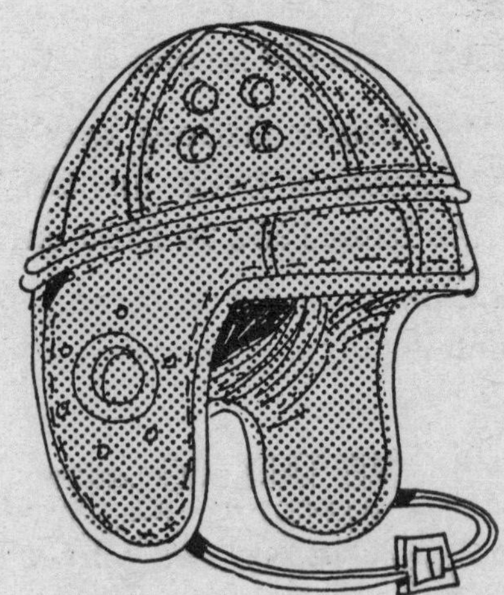

When the referee makes the official signal pictured, what does it mean?

It means that a player has committed a personal foul, for which a 15-yard penalty is imposed on his team.

Which man was *not* a member of the New York Giants pro football team in 1956: (1) Charlie Conerly, (2) Sam Huff, (3) Andy Robustelli, or (4) Y.A. Tittle?

The answer is number 4, Y. A. Tittle. Y.A. was a quarterback for the San Francisco 49ers in 1956 and did not join the Giant squad until 1961.

The first National Small College Football Championship was held on December 15, 1972. Which small college team won the first championship? Was it Louisiana Tech, Western Kentucky, or the University of Delaware?

Louisiana Tech won the first National Small College Football Championship by defeating Western Kentucky, 34 to 0, in the Camellia Bowl, which is played in Sacramento, California.

The winners of the Canadian Football League's Eastern and Western Conferences play a championship game for the Grey Cup. True or false?

True. The Grey Cup, named for Earl Grey, a popular Canadian governor-general who donated it, is the trophy awarded to the winner of the annual playoff game between the two Canadian Football League Conferences.

In what year was the first game played in the American Football League?

The old American Football League was developed in 1959, and play amongst its eight teams began in 1960.

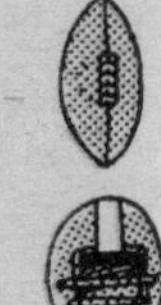

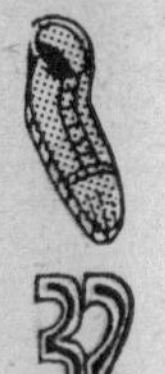

True or false? Former pro football players Tucker Frederickson, Lance Rentzel, and Dick Butkus were members of the 1960 High School All-American Football Team.

True. Butkus of the Chicago Bears, Rentzel of the Dallas Cowboys, and Frederickson of the New York Giants were high school All-American football players in 1960.

In college football, is a defensive player allowed to advance a fumble?

No. In college football, a defensive player is *not* allowed to advance a fumble. However, in high school and pro football, a defensive player *is* allowed to pick up a fumble and advance it.

True or false? Johnny Unitas holds the NFL record for most career TD passes.

False. Fran Tarkenton holds the lifetime record with 317 touchdown passes — a record he established from 1961 to 1977.

Can you name the pro football player who scored the most points in a single game? Is it O.J. Simpson, Jim Brown, or Ernie Nevers?

Ernie Nevers is the correct answer. On November 28, 1929, as a Chicago Cardinal, Nevers scored 6 touchdowns and 4 points after touchdown against the Chicago Bears, for a total of 40 points.

Actor and sports announcer Don Meredith played quarterback for which NFL team?

"Dandy" Don Meredith was a quarterback for the Dallas Cowboys from 1960 to 1968.

From which yard line do football teams kick off?

Unless there is a penalty, high school and college football teams kick off from their 40-yard line, while in the professional league, it's from the 35-yard line.

In the 1940 NFL Championship game, the Washington Redskins were beaten, 73 to 0. Which team slaughtered the Redskins?

The team that trounced Washington and won the National Football League Championship in 1940 was the Chicago Bears.

Which college quarterback threw the most touchdown passes in one season? Was it Dennis Shaw, Scott Hunter, or Archie Manning?

In 1969, quarterback Dennis Shaw of San Diego State set the major college record for touchdown tosses by hurling 39.

True or false? Paul Warfield, one of the greatest receivers in NFL history, was a running back in college.

True. At Ohio State University, Paul Warfield was a running back and was switched to the flanker position after being drafted by the Cleveland Browns.

A Green Bay Packer established the NFL record for scoring the most points in a single season during the 1960 season. Was that Packer Bart Starr, Jimmy Taylor, or Paul Hornung?

The halfback and kicker who established the record of 176 points was Paul Hornung, with 15 TDs, 41 PATs, and 15 FGs.

Who holds the major college record for the highest average gain per rush in a single season? Is it Steve Owens, Jim Nance, or Greg Pruitt?

Oklahoma's Greg Pruitt established the record in 1971 by averaging an amazing 9.35 yards per carry.

True or false? Howard Twilly of Tulsa holds the major college record for the most passes caught in a season.

True. Twilly snared 134 passes in 1965 to set the record.

How much playing time is there in a football game?

College and professional football games are 60 minutes long. The time is broken down into four 15-minute quarters with a 15- to 20-minute intermission called *half-time* in the middle.

Calvin Hill of the Dallas Cowboys was voted the NFL's Rookie of the Year in 1969. True or false?

True. During his first year with the Dallas Cowboys, Calvin Hill, a graduate of Yale, gained 942 yards and earned Rookie of the Year honors.

Colorado and Oklahoma are in the same conference. What is the name of that conference?

Colorado and Oklahoma are in the Big Eight Conference, along with Missouri, Kansas State, Nebraska, Oklahoma State, Kansas, and Iowa State.

Can you name the NFL teams that played in Super Bowl XII? And who was the winner?

The Dallas Cowboys defeated the Denver Broncos, 27 to 10, in Super Bowl XII.

True or false? The Cotton Bowl is in Atlanta, Georgia.

False. The Cotton Bowl is in Dallas, Texas.

The Baltimore Colts played the Dallas Cowboys in the 1971 Super Bowl. Which team won?

The Colts, led by Johnny Unitas, edged the Cowboys, 16 to 13.

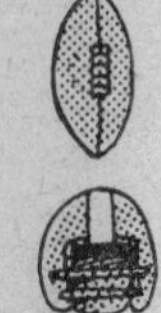

True or false? John Brodie and Jim Plunkett were both All-American quarterbacks at Stanford University.

True. John Brodie was an All-American at Stanford in 1956, and Jim Plunkett was an All-American there in 1970.

Which NFL team holds the record for winning the most consecutive games during regular season play? Is it the Miami Dolphins, the Green Bay Packers, or the New York Giants?

In 1972, the Miami Dolphins won 17 straight games to establish an NFL record.

How deep is the end zone on a football field? Is it 5 yards, 10 yards, or 15 yards?

The end zone is 10 yards deep.

Alex Karris, the actor and sports announcer, was a former NFL All-Star. What position did Karris play?

Alex Karris was a defensive tackle for the Detroit Lions for twelve years before his retirement in 1971. Before that, Karris starred with the linemen of the University of Iowa.

Only two linemen have ever won the Heisman Trophy. End Larry Kelley of Yale won it in 1936. Who was the other lineman?

Leon Hart, an end at Notre Dame, won the Heisman Trophy in 1949.

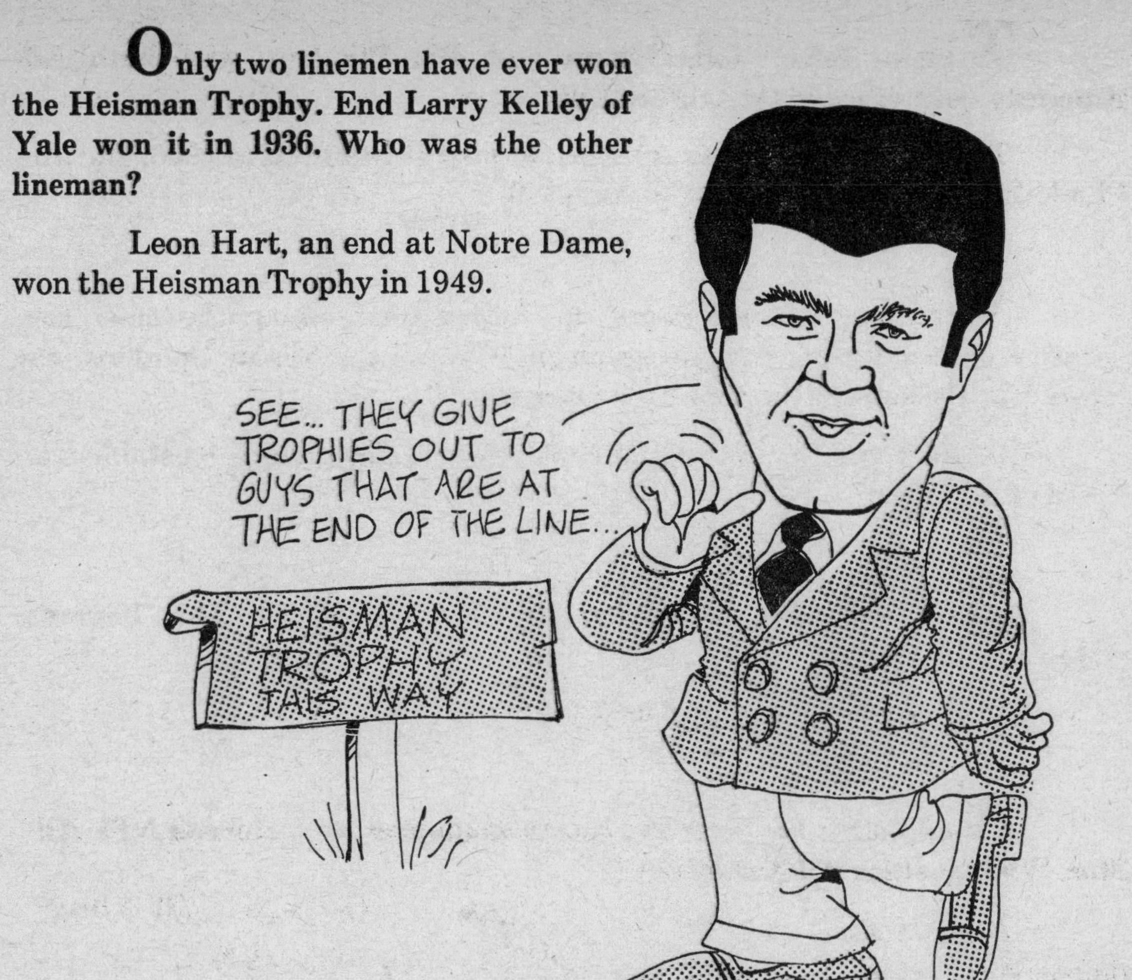

Who was the first black football coach in the NFL? Was it Emlen Tunnell, Rosey Grier, or Jim Brown?

After playing for the Giants from 1948 to 1958 and the Packers from 1958 to 1961, Emlen Tunnell became the first black coach in the NFL when he joined the New York Giants' staff in 1965. He was also the first black player elected to the National Professional Football Hall of Fame.

Who holds the NFL record for the most pass receptions in a single season? Is it Charley Hennigan, Pat Studstill, or Danny Abramowicz?

Charley Hennigan of the Houston Oilers set the record in 1964 by catching 101 passes.

In 1962, the New York Titans of the American Football League changed their name. What was their new name?

When Sonny Werblin became the new owner of the financially troubled New York Titans, he was instrumental in having the team's name changed to the New York Jets.

Which NFL quarterback gained the most yards passing in a single season?

In 1967, Joe Namath of the New York Jets set the record by passing for 4,007 yards.

True or false? Jim Bakken of the St. Louis Cardinals holds the NFL record for kicking the most field goals in one game.

True. Jim Bakken kicked 7 field goals in a game against the Pittsburgh Steelers on September 24, 1967.

In professional football, the clock is stopped under five conditions: (1) if a player is injured, (2) if the ball carrier crosses a sideline and goes out of bounds, (3) after a team scores, (4) after a first down. What is the fifth?

The clock is also stopped after each incomplete pass.

Who holds the Super Bowl rushing record? Here's a hint. The record was set in Super Bowl IX.

In 1975, fullback Franco Harris of the Pittsburgh Steelers set the Super Bowl rushing record by gaining 158 yards against the Minnesota Vikings.

The Minnesota Vikings have played in four Super Bowl games. Have they ever won the Super Bowl?

No. The Kansas City Chiefs beat the Vikings, 16 to 0, in Super Bowl IV in 1970. The Vikings lost Super Bowl VIII in 1974 to the Miami Dolphins by the score of 24 to 7. The Pittsburgh Steelers beat them, 21 to 6, in Super Bowl IX in 1975, and the Oakland Raiders defeated Minnesota, 32 to 14, in Super Bowl XI in 1977.

In what year was professional football first seen on nationwide TV?

Professional football games were seen on national television for the first time in 1956.

In the early 1960s, the Los Angeles Rams had a great defensive line that consisted of tackles Rosey Grier and Merlin Olsen, and ends Deacon Jones and Lamar Lundy. What was the nickname of that famous defensive front four?

Because of their exceptional ability and aggressive play, that quartet was nicknamed "The Fearsome Foursome."

A National Football League game has never been cancelled due to bad weather. True or false?

It's true. Pro football games are played no matter what the weather conditions are.

True or false? Amos Alonzo Stagg coached college football longer than anyone else.

True. "Football's Grand Old Man," as Stagg was called, coached college football for 59 years! His first 41 years were spent at the University of Chicago, but even after his retirement at the age of 70, Stagg spent the years from 1933 to 1946 coaching at the College of the Pacific, and from 1947 to 1952 at Susquehanna University in Pennsylvania.

Texas Christian University and Marquette played in the first Cotton Bowl game. Which team won the first Cotton Bowl?

Texas Christian University won the first Cotton Bowl game, beating Marquette, 16 to 6.

Which college fullback scored the most points in an intercollegiate football game?

The answer is the great Jim Brown of Syracuse. He scored 43 points in a game against Colgate in 1956.

An Ivy League football team has never been declared the Champion of the NCAA. True or false?

False. In 1925, Dartmouth, a member of the Ivy League, was declared the Champion of the National Collegiate Athletic Association.

In 1962, quarterback Roman Gabriel of North Carolina State was the first draft pick of a pro football team. Was that team the Oakland Raiders, the Philadelphia Eagles, or the Los Angeles Rams?

The Oakland Raiders selected Roman Gabriel as their first draft pick in 1962.

Which pro football player was the first back to rush for more than 2,000 yards in a single season? Was it O.J. Simpson, Gregg Pruitt, or Jimmy Taylor?

If you said O.J. Simpson, you're right. During the 1973 season, O.J. rushed for 2,003 yards.

By 1974, there were two major professional football leagues in the United States. True or false?

True. In addition to the National Football League, which was established in 1922, the World Football League, a second pro football league, began play in 1974. But its twelves teams were plagued with financial problems, and the WFL was dissolved in 1975.

In football, what does the term *offsetting penalties* mean?

Offsetting penalties means that both teams have committed fouls which cancel each other out.

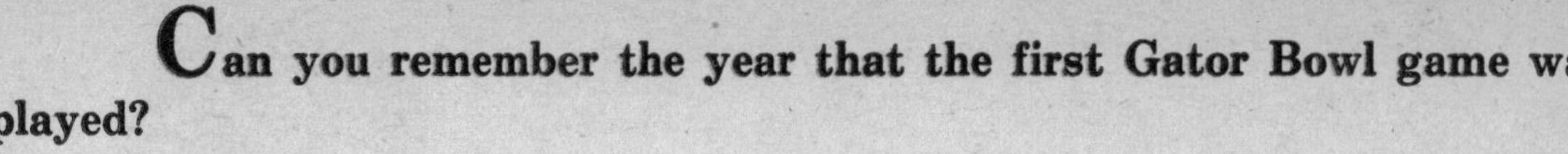

Can you remember the year that the first Gator Bowl game was played?

If you said 1946, you're right. Wake Forest defeated South Carolina, 26 to 14, in the first of the annual Jacksonville, Florida, classic games.

Which NFL back holds the record for scoring the most points in his rookie season? Is it Gale Sayers, Jim Brown, or O.J. Simpson?

Playing for the Chicago Bears, Gale Sayers scored 132 points as a rookie in 1965 to set the NFL record.

Where is the Sugar Bowl played?

The Sugar Bowl is played in New Orleans, Louisiana.

Which college football team won the National Championship in 1969? Here's a hint. The team is a powerful member of the Southwest Conference.

Coach Darrell Royal's Texas Longhorns won the National Championship in 1969.

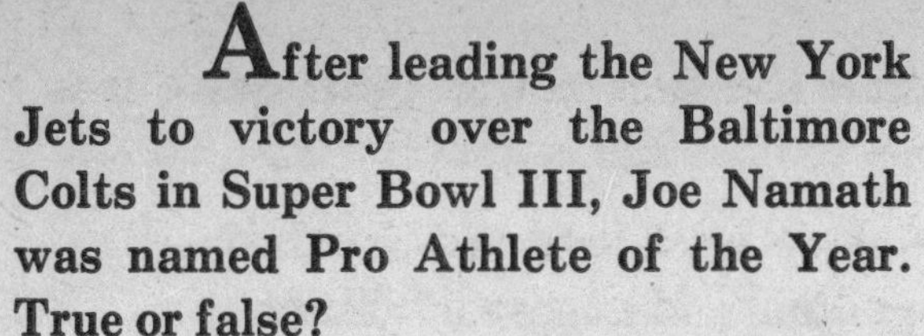

After leading the New York Jets to victory over the Baltimore Colts in Super Bowl III, Joe Namath was named Pro Athlete of the Year. True or false?

True. In 1969, Joe Namath was named Pro Athlete of the Year by the Sportswriters of America.

Which National Football League quarterback holds the record for completing the most passes in one game? Is it George Blanda, Joe Namath, or Y.A. Tittle?

George Blanda holds the record. Playing for the Houston Oilers against the Buffalo Bills on November 1, 1964, Blanda completed 37 passes.

Who made the longest field goal on record?

Tom Dempsey's record-setting field goal of 63 yards, kicked in a 1970 game between the New Orleans Saints and the Detroit Lions, was made more remarkable by the fact that Dempsey has only half a foot on his kicking leg.

In 1970, Penn State's backfield was made up of two running backs who went on to become all-pro performers in the NFL. Can you name them?

Fullback Franco Harris and halfback Lydell Mitchell starred for Penn State before Harris joined the Pittsburgh Steelers and Mitchell, the Baltimore Colts.

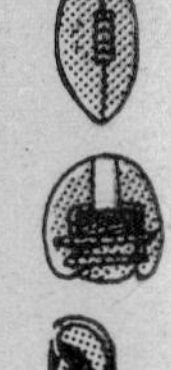

Only five pro football quarterbacks have thrown 7 TD passes in a single game. Four of them are Y.A. Tittle, Sid Luckman, George Blanda, and Adrian Buck. Who is the fifth?

It's Joe Kapp of the Minnesota Vikings. He tossed 7 TD passes in a game against the Baltimore Colts on September 28, 1969.

True or false? The team that has won the most National Football Conference Championships is the New York Giants.

False. The Green Bay Packers won their league title eleven times — more than any other team in the NFL. They took the title in 1929, 1930, 1931, 1936, 1939, 1944, 1961, 1962, 1965, 1966, and 1967. The Giants won the championship only three times — first in 1934, then in 1938 and 1956.

George Blanda spent twenty-six seasons in the National Football League. Can you name the team that Blanda began his NFL playing career with?

George Blanda started playing professional football with the Chicago Bears in 1949. He then went on to play with the Baltimore Colts, the Houston Oilers and ended his career as an Oakland Raider.

Glenn Davis and Felix "Doc" Blanchard, West Point's famous backfield duo, were voted to the All-American team in 1945, 1946, and 1947. What were the nicknames given to Davis and Blanchard?

Davis was known as "Mr. Outside," and Blanchard was known as "Mr. Inside."

Joe Namath was a great pro football quarterback for the New York Jets and the Los Angeles Rams. Where did Joe play college football?

Joe Namath played college football at the University of Alabama and led his team to the 1964 National Championship.

On December 15, 1974, in a game against the New York Jets, quarterback Bert Jones of the Baltimore Colts set an NFL passing record. What record did he set?

Bert Jones completed 17 passes in a row to set a new NFL record.

Which college football player scored the most points in one season? Was it Lydell Mitchell, O.J. Simpson, or Tony Dorsett?

Penn State's Lydell Mitchell holds the record. In 1971, the swift halfback scored 174 points.

True or false? Brown and Dartmouth are members of the Big Ten Conference.

False. Brown and Dartmouth are members of the Ivy League, along with Yale, Harvard, Cornell, Pennsylvania, Columbia, and Princeton.

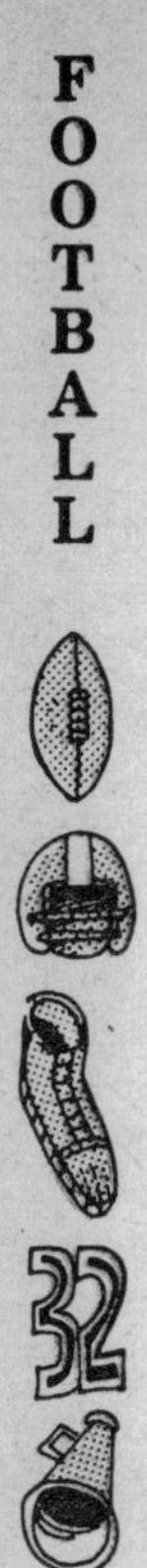

Which coach invented the single wing-back and double wing-back formations? Was it Knute Rockne, Glenn Warner, or Tom Landry?

Glenn "Pop" Warner, a coach for over forty-five years at Carlisle, Pittsburgh, Stanford, Temple, and other schools, invented the single- and double-wing formations.

How many points are awarded for a *safety*?

When a ball carrier is downed in the end zone his team is defending, the defensive team scores a *safety* and is awarded 2 points.

What is the major college record for the most touchdown passes caught in a season?

The record for the most touchdown passes caught in a season is 18. It was established by Tom Reynolds of San Diego State in 1969.

Y.A. Tittle was a super NFL quarterback with the San Francisco 49ers and the New York Giants. Can you guess what Y.A.'s initials stand for?

Y.A. Tittle's full name is Yelberton Abraham Tittle.

What is a *rollout* play?

A *rollout* is a passing play in which the quarterback retreats from the line of scrimmage and runs toward the sideline before throwing the ball.

Which college holds the record for the longest winning streak? Is it Texas, Notre Dame, or Oklahoma?

Oklahoma holds the record with 47 consecutive wins.

Which college football team won the first Sugar Bowl game?

Tulane beat Temple by the score of 20 to 14 in the 1935 Sugar Bowl classic.

True or false? In the Pro Canadian Football League, the offensive team gets only 3 downs to make a first down.

True. In the U.S., a team gets 4 downs to go 10 yards, but in Canada, teams get only 3 downs to advance those 10 yards.

The Pittsburgh Steelers defeated the Dallas Cowboys in Super Bowl X. What was the score in that game?

In Super Bowl X in 1976, Pittsburgh defeated Dallas, 21 to 17.

Has any team ever scored over 200 points in a single intercollegiate football game?

Yes. On October 7, 1916, Georgia Tech beat Cumberland University of Lebanon, Tennessee, by the score of 222 to 0.

Ohio State and Michigan are members of the Big Ten, one of the strongest college football conferences in the country. Can you name the other eight teams in the Big Ten?

Purdue, Michigan State, Illinois, Indiana, Northwestern, Wisconsin, Minnesota, and Iowa complete the list of the Big Ten Conference.

Who holds the NFL record for scoring the most touchdowns rushing in a single season? Is it Jimmy Taylor, Alex Webster, or Larry Csonka?

Jimmy Taylor, the great Green Bay Packer fullback, holds the record. He rushed for 19 touchdowns in 1962.

Bob Lilly was an all-pro defensive tackle with the Detroit Lions. True or false?

False. Bob Lilly was an all-pro defensive tackle for the Dallas Cowboys.

At age thirty-four, quarterback Y.A. Tittle left the San Francisco 49ers to join the New York Giants and accomplished an amazing feat. What was that feat?

After many experts said his playing career was over, Y.A. Tittle led the Giants to victory in three consecutive conference championship games: in 1961, 1962, and 1963.

In 1971, Heisman Trophy winner Jim Plunkett of Stanford was the number-one draft pick of which NFL team?

Jim Plunkett was selected in the first round by the then Boston Patriots (now the New England Patriots).

True or false? While at Pittsburgh, Tony Dorsett established the major college record for scoring the most points in a career.

True. Dorsett scored 356 points from 1973 to 1976, which is the current collegiate record.

Emlen Tunnell, a defensive back with the New York Giants and the Green Bay Packers, holds the NFL record for the most interceptions in a lifetime. How many interceptions did Tunnell make in his pro career?

Emlen Tunnell intercepted 79 passes during his NFL career from 1948 to 1958 with the Giants and from 1959 to 1961 with the Packers.

The winners of two college conferences receive automatic invitations to play in the Rose Bowl game. Which two conferences are they?

The top team in the Big Ten Conference is invited to play against the top team in the Pacific Ten Conference in the Rose Bowl.

Jim Turner kicked 34 field goals during the 1968 season, an NFL record. When Turner established the record, which team was he playing for?

In 1968, Jim Turner was a member of the New York Jets.

True or false? Quarterback Sammy Baugh of the Washington Redskins was also a punter.

True. Sammy Baugh holds many NFL records in both passing and punting, including the most seasons leading the league in both (passing — 6 and punting — 4).

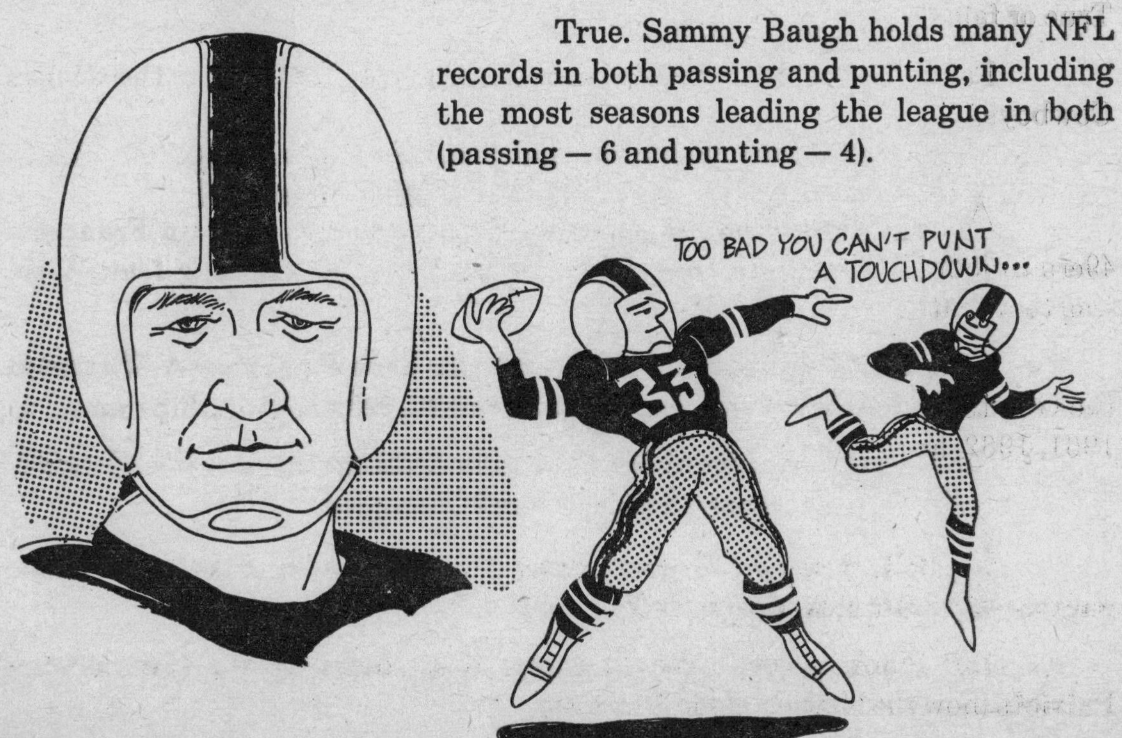

Which NFL player led the league in rushing yards in 1976? To help you answer the question, here is a hint. He's a former Heisman Trophy winner from the University of Southern California.

O.J. Simpson, the Heisman Trophy winner from USC, gained 1,503 yards playing for Buffalo in 1976 to lead the league.

Which player holds the NFL record for playing in the most consecutive games? Is it Jim Ringo, Jerry Kramer, or Jim Marshall?

It's Jim Marshall. Playing for the Minnesota Vikings and the Cleveland Browns, Marshall appeared in 236 consecutive games.

When did the Associated Press start polling sportswriters and broadcasters to determine its National Champion of college football?

The Associated Press first polled its members in 1936 and has been awarding a trophy each year to the team it chooses as National Champion. The United Press International offers a trophy too, based on selections made by college coaches.

When a receiver runs a *post* pattern, he sprints straight down the field and then scants in toward the middle of the field. True or false?

True.

Which college football team won the Rose Bowl and the National Championship in 1975? Was it Michigan, Stanford, or USC?

The University of Southern California defeated Ohio State, 17 to 16, in the Rose Bowl and was named the National Champion in 1975.

What is a *turnover*?

A *turnover* occurs when a team loses possession of the ball due to a misplay.

Which college halfback holds the major college record for scoring the most career touchdowns? Is it Glenn Davis or Tony Dorsett? Be careful. This is a tricky question.

Glenn Davis of Army and Tony Dorsett of Pittsburgh share the record for scoring the most career touchdowns. Davis scored 59 TDs playing from 1943 to 1946, and Dorsett equaled that record in the 1973 to 1976 seasons.

True or false? Dick Butkus was an all-pro defensive end for the Cleveland Browns.

False. Dick Butkus was an all-pro middle linebacker for the Chicago Bears.

What is the NFL record for the most touchdown passes caught in a single game?

The NFL record for TD catches in a single game is 5. It was set by Bob Shaw of the Chicago Cards in a game against the Baltimore Colts on October 2, 1950.

How many times was Don Hutson, the great Green Bay Packer receiver, selected as the Most Valuable Player in the National Football League?

Don Hutson was named the MVP twice, once in 1941 and again in 1942.

How many officials are there in a college football game?

There are six officials in a college football game. They are the *referee,* the *umpire,* the *linesman,* the *field judge,* the *back judge,* and the *time keeper* or *clock operator.*

Can you name the team that beat Colorado in the 1977 Orange Bowl?

Ohio State defeated Colorado, 27 to 10, in the 1977 Orange Bowl.

The great Jim Thorpe won All-American football honors in 1911 and 1912 during his college years. For which college did Jim Thorpe play?

Jim Thorpe played college football for Carlisle Institute, a small U.S. Indian industrial school which was brought to national prominence by Thorpe's gridiron heroics.

Johnny Lujack won the Heisman Trophy in 1947. What position did Lujack play and which college did he attend?

Johnny Lujack was an All-American quarterback for the Fighting Irish of Notre Dame.

Can you name the two college teams that played in the 1978 Orange Bowl? And who won?

The Arkansas Razorbacks defeated the Oklahoma Sooners in the 1978 Orange Bowl by the score of 24 to 0.

Who won the 1978 Cotton Bowl?

The Fighting Irish of Notre Dame beat the Texas Longhorns, 38 to 10, in the Dallas, Texas, annual New Year's Day classic.

In 1974, the Miami Dolphins beat the Minnesota Vikings in Super Bowl VIII. Where was Super Bowl VIII played?

Super Bowl VIII was played in Rice Stadium in Dallas, Texas.

On January 1, 1978, an Arkansas back established a new Orange Bowl record for rushing. Can you name that back?

Roland Sales of Arkansas set the new Orange Bowl rushing record by gaining 205 yards against Oklahoma.

South River, New Jersey, High School had two talented quarterbacks on its roster in 1966. They were Joe Theisman and Drew Pearson. Both men went on to make their marks in pro football. Which teams did Theisman and Pearson play for in 1977?

Joe Theisman became a quarterback for the Washington Redskins, and Drew Pearson was a wide receiver for the Dallas Cowboys.

True or false? Ken Stabler, the man who quarterbacked the Oakland Raiders in 1977, is a left-handed quarterback.

True. Although most quarterbacks are right-handed, the great Ken Stabler is a southpaw.

Harold "Red" Grange was a University of Illinois halfback famous for his dazzling speed and deceptiveness. Grange's phenomenal skill earned him an unusual nickname. Can you guess it?

Harold "Red" Grange was nicknamed the "Galloping Ghost" when he scored 5 touchdowns the first five times he carried the ball for the University of Illinois against the University of Michigan in 1924. Grange went on to play pro ball with the New York Yankees and the Chicago Bears.

Which NFL team did Vince Lombardi coach before he became the head coach of the Green Bay Packers in 1959?

From 1954 to 1959, Vince Lombardi was the offensive coach of the New York Giants.

How much must an official pro football weigh? Is it 13-14 ounces, 14-15 ounces, or 15-16 ounces?

An official pro football must weigh 14-15 ounces. The leather case contains a rubber lining blown up to an air pressure of 12½-13½ pounds per square inch. The leather laces along one of its four seams provide a good grip for passing the ball. Manufactured by the Wilson Sporting Goods Company, the official pro football has the signature of the NFL commissioner on it.

True or false? Ray Nitschke, who played for the Green Bay Packers, was a great halfback.

False. Ray Nitschke of the Green Bay Packers was not a halfback. He was one of the greatest middle linebackers ever to play professional football.

In the National Football League, how many official footballs must the home team provide for testing before a game?

Before an NFL game, the home team must have twenty-four footballs ready for testing with a pressure gauge by the referee.

In pro football, how long does an offensive team have to start a play after the referee signals "Ready for Play"? Is it 15 seconds, 25 seconds, or 30 seconds?

The answer is 30 seconds. If an offensive team does not start a play within 30 seconds of the "Ready for Play" signal, a "Delay of Game" is called and that team is penalized 5 yards.

Which Oakland Raider was named the Most Valuable Player of Super Bowl XI by *Sport Magazine*?

In 1977, Raiders' wide receiver Fred Biletnikoff was named the MVP of Super Bowl XI by *Sport Magazine.* His four key catches inside the 10-yard line helped Oakland down the Minnesota Vikings, 32 to 14.

Who won the Heisman Trophy in 1977?

Running back Earl Campbell of the University of Texas was awarded the famed football trophy in 1977.

Tom Harmon, a back for Michigan, and Doak Walker, a back for Southern Methodist University, were both Heisman Trophy winners. Which of them was the first to win it?

Tom Harmon won the Heisman Trophy in 1940, and Doak Walker won college football's most coveted prize eight years later in 1948.

Quarterback Otto Graham led his NFL team to the conference championship of the Eastern Division six straight years during the 1950-55 seasons. Which NFL team did Otto Graham play for during those six years?

The great Otto Graham was the quarterback of the Cleveland Browns.

Jim Thorpe once called Ed Mahan "the greatest back in football." Where did Ed Mahan play college football?

Ed Mahan played at Harvard and was an All-American in 1913, 1914, and 1915.

True or false? Halfback Dicky Moegle of Rice University once scored on a 95-yard touchdown run, but ran only 53 yards.

True. It happened in the 1954 Cotton Bowl game when Rice beat Alabama, 28 to 6. Early in the game Moegle took the ball at his own 5-yard line, broke to the outside, and easily outraced the entire Alabama defense. He had a clear path down the sideline to the end zone, but was tackled by Tommy Lewis, who leaped off the Alabama bench to stop the Rice star. Moegle ran only 53 yards, but was awarded a 95-yard touchdown run by the officials who felt he would have scored if Lewis had not interfered with his progress.

True or false? In 1961, Allie Sherman, the rookie head coach of the New York Giants, was named the NFL's Coach of the Year.

True. In 1961, Sherman coached the Giants to the NFL's Eastern Conference title with a record of 10-3-1, and was named Coach of the Year in his rookie season.

Pro Quarterback Magazine **regularly selects its Quarterback of the Year. Who received that honor in 1977? Was it Ken Stabler of the Oakland Raiders, Roger Staubach of the Dallas Cowboys, or Craig Morton of the Denver Broncos?**

Roger Staubach of the NFL Champion Dallas Cowboys was *Pro Quarterback Magazine*'s Quarterback of the Year in 1977.

The Canton Bulldogs, of Canton, Ohio, were one of the first professional football teams to be formed. Which famous All-American joined the Bulldogs in 1915 as a player-coach?

After gaining national fame in college football, Jim Thorpe began his pro football career with the Canton Bulldogs as a player-coach.

Who has been called the "Father of American Football"? Is it Walter Camp, Vince Lombardi, or Knute Rockne?

Walter Camp is the correct answer. Camp coached Yale and Stanford between 1879 and 1895. He wrote many books on football, picked All-American teams from 1889 to 1924, and also played an important role in the formulation of football's rules and patterns of play.

Which team holds the record for the most fumbles in one season?

The 1938 Chicago Bears hold that dubious honor with 56 fumbles.

The Chicago Bears played the Washington Redskins in the 1940 NFL Championship game. In that game, two of the finest quarterbacks in history locked horns. Who were they?

Sid Luckman was the QB for the Bears while Sammy Baugh called the plays for the Redskins in the 1940 NFL Championship game. It was Luckman who led Chicago to a 73 to 0 victory over Washington.

Sid Luckman's sensational college passing earned him the nickname "Mr. Quarterback." Where did Sid Luckman play college football? Here's a hint. It's an Ivy League school.

Sid Luckman quarterbacked the Lions of New York's Columbia University in 1936, 1937, and 1938, before signing with the Chicago Bears in 1939.

Former U.S. President Gerald Ford played college football for the University of Michigan. Which position did Mr. Ford play?

Former President Gerald Ford played offensive center for the undefeated University of Michigan Wolverines in 1932 and 1933, and was chosen as the Most Valuable Player on the 1934 team. He was considered good enough to be offered a pro football tryout with the NFL's Green Bay Packers, but he chose to pursue a career in politics instead. He worked his way through Yale University Law School as an assistant football coach.

Halfback Steve Van Buren held nine NFL career rushing records when he retired in 1952. Which NFL team did Van Buren play for during his pro career?

Steve Van Buren played halfback for the Philadelphia Eagles from 1944 to 1952.

Who was the winner of the 1978 Rose Bowl game?

The Washington Huskies beat the Michigan Wolverines by the score of 27 to 20 in the annual Pasadena, California, New Year's Day classic.

TV sports commentator Pat Summerall played football for the New York Giants from 1958 to 1961. What position did he play?

Pat Summerall, though a college defensive end at Arkansas, became a field goal kicker in the professional ranks.

Quarterback Bobby Douglas of the Chicago Bears once scored 4 touchdowns by rushing for only 5 yards. True or false?

True. On November 4, 1973, in a game against the Green Bay Packers, Douglas made three 1-yard touchdowns and scored a fourth TD on a 2-yard scamper into the end zone.

FOOTBALL

Knute Rockne was one of college football's most famous coaches. Did Rockne ever *play* college football?

Yes. Knute Rockne played college football at Notre Dame and earned All-American honors at the end position in 1913.

December 28, 1958 was the first time in the history of the National Football League that a championship game went into sudden-death overtime. Which two teams were involved in that famous sudden-death overtime?

When time ran out in the 1958 NFL Championship game, the Baltimore Colts and the New York Giants were tied, 17 to 17. Baltimore won the championship 8 minutes and 15 seconds into the sudden-death period when Alan Ameche took a handoff from Johnny Unitas and scored a touchdown from the Giants' 1-yard line.

O.J. Simpson is one of the greatest backs to ever play the game of football. Do you know O.J.'s full name?

Orenthal James Simpson is better known to most football fans simply as O.J. Simpson.

Before becoming head coach of the Pittsburgh Steelers in 1977, Dick Nolan played professional football for the New York Giants and the Chicago Cardinals from 1954 to 1961. What position did Nolan play?

Dick Nolan was a defensive halfback with the Giants and Cardinals.

True or false? Only *players* can be voted into the National Professional Football Hall of Fame.

False. The Hall of Fame, established in 1962 in Canton, Ohio, is not limited to players. Coaches and others who have made outstanding contributions to professional football are eligible as well.

Match the following New York Giants with the year they were inducted into the Pro Football Hall of Fame.

(1) Ken Strong, New York Giants' running back, 1933-35, 1939-47	**(a) Inducted into the Pro Football Hall of Fame in 1963**
(2) Mel Hein, New York Giants' center, 1931-45	**(b) Inducted into the Pro Football Hall of Fame in 1967**
(3) Cal Hubbard, New York Giants' tackle, 1927-29, 1936	**(c) Inducted into the Pro Football Hall of Fame in 1966**

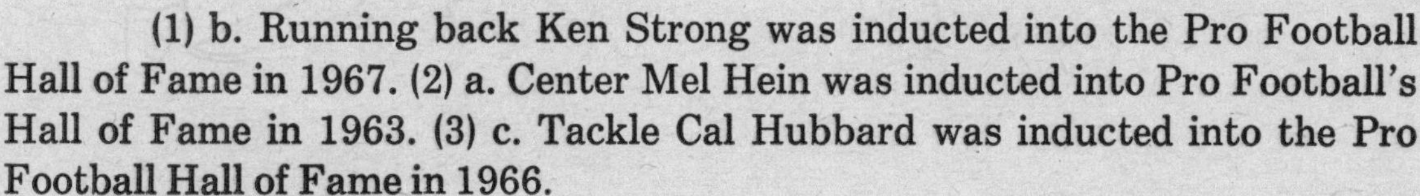

(1) b. Running back Ken Strong was inducted into the Pro Football Hall of Fame in 1967. (2) a. Center Mel Hein was inducted into Pro Football's Hall of Fame in 1963. (3) c. Tackle Cal Hubbard was inducted into the Pro Football Hall of Fame in 1966.

Why is a football playing field often referred to as a *gridiron*?

The playing field is so called because the yard-line markings look like the parallel metal bars and wires on a cooking utensil for grilling meat called a *gridiron.*

For whom was the Heisman Trophy named?

Every year since 1935, a trophy has been awarded to the outstanding college football player in the United States by the Downtown Athletic Club of New York City. The winner is selected by a group of sportswriters and sportscasters. In 1936, the trophy was named for John W. Heisman, who had been a college football coach for thirty-five years from 1892 to 1927. During those years, Heisman helped map football strategy and revolutionize its rules.

Who was called *Mr. Pro Football*?

George Halas, the player-owner-coach of the Chicago Bears for more than fifty years is regarded as *Mr. Pro Football.*

Which team won the Super Bowl in 1969? Here is a hint to help your memory. The man who quarterbacked the winning team was Lenny Dawson.

Lenny Dawson led the Kansas City Chiefs in upsetting the heavily favored Minnesota Vikings, 23 to 7, in the 1969 Super Bowl.

When the referee makes the official signal pictured, what does it mean?

It means that a *time out* has been called.

Only one college player ever won the Heisman Trophy for two consecutive years. Was it O.J. Simpson, John Cappelletti, or Archie Griffin?

The great Ohio State halfback Archie Griffin was the only two-time Heisman winner, receiving the trophy in 1974 and 1975.

Where did Dallas quarterback Roger "The Dodger" Staubach play college football?

Roger Staubach, the Heisman Trophy winner in 1963, played for the U.S. Naval Academy and later served as an officer in the Navy before becoming a professional athlete.

True or false? Walter Payton broke O.J. Simpson's single game rushing record in 1977.

True. The old record of 273 yards, set by Buffalo Bill O.J. Simpson in a game against Detroit in 1976, was broken when Chicago Bear Payton rushed for 275 yards against the Minnesota Vikings on November 20, 1977.

Southern California won the Rose Bowl in 1973, 1975, and 1977. Can you name the teams they defeated?

Southern Cal beat Ohio State twice — first in 1973 by a score of 42 to 17, and then in 1975 by a close 18 to 17. Their 1977 victory was over Michigan, outscoring them, 14 to 6.

In 1975, Alabama, the number-1-ranked college team in the country, lost its chance to become the National Champion when it was upset in the Orange Bowl game. Which team defeated Alabama and shattered its dream of a national title?

Notre Dame edged Alabama by the score of 13 to 11 to win the 1975 Orange Bowl.

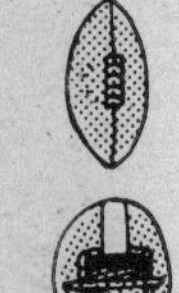

Frank Hinkey, an All-American end at Yale, and T. Truxton Hare, an All-American guard at the University of Pennsylvania, shared the same record in the 1890s. What was that record?

Hinkey and Hare were both named to All-American football teams for four consecutive years — Hinkey from 1891 to 1894, and Hare from 1897 to 1900.

Which quarterback holds the record for completing the most passes in a single season? Is it Joe Namath, Sonny Jurgensen, or Roman Gabriel?

Sonny Jurgensen of the Washington Redskins completed the most passes in a single season — 1,288 — in 1967.

In his now-famous "Win one for the Gipper" speech, who was Knute Rockne referring to as "The Gipper"?

George Gipp, a Notre Dame player who died in the middle of the season at the height of his career, was immortalized by Coach Knute Rockne in a pep talk to his team. Gipp was an All-American back in 1920.

How do teams in the American Conference and National Conference obtain college football players?

The teams in both conferences bolster their squads through a draft. When college players have finished their playing careers, the pro team with the poorest record in both conferences gets first choice, with the winner of the Super Bowl choosing last. This procedure was started in 1936 by the NFL.

Prior to 1880, the game of football was played with as many as 25 players on each side. True or false?

True. In those days, games were played with 25, 20, 15, or 11 men on a side. At an 1880 football convention, Walter Camp of Yale University persuaded the delegates to agree upon a binding rule calling for a limit of 11 players on a side.

True or false? President Franklin D. Roosevelt played college football.

True. Franklin D. Roosevelt was captain of Harvard's Freshman Scrub Team in 1900.

Who did Miami of Florida defeat in the first Orange Bowl game?

Miami defeated Manhattan College of New York, 7-0, in the first Orange Bowl game in 1933.

What is an *option play*?

On an *option play*, the quarterback has a choice of handing the ball off to another runner, running with the ball himself, or passing the ball. Sometimes halfbacks run option plays and then they can choose to run with the ball or to pass it.

Alphonse Emil "Tuffy" Leemans, a standout performer for the New York Giants from 1936 to 1943, was one of the five men inducted into the National Professional Football Hall of Fame on July 29, 1978. Can you name the other four football greats inducted into the Hall of Fame that year?

In addition to Alphonse Leemans, Weeb Ewbank, Lance Alworth, Larry Wilson and Ray Nitschke were the 1978 selections for the Hall of Fame. Weeb Ewbank coached championship teams in both the AFL and the NFL. Lance Alworth was an All-AFL selection as a wide receiver seven times while playing for the San Diego Chargers. Larry Wilson was an NFL All-Star at safety six times while playing for the St. Louis Cardinals. And Ray Nitschke starred as a middle linebacker for the Green Bay Packers during their championship years.

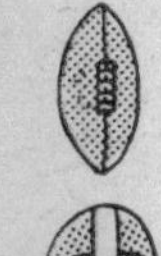

Felix "Doc" Blanchard and Glenn Davis, Army's famous backfield duo, won the Heisman Trophy in successive years. Who won it first, Blanchard or Davis?

In 1945, the sportswriters and sportscasters of America selected Felix Blanchard as the Outstanding College Football Player in America, and the Downtown Athletic Club of New York City presented him with the Heisman Trophy. The following year, 1946, Glenn Davis, Blanchard's backfield mate, won the Trophy.

True or false? The game of football was almost outlawed in the United States.

True. In the early 1900s, the game of football was so rough that many groups attacked the game as a brutal sport and called for legislation banning football in the United States. Conditions were so bad that some colleges abandoned the sport. The game, however, was saved by President Theodore Roosevelt, who called a meeting of representatives from Yale, Harvard, and Princeton for the purpose of reforming and improving football. The end result was the modification of rules and the introduction of the forward pass, which made football a faster, cleaner sport.

What happens on a *trap play*?

On a *trap play*, a defensive player is allowed to penetrate into the offensive backfield without any interference, so he can be blocked from the side by an offensive lineman.

Who was the Commissioner of the National Football League in 1978?

Pete Rozelle was the NFL Commissioner in 1978.

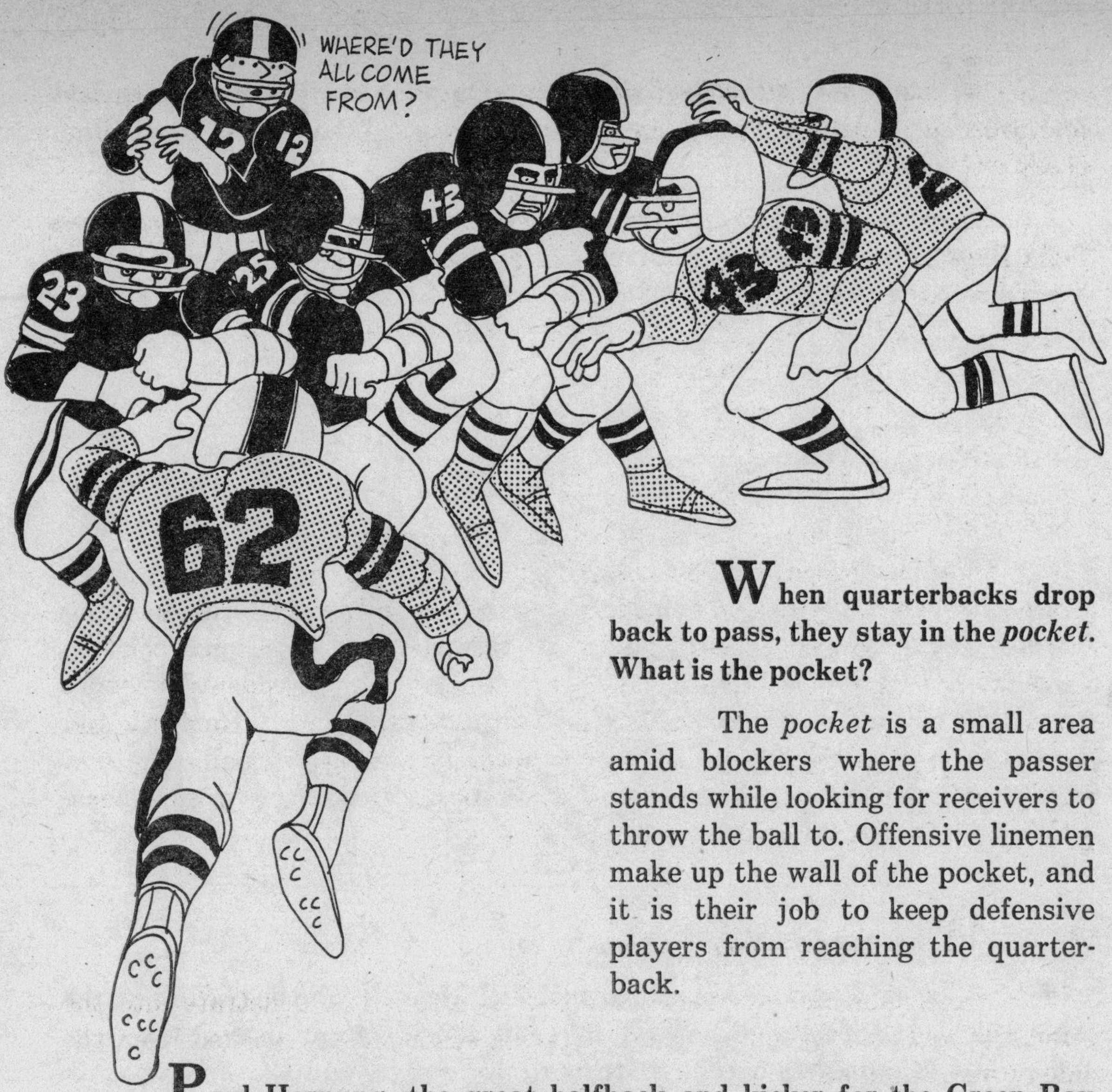

When quarterbacks drop back to pass, they stay in the *pocket*. What is the pocket?

The *pocket* is a small area amid blockers where the passer stands while looking for receivers to throw the ball to. Offensive linemen make up the wall of the pocket, and it is their job to keep defensive players from reaching the quarterback.

Paul Hornung, the great halfback and kicker for the Green Bay Packers, won the Heisman Trophy in 1956. For which college did he play?

Paul Hornung won the 1956 Heisman Trophy while playing for the University of Notre Dame.

When a pass receiver runs a *look-in* pattern, what does he do?

A receiver running a *look-in* pattern breaks quickly downfield and then turns instantly to look over his shoulder for a pass.

The Rose Bowl has been played 63 times from 1916 to 1978. How many of those games ended in a tie? Is the answer 3, 10, or 17 games?

Only 3 of the 63 Rose Bowl games played from 1916 to 1978 ended in ties. Washington and Jefferson ended their game with California in a 0 to 0 tie in 1922; Navy and Washington tied, 14 to 14, in 1924; and Alabama and Stanford played to a 7 to 7 tie in 1927.

Where does a *slotback* line up?

A *slotback* lines up at least one yard behind the line of scrimmage between a wide receiver and the interior linemen.

In football, what is a *bomb*?

A *bomb* is a long pass to a receiver speeding down the field toward the goal line. It is a play intended to make a quick score.

What is a *lateral*?

A *lateral* is a pass tossed parallel with the goal line or back toward a team's goal. If a lateral is dropped, it is not considered an incomplete pass. Instead, it is considered to be a free ball or fumble, and the first team to recover the ball retains possession.

What does the quarterback do on a *bootleg play*?

On a *bootleg play*, the quarterback runs to the side opposite the direction his blockers have moved. Since most defenders follow the movement of the blockers, it is a play designed to confuse the defense.

Felix Blanchard and Glenn Davis made up West Point's nationally famous backfield in 1944-45. Only one of them ever won the Sullivan Trophy, which is awarded by the Amateur Athletic Union of the United States. Which player was it?

In 1945, the AAU named Felix "Doc" Blanchard as the recipient of the Sullivan Trophy, which is awarded annually to the amateur athlete who, by performance, example, and influence, does the most to advance the cause of good sportsmanship.

Gary Beban, Steve Spurrier, and John Huarte were all college quarterbacks who won the Heisman Trophy during their senior years. Can you name the schools those three Heisman Trophy winners attended?

Gary Beban, who won the Heisman in 1967, attended UCLA; Steve Spurrier, the Heisman Trophy winner in 1966, graduated from the University of Florida; and John Huarte, who took the Heisman in 1964, attended the University of Notre Dame.

Has an Ivy League team ever won the Rose Bowl?

Yes, the Rose Bowl was won by an Ivy League team on two occasions. In 1920, Harvard beat Oregon by the score of 7 to 6, and in 1934, Columbia defeated Stanford, 7 to 0. On the two other occasions that Ivy League teams played in the Rose Bowl, Washington State beat Brown, 14 to 0, in 1916, and Oregon defeated Pennsylvania, 14 to 0, in 1917.

In what year did the American Football League merge with the National Football League? Was it in 1968, 1969, or 1970?

The AFL and the NFL merged in 1970, after the American Football League had been in operation for ten years.

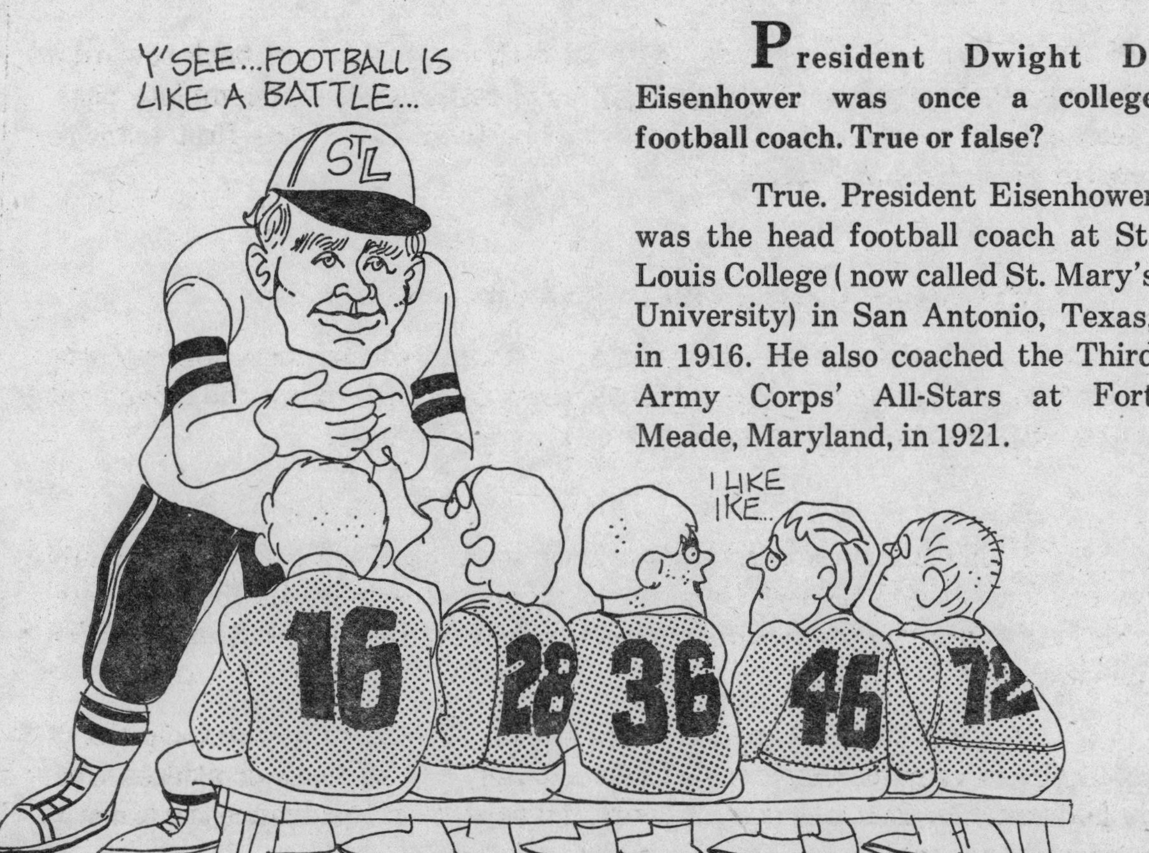

President Dwight D. Eisenhower was once a college football coach. True or false?

True. President Eisenhower was the head football coach at St. Louis College (now called St. Mary's University) in San Antonio, Texas, in 1916. He also coached the Third Army Corps' All-Stars at Fort Meade, Maryland, in 1921.

Gerrard "Buster" Ramsey, Ron Kramer, and Bill Wallace were all voted into the College Football Hall of Fame in 1978. Can you match each Hall-of-Famer with the school he attended?

(1) Gerrard "Buster" Ramsey **(a) William and Mary**

(2) Ron Kramer **(b) Rice University**

(3) Bill Wallace **(c) University of Michigan**

The correct match-ups are (1) a. Gerrard "Buster" Ramsey was an All-American guard who captained the William and Mary team in 1942. He was later All-Pro with the Chicago Cardinals and coached in the pro ranks with the Detroit Lions and the Buffalo Bills. (2) c. Ron Kramer earned All-America honors at the end position for the University of Michigan in 1955 and 1956. He later played on two world championship Green Bay Packer teams and ended his pro career playing for the Detroit Lions. (3) b. Bill Wallace was the first football Hall-of-Famer Rice University ever had. He is regarded by many as the greatest running back ever developed in the Southwest. In 1934, Wallace was named to the All-America squad.

What is a *screen play*?

On a *screen play,* the defensive linemen are allowed to rush toward the quarterback while a receiver takes up a position behind the line of scrimmage that is protected by a wall of offensive linemen. Once the defenders are out of position, the quarterback throws the ball to the receiver who sprints down the field protected by a wall of interference which the offensive linemen form.

Which side of the offensive line is referred to as the *weak side*?

The side of the offensive line where the split end lines up is referred to as the *weak side* of the line. It is called the weak side because there are only two offensive blockers on that side of the center. The *strong side* of the line has three offensive blockers: the tight end, a tackle, and guard.

Can you explain what a *flare pass* is?

A *flare pass* is a short pass swinging wide or flaring out of the backfield. Flare passes are usually thrown to backs.

If a defensive team goes into a *prevent defense,* what do they want to protect against? Is it a long pass completion or short gains made by runs and passes?

When a team goes into a *prevent defense*, they are attempting to stop long gains made by pass completions. Usually, the defensive team will lessen their front line strength by removing a lineman and increase their deep defense by bringing an additional defensive back into the game. Prevent defenses are structured to allow short gains while cutting off long gains.

President John F. Kennedy played football for Harvard in 1936 and 1937. Which position did he play?

John F. Kennedy played end for the Freshman team in 1936 and for the Junior Varsity team in 1937.

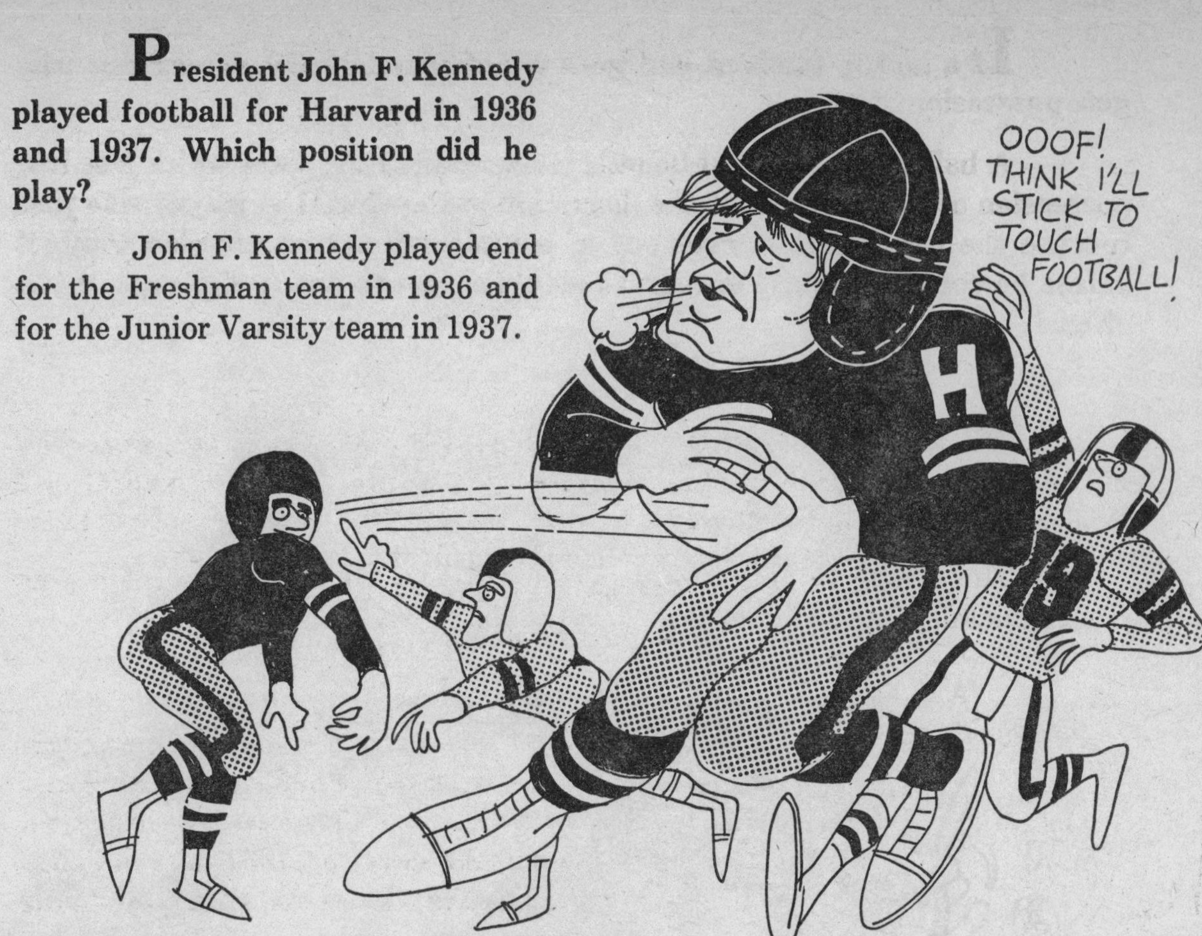

What is an *onside kick*?

An *onside kick* is a special kick the kickoff team uses when they want to retain possession of the ball. It is a short kick which the kicker attempts to angle away from any members of the opposing team. After the ball travels 10 yards on a kickoff, the team that gets the ball first retains possession of it. So the kicker attempts to kick the ball a minimum of 10 yards to a spot not occupied by any opponents, in the hopes that one of his teammates will be the first to reach it. If the ball does not travel 10 yards, the kicking team is penalized. The risk involved in an onside kick is that if the ball is recovered by the opposing team, they will have an excellent field position.

What is the name of the Michigan State football team?

The Spartans are Michigan State's team in the Big Ten Conference.

Which college football stadium holds more people? Is it Notre Dame Stadium at South Bend, Indiana, or the Yale Bowl at New Haven, Connecticut?

Yale's home field has a larger seating capacity. The Yale Bowl holds 70,874 people, while Notre Dame Stadium holds only 59,075.

If a ball is fumbled and goes out-of-bounds, what determines who gets possession of it?

A ball fumbled out-of-bounds is awarded to the team which last had possession of it, according to the discretion of the official. A player who just touches the ball before it goes out of bounds will not be awarded the ball unless he controls it long enough to establish possession in the eyes of the official.

When *Sport Magazine* picked its All-Time All-American Team, who did they name as coach of that team? Was it Knute Rockne, Glenn "Pop" Warner, or Amos Alonzo Stagg?

The coach of *Sport Magazine*'s All-Time All-American Team was Knute Rockne, the immortal head coach of Notre Dame.

The first Super Bowl game between the Green Bay Packers and the Kansas City Chiefs was played on January 5, 1967 at the Los Angeles Coliseum. Can you name the man who scored the first touchdown in the first Super Bowl game and the team he played for?

End Max McGee of the Packers scored the first Super Bowl touchdown in a 37-yard pass from Bart Starr. In Green Bay's 35 to 10 victory over Kansas City, McGee snared 2 TD passes. His other score was a 13-yard touchdown reception from Starr.

Who was the first college varsity football player to become President of the United States?

The answer is Dwight David Eisenhower. In 1912, "Ike" was a starting halfback for the Military Academy of West Point. His football playing career was cut short when he broke his leg in a game against Carlisle College on November 9, 1912. The break was so bad that Ike was never able to play football again. The accident occurred as 22-year-old Dwight David Eisenhower was bowled over while attempting to stop one of Carlisle's backs from scoring a touchdown. The back who bowled over young Eisenhower was a young Indian named Jim Thorpe!

HOCKEY

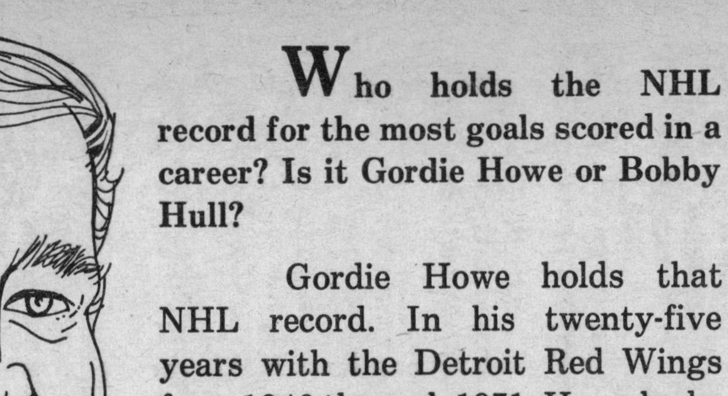

Who holds the NHL record for the most goals scored in a career? Is it Gordie Howe or Bobby Hull?

Gordie Howe holds that NHL record. In his twenty-five years with the Detroit Red Wings from 1946 through 1971, Howe had a total of 786 goals in regular-season play. Along with this record, he also holds records for the most career points (1,809), the most assists (1,023), the most games played (1,687), the most seasons played (25), and the most Most Valuable Player Awards (5 — 1952, 1953, 1957, 1958, 1960, and 1963).

Can a hockey game end in a tie during the regular season?

Yes. A hockey game ends after three periods of play during the regular season even if the score is tied. However, in the NHL, the WHL, and many other leagues, a tie in a playoff game results in a sudden-death overtime period. The tied teams then continue to play extra periods until one team scores to win the game.

The Most Valuable Player in the Stanley Cup Playoffs is awarded a trophy. What is the name of that trophy?

The Conn Smythe Trophy is awarded by the NHL to the Most Valuable Player in the Stanley Cup Playoffs. It was named for the former owner and manager of the Toronto Maple Leafs, who was a major influence in the NHL for many years.

Which NHL team calls Los Angeles, California, its home?

The correct answer is the Los Angeles Kings — a team which entered the NHL in 1967-68 along with five other teams to form the Western Division.

In hockey, what is a *breakaway* play?

A *breakaway* is considered to be one of the most exciting plays in hockey. An offensive player takes the puck and outraces the defensive players to go in one-on-one against the opposing goalie.

Who was the first NHL rookie to win the Conn Smythe Trophy as the Most Valuable Player in the Stanley Cup Playoffs?

In 1971, goal tender Ken Dryden of the Montreal Canadiens became the first rookie to win the Conn Smythe Trophy by leading his team to victory over the favored Chicago Black Hawks in the Stanley Cup Playoff Finals.

True or false? The trophy awarded to the National Hockey League championship team is the Grey Cup.

False. The NHL champions receive the Stanley Cup.

Boston College played against Boston University in the NCAA Hockey Championship game in 1978. Which team won the title?

Boston University was the NCAA Hockey Champion in 1978. They defeated Boston College by the score of 5 goals to 3.

True or false? In the NHL, the penalty for fighting is two minutes in the penalty box.

False. An NHL player has to serve *five* minutes in the penalty box for fighting.

Which NHL star holds the record for playing in the most consecutive games? Is it Garry Unger, John Bucyk, or Jean Ratelle?

Garry Unger, playing for Toronto, Detroit, and St. Louis, holds that record. During ten seasons, from 1968 through 1978, Unger played in 803 consecutive games.

Which trophy is awarded to the NHL's Rookie of the Year?

The Calder Memorial Trophy is awarded annually to the outstanding rookie in the NHL. It was established in 1936-37 by Frank Calder, the first president of the NHL.

In what year was the National Hockey League formed?

The National Hockey League was formed in 1917 from an earlier professional league, the National Hockey Association. The four teams that made up the original NHL were all Canadian teams: the Montreal Wanderers, the Montreal Canadiens, the Toronto Arenas, and the Ottawa Senators. It wasn't until the 1920s that American teams joined the league.

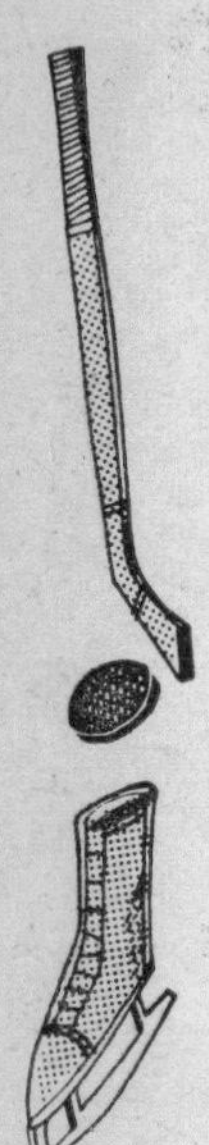

Terry Sawchuck, Jacques Plante, and Glenn Hall are all former NHL stars who played the same position. What was that position?

Sawchuck, Plante, and Hall were all great goal tenders in the National Hockey League. In 1953 and 1955 with Detroit and in 1965 with Toronto, Sawchuck led the league in the least goals scored against him. Plante duplicated that feat with Montreal from 1956 to 1960 and in 1962, and Hall did the same with Chicago in 1963.

Which Montreal Canadien star is nicknamed "The Road Runner"? Is it Yvan Cournoyer, Henri Richard, or Guy Lafleur?

Yvan Cournoyer, the Canadiens' right-winger, was dubbed "The Road Runner" because of his dazzling speed on the ice.

The James Norris Memorial Trophy is awarded annually to the outstanding goalie in the NHL. True or false?

False. The Norris Trophy is awarded annually by the National Hockey League to its top *defenseman*. The trophy was named after James Norris, who purchased the Detroit Falcons in 1933 and changed their name to the Red Wings.

Who was the first NHL star to score 50 goals in a single season? Was it Gordie Howe, Bobby Hull, or Maurice Richard?

In 1944-45, right-winger Maurice Richard of the Montreal Canadiens became the first man in NHL history to score 50 goals in one season. Bobby Hull duplicated that record in the 1960-61 season. Gordie Howe came close with 49 goals in 1952-53, but never hit the 50 mark.

Who holds the World Hockey Association's record for scoring the most points in a single game?

Jim Harrison, playing for the Alberta Oilers, established the WHA single-game scoring record by scoring 3 goals and 7 assists for a total of 10 points in a 1973 game against Toronto.

Which NHL player receives the Hart Memorial Trophy at the end of the season?

The Hart Memorial Trophy is awarded by the NHL to the player voted "the most useful" to his club. The trophy was donated to the NHL in 1923 by David A. Hart, father of Cecil Hart — the coach of the Montreal Canadiens for many years.

Which player was nicknamed "The Crown Prince of Hockey"?

Jean Beliveau, the Montreal Canadiens' center who appeared in sixteen consecutive All-Star games and scored 500 goals in his career, holds the honorary title of "The Crown Prince of Hockey."

Who holds the World Hockey Association record for goal-scoring in a single season? Is it Bobby Hull, Gordie Howe, or Anders Hedberg?

Swedish hockey player Anders Hedberg of the Winnipeg Jets established the WHA single-season goal-scoring record in 1976-77 by shooting 83 pucks into the net.

Who coached the Boston Bruins of the NHL in 1977-78?

Don Cherry was the Bruins' coach during the 1977-78 season.

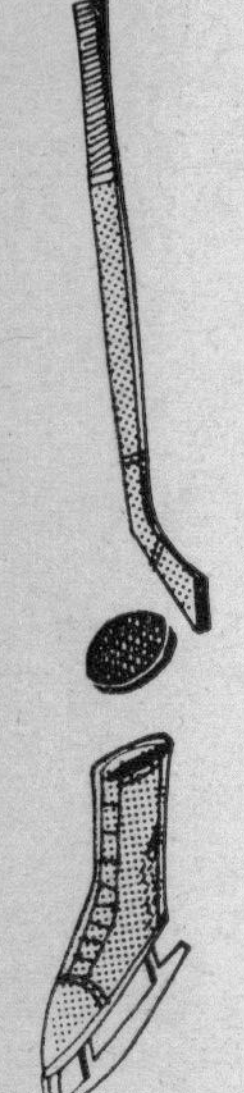

Who holds the NHL record for the most penalty minutes served in a single season? Here's a hint. The record was set by a Philadelphia Flyer in 1974-75.

Dave Schultz, playing for the Philadelphia Flyers in 1974-75, set the record by serving 472 minutes in penalties.

True or false? Steve Shutt of the Montreal Canadiens scored 50 goals in 1976-77.

False. Versatile Steve Shutt of the Canadiens fired a total of 60 goals into the net in 1976-77.

The champions of the NHL win the Stanley Cup. What do the winners of the WHA Finals receive?

The Avco World Trophy, named after a commercial television sponsor, is awarded to the top team in the World Hockey Association.

True or false? Clarence Campbell was President of the National Hockey League for 31 years.

True. Clarence Campbell was at the head of the NHL from 1946 to 1977, when he retired and turned the job of president over to John Augustus Ziegler.

The Vezina Trophy is awarded annually to a player in which position?

The NHL goal tender who has the least number of goals scored against him in a season is awarded the Vezina Trophy. This trophy was first donated to the NHL by the Montreal Canadiens in 1926-27, in memory of George Vezina, a great Canadien goal tender who died during the 1925 season.

Has a New York Ranger goal tender ever won the NHL's Vezina Trophy?

Yes. Ed Giacomin and Gilles Villemure, alternating in goal tending for the Rangers, shared the Vezina Trophy in 1970-71.

In most indoor hockey rinks, how many coats of ice are there? Is it one, two, or three coats?

Most indoor hockey rinks consist of two coats of artificial ice. The bottom coat is painted white with red and blue markings, and is covered with a coat of clear ice.

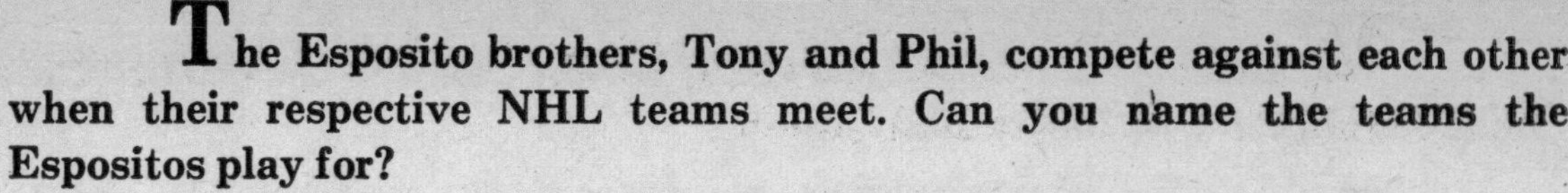

The Esposito brothers, Tony and Phil, compete against each other when their respective NHL teams meet. Can you name the teams the Espositos play for?

Tony Esposito is a goal tender for the Chicago Black Hawks, and Phil Esposito, a former Boston Bruin, is a center for the New York Rangers.

Can you explain what *offside at the blue line* means?

It means that an attacking hockey player crossed over the blue line into his opponents' zone before his attacking teammates brought the puck over the blue line into that zone. The puck must *precede* an offensive player into the opponents' zone, or it is an *offside.*

Which trophy is awarded to the leading scorer in the NHL?

At the end of the season, the leading scorer in the NHL is awarded the Art Ross Trophy. Former Boston Bruin manager Art Ross donated the trophy to the league in the 1947-48 season.

In 1976, which NHL hockey team was nicknamed "The Broad Street Bullies"?

The Philadelphia Flyers were nicknamed "The Broad Street Bullies" because of the very aggressive brand of play by these skaters whose stadium is on Philadelphia's Broad Street.

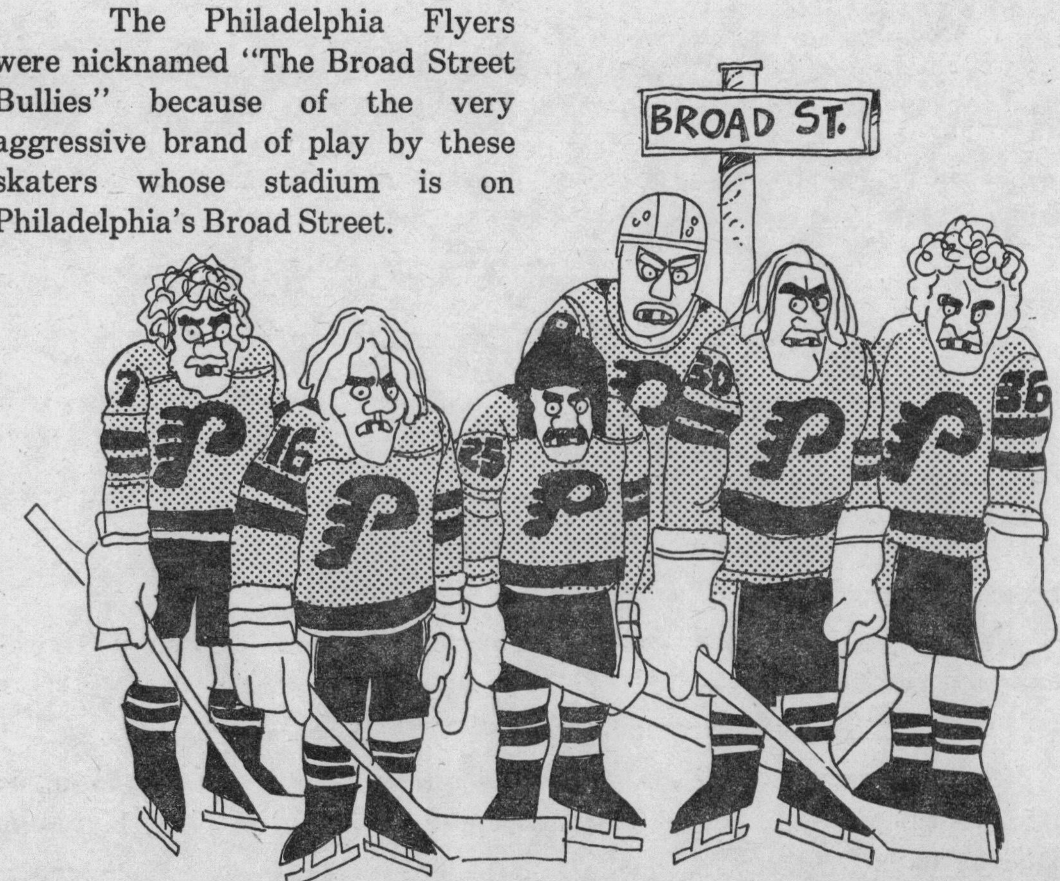

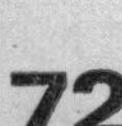

Which player was clocked as the fastest skater in the NHL? Was it Bobby Hull, Ed Westfall, or Rod Gilbert?

The answer is Bobby Hull. He has been clocked on the ice at a speed of 29.7 mph.

Which NHL team won the Stanley Cup for the most consecutive years? Is it the Toronto Maple Leafs, the Detroit Red Wings, or the Montreal Canadiens?

The correct answer is the Montreal Canadiens. The Canadiens won the Stanley Cup every year from 1955 to 1960.

Although hockey is hardly a "gentlemanly" sport, does the NHL give an award for gentlemanly conduct?

Yes. Since 1925, the Lady Byng Award has been given to the NHL player who best combines gentlemanly conduct with hockey talent. It was named for the wife of Canada's then governor general.

The Boston Bruins and the Montreal Canadiens are two of the four teams that competed in the 1977-78 Stanley Cup Semi-finals. Can you name the other two NHL teams that played in the Semi-finals?

The Boston Bruins met the Philadelphia Flyers, and the Montreal Canadiens played against the Toronto Maple Leafs in the 1977-78 Stanley Cup Semi-finals.

How many times did Bernie "Boom Boom" Geoffrian lead the NHL in scoring?

Bernie Geoffrian of the Montreal Canadiens led the NHL in scoring for two seasons. In 1954-55, his 75 points were the highest in the league, and in 1960-61, he won the scoring title again with a total of 95 points.

How are All-Star Teams selected?

Hockey writers and broadcasters choose a first and second All-Star Team from both NHL divisions. These selected East All-Stars have been meeting selected West All-Stars since the NHL had its first All-Star Game in 1947.

How many times have the Chicago Black Hawks won the Stanley Cup?

The Chicago Black Hawks won hockey's coveted award three times: in 1934, 1938, and 1961.

True or false? Boston University won the National Collegiate Athletic Association Hockey Championship in 1971 and again in 1972.

True. In 1971, Boston University defeated the University of Minnesota, 4 goals to 2, to win the crown. They held onto that championship in 1972 by beating Cornell, 4 to 0.

True or false? Bob Ganey, who played forward for the Montreal Canadiens in 1977-78, is best known for his ability as a puck handler.

False. Bob Ganey is best known for his *checking* ability. He is probably one of the best checking forwards ever to play in the NHL.

Can you name the college that won the NCAA Hockey Championship in 1973? Was it Cornell, Wisconsin, or Denver University?

Wisconsin won the NCAA Hockey Championship in 1973 by defeating Denver by the score of 4 to 2.

Who won the Stanley Cup in 1977?

The Montreal Canadiens defeated the Boston Bruins in the 1977 playoff finals to win the Stanley Cup.

In hockey, what is a *hand pass*?

A *hand pass* is called when a hockey player uses his hand to direct the puck to a member of his own team. A hand pass is not legal, and when it occurs, play is stopped and a face-off restarts the game.

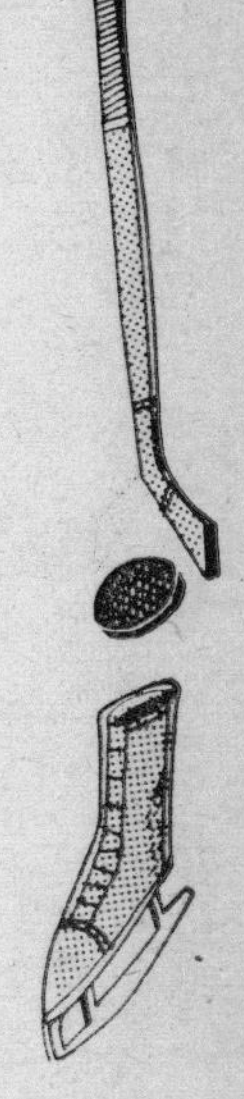

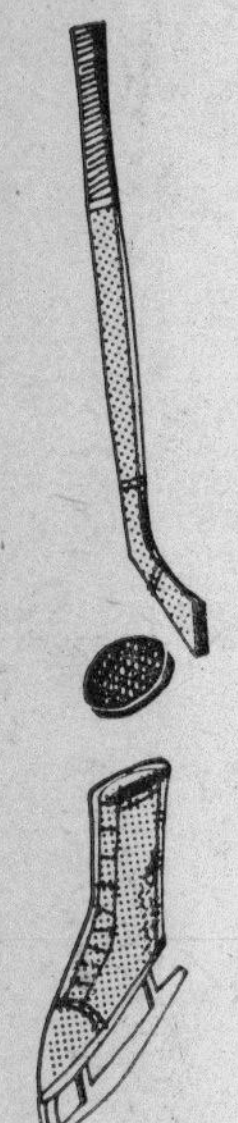

True or false? The last time the New York Rangers won the Stanley Cup was in the 1939-1940 season.

True. The Rangers haven't won the Stanley Cup since 1940.

True or false? Steve Vickers is *not* a former NHL Rookie of the Year.

False. Steve Vickers, playing for the New York Rangers, *was* the NHL's Rookie of the Year in 1972-73.

Can you name the NHL division the New York Rangers are in?

The New York Rangers are in the Lester Patrick Division of the Clarence Campbell Conference, along with the Philadelphia Flyers, the Atlanta Flames, and the New York Islanders.

Who was voted the Most Valuable Player in the 1976-77 Stanley Cup Playoffs?

Guy Lafleur of the Montreal Canadiens was voted the Most Valuable Player in the 1976-77 Stanley Cup Playoffs.

Swedish-born Borje Salming, an NHL All-Star, played defense for which pro hockey team in 1977-78? Was it the Toronto Maple Leafs, the Quebec Nordiques, or the New York Rangers?

Borje Salming was an All-Star defenseman for the Toronto Maple Leafs in 1977-78.

Under normal conditions, how many players does a hockey team have on the ice at one time?

If no penalties are being served, a hockey team has six players on the ice at one time. The forward line of attackers is made up of two wingers and a center; the second line has two defensemen who seldom cross their opponents' blue line; and the sixth player is the goal tender.

How many periods are there in an ice hockey game?

In an ice hockey game, there are three 20-minute periods of actual playing time, separated by two 10- or 15-minute intermissions.

Who won the Hart Memorial Trophy in 1975 and 1976? Here's a hint. He was a center for the Philadelphia Flyers.

Bobby Clarke of the Philadelphia Flyers won the Hart Trophy in 1975 and 1976 as the most useful player to his club.

Goal tender Gerry Cheevers of the Boston Bruins holds the record for playing the most games without a defeat. How many games did Cheevers go without losing to set the record?

In 1971-72, goalie Gerry Cheevers played 33 games without suffering a defeat to establish the record.

How many times have the Detroit Red Wings won the Stanley Cup? Is it five, seven, or nine times?

The Red Wings won the Stanley Cup in 1936, 1937, 1943, 1950, 1952, 1954, and 1955 — a total of seven times.

Can you name the two goal tenders who played for the New York Islanders during the 1977-78 season?

Glenn "Chico" Resch and Billy Smith were the New York Islanders' goalies during the 1977-78 season.

What is the name of the NHL team located in Atlanta, Georgia?

Georgia's pride in the NHL is the Atlanta Flames.

Can you name the WHA team that Gordie Howe played for during the 1977-78 season?

Gordie Howe was a member of the New England Whalers in 1977-78. But before joining them, he also played for the WHA's Houston Aeros and the NHL's Detroit Red Wings.

True or false? A teammate may serve a goalie's penalties.

True. A teammate may serve any goalie's penalties other than a game misconduct.

Can you name the NHL player who scored the most goals in one year?

If you said Reggie Leach, you're absolutely correct. As a Philadelphia Flyer in 1975-76, Leach scored a total of 80 goals in the regular season and the playoffs.

In 1973, the Montreal Canadiens played the Chicago Black Hawks in the Stanley Cup Finals. Which team won that best-of-seven series?

The Montreal Canadiens clinched the Stanley Cup on May 10, 1973 by defeating the Chicago Black Hawks, 4 games to 3.

Punch Imlach was the general manager of which NHL team during the 1977-78 hockey season?

Colorful Punch Imlach was the general manager of the Buffalo Sabres in 1977-78.

A 1977 motion picture, *Slap Shot*, told the story of a professional hockey team and its aging, but spirited, captain. Do you remember who starred in the role of that team captain?

Paul Newman took his lumps on the ice as the film's gutsy captain.

Gil Perreault and René Robert are two of the three NHL stars on the Buffalo Sabres' high-scoring "French Connection" line. Who was the third member of the Sabres' famous 1977-78 line?

Winger Rick Martin was the third member of Buffalo's "French Connection" line.

Which team holds the infamous NHL record of going the longest without winning a game? Is it the Detroit Red Wings, the Kansas City Scouts, or the Washington Capitals?

The old Kansas City Scouts hold that infamous record. From February 12 to April 5, 1976, they played in 27 NHL contests and didn't win a single one. They lost 21 and tied 6 before they finally won a game.

True or false? A hockey team named the Ottawa Silver Seven once won the Stanley Cup.

True. Although you'd have to go back to the record books for the early 1900s, the Ottawa Silver Seven did win the Stanley Cup — three times! They won it in 1903, 1904, and 1905.

Who won the Norris Trophy the first year it was awarded?

Doug Harvey of the Montreal Canadiens was named the Outstanding Defenseman in the NHL the first time the Norris Trophy was awarded in 1957-58. Harvey won this award again in 1959-60 and 1960-61. Joining the New York Rangers in 1961-62, Harvey was once more the Norris Trophy winner.

How many times did Alex Delvecchio win the NHL's Lady Byng Award?

Alex Delvecchio of the Detroit Red Wings won the Lady Byng Award for skillful and sportsmanlike play in 1958-59, 1965-66, and 1968-69 — a total of three times.

Where is the Hockey Hall of Fame located?

Exhibition Park in Toronto, Canada, is the site of the Hockey Hall of Fame. Opened in 1961, the museum honors former players, referees, and other people who helped develop and popularize the sport of hockey.

How long must a hockey player remain in the penalty box if he receives a misconduct penalty?

A misconduct penalty, given chiefly for improper behavior toward officials, results in a ten-minute penalty. However, if two players are already in the penalty box, a substitute may go into the game as a replacement for the player serving the misconduct penalty, since a team must *always* have at least four men on the ice.

Left-winger Ross Lonsberry once played in 82 pro hockey games in a 78-game NHL hockey season. True or false?

Impossible as it seems, the answer is true. Lonsberry began the 1971-72 season with the Los Angeles Kings, where he played in 50 games. Then he was traded to the Philadelphia Flyers, who had played only 46 games on their schedule to date. Ross finished out the season by playing in 32 more games. Therefore in 1971-72, Ross Lonsberry played in 82 pro hockey games in a 78-game NHL season.

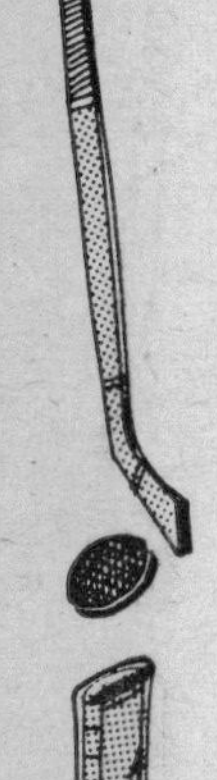

In 1977-78, which team finished first in the Lester Patrick Division of the NHL?

The New York Islanders won out over the Atlanta Flames, the Philadelphia Flyers, and the New York Rangers in the Lester Patrick Division in 1977-78.

Can you name the man who was the head coach of the New York Islanders hockey team in 1977-78?

If you said Al Arbour, you're right. Arbour coached the New York Islanders in 1977-78, bringing them out of virtual obscurity and into the Stanley Cup Playoffs.

In 1976-77, Willie Plett of the Atlanta Flames was named Rookie of the Year. True or false?

True. Plett scored 33 goals in his first NHL season and won Rookie of the Year honors.

Did Ted Lindsay of the Detroit Red Wings ever lead the NHL in scoring?

Yes. "Terrible" Ted Lindsay of the Red Wings was the NHL's leading scorer in 1949-50. In 69 games, he scored 23 goals and 55 assists for a league-leading total of 78 points.

What does the hockey term *hat trick* mean?

The term *hat trick* means that one player has scored 3 goals in a single game.

How many times did Henri Richard, the former team captain of the Montreal Canadiens, play in the Stanley Cup Finals?

Henri "The Pocket Rocket" Richard, played in eleven Stanley Cup Championship Finals.

True or false? The Philadelphia Flyers hold the NHL record as the most penalized team in a single season.

True. In 1975-76, the Flyers had 1,980 minutes in penalties assessed against them — an NHL record!

Do you know which NHL team Scott Bowman coached in 1977-78?

In 1977-78, Scott Bowman was the head coach of the Montreal Canadiens.

In the 1976-77 NHL season, the Montreal Canadiens won 60 games. How many games did they lose that year?

In 1976-77, the Montreal Canadiens lost only 8 games. Their regular-season record was 60 wins, 8 losses, and 12 ties.

True or false? Guy Lafleur, Steve Shutt, and Jacques Lemaire of the Montreal Canadiens hold the NHL record for scoring by a single line.

True. Lafleur, Shutt, and Lemaire set the NHL record in 1976-77 by scoring a total of 150 goals as linemates.

Can you name the goal tender who holds the NHL record for career shutouts?

Goalie Terry Sawchuck is the record holder. Playing for the Toronto Maple Leafs, the Detroit Red Wings, the Boston Bruins, the Los Angeles Kings, and the New York Rangers during his twenty seasons in the NHL, Sawchuck recorded 103 shutouts.

Of the three officials on the ice during an NHL hockey game, which ones can call penalties?

With two linesmen and a referee on the ice during an NHL game, only the referee can call penalties. The linesmen watch for offsides, drop the puck for face-offs, and call icings. They cannot call an infraction, but they can alert the referee to one.

Ice hockey pucks have been found to travel at speeds of over 100 mph. Whose powerful shots have been timed as fast as 118 mph? Is it Bobby Hull, Gordie Howe, or Marcel Dionne?

Bobby Hull, "The Golden Jet," not only has skating speed, but also the power to send a puck traveling at a clocked speed of 118.3 miles per hour.

True or false? Clark Gillies was the team captain of the Toronto Maple Leafs during the 1977-78 season.

False. During the 1977-78 season, Clark Gillies was the team captain of the New York Islanders. The Toronoto Maple Leafs were captained by Darryl Sittler.

True or false? Robbie Ftorek, as a member of the Phoenix Road Runners, was named the Most Valuable Player in the WHA in 1976-77.

True. Ftorek, who scored 117 points for the Road Runners during the 1976-77 season, was named the MVP of the World Hockey Association.

The Detroit Red Wings finished first in the NHL's Norris Division in 1977-78. True or false?

False. The Montreal Canadiens finished first in the Norris Division in 1977-78, clinching the division title early in the season.

True or false? At the start of some Philadelphia Flyers' home games, a recording of Kate Smith singing "God Bless America" is played instead of the National Anthem.

True. For special or important games, the Flyers substitute Kate Smith's rendition of "God Bless America" — their good-luck sign — for the National Anthem.

Which player holds the National Hockey League record for scoring the most goals as a rookie? Is it Mike Bossy, Garry Unger, or Gil Perrault?

Mike Bossy of the New York Islanders set the NHL record in 1977-78 by scoring 53 goals in his rookie season.

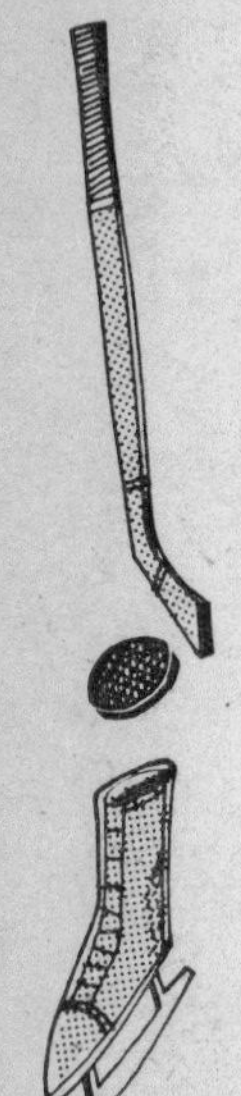

True or false? A Canadian college hockey player once scored a goal after only three seconds of play.

True. Kim D. Miles, playing for the University of Guelph, scored a goal after only three seconds of play in a game against the University of Western Ontario on November 9, 1957.

Maurice Richard, the famouse right-winger for the Montreal Canadiens, had an interesting nickname. What was it?

Richard was nicknamed Maurice "The Rocket" Richard because of his explosive scoring ability.

True or false? Bryan Trottier of the New York Islanders won the Hart Memorial Trophy in 1977-78 as the NHL's Most Valuable Player.

False. Montreal Canadien Guy Lafleur was the 1977-78 winner of the Hart Memorial Trophy. He also captured the Art Ross Trophy as the NHL's top scorer that same year.

True or false? Stefan Persson, a defenseman for the New York Islanders in 1977-78, is originally from Canada.

False. Defenseman Stefan Persson is a native of Sweden.

What is a *penalty shot*?

A free shot at the oppontents' goal with only the goalie defending it is called a *penalty shot*. A penalty shot is imposed when an attacking player has a clear shot at the goal and is pulled down from behind, thus preventing him from taking that shot.

In what year was the first professional hockey league formed? Was it 1893, 1900, or 1904?

The International Pro Hockey League, hockey's first professional league, was started in 1904. It included teams from Canada and the United States.

The Boston Bruins and the Chicago Black Hawks were both champions of their divisions in 1977-78. Can you name each team's division?

The Bruins captured the Adams Division title in 1977-78, while the Black Hawks were the champs in the Conn Smythe Division.

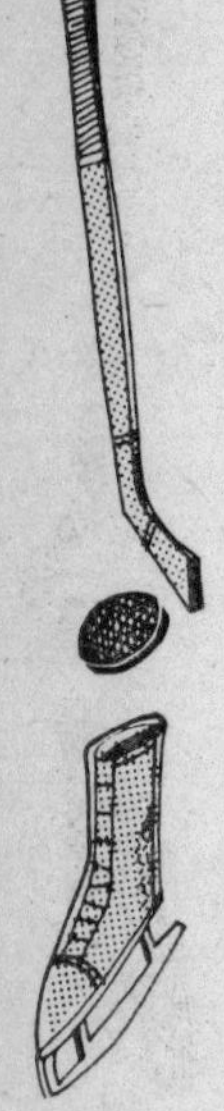

Defenseman Jerry Korab of the Buffalo Sabres has a catchy nickname. Can you guess what it is?

Because of his size, the 6'3", 218-pound defenseman of the Sabres is nicknamed "King Kong Korab."

The Chicago Black Hawks and the Minnesota North Stars are in the NHL's Conn Smythe Division. Can you name the other three teams in that division in 1977-78?

If you answered the Vancouver Canucks, the Colorado Rockies, and the St. Louis Blues, you're correct.

World amateur hockey is regulated by the International Ice Hockey Federation. Where is the headquarters of the IIHF? Is it in the United States, England, or the Soviet Union?

The International Ice Hockey Federation, founded in 1908, governs world amateur ice hockey in about thirty countries from its headquarters in London, England.

True or false? Dennis Potvin, Clark Gillies, and Mike Bossy were all former first-round draft choices of the New York Islanders.

True. NHL stars Potvin, Bossy, and Gillies were all first-round draft picks of the New York Islanders — Potvin, in 1973; Gillies, in 1974; and Bossy, in 1977.

Eddie Shore, called by many the "firebrand of hockey," had all his teeth knocked out, 19 scars in his scalp, and 600 stitches all over his body by the time he retired. For which team did Shore play?

Eddie Shore, one of the roughest players in the history of hockey, played for the Boston Bruins during the late 1920s and the early 1930s.

Joe Malone of the old Quebec Bulldogs holds the record for scoring the most goals in a single game. How many goals did Malone score to set that record?

Joe Malone set the scoring record with 7 goals as the old Quebec Bulldogs beat the old Toronto St. Patricks, 10-6, on January 31, 1920.

Can you name the college team that won the NCAA hockey championship in 1977? Was it Wisconsin, New Hampshire, or Boston University?

Wisconsin won the NCAA hockey championship in 1977, defeating a stubborn New Hampshire squad by the score of 4 to 3 in overtime.

Maurice Richard of the Montreal Canadiens holds the NHL record for scoring the most hat tricks (3 goals or more in one game) in the Stanley Cup Playoffs. How many hat tricks did Richard score in Stanley Cup competition to set the record?

Maurice "The Rocket" Richard set the National Hockey League record by scoring 7 hat tricks in Stanley Cup play.

Who was the first defenseman in NHL history to win a scoring championship? Was it Bobby Orr, Brad Park, or Dennis Potvin?

During the 1968-69 season, Bobby Orr of the Boston Bruins scored 33 goals and 87 assists for a total of 120 points to become the first defenseman in history to capture the NHL scoring crown.

Who won the Conn Smythe trophy in 1977-78? Was it Larry Robinson, Gerry Cheevers, or Steve Shutt?

Defenseman Larry Robinson of the Montreal Canadiens won the Conn Smythe Trophy as the Most Valuable Player in the 1977-78 Stanley Cup Playoffs.

Which player holds the NHL record for scoring the most assists in a single season?

The great defenseman Bobby Orr holds the NHL record for scoring the most assists in a single season. As a Boston Bruin in 1970-71, Orr assisted on 102 goals to establish the record.

Which NHL team did Fred Shero coach in 1978-79?

In 1978-79, Fred Shero was the head coach and general manager of the New York Rangers, the team for which he played in the late 1940s.

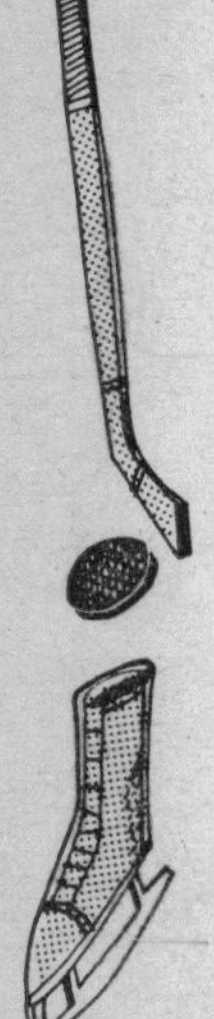

The first American hockey team to compete in the NHL was the New York Rangers. True or false?

False. The correct answer is the Boston Bruins. The Boston team became a member of the formerly all-Canadian National Hockey League in 1924. The New York Rangers joined the NHL the following season, along with four other U.S. teams.

The Pittsburgh Penguins and the Detroit Red Wings are in which NHL division?

In 1977-78, Pittsburgh and Detroit were in the Norris Division of the Wales Conference, along with the Los Angeles Kings, the Montreal Canadiens, and the Washington Capitals.

Who was the team captain of the Buffalo Sabres during the 1977-78 season? Was it Jim Schoenfeld or Danny Gare?

Right-winger Danny Gare was captain of the Sabres' squad in 1977-78. Defenseman Jim Schoenfeld was the previous captain of the Buffalo team.

True or false? The Stanley Cup was once used by a cleaning woman as a flower pot.

True. In 1906, the Montreal Wanderers, winners of the Stanley Cup that year, left the silver bowl behind in a photo studio where team pictures were being taken. It was found there by a cleaning woman, who used it as a flower pot until it was recovered by its rightful owners.

The Stanley Cup, symbol of supremacy in the National Hockey League, was donated by Lord Stanley of Preston in 1893. How much did that original Stanley Cup cost? Was it $48.67, $55.71, or $100.03?

The original Stanley Cup, a silver bowl, cost a mere $48.67, but its current value, as it is passed on each year to the new NHL champ, is priceless.

Hockey has an unusual rule about making substitutions which no other major sport in the world has. What does that rule allow hockey teams to do?

In order to keep the action fast, hockey rules allow teams to substitute players while the game is in progress.

Goalie Jacques Plante was once named the Most Valuable Player of the NHL. True or false?

True. In 1961-62, Montreal Canadien goal tender Jacques Plante was named the MVP of the National Hockey League. That same year, he also won the Vezina Trophy for having the best goal-tending record in the NHL.

Defenseman Mike Milbury, an American-born hockey player with the Boston Bruins in 1977-78, also starred in college hockey. Did Milbury play for Colgate, Boston Univerisity, or Denver?

Mike Milbury, who was born and raised near Boston, played college hockey at Colgate University before going to the NHL.

In hockey, what is a *face-off*?

When an official drops the puck between the sticks of two opposing players, that is a *face-off*. The players each then try to hit the puck to one of their teammates or in the direction of their opponents' net.

Can you name the two NHL players who tended goal for the Montreal Canadiens during the 1976-77 season?

Ken Dryden and Bunny Laroque were the Montreal goalies in the 1976-77 season.

A hockey puck is 1 inch thick and 3 inches in diameter. Can you guess its weight? Is it 4½-5ounces, 5½-6 ounces, or 6½-7 ounces?

The hard rubber hockey puck weighs 5½-6 ounces.

What does the term *icing the puck* mean?

Icing is a violation that occurs when a defending player shoots the puck from his team's half of ice across the opponents' goal line. If the offending team has fewer players on the ice than the other team or if the puck ends up as a shot on goal, icing is not called.

Can you name the four teams in the Charles F. Adams Division of the NHL in 1977-78?

The Boston Bruins, the Buffalo Sabres, the Toronoto Maple Leafs, and the Cleveland Barons made up the NHL's Adams Division in 1977-78.

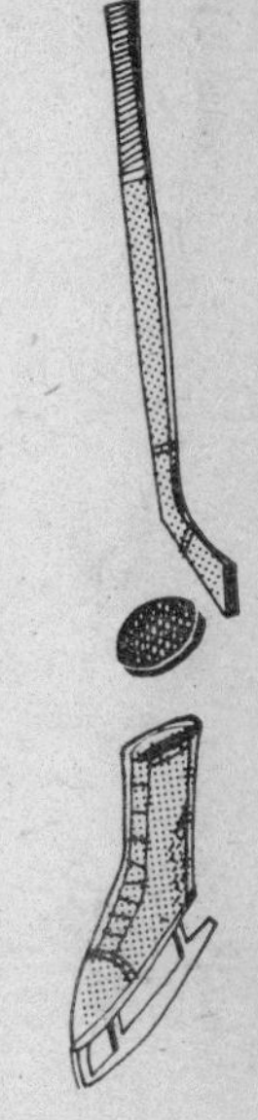

During the 1977-78 hockey season, the Montreal Canadiens set an NHL record for winning the most consecutive games. How many games did the Canadiens win to establish the record?

In 1977-78, Montreal won 28 straight games to set the new NHL record.

True or false? No NHL player has ever scored 3 goals in 21 seconds in a hockey game.

False. Bill Mosienko of the Chicago Black Hawks did it on March 23, 1952. He scored 3 goals in 21 seconds against the New York Rangers.

When a player uses a *stick check*, what is he doing?

When a player uses his hockey stick to hook or poke the puck away from his opponent's stick, that is called a *stick check*.

Chicago Black Hawk Stan Mikita has won the Art Ross Trophy, the Hart Trophy, and the Lady Byng Award. True or false?

True. Stan Mikita has won all three awards during his illustrious playing career which began in 1961 and saw him still on the ice in 1978.

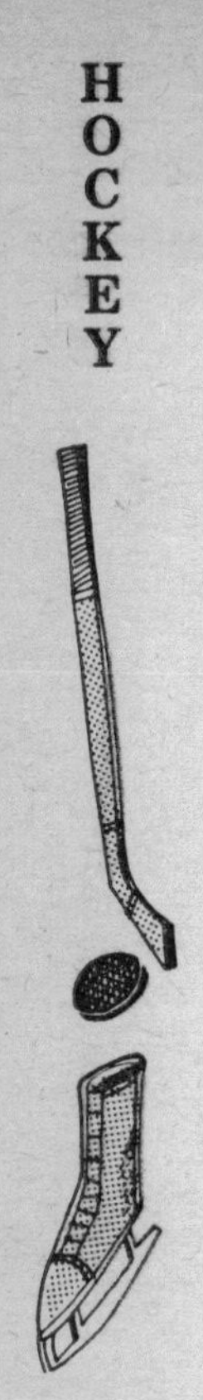

Right-winger Don Saleski of the 1977-78 Philadelphia Flyers has an amusing nickname. Do you know it?

Because of Saleski's curly hair, tall, gawky frame, and long, beaklike nose, he has been named after the "Sesame Street" character "Big Bird."

Bobbie Hull of the Winnipeg Jets won the first Gordie Howe Trophy in 1973 and repeated his win in 1975. To whom is that trophy awarded annually?

The Gordie Howe Trophy is awarded annually to the Most Valuable Player in the World Hockey Association. Howe, himself, was the 1974 winner when he played for the Houston Aeros of the WHA.

Gus Bodar of the Toronto Maple Leafs holds the NHL record as the player to score the fastest first goal as a rookie. True or false?

True. In his first NHL game on October 30, 1943, Gus Bodar scored a goal against the New York Rangers at 15 seconds of the first period.

True or false? The Stanley Cup is the oldest trophy competed for by professional athletes in North America.

True. The Stanley Cup, presented by the governor general of Canada, Lord Stanley, for the first time in 1893, is the oldest trophy competed for by professional athletes in North America. Although the trophy was originally put up for amateur hockey teams, the Stanley Cup was later turned over to the NHL.

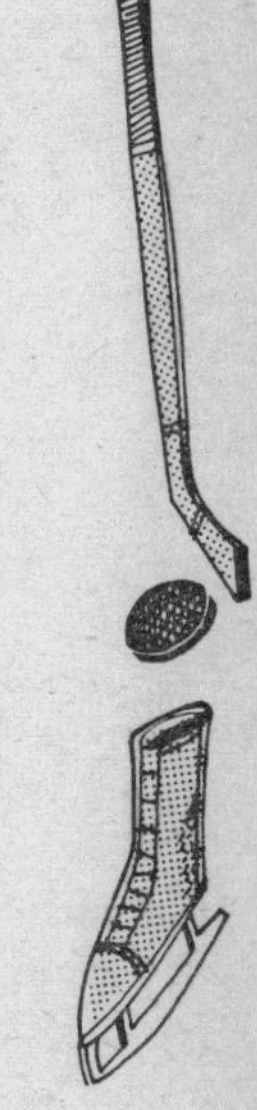

How many times have the Philadelphia Flyers won the Stanley Cup? Is it two, three, or five times?

The Philadelphia Flyers have won the Stanley Cup twice — first in 1974 and again in 1975.

Fred Shero, who coached the NHL's Philadelphia Flyers to Stanley Cup victories in 1974 and 1975, was a hockey player for the New York Rangers from 1947 to 1950. What position did Shero play?

Fred Shero was a defenseman for the New York Rangers.

In 1977-78, Bobby Hull entered his twenty-first season as a pro hockey player. For which WHA team did Bobby play that year? Was it the New England Whalers, the Winnipeg Jets, or the Birmingham Bulls?

The great Bobby Hull started his twenty-first pro hockey season as a member of the WHA's Winnipeg Jets, with whom he had signed a $2¾ million contract in 1972. Before that, from 1957 to 1972, Bobby played for the NHL's Chicago Black Hawks.

Which position does Bryan Trottier of the New York Islanders play?

Bryan Trottier is a center for the New York Islanders.

When the referee makes the signal pictured, what does it mean?

This signal means that a player is being penalized for *holding*. It is a minor penalty, and the guilty player must serve two minutes in the penalty box while his team plays short-handed.

Can you name the NHL team whose home ice is in Vancouver, British Columbia?

The Vancouver Canucks are the NHL team located on Canada's Pacific Coast.

What is a *power play*?

A *power play* occurs when one or two players on the same team are in the penalty box and the opposing team, having the manpower advantage, sends all of its players except its goal tender into the opposing zone in an all-out attempt to score a goal.

Who won the first Rookie of the Year Award in the NHL, and in what year was it presented?

Howie Meeker of the Toronto Maple Leafs won the first Rookie of the Year Award in 1946-47.

From 1920 to the 1950s, Canada dominated world amateur hockey. Which country then took over as the power in amateur hockey?

In the 1950s, Russia began a long string of victories in amateur hockey, however the spirit of competition between the two countries continued.

Who was the 1977-78 Rookie of the Year in the NHL? Was it Mike Bossy of the New York Islanders or Barry Beck of the Colorado Rockies?

The answer is Mike Bossy. The Islander scored more than 50 goals in his rookie year, to win the Calder Memorial Trophy. Beck finished second in the voting.

Which player holds the NHL record for scoring the most points in a single game? Is it Bryan Trottier, Guy Lafleur, or Darryl Sittler?

Darryl Sittler of the Toronto Maple Leafs holds the NHL record. He scored 10 points in a game against the Boston Bruins in 1976, on 6 goals and 4 assists.

Stan Mikita of the Chicago Black Hawks once led the NHL in scoring for four out of five years. True or false?

True. The Black Hawks' Stan Mikita took the NHL scoring honors in 1963-64, 1964-65, 1966-67, and 1967-68.

Hockey superstars Guy Lafleur and Steve Shutt were both first-round draft choices of which NHL team? Was it the Montreal Canadiens, the New York Islanders, or the Toronto Maple Leafs?

If you said the Montreal Canadiens, you're absolutely correct. Lafleur was the first-round draft choice in 1971, and Shutt was selected in 1972.

Only once in the history of the Stanley Cup was there no winner. Can you remember why?

During the 1918-19 Stanley Cup Finals in Seattle, Washington, the playoff games between the Montreal Canadiens and the Seattle Metropolitans were never finished due to a severe influenza epidemic in Seattle.

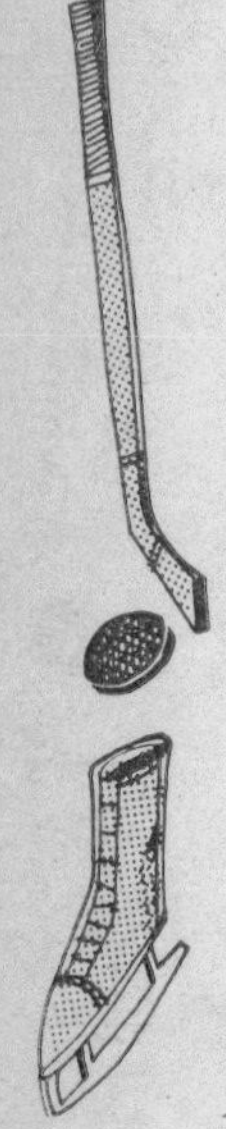

The first time the Toronto Maple Leafs won the Stanley Cup was in 1932. When was the last time they won the coveted hockey cup?

The Maple Leafs last won the Stanley Cup in 1967. But in the thirty-five years between 1932 and 1967, they took the title eleven times.

Who won the Norris Trophy at the end of the 1976-77 season?

Defenseman Larry Robinson of the Montreal Canadiens won the Norris Trophy in 1976-77 as the outstanding defenseman in the NHL.

What is the size of a standard hockey rink?

Although rinks differ in size, most conform to the standard measurements of 200 feet (61 meters) in length by 85 feet (26 meters) in width.

In hockey, how many penalty minutes must a player serve if he trips an opponent?

Tripping an opponent will send a player to the penalty box for two minutes.

During the 1928 Stanley Cup Championship game, the manager of the New York Rangers, a 50-year-old, white-haired former player, put himself in as goalie when the Ranger goalie was seriously injured, and sparked his team to a Stanley Cup victory. Who was that man?

The legendary "Mr. Hockey" was Lester Patrick, who as a player and manager participated in 20 Stanley Cup victories.

Which NHL team won the Stanley Cup in 1978? Was it the Boston Bruins or the Montreal Canadiens?

The Montreal Canadiens defeated the Boston Bruins, 4 games to 2, to win the 1978 Stanley Cup.

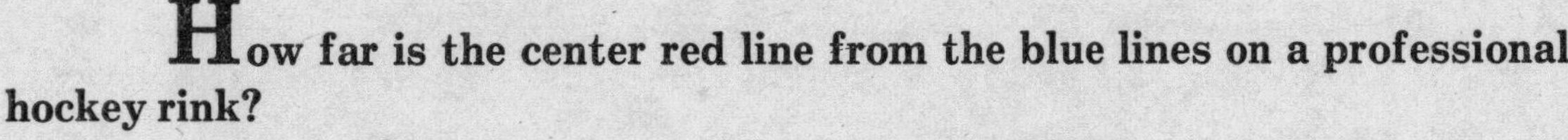

How far is the center red line from the blue lines on a professional hockey rink?

Each blue line is 30 feet from the center red line.

What is a *body check*?

When a player bumps against an opponent with his hip or shoulder in an attempt to block his progress or to throw him off balance, that is called a *body check*. Body checks are legal defensive hockey tactics.

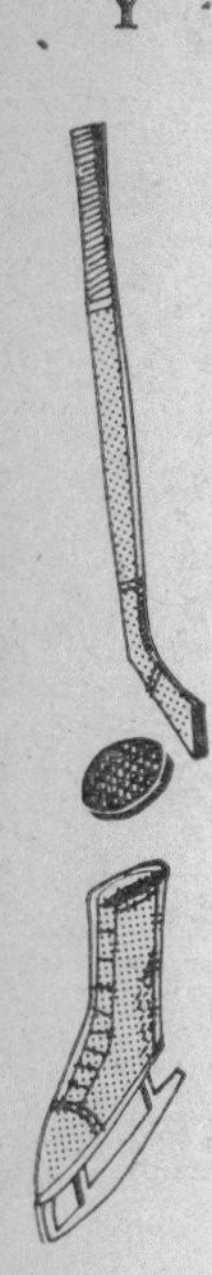

Who holds the NHL record for goal-scoring during the regular season? Is it Phil Esposito, Bobby Hull, or Gordie Howe?

Playing for the Boston Bruins in 1970-71, Phil Esposito scored 76 goals during regular-season play to set the NHL record. Bobby Hull holds the WHA record, with 77 goals scored during the 1974-75 season.

In what country was the game of ice hockey first developed? Was it in Canada, Sweden, or Norway?

According to the Canadian Amateur Hockey Association, ice hockey was developed in Canada, probably as an outgrowth of field hockey, which was played with a rubber ball. British soldiers in Ontario and Nova Scotia played the first ice hockey games around 1855. Hockey went on to become the national sport of Canada.

Which team established an NHL record by losing 17 straight games? Was it the Washington Capitals, the Colorado Rockies, or the Atlanta Flames?

The answer is the Washington Capitals. They went from February 18 to March 26, 1975 without a victory or a tie in 17 straight NHL games.

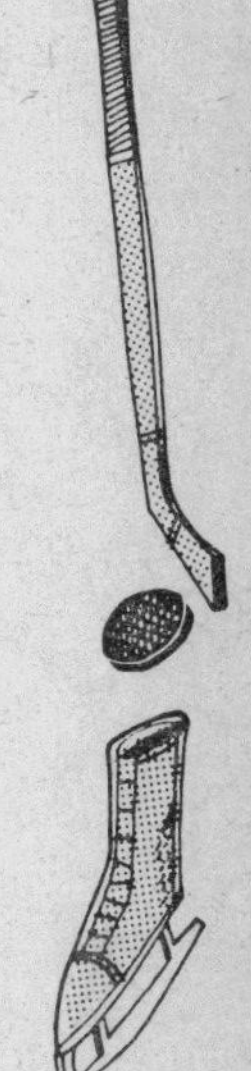

Can you name the men who won the following NHL trophies in 1977-78: (1) the James Norris Memorial Trophy, (2) the Lady Byng Award, and (3) the Frank J. Selke Trophy?

(1) Dennis Potvin of the New York Islanders won the Norris Trophy as the NHL's top defenseman. (2) Butch Goring of the Los Angeles Kings won the Lady Byng Award for combining playing ability with good sportsmanship. (3) Montreal's Bob Gainey won the Frank J. Selke Trophy as the league's best defensive forward.

Since the 1972-73 season, when the first Avco World Trophy Finals were held in the WHA, only two teams have won the championship more than once. Which teams are they?

The New England Whalers and the Houston Aeros share that honor. New England took the first title in 1973 by beating the Winnipeg Jets, 4 games to 1, then repeated their win over the Jets in 1978, shutting them out, 4 games to 0. Houston won the trophy in 1974, trouncing the Chicago Cougars, 4 games to 0. The Aeros retained their crown in 1975 with a 4-0 win over the Quebec Nordiques.

St. Louis Arena, the home rink of the NHL's St. Louis Blues, has been renamed recently. What is the new name of the St. Louis Blues' home rink?

When the Ralston-Purina Company bought the NHL's St. Louis Blues, they renamed St. Louis Arena "Checker Dome," in keeping with the checkerboard identifying logo on their many products.

Yvan Cournoyer of the Montreal Canadiens was named the Most Valuable Player in the 1973 Stanley Cup Playoffs. True or false?

True. Cournoyer scored a total of 15 goals in the 1973 Stanley Cup Playoffs and was voted the MVP of the series.

Defensemen Joe Watson and Jim Watson of the 1976-77 Philadelphia Flyers are not related. True or false?

False. Joe and Jim Watson are brothers, with Joe the older of the two.

A player who joins a fight between two other players is subject to a *misconduct penalty*. True or false?

True. That *misconduct penalty* causes the player to be removed from the game.

How long does the regular hockey season last?

Regular-season play begins in October and runs through early April.

In 1971, Gil Perrault was voted the NHL's Rookie of the Year. Which team did Perrault play for when he won the award?

Gil Perrault was a member of the Buffalo Sabres in 1971.

Who was the originator of the face mask now worn by all NHL goal tenders?

Goalie Jacques Plante of the Montreal Canadiens designed and introduced the face mask to the NHL in 1959. Prior to that, goal tenders had nothing to protect their faces.

BOXING

Who held the world heavyweight boxing title longer than any other fighter in history?

The twelve-year record is held by Joe Louis. He was the heavyweight champion of the world from 1937 until his retirement in 1949.

Which heavyweight fight had the biggest gate receipts? Was it the Tunney-Dempsey fight in 1927, the Frazier-Ali bout in 1971, or the second Ali-Spinks fight in 1978?

The $5 million gate for the second Ali-Spinks championship fight on September 15, 1978 goes down in boxing records as the largest gate in history. Over 70,000 fans gathered at the New Orleans, Louisiana, Superdome to watch Ali get his heavyweight crown back for the third time — a record in boxing history. The Tunney-Dempsey fight at Soldiers Field in Chicago, Illinois, on September 22, 1927 had the second biggest gate, with $2,658,660 collected, as 104,943 people watched Gene Tunney keep the heavyweight title by decisioning Jack Dempsey in 10 rounds. The March 8, 1971 Frazier-Ali fight ranks sixth on the all-time gate list. Held at New York's Madison Square Garden, the fight brought in $1,352,951 in gate receipts, as 20,455 people watched Joe Frazier decision Muhammad Ali in 15 rounds.

How many times was the great Joe Louis selected Fighter of the Year by *Ring Magazine?*

Joe Louis was selected as Fighter of the Year four times. *Ring Magazine* voted "The Brown Bomber" that honor in 1936, 1938, 1939, and 1941.

On June 21, 1932, Jack Sharkey won the heavyweight championship of the world. Who did he defeat to win the title?

Jack Sharkey faced the defending title holder, Max Schmeling, and captured the heavyweight boxing crown by a decision in 15 rounds.

Can you name the first black heavyweight champion of the world?

Jack Johnson became the first black heavyweight champion of the world when he defeated Tommy Burns in 1908. Johnson held the heavyweight crown for seven years.

James J. Corbett was considered to be the first professional fighter to skillfully "box" his opponents, rather than engage in a free-for-all brawl. Because of these boxing skills, Corbett was given an interesting nickname. What was it?

James J. Corbett was nicknamed "Gentleman Jim" Corbett.

What was the famous "long-count" fight?

The second Jack Dempsey-Gene Tunney fight, which took place in Chicago in 1927, saw Dempsey knock down Tunney in the seventh round. Because Dempsey did not go to a neutral corner immediately, the referee delayed starting the count over Tunney. When Tunney rose on the count of nine (or what would have been the count of fourteen) and went on to defeat Dempsey, the boxing world was left with the biggest controversy in its history — the famous "long-count" fight.

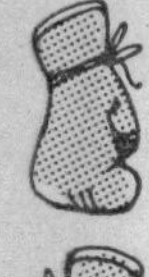

In 1935, one of the biggest upsets in ring history occurred when James J. Braddock took the heavyweight title away from the defending world champion. Can you name the fighter who lost his heavyweight crown to Braddock?

Max Baer, the flashy, well-dressed, headline-making "Playboy of Pugilism," was the heavyweight champ upset by Braddock.

True or false? In 1978, Muhammad Ali was selected as the "Athlete of the Decade" by a special panel of sportswriters and broadcasters.

True. Muhammad Ali was the top vote-getter after the panel reduced the field to thirteen elite candidates from all major sports. Golfer Jack Nicklaus finished second, followed by baseball's Hank Aaron, Pele — the king of soccer, John Havlicek of the NBA, O.J. Simpson of the NFL, and Bobby Orr of the NHL.

Which boxer holds the records for the most knockouts in his career? Was it Gene Tunney or Jack Dempsey?

The right answer is Jack Dempsey. Of the 60 wins in his 73 fights, Dempsey won 36 by KOs and was knocked out himself only 3 times. Gene Tunney has a total of 20 knockouts in his 47 wins and was never KO'd by an opponent.

In boxing, what do the letters *TKO* stand for?

A *TKO* is a *technical knockout*. It refers to a win decision given one fighter when the other is too badly hurt, too tired, or too dazed to continue the fight.

On February 16, 1970, Joe Frazier and Jimmy Ellis fought for the undisputed heavyweight title. How many rounds did that fight go before Frazier was declared the winner?

After being knocked down twice in the fourth round, Jimmy Ellis couldn't answer the bell in the fifth, and Joe Frazier was declared the winner.

Who was the lightest fighter ever to hold the world heavyweight boxing title? Was it Tommy Burns, James Fitzsimmons, or James J. Jeffries?

James Fitzsimmons was the lightest heavyweight champion of the world. He weighed only 167 pounds when he won the title by knocking out 183-pound James Corbett in 1897. Burns' fighting weight ranged between 176 and 180 pounds, while Jeffries' was well over 200.

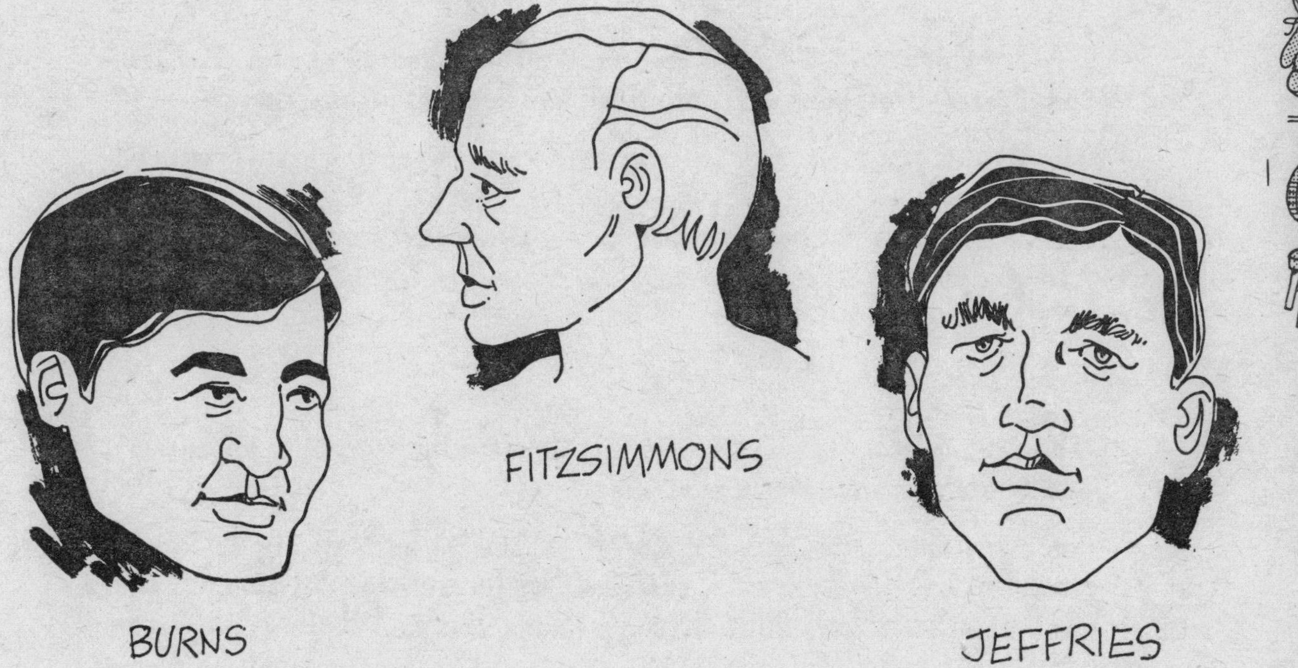

True or false? Joe Louis knocked out five world heavyweight boxing champions during his career.

It's unbelievable, but true. Joe Louis, "The Brown Bomber," KO'd five world champions. In 1935, he decked Primo Carnera in the 6th round of their non-title fight. Carnera, who outweighed Louis by 60 pounds, had been the world champion in 1933. In 1935, Louis put Max Baer on the canvas in the 4th round of their non-title bout. Baer was the heavyweight champion in 1934. In 1936, Jack Sharkey, the world heavyweight boxing champion in 1932, was KO'd by Joe Louis in the 3rd round of their non-title fight. In 1937, Jim Braddock, the reigning heavyweight title holder since 1935, lost his title when he was knocked cold by Louis in the 8th round of their championship bout. Lastly, Louis decked Max Schmeling, the 1930 champ, in the first round of their historic battle in 1938.

In order to compete in the bantamweight division, what is the most a fighter can weigh? Is it 118, 120, or 122 pounds?

The maximum weight in the bantam class is 118 pounds.

On February 15, 1978, Leon Spinks fought Muhammad Ali, the defending title holder, for the heavyweight championship of the world. In what city was that fight held?

The first 1978 Ali-Spinks heavyweight championship bout was held at the Sports Pavilion of the Hilton Hotel in Las Vegas, Nevada. Spinks won the 15-round title bout on a split decision, scored on the point system.

Did prize fighters always wear boxing gloves?

No. Professional boxers fought with bare knuckles until 1867.

In Ancient Rome, boxing was conducted pretty much as it is today. True or false?

False. Ancient Roman boxers fought a bloody death struggle, with leather straps embedded with metal spikes wrapped around their hands. They battled until death claimed the loser.

What are the three chief targets for a knockout punch?

If you guessed the chin, the temples, and the stomach, you've scored a KO.

How much do professional boxing gloves weigh?

The padded leather mitts which soften the blows and protect a fighter's hands usually weigh 6 - 8 ounces.

A British sportsman, the Marquis of Queensbury, established a set of rules which still governs amateur and professional boxing today. Were those rules drawn up in 1807, 1867, or 1956?

The correct answer is 1867. According to the Marquis of Queensbury rules, boxers were required to wear padded gloves, rounds were set as 3 minutes long with a 1-minute rest period in between, and the 10-second count for a knockout was established.

True or false? "Slapsie" Maxie Rosenbloom, the light-heavyweight champion of the world from 1930 to 1934, became a movie actor when he retired from boxing.

True. Maxie Rosenbloom became an actor and is often seen on television in many old movies, including *Irish Eyes Are Smiling, Louisiana Purchase, To The Shores of Tripoli, There's Nothing Sacred,* and *Each Dawn I Die.*

When Leon Spinks became the heavyweight boxing champion of the world in 1978, he had only seven professional fights prior to the title bout. True or false?

True. Spinks, a 1976 Olympic champion, had only seven professional fights, winning six and drawing once, before taking the world heavyweight boxing crown away from Muhammad Ali.

A flyweight boxer can weigh up to 118 pounds. True or false?

False. In order to compete in the flyweight division, a boxer cannot weigh more than 112 pounds.

Was Dick Tiger a world light-heavyweight or middleweight champion of the world? Put on your thinking cap. This is a tricky one.

Dick Tiger was a world champion in *both* divisions. He held the middleweight crown twice, first in 1962-63 and then in 1965-66. Then with some extra pounds on him, Tiger reigned as light-heavyweight champion from 1966 to 1968.

Gene Fullmer was a two-time world champion of which boxing division? Was it the middleweight, welterweight, or light-heavyweight division?

In 1957 and from 1959 to 1962, Gene Fullmer was the middleweight champion of the world.

When did the great Roberto Duran win the lightweight championship of the world?

Roberto Duran became the lightweight boxing champion of the world in 1972 by taking the crown away from Ken Buchanan, and as of 1978 he still retained the title. In his career, Duran won 60 out of 61 fights, taking 50 of them by KOs.

Which heavyweight champion was nicknamed "The Manassa Mauler"? Was it Jack Dempsey, Rocky Marciano, or Ezzard Charles?

Jack Dempsey, a native of Manassa, Colorado, was nicknamed "The Manassa Mauler" because of the savage, murderous punching with his famous left hook.

What was the first "million-dollar gate" in boxing history?

The great championship fight between Jack Dempsey and Georges Carpentier in July, 1921, saw 80,000 fans pay nearly $2,000,000 for the privilege of seeing the Manassa, Colorado, hero meet the handsome French boxer. This also marked the first time that a championship fight was aired over the radio.

How many times did boxer Emile Griffith hold world championship titles? Was it three, four, or five times?

Emile Griffith held world championship boxing titles five times. He was the welterweight champion in 1961, 1962-63, and 1963-66, then went on to gain the middleweight title in 1966-67 and 1967-68.

A boxer who weighs 128 pounds can fight in the featherweight division. True or false?

False. In order to be classified as a featherweight, a boxer cannot weigh more than 126 pounds.

Who was the heaviest fighter to hold the world heavyweight boxing championship? Was it Primo Carnera, Max Baer, or Sonny Liston?

Primo Carnera topped the scales at 267 pounds when he took the heavyweight title from Jack Sharkey in a fight held in New York City on June 29, 1933. Baer and Liston had top fighting weights of 209½ and 214, respectively.

When did the first heavyweight title fight take place under the Marquis of Queensbury Rules?

The famous heavyweight title bout between John L. Sullivan and James J. Corbett in 1892 was the first held under the Marquis of Queensbury Rules. The choice of rules was made by Sullivan as the defending champion.

True or false? Nino Benvenuti never held a world boxing title.

False. Benvenuti took the middleweight title in 1967 from Emile Griffith. After losing the championship back to Griffith later that year, Benvenuti regained the middleweight crown in 1968 and held it until 1970.

In order to compete as a light-heavyweight, what is the most a fighter can weigh?

A light-heavyweight boxer cannot weigh more than 175 pounds.

True or false? No fighter ever held world titles in three different weight classes simultaneously.

False. Amazing as it seems, during the four-month span from August to December, 1938, Henry "Homicide Hank" Armstrong, an American boxer, held the featherweight, lightweight, and welterweight world titles simultaneously.

On October 26, 1951, Joe Louis came out of retirement to fight Rocky Marciano in a non-title bout. Who won that fight?

Rocky Marciano quashed the aging Joe Louis' comeback attempt by putting the former champion on the canvas in the eighth round.

True or false? Until 1867, prize fights usually lasted until one boxer was knocked out, no matter how long it took.

It's absolutely true. This was the procedure until the Marquis of Queensbury Rules were established.

Kid Gavilan, Tony DeMarco, and Fritzie Zivic were all world champion boxers. In which weight class did they fight?

Gavilan, DeMarco, and Zivic were all welterweights.

Ken Norton was the number-3-rated heavyweight fighter in the world in 1977. Can you name the heavyweights who were rated number 2 and number 1 in that year?

In the 1977 world heavyweight ratings, George Foreman was number 2 and Muhammad Ali was number 1.

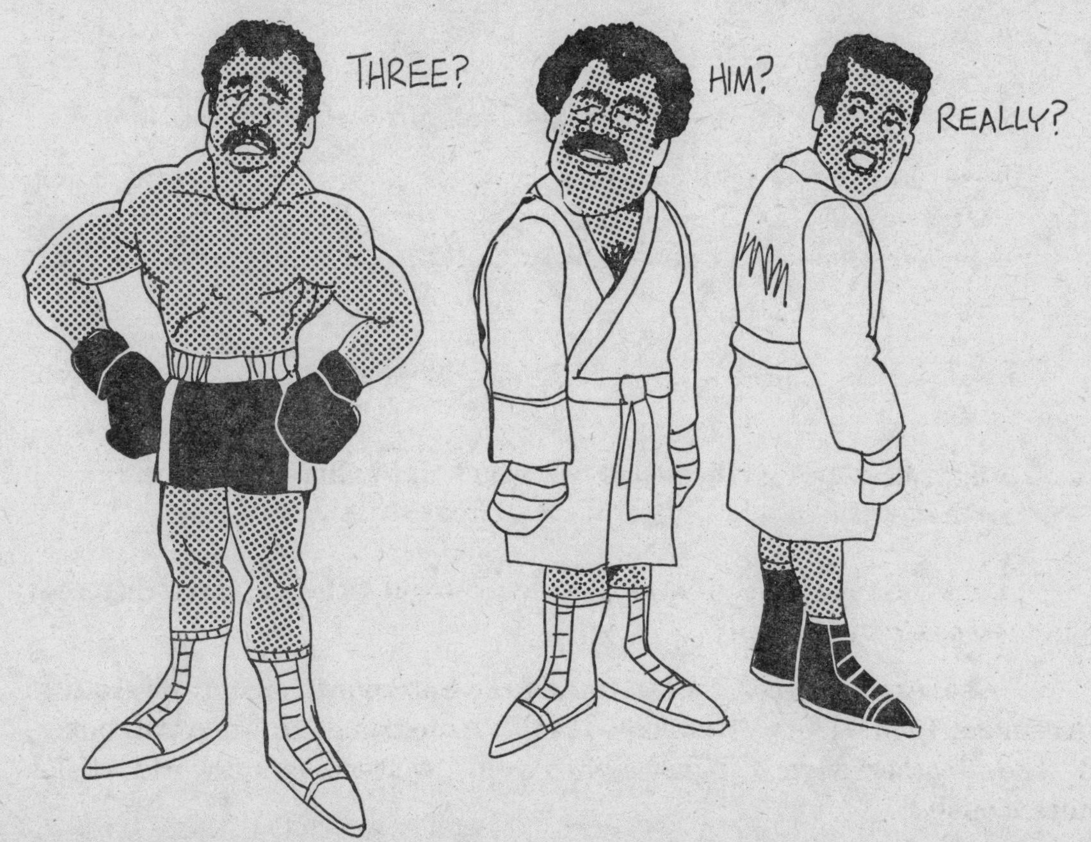

Heavyweight boxing champion Muhammad Ali began his ring career under his given name. Do you know what it was?

Before changing his name to Muhammad Ali in 1965, Ali was known as Cassius Clay.

Can you name the fighter who scored the greatest number of knockouts in a career? Was it Archie Moore, Joe Frazier, or Jimmy Ellis?

Former light-heavyweight champion Archie Moore holds the knockout record. From 1936 to 1963, Moore KO'd 141 opponents.

Who was the first heavyweight boxer to win back his championship after he had lost it? Was it Rocky Marciano, Joe Louis, or Floyd Patterson?

Floyd Patterson was the first heavyweight boxer to regain the title. After losing his crown to Ingemar Johansson in 1959, Patterson regained it in 1960 by KOing Johansson in the fifth round of their title bout.

Joe Burger was a national heavyweight champion in 1973. Did Burger hold that title in the United States, Great Britain, or Germany?

Joe Burger was the British heavyweight title holder in 1973.

Tony Zale and Jake LaMotta were both world champions in which weight division?

Tony Zale and Jake LaMotta were both middleweights, with Zale holding the title from 1940 to 1947 and LaMotta, from 1949 to 1951.

Which fighter defeated John L. Sullivan to become the second heavyweight champion of the world?

James J. Corbett defeated champion John L. Sullivan in 1892. Corbett retained the heavyweight title until 1897.

In which weight division did champion Bob Foster fight?

Bob Foster fought in the light-heavyweight division and was the light-heavyweight champion of the world from 1968 to 1970 and in 1972.

How many fights did the great Gene Tunney lose during his boxing career?

Gene Tunney lost only one fight during his 1922-28 career. As the defending American light-heavyweight champion, Tunney was beaten by Harry Greb in a title bout in 1922. Tunney later regained his crown by defeating Greb on February 23, 1923.

Who was the oldest fighter to hold the world heavyweight title? Was it Joe Walcott, Gene Tunney, or Jack Dempsey?

"Jersey" Joe Walcott, the 1951 world heavyweight champion, was the oldest fighter to win the title. At age 38, Walcott KO'd 30-year-old Ezzard Charles, the defending champ. Tunney was 29 when he took the title in 1926, and Dempsey, only 24 when he became champ in 1919.

True or false? Leon Spinks was the youngest fighter ever to become heavyweight champion of the world.

False. Although Spinks was only 24 when he took the heavyweight crown from Muhammad Ali, Floyd Patterson holds the record as the youngest heavyweight boxing champion. Floyd was only 21 years old when he knocked out Archie Moore in the fifth round of their title fight on November 30, 1956.

At what weight can a modern fighter qualify as a heavyweight?

In order to be classified as a heavyweight today, a fighter must weigh over 175 pounds.

What do you call a short punch delivered in an upward motion?

If you guessed an uppercut, you're right.

The movie *The Great White Hope* was based on the life of which prize fighter? Was it Jack Johnson, Floyd Patterson, or Ezzard Charles?

The Great White Hope was based on the life and career of Jack Johnson, the first black heavyweight champion of the world.

The Joe Louis-Max Schmeling heavyweight title fight in 1938 was one of the most famous championship bouts in history. Where was that fight held?

The Louis-Schmeling championship bout was held in New York's Yankee Stadium on June 22, 1938. Defending champ Louis kept his heavyweight crown by knocking out Schmeling in 2 minutes and 4 seconds of the first round.

What is the maximum a middleweight boxer can weigh?

In order to compete in the middleweight boxing division, a fighter cannot weigh more than 160 pounds.

George Foreman captured the world heavyweight boxing championship in 1973. Who did he beat to win the crown?

George Foreman won a victory by TKO over Joe Frazier to win the 1973 world heavyweight title.

Rocky Marciano retired from boxing with the world heavyweight title still in his possession. Did Marciano retire from the ring in 1950, 1956, or 1960?

Rocky retired as the heavyweight champion of the world in 1956.

From 1946 to 1951, Ray Robinson held which world title—lightweight, welterweight, or middleweight?

"Sugar" Ray Robinson was the world welterweight boxing champion.

In 1934, Max Baer challenged defending champion Primo Carnera for his world heavyweight title. Who won that fight?

Max Baer took the heavyweight crown away from Primo Carnera by knocking down the defending champion eleven times in 11 rounds before the fight was officially halted.

Max Baer, the heavyweight boxing champion from 1934 to 1935, was also a movie star during and after his fighting days. True or false?

True. Max Baer, who retired from the ring in 1940, acted in many movies, including *The Prize Fighter and the Lady* in 1933 and *The Harder They Fall* in 1956.

In boxing, what is a *feint*?

A *feint* is a fake punch. It is used by boxers as a decoy in an attempt to put their opponents off guard so a real punch can be delivered successfully.

Two boxers once battled for 276 rounds before their fight ended. True or false?

True. In 1825, Jack Jones and Patsy Tunney established a record by fighting 276 rounds in Cheshire, England. Jones knocked out Tunney to end the bout after they had been battling for 4 hours and 30 minutes.

True or false? The shortest world heavyweight title fight on record lasted only 1 minute and 28 seconds.

True. On March 17, 1908, in Dublin, Ireland, defending heavyweight champion Tommy Burns knocked out Jem Roche in 1 minute and 28 seconds of the first round of their title bout.

How much can a lightweight fighter weigh?

A lightweight fighter can weigh up to 135 pounds and no more.

The movie *The Harder They Fall* was a fictionalized version of which heavyweight champion's life story? Was it Primo Carnera, Jack Dempsey, or Jess Willard?

The Harder They Fall was based on the life of Primo Carnera, the 1933-34 heavyweight champion.

In 1967, Muhammad Ali was stripped of his heavyweight title and barred from professional boxing. Can you remember why?

This action was taken because Ali refused to be drafted into the U.S. Army. But he was permitted to return to the professional ring in 1970.

Can you name the four world-champion heavyweights who retired undefeated?

The undefeated champs were James J. Jeffries, who retired in 1905; Gene Tunney, in 1928; Joe Louis, in 1949; and Rocky Marciano, in 1956.

During a fight, how many men are in the ring?

In addition to the two boxers, there is a third man in the ring — the referee. It is his job to see that the boxers obey the rules.

The highlight of the 1942 film *Gentleman Jim* was the championship fight between Jim Corbett and John L. Sullivan. Do you remember who starred in those roles?

Errol Flynn played the role of Jim Corbett and Ward Bond was "The Great John L."

On September 25, 1962, Sonny Liston and Floyd Patterson met in the ring in the world heavyweight title bout. How did that fight end?

Liston knocked out Patterson in the first round of their title fight to win the world heavyweight crown in 1962.

Who was the shortest fighter to ever win the heavyweight boxing championship? Was it Tommy Burns, Leon Spinks, or Floyd Patterson?

The 1906-08 heavyweight champion, Tommy Burns, who stood 5 feet 7 inches tall, was the shortest boxer to hold the world title. Spinks was 6 feet ½ inch tall, and Patterson was 6 feet tall.

In order to compete in the welterweight boxing division, what is the most a fighter can weigh?

A welterweight boxer can weigh up to 147 pounds.

For a professional championship fight, the boxers may select the size of the ring, within certain size limitations, on the approval of the local boxing commission. What are those size limitations?

In a professional championship fight, the size of the ring may measure from 16 to 24 feet on each side. The ring stands 3 to 4 feet higher than the floor of the arena.

What are the three ways a boxer can win a fight?

A boxer can win a fight by a *knockout*, by a *technical knockout*, or by a *decision*.

How are fights won by a *decision*?

Decisions are judged on either the *point* or *round* system. In the point system, usually the referee and two judges separately award each fighter a number of points after each round, based on his performance. At the end of the fight, the referee and each judge total their points. The fighter with the greater number of points is declared the winner. In the round system, the referee and each judge award each round to one of the boxers, based on his performance. At the end of the fight, the boxer awarded the most rounds by the combined scores of the referee and judges is declared the winner.

When did the great Carlos Monzon win the world middleweight crown?

Carlos Monzon became the middleweight champion in 1970, and as of 1978 was still the reigning champ.

How many times did Sugar Ray Robinson hold the world middleweight boxing title? Was it three, five, or six times?

Sugar Ray Robinson held the world middleweight boxing title five different times: first, in 1951 when he took the title from Jake LaMotta; then from 1951 to 1952 when he dethroned Randy Turpin; from 1955 to 1956 when he defeated Bobo Olson; in 1957 after beating Gene Fullmer; and then from 1958 to 1959 when he took the crown from Carmen Basilio.

Which heavyweight title fight was held in Zaire, Africa?

The 1974 championship fight between Muhammad Ali and George Foreman took place in Zaire. Ali won by a KO in the 8th round.

The movie *Somebody Up There Likes Me* was based on the life story of which professional boxer? Was it Rocky Graziano, Dick Tiger, or Bobo Olson?

The life of Rocky Graziano was depicted in the film *Somebody Up There Likes Me,* with actor Paul Newman starring as the former middleweight champion.

How long does a round last in professional boxing? Is it two minutes, three minutes, or four minutes long?

In professional boxing, a round lasts three minutes.

Which former heavyweight contender was nicknamed "The Bayonne Bleeder"? Was it Chuck Wepner, Ernie Shavers, or Ron Lyle?

Chuck Wepner, the boxer who fought Muhammad Ali for the heavyweight crown in 1975 and lost, was nicknamed "The Bayonne Bleeder." The Bayonne, New Jersey, heavyweight was so named because of the profuse bleeding that resulted when he was cut during a fight.

Can you name the first world heavyweight boxing champion?

At the age of twenty-four, the great John L. Sullivan won the first world heavyweight title in 1882 by knocking out Paddy Ryan. Sullivan remained champion until 1892.

Which middleweight boxer was nicknamed "The Michigan Assassin"?

Stanley Ketchel, the middleweight champ in 1907 and 1908, was nicknamed "The Michigan Assassin" because of the blazing attacks that led him to KO 35 opponents in his first 39 bouts.

Jack Delaney, John Henry Lewis, and Gus Lesnevich were world champions in which weight class?

Delaney, Lewis, and Lesnevich were all world champion lightweights. Delaney held the title from 1926 to 1927; Lewis, from 1935 to 1939; and Lesnevich, from 1941 to 1948.

A 1977 movie was based on the life story of heavyweight champion Muhammad Ali. Can you name that movie and its star?

Ali's film biography was called *The Greatest,* and starred none other than Ali, himself, in the title role.

What kind of punch is the pictured fighter throwing? Is it a *left hook*, an *uppercut*, or a *left jab*?

This punch to the head is called a *left jab*. The boxer throwing it snaps his left wrist out in a straight line from his shoulder, while at the same time stepping toward his opponent with his left foot.

John L. Sullivan beat Jake Kilrain in the last bare-knuckle fight for the heavyweight championship under the London Prize Ring Rules. Can you guess how many rounds that 1889 fight lasted?

The Sullivan-Kilrain fight lasted 75 rounds under the boiling sun of Richburg, Mississippi. Since rounds were not timed under the London Prize Ring Rules, but rather ended when one fighter was knocked down, the 75 rounds took a total of 2 hours, 16 minutes, and 23 seconds.

On September 15, 1978, Muhammad Ali fought Leon Spinks in a last-chance effort to regain the heavyweight title which Ali had lost to Spinks seven months earlier. Who won that fight?

Muhammad Ali won back the world heavyweight title with a unanimous decision over Leon Spinks. At age 36, Ali completely dominated the bout, which was scored on rounds, and did not allow the 24-year-old Spinks to win more than four rounds on any of the judges' cards. This win made Ali the only fighter in boxing history to regain the heavyweight title three times.

In which weight class did Joey Giardello, Solly Krieger, and Tiger Flowers fight?

Giardello, Krieger, and Flowers were all middleweight champions: Giardello, in 1963; Krieger, in 1938, and Flowers, in 1926.

Was Muhammad Ali ever an Olympic champion?

Ali, then known as Cassius Clay, won the light-heavyweight gold medal at the 1960 Olympics in Rome. Later that year, he turned pro and embarked upon a historic ring career.

During his twelve-year reign as world heavyweight champion, how many times did Joe Louis defend his title? Was it 20, 25, or 30 times?

From June 22, 1937, when he took the heavyweight crown from James J. Braddock, until his retirement on March 1, 1949, Joe Louis successfully defended his title a record-setting 25 times, scoring 20 knockouts.

BASKETBALL

Former NBA superstar Wilt Chamberlain has an interesting and unusual nickname. Do you know what it is?

Because of his seven-foot height, Chamberlain is known as Wilt "The Stilt" Chamberlain.

During his college career, Pete Maravich scored more points than any other college basketball player. How many points did Maravich score? Was it 2,667, 3,667, or 4,667 points?

Playing for Louisiana State University from 1967 to 1970, Pete Maravich scored a record 3,667 points.

True or false? Louisiana State University's women's basketball team won the Association for Intercollegiate Athletes for Women Championship in 1977.

False. Delta State of Cleveland, Mississippi, defeated LSU in the championship game by the score of 68 to 55, to take the 1977 AIAW basketball title.

Which was the only college team to ever win both the NCAA and NIT Tournaments in one year?

Nat Holman's quintet at City College of New York accomplished what no other school had ever done when they won both the National Collegiate Athletic Association and National Invitation Tournaments in 1950. This is the only time that CCNY has won either tournament, but that double win is a record which will forever stand unbroken, for a team can no longer play in both tournaments.

Guard John Havlicek, playing for the Boston Celtics, set an NBA record by scoring 1,000 or more points in a season for the most seasons. How many times did Havlicek reach or surpass that 1,000-point season mark?

That great John "Hondo" Havlicek scored 1,000 or more points in a single season *fifteen* different times from 1963 to 1971.

With all the 6- and 7-footers in the NBA, one of the association's 1977 stars was only 5 feet 9 inches tall and weighed 165 pounds. True or false?

True. He is guard Calvin Murphy of the Houston Rockets. Even though Cal is only a 5'9" lightweight, he's one of the NBA's brightest stars and has been for several years.

The Portland Trail Blazers had first pick in the NBA's amateur draft in 1978. Did they select Mychal Thompson of Minnesota, Phil Ford of North Carolina, or Rick Robey of Kentucky?

The Portland Trail Blazers picked 6'11" Mychal Thompson. The second player selected was Phil Ford, who went to the Kansas City-Omaha Kings. The Indiana Pacers, picking third, selected Rick Robey.

Who was the NBA Coach of the Year in 1975-76?

Bill Fitch was the NBA Coach of the Year in 1975-76. Taking the third-place Cleveland Cavaliers of 1974-75, Fitch led them to the Eastern Conference Championship Playoffs the following year.

Dave Cowens was the NBA's Most Valuable Player in 1973. What position does he play?

Dave Cowens is a center for the Boston Celtics.

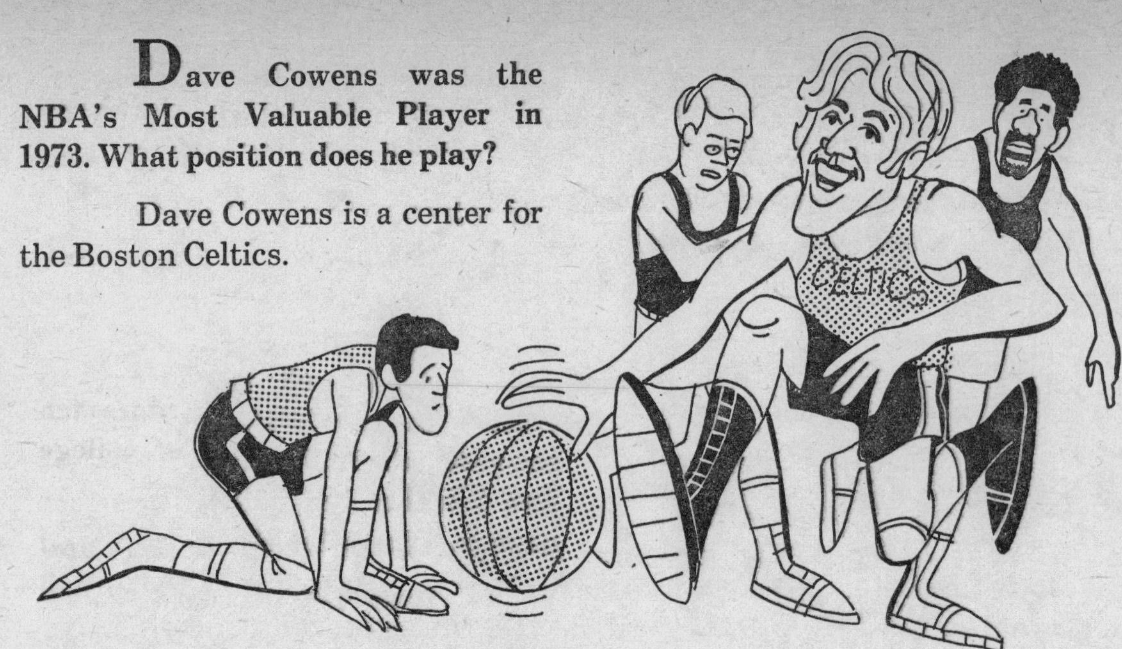

The U.S.S.R. is one of the two foreign countries that have won the Championship of the International Amateur Basketball Federation more than once. Can you name the other country?

If you said Brazil, you're right. They won the World Championship in 1959 and 1963. The U.S.S.R. won it in 1967 and 1974.

In 1973, the Sullivan Award for the United States Amateur Athlete of the Year went to a basketball player from UCLA. Can you guess who that player was? Here's a hint. He went on to star as a pro player with the Portland Trail Blazers.

Bill Walton, UCLA center, won the Sullivan Award in 1973.

After being named the Most Valuable Player in the National Invitation Tournament in 1967, a basketball player from Southern Illinois University went on to become a great pro star with the New York Knicks and the Cleveland Cavaliers. Can you name him?

The answer is Walter "Clyde" Frazier, one of the NBA's premier defensive guards.

During his college career at LSU from 1967 to 1970, Pete Maravich scored 3,667 points to become the highest scorer in the history of college basketball. Who is runner-up to Pete in the collegiate record books?

Get ready for a surprise answer! The runner-up is 5-foot 6-inch Carol "The Blaze" Blazejowski of the Montclair State College women's basketball team. From 1974 to 1978, the New Jersey superstar scored a college career total of 3,199 points.

As of 1978, how many times have the Boston Celtics won the NBA Championship?

The Celtics' win in 1976 marked the 13th time that the Boston team has taken the Championship of the National Basketball Association. The first time they won the NBA crown was in 1956-57. Their consecutive eight-year hold on the title from 1958-59 to 1965-66 is an NBA record. They later repeated as NBA Champions in 1967-68, 1968-69, 1973-74, and 1975-76.

Earl Monroe, who played for the New York Knicks in 1977-78, is one of the best shooting guards in the NBA. What is Earl Monroe's nickname?

Because of his flamboyant style and his excellent basketball skills, Monroe is known as "Earl the Pearl."

When a team is said to have a *ball-control offense*, what does that mean?

A *ball-control offense* is a team's attempt to keep prolonged possession of the ball while seeking a good scoring opportunity.

In what year was the first National Invitation Tournament held? Was it 1935, 1938, or 1940?

The first NIT was held in 1938. Top nationwide honors went to Temple University, with Colorado as the runner-up.

Can you name the man who originally formed and coached the Harlem Globetrotters?

If you said Abe Saperstein, you really know your Globetrotter history. The young immigrant from England became active in youth work in Chicago and set up and coached an all-black exhibition team, the Savoy Big Five. Later, in 1927, the Globetrotters were born, and Saperstein piloted them from small-time barnstormers to world famous athletic comedians.

How many times was Bill Russell named the Most Valuable Player in the National Basketball Association?

Bill Russell was the MVP of the NBA five times. He won the award in 1958, 1961, 1962, 1963, and 1965.

Who was the National Basketball Association's Rookie of the Year in 1975-76? Was it Bob McAdoo, Alvan Adams, or Adrian Dantley?

Phoenix Suns' star Alvan Adams was Rookie of the Year in the NBA in 1975-76. McAdoo, of the Buffalo Braves, was the NBA's Rookie of the Year in 1972-3, while Dantley, also of Buffalo, took the title in 1976-77.

In basketball, what is a *conversion*?

A *conversion* is the sinking of a free-throw attempt or a successful bonus shot.

Who was the first man in the history of the NBA to score over 20,000 career points? Was it Bob Pettit, George Mikan, or Neil Johnston?

Forward Bob Pettit of the St. Louis Hawks holds the honor of being the first NBA player to break the 20,000-point scoring mark. He did it in 1965, his eleventh season with the Hawks, with a record-breaking 20,880 points.

In the first intercollegiate basketball game ever played, the University of Chicago beat the University of Iowa by the score of 15 to 12. Can you guess when that game was played? Was it 1896, 1910, or 1925?

That precedent-setting game, which established five-man teams, was played on January 16, 1896, before 400 spectators in Iowa City.

When the referee blows his whistle and makes the hand signal pictured, what does it mean?

The hand signal pictured means that the player with the ball is guilty of *traveling* — he has taken illegal steps while holding the basketball. The team whose player is guilty of traveling must give up possession of the ball.

Who was voted the Most Valuable Player of the 1978 NBA Playoffs?

Wes Unseld, the veteran center of the Washington Bullets, was the MVP of the National Basketball Association's Playoffs in 1978. Unseld scored 63 points, pulled down 82 rebounds, and chalked up 27 assists to earn the Award.

Was a basketball team ever thrown out of a league for being too strong?

The Celtics of the old American Basketball League so dominated the game, winning 109 out of 120 games in one season, that they were thrown out of the league. Starting as a semi-pro team in 1915, the Celtics later traveled the country, playing about 150 games a year and winning 90 percent of them. Before the Celtics were disbanded in 1928, they had made stars out of Joe Lapchick, Nat Holman, Ernie Reich, Dave Banks, "Dutch" Dehnert, Chris Leonard, Johnnie Beckman, "Stretch" Meehan, "Chief" Mueller, and Jim Kane.

How long does a team have to move the ball across the division line? Is it 5, 10, or 15 seconds?

A basketball team has 10 seconds to get the ball across the division line. If they fail to do it in those 10 seconds, they lose possession of the ball.

Bob Cousy, who coached the Cincinnati Royals in 1972-73, was an NBA superstar on one team for thirteen years. Which team did Cousy play for?

Bob Cousy was a member of the Boston Celtics from 1950 until his retirement in 1963. During his brilliant career, in which he averaged almost 20 points a game, Cousy helped lead the Celtics to six NBA Championships.

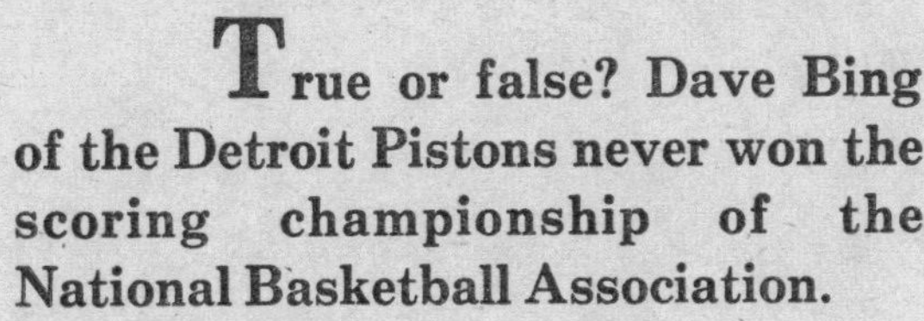

True or false? Dave Bing of the Detroit Pistons never won the scoring championship of the National Basketball Association.

False. Bing was the NBA's scoring champion in 1967-68, when he topped the league with 2,142 points. This was only Bing's second season in the NBA, coming on the heels of his Rookie of the Year Award in 1966-67.

From October 22 to November 16, 1976, Rick Barry set an NBA record for making the most free throws in a row. How many free throws established that record for Barry?

The magic number for Rick Barry was 63 free throws. In his illustrious pro career in the NBA and ABA with the Golden State Warriors, the Oakland Oaks, and the New York Nets, the star forward set many records, including scoring 50 or more points in a single game *fifteen* times.

True or false? An NBA player once scored more than 4,000 points in a single season.

True. The player who accomplished that amazing feat was the great Wilt Chamberlain. Playing for the 1962 Philadelphia Warriors, Chamberlain won the NBA scoring championship with a total of 4,029 points.

At the conclusion of the 1977-78 regular season, which college basketball team finished first in almost all of the national ratings? Was it Kentucky or Arkansas?

The Kentucky Wildcats, with a record of 22 wins and 2 losses at the end of the 1977-78 season, were the consensus choice for the number-one spot in the national rankings. The Arkansas Razorbacks, with a season record of 27 wins and 2 losses, were ranked second.

When the ABA was dissolved in 1976, four of its teams joined the NBA. Can you name those four teams?

The Denver Nuggets, the New York Nets, the San Antonio Spurs, and the Indiana Pacers all joined the NBA when the ABA went out of existence.

Is there a difference in the size of a high school basketball court, a college basketball court, and a professional basketball court?

Yes. College and professional courts are longer than most high school basketball courts. A high school court is usually 84 feet long and 50 feet wide. Most college and pro courts are 94 feet long and 50 feet wide. However, courts can vary in size. The maximum legal length is 94 feet while the minimum is 74 feet. The maximum width allowed is 50 feet and the minimum is 42 feet.

Oscar Robertson of Cincinnati and Austin Carr of Notre Dame are both high on the list of NCAA career-scoring leaders. Which one scored more points during his college career?

Oscar Robertson, with a total of 2,973 points, tops Austin Carr's career total of 2,560. These scores place them second and third, respectively, in NCAA totals behind Pete Maravich's 3,667 points.

Which basketball player is taller — Wilt Chamberlain or Bill Walton?

The answer is Wilt "The Stilt" Chamberlain, who stands 7 feet tall, topping by one inch Bill Walton's 6 feet 11 inches.

True or false? Dave DeBusschere played pro basketball and pro baseball at the same time.

True. In 1962, young Dave DeBusschere was a pitcher with baseball's Chicago White Sox of the American League and a forward for the Detroit Pistons of the NBA. He later gave up pro baseball to become the player-coach of the Pistons.

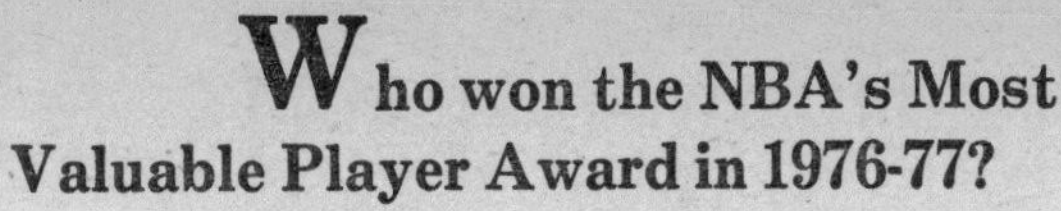

Who won the NBA's Most Valuable Player Award in 1976-77?

Kareem Abdul-Jabbar of the Los Angeles Lakers was selected by a poll of the players as the MVP of 1976-77. This was the second year in a row that he won the Award.

How many players are on a basketball team and what are their positions?

There are five players on a basketball team: two *forwards*, who play near the corners of the court; one *center*, who is usually the tallest player on the team because he plays nearest the basket; and two *guards*, who are usually the shortest but quickest and most agile players on the team because they handle the ball most of the time when their team is on the offense.

True or false? The great Bill Russell, who played for the world champion Boston Celtics, was best known for his offensive ability.

False. Even though he played well offensively, Bill Russell was best known for his ability as a defensive center. Russell, with his uncanny talent for stealing the ball and for blocking shots, led the Celtics to 11 titles in 13 seasons between 1957 and 1969.

How many points did the great Jerry West score in his career? Was it 15,192 points, 20,192 points, or 25,192 points?

In his fourteen seasons in the NBA, Jerry West scored 25,192 points, making him the fourth highest scorer in NBA history behind Wilt Chamberlain (31,449), Oscar Robertson (26,710), and John Havlicek (25,716).

Which two players have been called "the greatest scoring combination in the history of basketball"?

Jerry West and Elgin Bayor of the Los Angeles Lakers make up this dream combination. West has such spring in his legs and gets up so high, it's almost impossible to block his shots. In addition, he's a star on defense. His teammate, Baylor, has such incredible moves that he's probably the best offensive player in the history of basketball.

Which NBA team did superstar Walt Frazier play for in 1977-78?

Walt Frazier, a former New York Knickerbocker, played for the Cleveland Cavaliers in 1977-78.

True or false? Red Holzman was never named Coach of the Year.

False. Holzman was named Coach of the Year in 1969-70, when he led the New York Knicks to the NBA Championship.

In basketball, what is a *fast break*?

A *fast break* describes the play when the offensive team regains possession of the ball and races down court in an attempt to get into scoring position before the defensive team can regain its back court posts.

Can you name the NBA team that Lenny Wilkens coached in 1977-78?

In 1977-78, Lenny Wilkens coached the Seattle Supersonics. The former NBA All-Star had previously played with the St. Louis Hawks, the Seattle Supersonics, and the Cleveland Cavaliers before he returned to the Supersonics as their coach.

In the early days of basketball, the balls used in the game were soccer balls. True or false?

True. Soccer balls were used to play the game of basketball until 1894, when larger balls were introduced to the sport. The early basketballs were made of leather with a rubber lining, and were held together by laces. A laceless ball became official in 1937, and our modern basketball took its place in 1950.

Immaculata, a small Catholic college in suburban Philadelphia, has been a national power in women's basketball for several years. How many times has Immaculata won the AIAW Basketball Championship?

The correct answer is three times. Immaculata won the championship the first year the AIAW was formed, 1972, and successfully defended the title in 1973 and 1974.

In basketball, what is a *dunk* shot?

When a player leaps above the rim of the hoop with the ball in his hand and slams or stuffs it into the basket for a score, that is a *dunk* shot.

What is a *tipoff*?

A *tipoff* is a jump ball that starts the game and the second half.

Can you name the first NBA player to pull down over 1,000 rebounds in a single season?

The answer is big Dolph Schayes, who played for sixteen years with the old Syracuse Nationals. Schayes was not only the first NBA player to grab 1,000 rebounds in a season, but he was also the first NBA star to score 15,000 points.

True or false? In basketball, a *one-handed pass* is used chiefly for very short passes.

False. A one-handed pass is usually used for very *long* passes. The ball is held in one hand and thrown like a baseball. Although one-handed passes cover long distances, they are not always accurate.

How many times was Wilt Chamberlain the scoring champion of the National Basketball Association?

Playing for the Philadelphia (later the San Francisco) Warriors and then the Philadelphia 76ers, Wilt "The Stilt" Chamberlain reigned as the scoring champion of the NBA from 1959 to 1966. These seven consecutive years represent a feat that no other pro player has ever duplicated.

True or false? In 1968, the NBA's Rookie of the Year was Walt Frazier of the New York Knicks.

False. Walt Frazier never won the Rookie of the Year Award. The NBA's top rookie in the 1967-68 season was Earl Monroe of the Baltimore Bullets.

Where is the *back court* area on a basketball court?

The *back court* is the area between the center line and the basket, which the offensive team leaves as it moves toward its own basket.

From 1967 to 1975, how many times did UCLA win the NCAA Basketball Championship?

UCLA won the NCAA basketball title nine times between 1967 and 1975. They won the championship every year except 1974, when North Carolina State captured college basketball's crown.

Who holds the NBA record for making the most consecutive free throws in one game without a miss?

On November 22, 1961, Bob Pettit, playing for the St. Louis Hawks, made 19 free throws in a row against the Boston Celtics, to establish an NBA record.

The Duke Blue Devils played the Kentucky Wildcats in the 1978 NCAA Basketball Championship game. Who were the head coaches of those two teams?

In 1977-78, Joe Hall was the head coach at the University of Kentucky, and Bill Foster guided the Blue Devils of Duke.

Independence of Kansas played Niagara of Sanborn, New York, in the National Junior College Athletic Association's Basketball Championship in 1978. Can you guess which team won the title?

If you guessed it was Independence, you're right. The Kansas team beat Niagara, 62 to 61, to win the NJCAA title in 1978.

BASKETBALL

Because of his uncanny ability to shoot the ball into the basket, NBA star Pete Maravich has an amusing nickname. Do you know it?

You scored two points if you said "Pistol Pete" Maravich.

When professional sportswriters chose basketball's Man of the Half-Century in the 1950s, they selected a 6'10" center from the Minnesota Lakers. Who was their choice?

George Mikan, who was the first big man to dominate the game of basketball and who scored 11,764 points in his seven-year pro career, was named Basketball's Man of the Half-Century.

Artis Gilmore and Tom Burleson are two of the tallest players in the National Basketball Association. Which of them is taller?

Tom Burleson, who played for the Kansas City Kings in 1977-78, is the tallest man in the NBA at 7 feet 4 inches. The Chicago Bulls' Artis Gilmore is a "mere" 7 feet 2 inches tall.

Only four players have ever reached the 1000-point mark thirteen times in their career. Can you name those four stars?

If you named Oscar Roberston, Bob Cousy, Wilt Chamberlain, and Jerry West, you can consider yourself a true basketball fan.

Walt Frazier is one of the greatest stars in the National Basketball Association. What position does Frazier play?

Walt Frazier is a guard.

In 1968-69, the Boston Celtics defeated the Los Angeles Lakers for the NBA Championship, but the award for the Most Valuable Player in the playoffs went to a member of the *losing* team. Can you name the Laker who won it?

The answer is Jerry West. Even though his Los Angeles Lakers lost the championship, West had such an outstanding series that he was voted the MVP of the Playoffs.

True or false? Wilt "The Stilt" Chamberlain once played for the Harlem Globetrotters.

True. Chamberlain, who turned pro after his junior year at the University of Kansas, played for the Globetrotters in 1958-59 before joining the Philadelphia Warriors of the NBA in 1960.

Can you name the team that the Washington Bullets defeated in the 1978 Eastern Division Playoffs to advance to the NBA Championship?

In 1978, the underdog Bullets beat the Philadelphia 76ers in six games, to advance into the finals and take the National Basketball Association Championship.

When Kareem Abdul-Jabbar was voted the Outstanding Player in the NCAA in 1967, 1968, and 1969, he was known by a different name. Do you remember it?

Before changing his name to Kareem Adbul-Jabbar, the UCLA star and winner of the NCAA's Outstanding Player Award was known as Lew Alcindor.

In 1968, the Detroit Pistons traded Dave DeBusschere to the New York Knickerbockers. Who did the Pistons receive in return for DeBusschere?

Star center Walt Bellamy went to the Pistons in the trade that sent DeBusschere to the Knicks. There, DeBusschere immediately gained superstar status and was voted the NBA's Defensive Player of the Year in 1969.

Which NBA team set the record for losing the most games in a season? Was it the Los Angeles Lakers or the Philadelphia 76ers?

It was the Philadelphia 76ers who established that dubious record by losing seventy-three games during the 1972-73 season. The Lakers, on the other hand, hold the NBA record for *winning* the most games in a single season. In 1971-72, they were victorious in sixty-nine contests.

Can a basketball game end in a tie?

No. If a game is tied at the end of regulation time, overtime periods are played to determine a winner. High school teams play 3-minute overtime periods. College and pro teams' overtime periods are five minutes long.

True or false? Elgin Baylor holds the NBA record for scoring the most points in one game of an NBA Championship series.

False. That record is held by Wilt Chamberlain. As a Philadelphia Warrior, Chamberlain scored 100 points against the New York Knicks in a championship game on March 2, 1962.

In 1975, the Most Valuable Player in the NBA Playoffs and the NBA's Rookie of the Year were on the same team. Can you name that team and those two players?

The answer is the Golden State Warriors. In 1975, Warrior Rick Barry was the MVP of the Playoffs, and teammate Keith Wilkes was the league's top rookie.

What is a *free throw*?

A *free throw* is a bonus shot awarded to a fouled player. The player must shoot the ball from behind the free-throw line, and no other players may enter the free-throw lane or circle until the ball hits the backboard or the basket. A successful free throw counts as 1 point.

Willis Reed of the New York Knicks was named the Most Valuable Player in the NBA in what year? Was it 1969, 1970, or 1972?

Willis Reed won the National Basketball Association's MVP Award in 1970 and went on to be named the playoffs' MVP as well. Reed captured the playoffs' Award again in 1973.

In what year was the first standard set of basketball rules drawn up? Was it 1900, 1915, or 1918?

Basketball's rule-making groups met and developed the first standard set of rules in 1915, using James Naismith's original thirteen rules as a guide. Most notable of these new rules was the one limiting the number of players on a team to five.

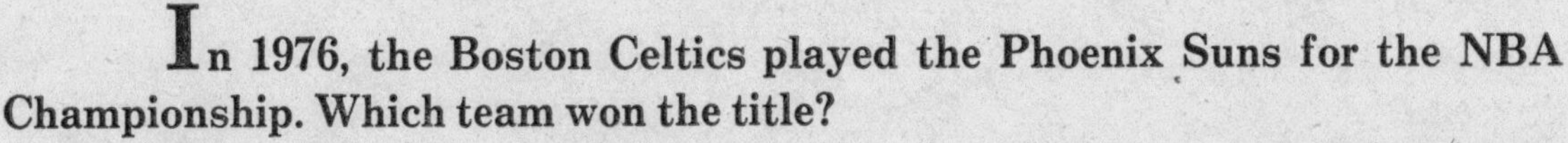

In 1976, the Boston Celtics played the Phoenix Suns for the NBA Championship. Which team won the title?

The Celtics beat the Suns, 4 games to 2, to become the 1976 Champions of the National Basketball Association.

Has Holy Cross College ever won the National Collegiate Athletic Association's Basketball Championship?

Yes. Holy Cross was the NCAA Basketball Champion in 1947.

Bill Bradley, who played professionally for the New York Knicks, was a college All-American at which university? Was it UCLA, Princeton, or Ohio State?

In 1965, Bill Bradley was an All-American at Princeton University and was voted the outstanding player in the NCAA.

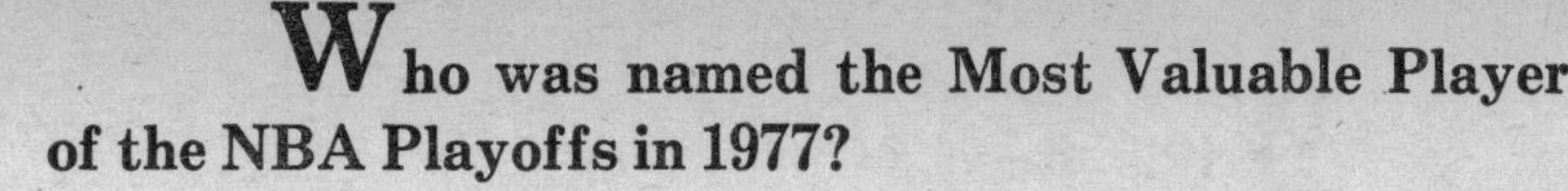

Who was named the Most Valuable Player of the NBA Playoffs in 1977?

Center Bill Walton of the Portland Trail Blazers was named the MVP of the 1977 playoffs. In the game that clinched the championship for Portland against the Philadelphia 76ers, Walton scored 20 points, pulled down 23 rebounds, and blocked 8 shots.

BILL WALTON

What is a *double dribble*?

A *double dribble* is a violation which occurs when a player who has already dribbled grasps the ball with both hands and starts to dribble again. For this violation, possession of the ball is automatically awarded to the other team.

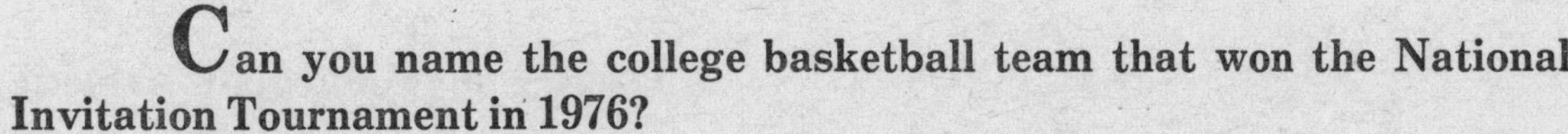

Can you name the college basketball team that won the National Invitation Tournament in 1976?

The Kentucky Wildcats were the victors in the 1976 NIT, with North Carolina-Charlotte as the runner-up.

The NBA awards the Maurice Podoloff Cup annually. To which player is that trophy awarded?

The Maurice Podoloff Cup is awarded to the Most Valuable Player in the NBA at the end of each season. The cup was named for Maurice Podoloff, who was president of the Basketball Association of America when it merged with the NBA in 1949. Podoloff brought the NBA to national prominence during his 17-year reign as commissioner.

What is an *all-court,* or *full-court, press?*

Both terms mean the same thing — a pressure type defense in which the defenders guard the offensive players very closely at all points on the court in an attempt to force them to commit errors.

True or false? Superstar Connie Hawkins was 29 years old in his rookie season in the NBA.

True. Before joining the NBA's Phoenix Suns as a 29-year-old rookie, 6-foot 8-inch Connie Hawkins played in the American Basketball League, the American Basketball Association, and with the Harlem Globetrotters. During that eight-year period, he won the MVP Awards of both the ABL and the ABA.

Which team won the ABA Championship in 1976? Was it the Denver Nuggets or the New York Nets?

New York beat Denver, 118 to 110, in the sixth game of their championship series to clinch the 1976 ABA title. It was the second time the Nets won the ABA crown, their first win coming in 1974.

How many times did the great Neil Johnston lead the NBA in scoring?

Playing for the Philadelphia Warriors, Neil Johnston topped all NBA scorers for three consecutive years, from 1953 to 1955.

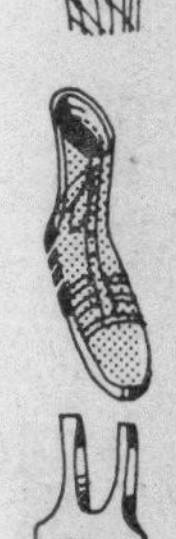

Johnny Kerr, who was a member of the Syracuse Nationals, the Philadelphia Warriors, and the Baltimore Bullets, holds the NBA record for playing in the most consecutive games. Can you guess how many games he played in to set that record?

From October 31, 1954 to November 4, 1965, Johnny Kerr played in 844 consecutive basketball games.

Kentucky, UCLA, Louisville, and Syracuse all battled for the championship in the 1975 NCAA Basketball Tournament. Can you rank the four teams in the order in which they finished?

The four teams finished in the following order: (1) UCLA, (2) Kentucky, (3) Louisville, and (4) Syracuse. UCLA beat Kentucky, 92 to 85, to win the championship, and Louisville defeated Syracuse, 96 to 88, in the consolation game.

True or false? The ancient Aztec Indians played a game similar to basketball.

True. The Aztecs' game, called *Ollamalitzli*, required a team to put a solid rubber ball through a fixed stone ring placed high on the side of the stadium wall. This primitive game was a brutal one, and the captain of the losing team was often beheaded. The winning team was also entitled to the clothing of all of the spectators as a prize.

What is *goal tending*?

Goal tending is touching the ball during its downward arch toward the basket or knocking the ball back from the basket when it's above or in the opponent's basket. Goal tending results in an automatic field goal for the team that shot the ball.

Which team in the American Basketball Association won the championship the most times? Is it the Indiana Pacers, the New York Nets, or the Pittsburgh Pipers?

The correct answer is the Indiana Pacers. They won the ABA Championship three times: in 1969-70, 1971-72, and 1972-73. The New York Nets won the title twice: in 1973-74 and 1975-76; while the Pittsburgh Pipers took the title only once — in 1967-68.

True or false? The Oakland Oaks have never won the ABA Championship.

False. The Oaks, who topped the Western Division with 60 wins and only 18 losses in 1968-69, went on to capture the ABA crown that year.

What is a *bounce pass*?

When an offensive player passes the ball to a teammate by first bouncing it a single time off the floor, that pass is called a *bounce pass*.

True or false? Bob Pettit of the old St. Louis Hawks was named to the NBA All-Star Team every year of his eleven-year career.

True. Pettit made the All-Star Team for eleven consecutive years, from 1954 to 1965.

The coach of the Denver Nuggets was named the ABA Coach of the Year in 1975-76. Who was he?

Denver's Larry Brown was the 1975-76 ABA Coach of the Year. This was the third win for Brown, who won the same award in 1971-72 and in 1974-75.

Who was the first player picked in the 1976 NBA amateur draft? Was it Scott May of Indiana or John Lucas of Maryland?

Guard John Lucas became the first player selected in the 1976 NBA draft when the Houston Rockets named him as their choice. Center Scott May was the second player picked and went to the Chicago Bulls.

Which NBA player holds the record for making the most free throws in a lifetime? Is it Oscar Robertson, John Havlicek, or Jerry West?

Playing for the Cincinnati Royals and the Milwaukee Bucks from 1961 to 1974, Oscar Robertson, "The big O," made 7,694 free throws, to set the NBA record.

Who coached the New York Knickerbockers in 1977-78?

Willis Reed, who was a center for the Knickerbockers from 1964 to 1974, rejoined the team in 1977-78, replacing Red Holzman as head coach. In the 1978-79 season, Holzman returned to replace Reed.

In 1954, Clarence Francis of Rio Grande College, Rio Grande, Ohio, set the college basketball record for scoring the most points in a single game. How many points did he score to set that record?

Clarence Francis scored an amazing single-game total of 150 points to set that record.

Which player holds the NBA record for committing the most personal fouls during his career? Is it Hal Greer, Walt Bellamy, or Dolph Schayes?

The answer is Hal Greer. During his career with the Syracuse Nationals and the Philadelphia 76ers, personal fouls were called against Greer on 3,855 occasions. Schayes is second on the all-time list and Bellamy is third.

In basketball, what does the term *give-and-go* mean?

Give-and-go is a strategy in which the player with the ball passes it to a teammate and then races toward the basket, anticipating a return pass.

What is the diameter of a basketball hoop? Is it 16 inches, 18 inches, or 20 inches in diameter?

A basketball hoop is 18 inches in diameter.

Which basketball player won the NCAA Outstanding Player Award more than once? Was it Jerry Lucas, Jerry West, or Elgin Baylor?

The answer is Jerry Lucas. Playing for Ohio State, Jerry was the NCAA's Outstanding Player in 1960 and 1961. Jerry West won the award in 1959 while he was at West Virginia, and Elgin Baylor won it in 1963, playing for Seattle.

What is the distance from the free throw line to the basket?

The free throw line is 15 feet from the basket.

The NBA record for assists in one season is 910. Was that record set by Nate Archibald, John Havlicek, or Oscar Robertson?

The answer is Nate "Tiny" Archibald. Playing for Kansas City-Omaha in 1972-73, Nate had a record-setting 910 assists.

The game of basketball was invented in 1891. Was it first played in England, the United States, or France?

Basketball is a native American game devised by James A. Naismith, a physical education instructor at the International YMCA Training School (now Springfield College) in Springfield, Massachusetts, in response to his department head's request to create a team sport which could be played indoors during the winter.

True or false? More people in more nations play basketball than any other team sport.

True. Even though soccer is the most *watched* game, the game of basketball is *played* in about 130 countries all around the world.

How long is a high school basketball game? Is it 30 minutes, 32 minutes, or 60 minutes long?

High school basketball games are 32 minutes long. They are divided into two 16-minute halves, broken down into two 8-minute quarters.

True or false? Two professional basketball teams set a record by scoring over 300 points in a single game.

True. The San Diego Conquistadors and the New York Nets of the ABA scored a record total of 342 points in a single game on February 14, 1975. San Diego won the game, 176 to 166.

The Portland Trail Blazers played the Philadelphia 76ers for the NBA Championship in 1977. Which team won the title that year?

After losing the first two games of the championship series to Philadelphia, Portland bounced back with four straight wins to take the 1977 NBA title.

Which NBA division are the Seattle Supersonics in?

The Supersonics are in the Pacific Division of the Western Conference, along with the Golden State Warriors, the Los Angeles Lakers, the Portland Trail Blazers, and the Phoenix Suns.

How many officials supervise a basketball game?

Two officials — a *referee* and an *umpire* — supervise most college basketball games. The referee is the chief official, but the umpire has equal rights to call fouls and violations and to enforce penalties. In professional basketball, both officials are called referees, with the referee with the greatest seniority in charge.

In 1971-72, the Los Angeles Lakers established an NBA record for the most consecutive victories. How many games did they win to set that record? Was it 30, 33, or 37 games?

The Lakers set the NBA record by winning 33 games in a row.

What is a *pick* play?

In a *pick* play, an offensive player uses his body to block a defender, setting up one of his teammates for an unmolested field goal attempt.

In the 1975 AIAW Championship game, two of the top women basketball powers in the country faced each other. Can you name those two AIAW basketball powers?

Delta State College of Mississippi faced Immaculata College of Pennsylvania, with Delta defeating Immaculata, 90 to 81, for the 1975 AIAW Basketball Championship.

Which NBA star is known to his fans as "Doctor J"?

Julius Erving, formerly of the Virginia Squires and the New York Nets, and currently under a $3½ million contract to the Philadelphia 76ers, has been fondly nicknamed "Doctor J." This started during Erving's college days at the University of Massachusetts, when Erving jokingly nicknamed a very bright friend "The Professor." The Professor, in turn, jokingly called Erving "The Doctor," and when Erving joined the Virginia Squires, a teammate picked up on that nickname and labeled him "Doctor J."

A basketball announcer states that one team has *"control of the boards."* What does that mean?

When a team has *"control of the boards,"* that team is getting most of the rebounds.

Is a college basketball game as long as a professional basketball game?

No. A pro game is longer. College teams play two 20-minute halves, with a 15-minute rest between halves. Pro basketball teams play four 12-minute quarters, with a 1½-minute rest between quarters and a 15-minute rest between halves.

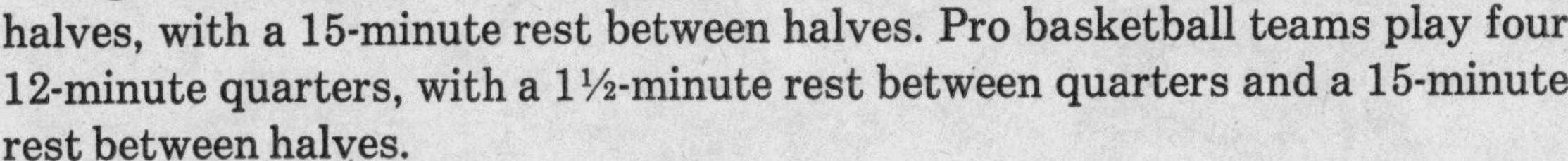

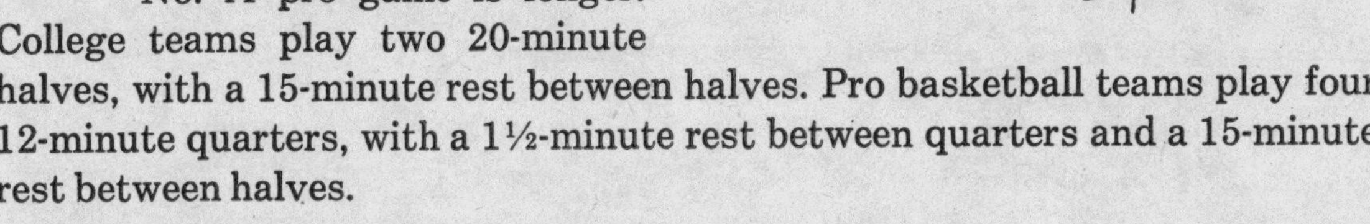

Oscar Robertson, Bill Russell, and Elgin Baylor have all become basketball superstars. Two of them won Rookie of the Year honors during their first NBA season. Which one did not?

Oscar Robertson was the NBA's Rookie of the Year in 1961, and Elgin Baylor was voted the top newcomer in the league in 1959. So the answer is Bill Russell. His first year in the NBA was 1956, when Maurice Stokes of the Rochester Royals won the Rookie of the Year Award.

The NBA record for making the most consecutive free throws is 60. Who holds that record?

From October 22 to November 16, 1976, Rick Barry of the Golden State Warriors made those 60 free throws in a row.

Which team won the first ABA Championship when the association was first established?

The ABA's premier season, 1967-68, saw the Pittsburgh Pipers take the first championship.

Two of these stars played in the ABA before coming to the NBA. Which one did not? Is it Julius Erving, Dan Issel, or Bill Walton?

Bill Walton is the correct answer. Julius Erving played for the New York Nets, and Dan Issel played for the Kentucky Colonels, both ABA teams, before coming to the NBA.

True or false? The Syracuse Nationals and the Rochester Royals have never won NBA titles.

False. The Rochester Royals captured the NBA crown in 1950-51, and the Syracuse Nationals were the NBA champions in 1954-55.

When the referee makes the hand signal pictured, what does it mean?

The hand signal means that the referee has called a *technical foul*. Technical fouls may be called on players or coaches for unsportsmanlike conduct; they can also be called on teams for taking too many time outs, delaying the game, or having a player enter or leave the game illegally.

Is a zone defense legal in professional basketball?

No. The zone defense is legal only in high school and college ranks, but is illegal in professional basketball. Zone defenses tend to limit scoring opportunities, which is why it is outlawed among the pros.

Can you match the following NBA superstars with the year they led the National Basketball Association in scoring?

(1) Jerry West, playing for the Los Angeles Lakers

(2) Nate Archibald, playing for the Kansas City-Omaha Kings

(3) Bob McAdoo, playing for the Buffalo Braves

(a) Led the NBA in scoring in 1972-73 with 2,719 points

(b) Led the NBA in scoring in 1973-74 with 2,261 points

(c) Led the NBA in scoring in 1969-70 with 2,309 points

The answers are: 1. (c) Jerry West of the Los Angeles Lakers led the NBA in scoring in 1969-70 with 2,309 points. 2. (a) Nate Archibald, playing for the Kansas City-Omaha Kings, led the NBA in scoring in 1972-73 with 2,719 points. 3. (b) Bob McAdoo, playing for the Buffalo Braves, led the NBA in scoring in 1973-74 with 2,261 points.

A member of the original 1923 Celtics went on to become one of the greatest collegiate and professional coaches in basketball history. Can you name him?

That playing and coaching star was Joe Lapchick. As coach of New York's St. John's University from 1937 to 1947 and from 1957 to 1965, Lapchick led his collegiate team to four National Invitational Tournament Championships—in 1943, 1944, 1959 and 1965. At the helm of the NBA's New York Knicks from 1948 to 1956, he won two Eastern Division titles—in 1953 and 1954.

What is a *lay-up*?

A *lay-up* is an easy shot that a player takes after he breaks away from defenders under the basket. The shot is pushed rather than thrown, and is usually banked off the backboard.

Do basketball teams have offensive and defensive squads like football teams do?

No. The five players on the court during the game must play both offensive and defensive basketball.

The American Basketball Association had a relatively short life. How long was the ABA in existence? Was it five years, nine years, or twelve years?

The ABA had a nine-year, four-month, and five-day life which ended June 17, 1976. The last ABA Champions were the New York Nets.

What is the difference between a *zone defense* and a *man-to-man defense*?

In a *zone defense*, each defending player is responsible for a certain area of the court. While playing *zone*, a defender keeps his attention on the movement of the ball and guards any opposing player who enters his zone. In a *man-to-man defense*, each defender guards a particular opponent and shadows that player wherever he goes, attempting to stay between him and the basket.

Which NBA player holds the record for scoring the most points in playoff competition? Is it Elgin Baylor, Bob Cousy, or Jerry West?

The answer is Elgin Baylor of the Los Angeles Lakers. During his thirteen-year career, Baylor scored 3,010 points in playoff competition, averaging 30 points per game.

Where is the *front court* on a basketball court?

The *front court* is the area from the center line to the offensive team's basket. This area must be reached by the offensive team within ten seconds after gaining possession of the ball.

Which NBA basketball team did Dick Motta coach in 1978?

Dick Motta coached the Washington Bullets to the NBA Championship in 1978.

In what year was the first professional basketball All-Star Game played? Was it in 1948, 1951, or 1955?

The year 1951 marked the first time that the East All-Stars met the West All-Stars. The East took that game by the score of 111 to 94. In the years between 1951 and 1977, the East has won that game a total of seventeen times to the West's ten.

How many times was Julius Erving voted the Most Valuable Player in the old American Basketball Association?

Julius Erving, playing for the New York Nets at the time, won the ABA's Most Valuable Player Award three times. He was named the MVP in 1974 and 1976, and shared the award with George McGinnis in 1975.

In basketball, what does it mean when two defenders *switch*?

A *switch* occurs when defenders are using a man-to-man defense. In order to avoid being blocked out when offensive players crisscross, defenders call "switch" and automatically change the man they are assigned to guard, with each picking up the player closest to him.

The man who directs the Globetrotters' zany on-court antics is considered to be the "Clown Prince of Basketball." Is it Meadowlark Lemon, Clarence Wilson, or Marques Haynes?

Although all three players have been stars of the Globetrotters, Meadowlark Lemon is the undisputed "Clown Prince of Basketball."

Which American Basketball Association team won the league championship in 1974-75?

The Kentucky Colonels won the ABA Championship in 1974-75 by defeating the Indiana Pacers, 4 games to 1.

Who holds the record for sinking the most free throws in one game? Is it Wilt Chamberlain, Jerry West, or Walt Frazier?

Even though he wasn't known for his foul-shooting ability, Wilt Chamberlain is the record holder. On March 2, 1962, playing for the old Philadelphia Warriors in a game against the New York Knicks, Wilt sank 28 free throws in 32 attempts, to establish that record.

In professional basketball, a team can score in two ways: 2 points on a field goal or 1 point on a free throw. However, in the old American Basketball Association, there was a third way. What was it?

According to the rules of the old ABA, a field goal shot from more than twenty-five feet from the basket counted as 3 points, thereby providing teams with a third scoring possibility.

Hal Greer and Oscar Robertson were great NBA stars. Which player scored more points in his career?

The answer is Oscar Robertson. In fourteen years as a pro basketball player, Robertson scored a total of 26,710 points. Hal Greer scored 21,586 points during his fifteen-year career.

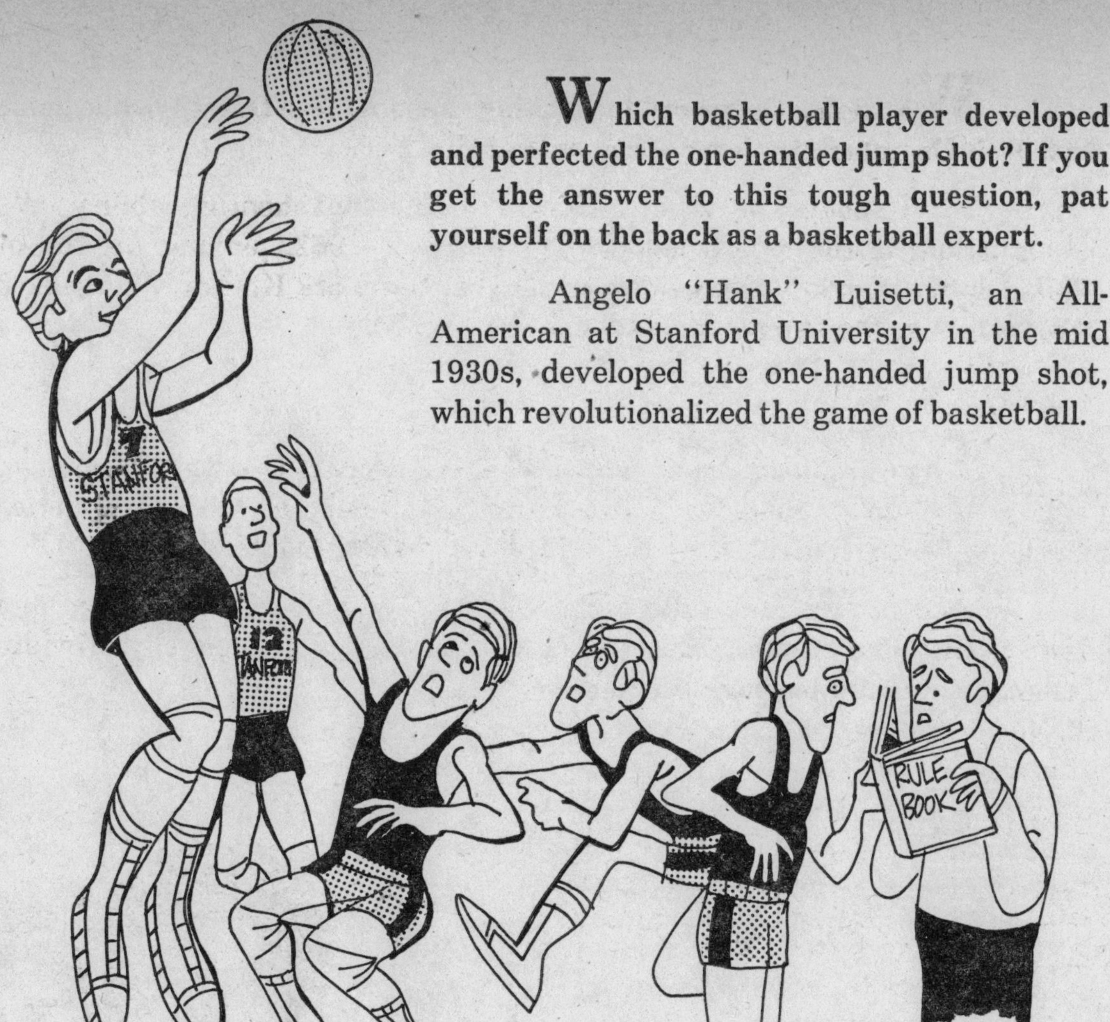

Which basketball player developed and perfected the one-handed jump shot? If you get the answer to this tough question, pat yourself on the back as a basketball expert.

Angelo "Hank" Luisetti, an All-American at Stanford University in the mid 1930s, developed the one-handed jump shot, which revolutionalized the game of basketball.

True or false? A basketball measures about 20 inches in circumference.

False. A basketball measures about 30 inches in circumference. The molded 20- to 22-ounce ball is made of leather, plastic, rubber, or a similar material.

Which team won the National Invitation Tournament in 1978? Was it the University of Texas, North Carolina State, or Rutgers?

The University of Texas took the 1978 NIT title by defeating North Carolina State, 101 to 93, in the finals.

Can you give the definition of a *set shot*?

A *set shot* is an attempted field goal a player takes with deliberation as he stands with both feet on the floor, well away from the basket.

True or false? Basketball players were always allowed to dribble the ball.

False. In the early stages of basketball's development, the only way players were allowed to advance the ball was by passing it. The technique of dribbling wasn't incorporated into the game until around 1900.

In the Association for Intercollegiate Athletes for Women, the 1978 basketball championship game saw UCLA play the University of Maryland. Which team won?

The University of California at Los Angeles won the AIAW basketball title in 1978 by beating Maryland, 90 to 74.

If an offensive player is fouled in the act of shooting and his shot is *not* good, how many free throws does he get?

Two free throws are given to a player fouled in the act of shooting if his shot does not go into the basket. If, however, the ball *does* go into the basket on that fouled shot and the referee rules that the shot is good, the player gets one free throw. This is called a *three-point play*.

Can you explain basketball's *three-second rule*?

The *three-second rule* prohibits offensive players from remaining in the free-throw lane for more than three seconds. Offensive players are not allowed to hang under their basket and must continually move in and out of the lane. If an offensive player violates the three-second rule, play is stopped and possession of the ball is awarded to the opposing team.

Which college basketball team won the NCAA Championship in 1977?

Marquette won the NCAA Championship by beating North Carolina, 67 to 59, giving their dynamic coach, Al McGuire, a fine retirement 1977 gift.

The National Basketball Association was originally called the Basketball Association of America. True or false?

True. The Basketball Association of America became the National Basketball Association when it merged with the National Basketball League in 1949.

Can you define a *high post* and a *low post*?

A *high post* refers to a position near the outer circle of the free-throw line. A *low post* is at the side of the basket outside the free-throw lane.

True or false? The game of basketball always allowed five players on each team.

False. When the game was first devised by Dr. James Naismith, there were *nine* players on each team. Why? Simply because Dr. Naismith's physical education class had eighteen students in it, and he had to divide them into two teams to keep them occupied during the winter months.

Where is the basketball Hall of Fame located? Is it in New York, Massachusetts, or Ohio?

The Naismith Memorial Basketball Hall of Fame, which was established in 1959, is located in Springfield, Massachusetts. The memorial to Dr. James A. Naismith, the inventor of basketball, honors players, coaches, teams, and others who have made contributions to basketball.

True or false? The first basketball baskets in the 1890s were half-bushel fruit baskets which did not have holes in them.

Absolutely true. In early basketball games, a ladder had to be brought out onto the court to retrieve the ball from the basket every time a player scored. Later, metal baskets with holes in them were used so the ball could be pushed out with a pole. Basketball hoops that allowed the ball to drop through a net after a successful shot did not come into use until about 1913.

From 1964 to 1973, UCLA took the NCAA Championship every year except one. Can you name the college that interrupted UCLA's championship reign and the year they won the NCAA title?

The answer is Texas Western College. They interrupted UCLA's streak by winning the NCAA Basketball Championship in 1966.

Did Oscar Robertson ever win the Podoloff Cup?

Yes. Robertson was voted the Most Valuable Player in the NBA and awarded the Podoloff Cup in 1964, when he was a starting guard for the old Cincinnati Royals.

How tall is Kareem Abdul-Jabbar? Is he 6 feet 11 inches, 7 feet, or 7 feet 2 inches tall?

Kareem Abdul Jabbar, who played for the Los Angeles Lakers in 1977-78, is 7 feet 2 inches tall, but he combines the speed, grace, and ability of a swift 6-foot guard.

Princeton played against Providence for the Championship of the 1975 National Invitation Tournament. Which team won?

Princeton won the NIT in 1975, defeating Providence by the score of 80 to 69.

Where did Bob Cousy play college basketball?

Cousy starred for Holy Cross and set an all-time scoring mark of 582 points.

What is a *held ball*?

A *held ball* is called when a player from each team has a firm hold on the ball but neither is in complete control of it. The referee immediately stops play, and a jump ball determines which team takes possession of the ball.

How many times has Saint John's University of Brooklyn won the National Invitation Tournament?

As of 1977, Saint John's won the NIT a total of four times. They were the NIT Champions in 1943, 1944, 1959, and 1965.

The Philadelphia 76ers set an NBA record for losing the most games in a row. How many consecutive games did they lose?

In 1973, the hapless Philadelphia 76ers lost twenty games before they finally won one.

True or false? Ohio State has never won the NCAA Basketball Championship.

False. Ohio State won the NCAA Basketball crown in 1960.

In 1969, the Most Valuable Player in the NBA, a Baltimore Bullet, was also the NBA's Rookie of the Year. Can you name that player?

The correct answer is Wes Unseld. As a center for the Baltimore Bullets, Unseld won both awards in 1969.

The Seattle Supersonics squared off against the Washington Bullets for the 1978 National Basketball Association Championship. Which team won the title?

After six hard-fought playoff games, the Bullets and the Supersonics were tied three games apiece. In the fourth and final game of the series, Washington beat Seattle by the score of 105 to 99, to win the 1978 NBA Championship.

In 1977, which NBA team did Jerry West coach?

Jerry West, one of the greatest players in NBA history, was a coach for the Los Angeles Lakers in 1977.

What is a *rebound*?

A *rebound* occurs after a shot taken at the basket fails to go into the hoop. When the ball bounces off the backboard or rim, it is a free ball and is called a rebound. The team that gets the rebound retains possession of the ball.

Which NBA teams are located in the following cities: New York, Philadelphia, Cleveland, and Chicago?

If you came up with the New York Knickerbockers, the Philadelphia 76ers, the Cleveland Cavaliers, and the Chicago Bulls, you're correct.

Do you remember the name of the movie that was based on the story of the Harlem Globetrotters?

The name of the movie was *Go, Man, Go!* and starred actor Dane Clark as Globetrotter owner-manager Abe Saperstein, along with the Globetrotters themselves.

In basketball, how many points does a team score on a field goal?

A field goal is worth 2 points on the scoreboard.

Can you name the two college basketball teams that played in the 1978 NCAA Championship game?

The Blue Devils of Duke faced the Kentucky Wildcats, with Kentucky beating Duke, 94 to 88, to take the 1978 NCAA Basketball Championship.

Of the three college stars up for grabs by the pros in 1950, the "least wanted" one had his name picked out of a hat by the Boston Celtics. Who was that college star?

Bob Cousy was that unwanted star, but that drawing proved to be the luckiest break a team ever had, for Cousy went on to become one of the most spectacular stars the game has ever seen. In his thirteen seasons with Boston, Cousy sparked the Celtics to six NBA Championships.

Match the following NBA teams to their home cities.

(1)	**Bucks**	**(a)**	**Atlanta**
(2)	**Rockets**	**(b)**	**Rutherford**
(3)	**Nuggets**	**(c)**	**Boston**
(4)	**Spurs**	**(d)**	**New Orleans**
(5)	**Lakers**	**(e)**	**Houston**
(6)	**Cavaliers**	**(f)**	**San Antonio**
(7)	**Bulls**	**(g)**	**Denver**
(8)	**Trail Blazers**	**(h)**	**Los Angeles**
(9)	**Celtics**	**(i)**	**Chicago**
(10)	**Jazz**	**(j)**	**Portland**
(11)	**Nets**	**(k)**	**Milwaukee**
(12)	**Pistons**	**(l)**	**Detroit**
(13)	**Supersonics**	**(m)**	**Cleveland**
(14)	**Hawks**	**(n)**	**Seattle**

The answers are: (1) k. The Bucks are Milwaukee's team in the NBA; (2) e. It's the Houston Rockets; (3) g. The Nuggets play in Denver; (4) f. San Antonio claims the Spurs; (5) h. The Lakers make their home in Los Angeles; (6) m. Cleveland is the home city for the Cavaliers; (7) i. The Bulls play in Chicago; (8) j. The Trail Blazers are Portland's NBA team; (9) c. The long-time pride and joy of Boston is the Celtics; (10) d. New Orleans is the home town of the Jazz; (11) b. The former N.Y. Nets, now call Rutherford, New Jersey, home; (12) l. Detroit fans back the Pistons; (13) n. The Supersonics make their home in Seattle; and (14) a. The Hawks are Atlanta's team in the NBA.

SOCCER

Ron Newman was named the North American Soccer League's Coach of the Year in 1977. Which NASL team did he coach that year?

Ron Newman coached the NASL's Fort Lauderdale Strikers in 1977 and led them to the first-place spot in the Atlantic Conference's Eastern Division, with 19 wins and 7 losses.

What is *dribbling*?

Moving the ball down the field by kicking it gently or nudging it from one foot to the other is called *dribbling.*

In soccer, when a player directs the path of a ball in the air by using his forehead, he is said to be *heading the ball.* True or false?

True.

Which country won soccer's World Cup Championship in 1974?

West Germany won the 1974 World Cup Championship by defeating The Netherlands, 2 games to 1, in Munich, West Germany.

Michigan State was the National Collegiate Athletic Association Soccer Co-Champion for two years in a row. True or false?

True. In 1967, Michigan State tied St. Louis University, 0 to 0, to share the NCAA soccer crown, and in 1968, they tied Maryland, 2 to 2, to become co-champions for the second year in a row.

Edson Arantes do Nascimento is a world-famous soccer player from Brazil. Most soccer fans know him by a different name. Do you know that name?

Edson Arantes do Nascimento is known to soccer fans all over the world as Pele.

When were the official rules and regulations of soccer first set down? Was it in 1863, 1880, or 1900?

On December 8, 1863, the Football Association was formed by representatives of football clubs in London, England, and the first set of rules and regulations of soccer were set down.

Soccer has its equivalent to football's Super Bowl. What is the NASL Championship game called?

The North American Soccer League Championship game is The Soccer Bowl.

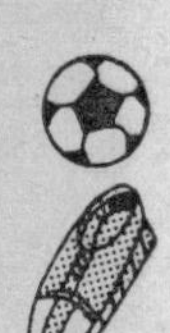

George Best, Derek Smethurst, and Steve David were the top scorers in the North American Soccer League in 1977. Can you arrange them in the order in which they led the league?

Steve David of Los Angeles had 26 goals and 6 assists for a league-leading total of 58 points. Derek Smethurst of Tampa Bay was second with 19 goals and 4 assists, totaling 42 points. George Best of Los Angeles was third with 11 goals and 18 assists, for a total of 40 points.

Which NASL team won the Soccer Bowl in 1977? Was it the Dallas Tornado, the Los Angeles Aztecs, or the New York Cosmos?

The New York Cosmos beat the Seattle Sounders to win the North American Soccer League Soccer Bowl in 1977.

True or false? Italy has never won soccer's World Cup.

False. Italy won the World Cup in 1934 in Rome by defeating Czechoslovakia, 2 games to 1. The Italians took the Cup again in 1938, when they downed Hungary, 4 games to 2, in Paris.

In what year did soccer's World Cup competition begin? Was it 1930, 1934, or 1940?

The World Cup competition was instituted by the *Federation Internationale de Football Associations* in 1930 when Jules Rimet, the President of FIFA, presented a cup for the winner of an international competition. Currently, more than 130 nations are members of the FIFA.

What is the size of the area around the net designated as the *goal area?* Is it 6 yards deep by 20 yards wide, 5 yards deep by 15 yards wide, or 7 yards deep by 21 yards wide?

The *goal area* is 6 yards (5.5 meters) deep by 20 yards (18.3 meters) wide.

Pele, the former New York Cosmos star from South America, scored over 1,000 goals in his career. True or false?

True. Pele's career total was 1,281 goals, which he achieved in his 1,363rd game.

Which country won soccer's coveted World Cup in 1970?

Brazil won soccer's World Cup in 1970 by defeating Italy, 4 games to 1, in Mexico City.

How often are the World Cup Soccer Championship games played?

Since their beginnings in 1930, the World Cup Soccer Championships have been played every four years, with the exception of a twelve-year break from 1938 to 1950.

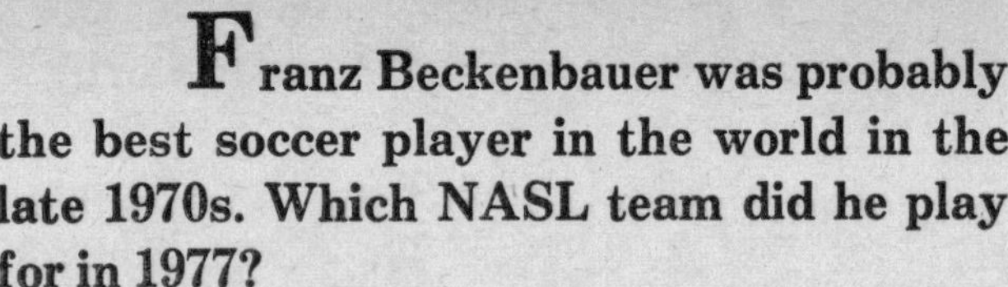

Franz Beckenbauer was probably the best soccer player in the world in the late 1970s. Which NASL team did he play for in 1977?

Beckenbauer, the former captain of West Germany's World Cup Champion soccer team, came to the United States in 1977 and joined the New York Cosmos of the NASL.

What is a *corner kick?*

A *corner kick* is a kick made by an offensive player when a ball last touched by a defensive player passes over the goal line without going into the goal. The offensive player puts the ball back into play by kicking the ball from the nearest corner of the field toward the goal mouth. Corner kicks usually result in scoring opportunities.

Which country won the first World Cup Soccer Championship? Was it Brazil, England, or Uruguay?

When the World Cup Soccer Championship was established in 1930, Uruguay was the first winner, defeating Argentina, 4 to 2, in the games played in Montevideo, Uruguay.

Who coached the New York Cosmos soccer team in 1978? Was it Eddie Firmani, Al Miller, or Freddie Goodwin?

Eddie Firmani coached the Cosmos. Miller was the coach of the Dallas Tornado, while Goodwin was at the reins of the Minnesota Kicks.

What is the soccer term for hooking or kicking the ball away from an opponent?

Hooking or kicking the ball away from an opponent is called *tackling.*

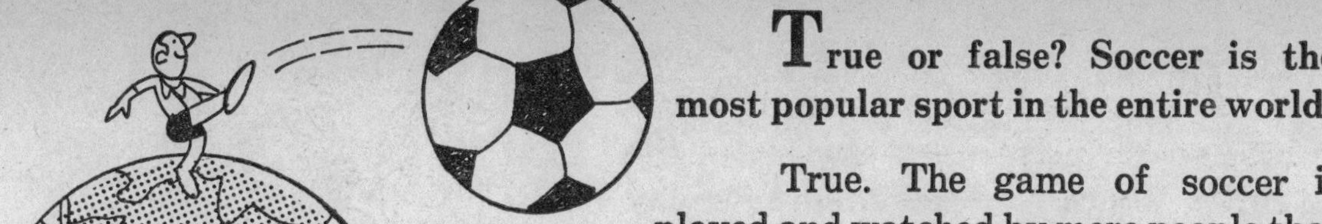

True or false? Soccer is the most popular sport in the entire world.

True. The game of soccer is played and watched by more people than any other sport in the world, and is the national sport of several European, Asian, and South American countries, where crowds of up to 200,000 people attend the games. Millions more wager in weekly soccer pools, in the hopes of winning large sums of money. World Cup matches arouse the same interest and excitement around the world as baseball's World Series does in the United States.

In what year was the North American Soccer League founded? Was it 1965, 1967, or 1968?

The North American Soccer League was founded in April, 1967, when two professional leagues, the National Professional Soccer League and the United Soccer Association, merged to form the NASL.

How many players are on a soccer team?

There are eleven players on a soccer team. The usual breakdown is five forwards, three halfbacks, two fullbacks, and a goalkeeper.

True or false? In 1973, Kyle Rote, Jr. was the Rookie of the Year in the North American Soccer League.

True. Rote earned 1973 Rookie of the Year honors by helping his Dallas Tornado team to finish first in the NASL's Southern Division.

How many officials are there in a soccer game?

A soccer game has three officials — a *referee* and two *linesmen.* The referee calls fouls and enforces the rules, while the linesmen make boundary and offside calls.

Can you name the only country to win the World Cup more than twice? Is it Italy, West Germany, or Brazil?

If you said Brazil, you're absolutely right. Brazil won soccer's coveted prize three times: first, in 1958, defeating Sweden; in 1962, defeating Czechoslovakia; and in 1970, defeating Italy. Italy and West Germany each won the World Cup twice.

In which country was the 1978 World Cup Soccer Championship played? Was it Argentina, West Germany, or Brazil?

The eleventh World Cup Soccer Championship, which is played every four years, was held in Argentina in 1978. In 1974, it was held in West Germany, and in 1970, Brazil won the bid for the game.

Which NASL team won the championship in 1976? Was it the Toronto Metros-Croatia, the Minnesota Kicks, or the Colorado Caribous?

The Toronto Metros-Croatia were the 1976 NASL Champions.

The Dallas Tornado and the Toronto Metros-Croatia are two of the twelve teams in the NASL's National Conference. How many more of those teams can you name?

The NASL's National Conference also includes the Rochester Lancers, the Washington Diplomats, the Minnesota Kicks, the Tulsa Roughnecks, the New York Cosmos, the Colorado Caribous, the Seattle Sounders, the Los Angeles Aztecs, the Portland Timbers, and the Vancouver White Caps.

Who is the only player to have played on three World Cup Championship teams?

Pele, the electrifying star of the Brazilian soccer team, led his team to three World Cup Championships: in 1958, 1962, and 1970.

Which NASL goalie was named to the 1977 All-Star team? Was it Ken Cooper, Gordon Banks, or Zeljko Bilnecki?

Gordon Banks of the Ft. Lauderdale Strikers was the All-Star goalkeeper on the 1977 team.

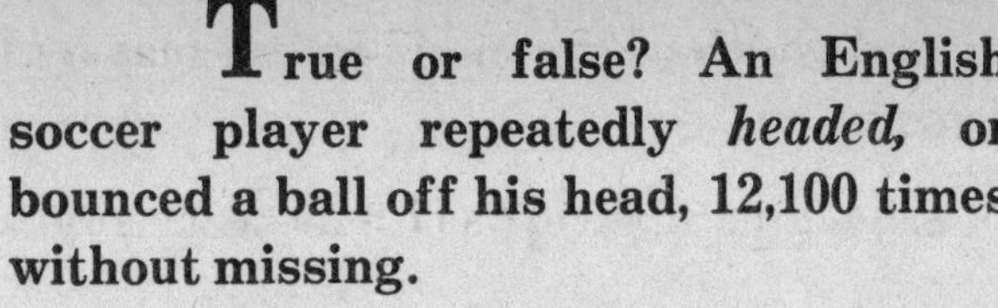

True or false? An English soccer player repeatedly *headed,* or bounced a ball off his head, 12,100 times without missing.

True. It was done by 17-year-old Michael Helliwell of Elland, England, on December 14, 1973. Helliwell repeatedly *headed* a ball 12,100 times in 54 minutes and 22 seconds. The reason? Simply to get into the *Guinness Book of World Records.*

How long is a soccer match?

A soccer match lasts 90 minutes. The game is broken into two 45-minute halves, with a halftime interval of about 10 minutes.

In 1978, Argentina played against Holland in the World Cup Championship game. Which team won?

Argentina, the host country for the 1978 World Cup games, defeated Holland, 3 games to 1, to win soccer's most coveted prize.

Who was the North American Soccer League's Rookie of the Year in 1977?

Jim McAlister of the Seattle Sounders won the NASL Rookie of the Year Award in 1977.

In soccer, what is a *dropped ball*?

A *dropped ball* in soccer is like a face-off in hockey. The referee drops the ball onto the ground between two opposing players. This starts play again after the referee has stopped it for some reason other than a foul.

In soccer, what is the height and width of the goal? Is it 6 feet by 6 yards, 7 feet by 7 yards, or 8 feet by 8 yards?

A soccer goal is 8 feet (2.4 meters) high and 8 yards (7.3 meters) wide.

Who was named the Most Valuable Player in the NASL in 1977? Was it Pele, Franz Beckenbauer, or Steve David?

Franz Beckenbauer of the New York Cosmos won MVP honors as he spurred his team to the 1977 NASL Championship.

True or false? The record number of goals scored by an individual in an international soccer match is 8.

False. Gottfried Fuchs set the record in 1912 by scoring 10 goals for his German team when they beat Russia, 16 to 0, in the 1912 Olympics.

How many teams were in the North American Soccer League in 1977?

There were twenty-four teams in the NASL in 1977 — twelve in the National Conference and twelve in the American Conference.

Name the North American Soccer League teams that were located in the following cities in 1978: Detroit, San Jose, and Memphis.

Detroit's NASL team was the Express; the Earthquakes played in San Jose; and Memphis' team was the Rogues.

How is play started at the beginning of a soccer game?

The team captains flip a coin to see who will get the ball first. The team that wins the toss gets the kickoff. The ball is placed at the center spot, which is a point in the middle of the halfway line. The players line up, then one of the attackers kicks the ball forward to a teammate to start play.

The old Philadelphia Atoms won the NASL Championship in 1973. Who did they beat?

The Philadelphia Atoms beat the Dallas Tornado, 2 to 0, to win the 1973 NASL Championship.

When do *throw-ins* take place during a soccer game?

A *throw-in* takes place after a player has knocked the ball over one of the touch lines. A member of the other team then throws the ball back into play. The thrower must keep both feet on the ground on the touch line or outside of the playing area, and must use two hands to throw the ball in.

Although Pele retired from soccer in 1974, he returned to competition the following year. Do you know what lured him out of retirement?

The three-year $4¾ million contract offered him by the New York Cosmos lured Pele back into NASL play. He stayed with the Cosmos until 1977. In his final game with New York — an exhibition game between the NASL Champion Cosmos and Pele's original Brazilian team — "The Black Pearl," as Pele is called, played the first half for New York and the second half for Brazil before a crowd of 75,646 fans.

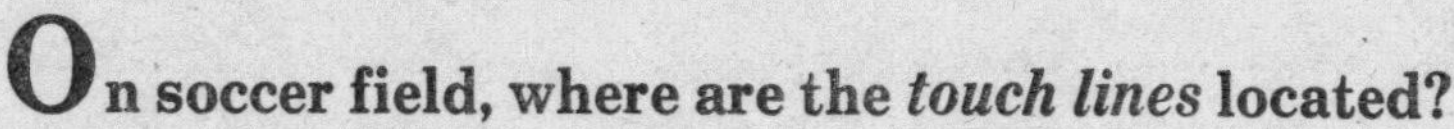

On soccer field, where are the *touch lines* located?

The *touch lines* are the boundary lines on the long sides of a soccer field.

Shep Messing is a well-known goalkeeper in the North American Soccer League. Which team did he play for in 1978?

The Oakland Stompers benefited from Shep Messing's goalkeeping in 1978.

True or false? Many authorities believe the Chinese originated the sport of soccer.

True. Many authorities believe that a game described in a Chinese military textbook of the Han Dynasty of some 2,000 years ago was the forerunner of today's soccer. In that textbook, the game is described as *Tsu Chu. Tsu* in Chinese means "to kick the ball with the feet." *Chu* means "the ball made of leather and stuffed."

Can you name the man who was voted the Most Valuable Player in the North American Soccer League in 1976?

The New York Cosmos' superstar, Pele, was soccer's MVP in 1976.

Italian soccer star Giorgio Chinaglia was a member of which North American Soccer League team in 1977? Was it the New York Cosmos, the Los Angeles Aztecs, or the Dallas Tornado?

In 1977, Giorgio Chinaglia played for the New York Cosmos and helped them in their drive towards the NASL Championship, with his 15 goals and 8 assists for a total of 38 points.

GOLF

Which LPGA rookie won more prize money than any other rookie woman golfer in history?

As of the end of 1978, Nancy Lopez of New Mexico had won $189,813 as a rookie on the professional golfers' tour, to become the all-time leading money winner as an LPGA rookie. Lopez was also named the 1978 Woman Athlete of the Year by the Associated Press.

In what year did Jack Nicklaus win the $250,000 Jackie Gleason Inverrary Classic Golf Tournament? Was it in 1977 or 1978?

An ardent golf fan will remember that Jack Nicklaus took top prize money in the Lauderhill, Florida, classic in 1977 *and* 1978.

A 7-under-par 281 won the 1978 Carlsbad, California, Tournament of Champions for which golfer?

Gary Player took the top spot in the 1978 Tournament of Champions, earning himself the lion's share of the $225,000 prize money.

Who is the only golfer to win all five major titles at least twice in his career? Is it Jack Nicklaus, Gary Player, or Arnold Palmer?

Jack Nicklaus holds that distinction. He won the U.S. Amateur title in 1959 and 1961; the U.S. Open in 1962, 1967, and 1972; the British Open in 1966, 1970, and 1978; the PGA in 1963, 1971, 1973, and 1975; and the Masters in 1963, 1965, 1966, 1972, and 1975.

Mary "Mickey" Kathryn Wright holds the women's record for the lowest recorded score on an 18-hole golf course. Can you guess that record score?

"Mickey" Wright shot a 62 on the Hogan Park Course in Midland, Texas, in November of 1964, to establish the record.

Is the oldest existing golf club in North America located in the United States or Canada?

The Royal Montreal Golf Club, founded in Canada in 1873, is the oldest existing golf club in North America. Foxbury Country Club in Pennsylvania claims to be the oldest United States golf club, listing 1887 as its founding date.

Can you name the pro golfer who was the PGA's leading money winner eight times between 1964 and 1976? Was it Jack Nicklaus, Tom Watson, or Billy Casper?

The correct answer is Jack Nicklaus, who led the PGA in earnings in 1964 ($114,284), 1965 ($140,752), 1967 ($188,988), 1971 ($244,490), 1972 ($320,942), 1973 ($308,362), 1975 ($298,149), and 1976 ($266,438).

During a golf match, what determines who tees off first after every hole?

The honor at each teeing ground after the first goes to the player who won the previous hole. If a hole is tied, the honor is given to the player who won the last hole that wasn't tied.

Who was the LPGA Tournament winner in 1977? Was it Kathy Whitworth, Chako Higuchi, or Betty Burfeindt?

Chako Higuchi took the LPGA Tournament title in 1977. Burfeindt was the 1976 winner and Whitworth, the 1975 champion.

Which LPGA golfer won the $100,000 Sun Star Classic in 1978? Was it Nancy Lopez, Debbie Austin, or Debbie Massey?

Nancy Lopez won the 1978 Sun Star Classic by shooting a 3-under-par 285. Debbie Austin and Debbie Massey tied for second with a 286.

Who is allowed to compete in the World Series of Golf?

The winners of four major golf tournaments — the British Open, the U.S. Open, the Masters, and the Professional Golf Association Championship — are allowed to compete in the World Series of Golf. This PGA-sponsored tournament is held every September at the Firestone Country Club in Akron, Ohio, with $100,000 in prize money going to the winners.

The woman golfer who helped to found the Ladies Professional Golf Association was also its first president. Can you name her?

The 1950 founder of the LPGA and its first president was champion golfer Patty Berg, winner of 83 pro tourneys in her 29 years on the links.

In golf, what is the number-1 wood club called?

The number-1 wood club is called a *driver*. The driver is used to achieve the longest distances without hitting the ball high when driving off from the tee.

How many times has Jack Nicklaus won the Tournament Players Championship?

Jack Nicklaus has won the TPC three times. His first win was in 1974 and his second, in 1976. His most recent win was in 1978, when he shot a 1-over-par 289, to finish one stroke ahead of Lou Graham.

True or false? During a golf game, the player whose ball is closest to the hole plays his ball first.

False. The player whose ball lies the *farthest* from the hole has the honor and always plays his ball first.

The 1977 World Cup Championship was played in Manilla, The Phillipines. Was the winner Gary Player, Hubert Green, or Seiichi Kanai?

Gary Player of South Africa took the 1977 World Cup Championship with a 289. Hubert Green of the United States tied with Rudy Lavares of The Phillipines for second place with a 292, and Seiichi Kanai of Japan came in third with a score of 293.

Who won the Colonial National Invitation Tournament in 1978?

Lee Trevino was the winner of the 1978 Colonial, finishing four strokes ahead of second-place Jerry Heard.

Which player staged what is probably the most amazing comeback in the history of golf?

The 1948 U.S. Open, PGA, and Western Open Champion, Ben Hogan, must be given that honor. A near-fatal auto accident in 1949 left "Little Ben" more dead than alive and with the prospect of never walking again. Not only did Hogan walk again, but he returned to the tee less than a year later, and, still limping, went on to win the U.S. Open in 1950, the U.S. Open and the Masters Tournament in 1951, and the U.S. Open, the Masters, and the British Open in 1953.

Only one golfer has ever had his life story made into a movie. Can you name him?

That golfer was Ben Hogan, and the 1951 movie was *Follow the Sun.* Actor Glen Ford starred as Hogan.

Only one golfer has ever won the NCAA Golf Championship three years in a row? Was it Hale Irwin, Ben Crenshaw, or Jack Nicklaus?

It was Ben Crenshaw, when he was a student at the University of Texas. He won the NCAA title in 1971, shared it with fellow schoolmate Tom Kite in 1972, and retained it in 1973.

How many times did the immortal Babe Didrikson Zaharias win the United States Women's Open Golf Championship?

Babe Didrikson Zaharias, one of the greatest woman athletes of all time, was the U.S. Women's Open Golf Champion three times: in 1948, 1950, and 1954.

Who was the first black golfer to play in the Masters Tournament?

Lee Elder, by winning the Monsanto Golf Tournament in April, 1974, qualified for the 1975 Masters — the first black golfer to do so. Elder also served as a good-will ambassador for the U.S. State Department to Africa, and became the first black American to compete in multi-racial sports in South Africa. Elder had previously been the All-Army Golf Champion and the winner of the Nigerian Open in 1972. Despite his loss in the 1975 Masters, Elder went on to win the Houston Open in 1976 and to compete in the 1977 Masters.

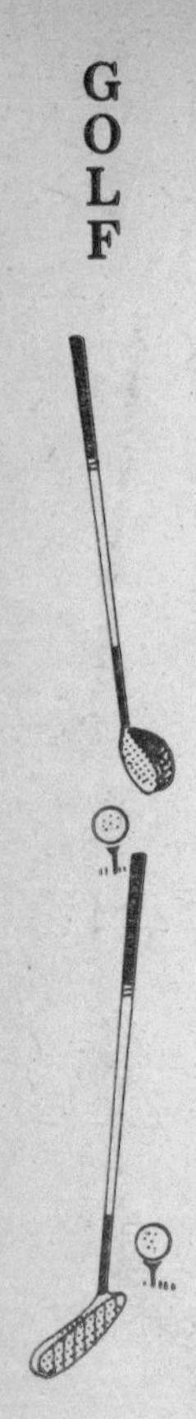

Which professional golfer holds the career record for winning the most major tournaments?

During his 40-year professional career, "Slammin' Sam" Snead won over 100 tournaments, including PGA Championships, Masters titles, and the British Open.

In 1978, who won the Bing Crosby Pro-Am Golf Tournament at Pebble Beach, California?

At the end of regulation play, Tom Watson and Ben Crenshaw were tied at 280, forcing the two men into a sudden-death playoff. On the second playoff hole, Watson birdied a three-foot putt, to take the championship of the Bing Crosby Pro-Am Tournament. Watson's earlier win of the Bing Crosby in 1977 established a tournament record for the Pebble Beach course at a 14-under-par 273.

Penny Pulz of Australia and Sandra Post of Canada were forced into a sudden-death playoff for the 1978 championship of the Colgate-Dinah Shore Winners Circle Golf Tournament. Who won the championship in that sudden-death playoff?

Both Penny Pulz and Sandra Post finished regulation play with scores of 5-under-par 283, sending them into a sudden-death playoff. Sandra clinched the championship of the 1978 Colgate-Dinah Shore Winners Circle Tournament on the second hole. This was only her second LPGA victory in 211 tournaments in her ten years of competition.

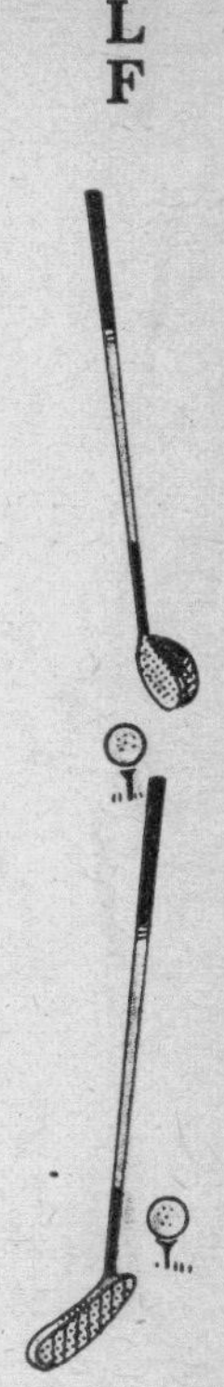

The PGA's leading career money winner had earned $3,349,393 as of the end of 1978. Was that superstar Arnold Palmer, Jack Nicklaus, or Lee Trevino?

From 1961, when he turned pro, to the end of 1978, Jack Nicklaus has earned over $3 million, outdistancing second-place earner Trevino, whose career prize money totaled $1,849,446, and Palmer, with $1,789,155.

Can you remember who won the $77,000 LPGA Classic in 1977? Was it Kathy Whitworth or Donna Caponi Young?

Kathy Whitworth took the 1977 LPGA Classic by shooting an 11-under-par 202. Donna Caponi Young was second, finishing three strokes behind Whitworth.

Which PGA golfer won the United States Open Golf Tournament in 1977? Was it Tom Weiskopf, Hubert Green, or Lou Graham?

Hubert Green finished the 1977 U.S. Open with a 2-under-par 278, to win the $45,000 in first-prize money. Graham's second-place score of 279 earned him $23,500, and Weiskopf was third with a 281, to win $16,000.

True or false? The ancient Romans played a game similar to golf.

True. The ancient Romans played a game called *paganica,* which is believed to be similar to modern golf. To play the game of *paganica,* the Romans struck a feather-stuffed ball with a bent stick.

Can you match the golfer with his 1978 Championship title?

(1) Andy North	**(a) The Masters Champion**
(2) John Mahaffey	**(b) The U.S. Open Champion**
(3) Gary Player	**(c) The PGA Champion**

The correct match-ups are (1) Andy North was (b), the 1978 U.S. Open Champion; (2) John Mahaffey was (c), the 1978 PGA title holder; and (3) Gary Player was (a), the 1978 Masters Champ.

Dean Prince, a 40-year-old insurance salesman from California, beat out 159 competitors to win the 53rd U.S. Amateur Public Links Golf Championship in 1978. Where was that tournament held?

Bangor, Maine, was the site of the 1978 U.S. Amateur Public Links Golf Championship. It was the first time that the six-day tournament was held in New England.

Can you name the world's oldest amateur golf team match?

The answer is the Walker Cup. Teams from the United States and Great Britain have been competing every two years for the Walker Cup ever since 1922.

True or false? The great golfer Harry Varden won the British Open title three times.

False. Harry Varden won the British Open six times between 1896 and 1914. He also won the United States Open in 1900.

Who won the Byron Nelson Classic Golf Tournament in 1977? Was it Ray Floyd, Ben Crenshaw, or Hale Irwin?

Ray Floyd shot an 8-under-par 276 on the Preston Trail Course in Dallas, Texas, to win the Byron Nelson Classic in 1977. Ben Crenshaw finished second with a score of 278.

What record was shattered when Tom Watson won the British Open in 1977?

Watson's score of 268 set a new British record for the Open, cutting by 8 shots the record of 276 set by Tom Weiskopf in the 1973 tournament.

When Dick Siderowf won the British Amateur Golf Tournament in 1973 and 1976, he became one of only three Americans to ever win the British Amateur twice. Who are the other two?

Lawson Little and Frank Stranahan of the United States each won the British Amateur Golf Tournament twice. Little did it in 1934 and 1935, and Stranahan duplicated the feat in 1948 and 1950.

How many golf clubs is a player allowed to use for a match?

A golfer is allowed to use a maximum of 14 clubs for a match. They usually consist of 4 woods, 9 irons, and a putter.

The first tournament Jim Simons won on the professional golfers' tour in 1977 was the $175,000 New Orleans Open. How many strokes under par did Simons finish to win that tournament? Was it 10, 15, or 18?

Jim Simons shot a 15-under-par 273 to win the $35,000 first prize in the 1977 $175,000 New Orleans Open.

What do golfers call a sand hole on a golf course?

A sand hole on a golf course is a *bunker*.

Tom Weiskopf defeated Jack Nicklaus in the 1978 $200,000 Doral Open in Miami. What was the difference in their scores?

Only one stroke gave Tom Weiskopf the Doral Open win. He completed the course with a 16-under-par 272.

Can you name the first LPGA title won by pro golfer Hollis Stacy? Here's a hint. The tournament was held at Roswell, Georgia, in 1977.

Hollis Stacy's first LPGA win was in the 1977 Lady Tara Classic. She shot a 10-under-par 209, to finish one stroke ahead of JoAnne Carner.

Which professional golfer holds the record for hitting the most holes-in-one during his career? Is it Art Wall Jr., Julius Boros, or Billy Casper?

Art Wall Jr. holds the record, with 41 career holes-in-one.

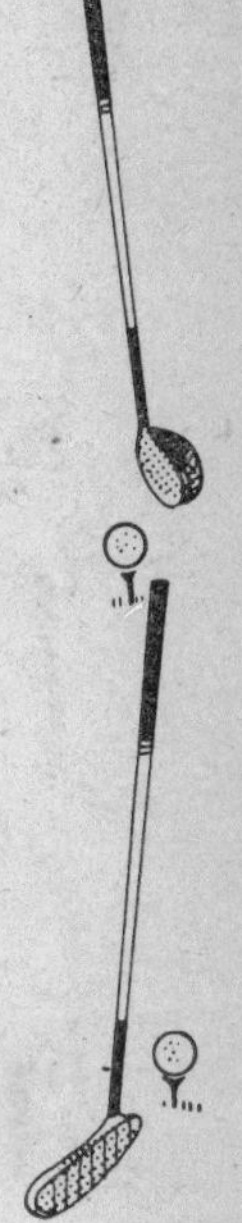

The modern Grand Slam of Golf refers to the winning of four major golf tournaments. Two of those tournaments are the Masters and the U.S. Open. Can you name the other two tournaments that make up Golf's Grand Slam?

The British Open and the PGA of America combine with the Masters Tournament and the U.S. Open to make up the Grand Slam of Golf.

Who holds the record for winning the most Professional Golf Association Championships? Is it Jack Nicklaus, Sam Snead, or Walter Hagen?

Walter "The Haig" Hagen captured the PGA Championship crown five times: first in 1921, then in 1924, 1925, 1926, and 1927. Nicklaus is second with four PGA titles, and Snead is among several golfers who have earned two championships.

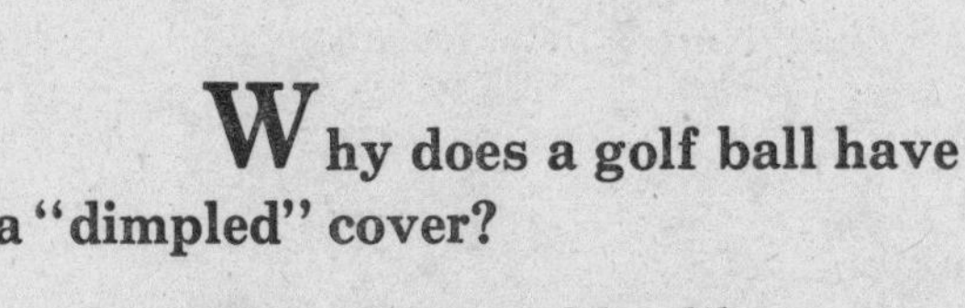

Why does a golf ball have a "dimpled" cover?

The thin, rubberlike cover on a golf ball has "dimples," or mesh markings, to increase distance and accuracy in the ball's flight.

If a golfer gives his opponent a *handicap*, what does that mean?

A *handicap* is an allowance of a certain number of strokes which one player gives to his opponent. That handicap is deducted from the opponent's total score. Handicaps are given when a golfer competes against an opponent who is less skillful than he.

True or false? The game of golf was once illegal.

True. In the middle of the 15th century, golf had become so popular in Scotland that it was banned by the parliament of King James II, himself a golfer. The parliament feared that golf would take the place of archery. At that time, archery wasn't only a sport, but also an important means of defending Scotland from her enemies. The ban ended in 1502 when Scotland and England signed a peace treaty.

How many holes are played in a round of golf?

A round of golf consists of 18 holes played in consecutive order. A course which has only 9 holes usually has its golfers play the course twice to complete a round.

Who is the LPGA's leader in career earnings? Is it Judy Rankin, Kathy Whitworth, or Jane Blalock?

As of the end of 1978, Kathy Whitworth led the LPGA in career earnings with a total of $813,214. Judy Rankin was second, with $652,095, and Jane Blalock was third, with $593,709.

Who won the 1975 British Open? Was it Tom Watson, Lee Trevino, or Johnny Miller?

If you said Tom Watson, you were correct. The 1975 British Open winner took the title again in 1977. Trevino won the British Open in 1971 and 1972, and Miller was the 1976 winner.

In 1978, Nancy Lopez set a record for the most consecutive victories by a woman professional golfer. How many tournaments did she win to establish the record?

Nancy Lopez, the 1978 rookie sensation, won five LPGA tournaments in a row to set the record. Her first win to start the consecutive streak came in the Greater Baltimore Golf Classic and was followed by the LPGA Coca-Cola Classic, the Kent Golden Lights Championship, the LPGA Championship, and the Bankers Trust Classic

A golfer once scored a hole-in-one by bouncing his ball off the trunk of a tree in the rough. True or false?

True. It happened to Woodrow Goldspinner at the Catskill Mountain Resort Golf Course in 1956. Goldspinner teed off and sliced his shot into the rough. The ball caromed off a tree trunk, rolled onto the green, and ended up dropping into the cup for a hole-in-one.

What does a *birdie* mean?

If a golfer scores a *birdie,* he has played the hole one stroke under par. Par is the number of strokes that course officials decide are required to hit the ball into a hole, depending on the distance and difficutly. Par ranges from 3 to 6 strokes.

What do you call this peg?

It is a golfing *tee*. A tee is a plastic or wooden peg on which the ball is placed at each teeing ground — a small, flat area on a golf course.

Where do most authorities believe that modern golf originated?

It is generally believed that golf, as we know it today, originated in Scotland in the middle 1400s. The Scots were the first ones to make holes in the ground and to play the game by attempting to shoot a ball into the hole.

Which golf tournament is the world's oldest amateur tournament?

The British Amateur Golf Championship, which has been played annually ever since 1885, holds the world record as the oldest amateur tournament.

Only four men have been Grand Slam winners in the history of golf. Can you name them?

The only players to win the U.S. Open, the British Open, the PGA Championship, and the Masters are Ben Hogan, Gene Sarazan, Jack Nicklaus, and Gary Player. But no one, to date, has ever captured all four titles in the same year.

Who won the PGA Championship in 1977? Was it Lanny Wadkins, Gene Littler, or Jerry Pate?

The answer is Lanny Wadkins. His score of 282 earned him the PGA title on the third hole of a sudden-death playoff against Gene Littler.

True or false? Sam Snead was never the United States PGA Champion.

False. "Slammin' Sam" Snead was the U.S. PGA Champion in 1942, 1949, and 1951. These represent three of the seven major titles Snead won during his career. The others are three Masters titles and one British Open.

True or false? An amateur golfer has never won a PGA tournament.

False. The 1976 Canadian Open Golf Tournament was won by Doug Sanders, an amateur golfer at the time.

How big is a golf hole? Is it 3½ inches inches in diameter, 4½ inches in diameter, or 5½ inches in diameter?

A golf hole is 4½ inches in diameter, although many golfers often wish it were larger.

Al Geiberger holds the United States PGA Tournament record score for 18 holes. What is that score?

The PGA record score is 59. Al Geiberger established that record on June 10, 1977, when he shot a 59 in 18 holes on a 72-par course in the second round of the Danny Thomas Classic in Memphis, Tennessee.

How many strokes are considered par on an average 18-hole golf course? Is it 66 to 68, 70 to 72, or 74 to 76?

On an average course of 18 holes, 70 to 72 strokes are considered par.

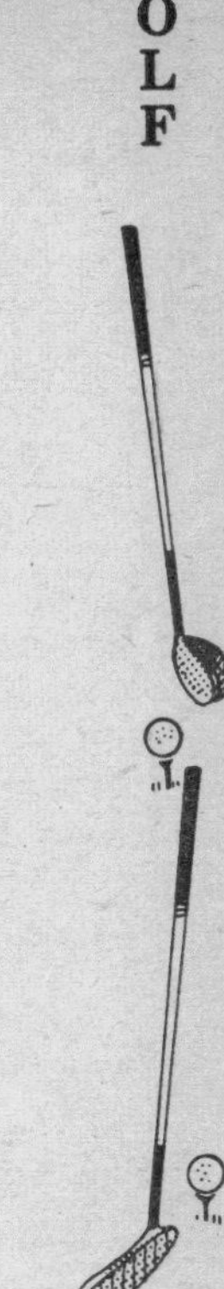

According to golf experts, what are the odds against a player making a hole-in-one? Are they 100,000 to 1, 300,000 to 1, or 500,000 to 1?

The experts claim that the odds against a golfer making a hole-in-one are 300,000 to 1.

Who was the winner of the 1978 Sea Pines Heritage Classic Golf Tournament? Was it Hubert Green or Hale Irwin?

Hubert Green finished three strokes ahead of Hale Irwin to win the $225,000 Hilton Head, South Carolina, classic in 1978.

Who was the first professional woman golfer to win over $100,000 in a single year? Was it Judy Rankin, Kathy Whitworth, or Laura Baugh?

Judy Rankin became the first woman golfer to earn over $100,000. She did it in the 1976 season, by earning $150,734, and setting an LPGA record at the same time.

Lee Trevino was the winner of British Open Golf Championship in 1971. Who captured the British Open title in 1972?

Texan Lee Trevino, nicknamed "The Merry Mexican" because of his witty personality and Mexican ancestry, repeated as the British Open Champion in 1972.

The winner of the 1935 Masters Tournament sank one of the most remarkable shots in the history of golf — a 235-yard shot which gave him a double eagle on the 15th hole. Do you remember who made that amazing shot?

If you said Gene Sarazan, you're absolutely correct. Sarazan made that double eagle to tie Craig Wood, then went on to win the Masters in a playoff, and, incidentally, only $750 in prize money. In Sarazan's 50-year professional golf career, from 1920 to 1970, he had two U.S. Open wins, three PGA wins, a British Open, and a Masters.

When was the U.S. Open Golf Championship inaugurated? Was it 1895, 1898, or 1900?

If you said 1895, you're correct. The Amateur Golf Association, now the U.S. Golf Association, was formed in 1894 as the governing body for the sport in the U.S. One year later, the first U.S. Open Championship was held at Newport, Rhode Island.

The 1973 World Series of Golf saw the following players meet: Tom Weiskopf, the winner of the British Open; Johnny Miller, the winner of the U.S. Open; Tommy Aaron, the winner of the Masters; and Jack Nicklaus, the PGA Champion. Who won the Series?

Tom Weiskopf won the $50,000 first-place prize in the 1973 World Series of Golf, with a 137 for 36 holes in the Akron, Ohio, annual classic. Miller and Nicklaus tied for second, with a 140, and Aaron was last.

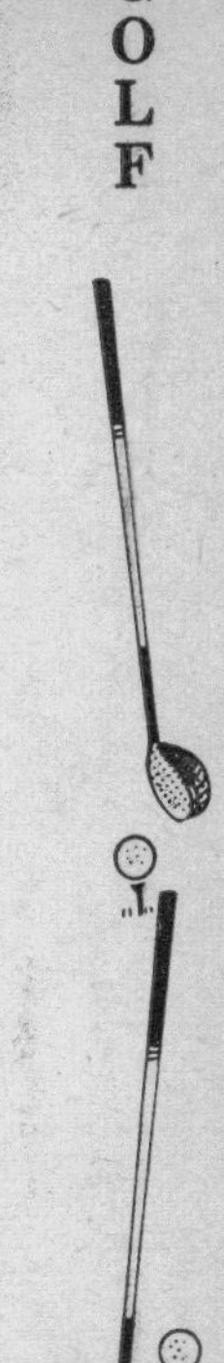

Can you name the pro golfer who won the most tournaments in a single season? Is it Bobby Jones, Ben Hogan, or Byron Nelson?

It's Byron Nelson. He won 19 out of 31 tournaments in 1945. Of these victories, 11 were consecutive and included the U.S. Open, the U.S. PGA, the Canadian PGA, and the Canadian Open.

For what accomplishment is the Vardon Trophy Awarded?

The Vardon Trophy is awarded to the golfer with the best average in the PGA.

When a hole is *halved* in match play, what has happened?

Halving means that both players took the same number of shots for the hole.

Which pro golfer holds the record for winning the most prize money in a single year? Is it Johnny Miller, Arnold Palmer, or Sam Snead?

Johnny Miller established that record by earning $353,021 in 1974.

Which two tournaments offer first-place prize money of $100,000?

The World Series of Golf, played at Akron, Ohio, and the World Open, played at Pinehurst, North Carolina, both offer $100,000 to first-place winners.

True or false? The man considered to be America's greatest amateur golfer, Robert T. "Bobby" Jones, Jr., won the United States Amateur Golf Championship three times.

False. The great Bobby Jones won the U.S. Amateur title a record-setting *five* times. He captured the crown in 1924, 1925, 1927, 1928, and 1930. In addition, in 1932, Jones won the British Amateur, the British Open, and the U.S. Open.

Did Babe Didrikson Zaharias ever win the U.S. Women's Amateur Golf Championship?

Yes. Babe was the United States Women's Amateur Golf Champion in 1946. The following year, she became the first American woman to win the British Women's Amateur title. These were only two of the 100 tournament titles Babe won.

Which professional golfer won four PGA Championships in a row? Was it Walter Hagen, Jack Nicklaus, or Byron Nelson?

From 1924 to 1927, Walter Hagen won four consecutive PGA Championships. His earlier win in 1921 brings his career total to five PGA titles. "The Haig" has 65 major golf tournaments to his credit, including two U.S. Opens and four British Opens.

True or false? The very first golf balls were carved out of wood.

False. The first golf balls were small bags of thin leather stuffed with feathers. In 1848, gutta percha balls replaced feather ones. Gutta percha is a rubberlike substance formed by the milky juice of the gutta percha tree of Malaysia. Today, a standard golf ball is made up of a long (about 36 yards), thin thread of rubber wound around a center core of liquid, rubber, or steel.

Which country boasts of the largest green in the world? Is it the United States, England, or Scotland?

The largest green in the world is on a golf course in the U.S.A. It's the 5th green at Runaway Golf Course in Bolton, Massachusetts, with a total area of more than 28,000 square feet.

England's two greatest golfers, Harry Vardon and Ted Ray, came to the American Open in 1913, only to finish in a tie with an unknown Boston teen-ager, Francis Ouimet. Who won that playoff?

Nineteen-year-old Ouimet played an amazing playoff round and finished five strokes ahead of Vardon and six strokes ahead of Ray. This victory marked the beginning of golf as a popular sport in the U.S.

The longest recorded holed putt in a major tournament was made by Cary Middlecoff in the 1955 Masters Tournament. How long was that putt? Was it 77 feet, 86 feet, or 95 feet?

It was an 86-foot putt, and Middlecoff made it on the 13th green of the Augusta, Georgia, National Golf Course.

The 1978 winner of the $150,000 Kathryn Crosby-Honda Civic Classic in San Diego, California, was determined by a playoff. Nancy Lopez was one of the two LPGA golfers involved in that playoff. Who was the other?

The answer is Sally Little. Sally beat Nancy Lopez on the first hole of their playoff, to win the 1978 Kathryn Crosby-Honda Civic Classic.

If a golfer hits his ball into the *rough*, is that good or bad?

It's bad. Hitting a ball into the *rough* means that it has been hit inaccurately and has landed in the area that borders the fairway on either side.

When did Orville Moody win the U.S. Open Championship? Was it in 1968, 1969, or 1970?

Orville Moody was the U.S. Open Champion in 1969.

Who won the 1977 Mayflower Classic in Noblesville, Indiana? Was it Judy Rankin, Jane Blalock, or Debbie Austin?

Judy Rankin's 4-under-par 212 earned her the 1977 Mayflower Classic win, four strokes in front of second-place Jane Blalock. Judy walked off with $7,500 in first-place prize money and her twenty-third career tournament championship.

Which golfer holds the PGA record for hitting the longest drive? Is it Sam Snead, Jack Nicklaus, or Lee Trevino.

Jack Nicklaus set the PGA record in July, 1963, when he drove a ball 341 yards.

How many times was Arnold Palmer the Professional Golf Association's leading money winner?

Arnold Palmer topped all money winners in the PGA four times: in 1958, he won $42,607; in 1960, $75,262; in 1962, $81,448; and in 1963, $128,230.

Can you identify the golf club pictured? Is it a *9-iron*, a *driver*, or a *putter?*

This straight-faced club, which is used on the green to stroke the ball into the hole, is a *putter.* The *9-iron* is used for accuracy and height, while the *driver* is used for teeing off on a long hole where distance is needed.

What is a *divot*?

A *divot* is a piece of turf knocked into the air when a club strikes the ground below the ball.

Which golfer's autobiography was entitled *Comeback*?

Comeback was the autobiography of Ken Venturi, who won the U.S. Open Championship in 1964 after a downhill slide in his career following his 1-stroke loss to Jack Burke in the 1956 Masters.

A golf course contains obstacles like sand traps, ponds, and streams. What are these obstacles called?

Natural and man-made obstacles on a golf course are called *hazards.* If the ball goes into a sand trap, the golfer must try to hit it out. But if the ball goes into a water hazard, the golfer lifts it out or puts another ball into play, taking an extra stroke as a penalty.

How many times has Gary Player won the Masters Tournament?

South African Gary Player has won the Masters Tournament three times. His first win came in 1961, when his winning score was 280. His second was in 1974, with a 278, and his third, in 1978, when he shot an 11-under-par 277. Player was also the PGA Champion in 1962 and 1972, the British Open Champion in 1968 and 1974, and the World Cup Champion in 1977.

Why are some golf tournaments called *opens*?

Open tournaments are open to amateur and professional golfers alike.

The great Jack Nicklaus was the NCAA Golf Champion in 1961. What university was Nicklaus attending when he won that title?

Jack Nicklaus was a student at Ohio State University when he won the 1961 NCAA Golf Championship.

Tom Kite beat Terry Diehl in a sudden-death playoff to win the $200,000 IVB-Philadelphia Classic in 1976. How many playoff holes did Kite and Diehl play before the match ended? Was it one, three, or five?

Sudden-death play continued to the fifth hole in the 1976 IVB-Philadelphia Classic until Tom Kite beat Terry Diehl.

What golf phrase is used to describe the person who starts play by hitting his ball first?

A golfer who starts play is said to *"have the honor."*

True or false? Billy Casper was the first professional golfer to win over $100,000 in one year.

False. Arnold Palmer claimed that honor in 1963, when his prize money totaled $128,230. Casper did not reach the $100,000 mark until 1966, when his earnings totaled $121,944.

Who won the British Open Golf Championship in 1978? Was it Jack Nicklaus, Ray Floyd, or Simon Owen?

Jack Nicklaus won the British Open in 1978 by shooting a 7-under-par 281. The victory was Nicklaus' 17th major tournament championship and his second British Open title. Ray Floyd and Simon Owen, a young golfer from New Zealand, tied for second, along with Ben Crenshaw and Tom Kite, two strokes behind Nicklaus.

Every two years, the United States and Great Britain compete in three team golf matches. Can you name those three matches?

American and British amateurs compete for the Walker Cup (men) and the Curtis Cup (women). Men professionals from the two countries vie for the Ryder Cup.

In golf, if a player scores an *eagle,* what does that mean?

If a golfer's score for any hole but a par-3 hole is two strokes under par, he is said to have scored an *eagle.*

TENNIS

Where were the U.S. Open Tennis Championships held in 1978?

The U.S. Open Tennis Championships, a Forest Hills tradition since 1951, moved to a new home in Flushing Meadows in 1978. With a newly built tennis stadium, the Open hoped to attract a larger number of spectators.

True or false? Bjorn Borg won the Men's U.S. Open Tennis Championship in 1978.

False. Jimmy Connors was the 1978 U.S. Open Champion, defeating Bjorn Borg in the finals, 6-4, 6-2, 6-2.

Who won the Women's U.S. Open Tennis Championship in 1978? Was it Pam Shriver, Chris Evert, or Wendy Turnbull?

Chris Evert won her fourth straight U.S. Open title in 1978 by defeating Pam Shriver in the finals. Chris thus became the only tennis player to ever win the title four years in a row, breaking the old record of three consecutive U.S. Open wins set by Maureen Connolly in 1951, 1952, and 1953.

Who is the only man to win the Grand Slam of Tennis twice?

Rod Laver of Australia performed this amazing feat in 1962 and again in 1969, thus making him the only two-time Grand Slam winner in the history of tennis.

How many Wimbledon titles did the great Billie Jean King win between 1961 and 1975? Is it twelve, sixteen, or nineteen?

Billie Jean King has won nineteen Wimbledon Championships, including six Singles, nine Doubles, and four Mixed Doubles.

In 1977, Jimmy Connors of the United States played Sweden's Bjorn Borg for the Wimbledon Men's Singles Championship. Who won?

Bjorn Borg defeated Connors, 3-6, 6-2, 6-1, 5-7, 6-4, to win the 1977 Wimbledon Men's Singles Championship.

Who won the 1978 Men's Singles Championship at Wimbledon?

In 1978, Sweden's Bjorn Borg blasted Jimmy Connors, 6-2, 6-2, 6-3, to win the Men's Singles Championship at Wimbledon for the third year in a row. Borg became the first man to record three consecutive Wimbledon victories since Fred Perry of Great Britain did it from 1934 to 1936.

Bernie Mitton of South Africa played John James of Australia for the top prize in the 1978 Hall of Fame Tennis Championship at Newport, Rhode Island. Who took home the top prize of $12,750?

Bernie Mitton won a 6-1, 3-6, 7-6 victory over John James to take the 1978 Hall of Fame Championship.

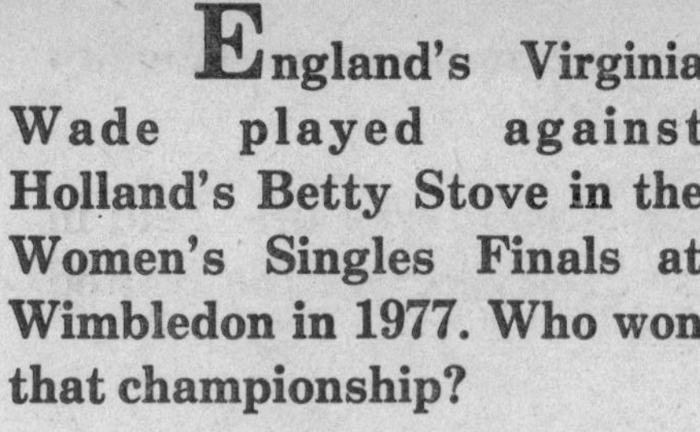

England's Virginia Wade played against Holland's Betty Stove in the Women's Singles Finals at Wimbledon in 1977. Who won that championship?

After fifteen earlier unsuccessful attempts at Wimbledon, Virginia Wade finally gained her first Wimbledon Singles Championship in 1977 by defeating Betty Stove, 4-6, 6-3, 6-1.

Who was the 1973 United States Men's Singles Champion? Was it John Newcombe, Ilie Nastase, or Stan Smith?

John Newcombe of Australia was the United States Men's Singles Champion in 1973, having succeeded Ilie Nastase of Romania who held the title in 1972, and Stan Smith of the U.S. who held it in 1971.

From 1962 to 1973, three women dominated the U.S. Women's Singles Championships by alternating as the Singles Champion. One was from Brazil; one was from Australia; and one was from the United States. Can you name these three women?

Maria Bueno of Brazil, Margaret Smith Court of Australia, and Billie Jean King of the United States alternated as U.S. Women's Singles Champions from 1962 to 1973, with the exception of 1968, when Virginia Wade of England won the title. Bueno was the champion in 1963, 1964, and 1966; Court won the title in 1962, 1965, 1969, 1970, and 1973; and King was the U.S. Singles Champion in 1967, 1971, and 1972.

In what year was the United States Women's Singles Championship held for the first time? Was it in 1915, 1918, or 1920?

The United States Women's Singles Championship was first held in 1920, and the winner of the title was Molla Bjurstedt Mallory of the United States.

True or false? Bobby Riggs was never the United States Men's Singles Tennis Champion.

False. Bobby Riggs was the U.S. Men's Singles Champion in 1939 and 1941, and runner-up in 1940.

Who was the youngest tennis player ever to compete in the Wimbledon Championships?

California's Tracy Austin holds the record as the youngest tennis player to compete at Wimbledon. She was only fourteen years old in 1977 when she entered the Wimbledon competition, only to be eliminated by Chris Evert. However, Tracy wound up the 1977 season ranked fourth in the United States Tennis Association National Rankings.

Who won the 1978 World Championship Tennis Finals in Dallas, Texas? Was it Eddie Dibbs, Vitas Gerulaitis, or Brian Gottfried?

The 1978 WCT winner was Vitas Gerulaitis of Kings Point, New York. He walked off with the $100,000 prize money by defeating Eddie Dibbs of North Miami Beach, Florida, 6-3, 6-2, 6-1, in only ninety-five minutes of play.

Can you match these tennis stars with the countries they played for?

(1) Ken Rosewall
(2) Suzanne Lenglen
(3) Bob Falkenburg
(4) Jaroslav Drobny
(5) Cilly Aussem
(6) Manuel Santana
(7) Jan Kodes
(8) Anita Lizana
(9) Ann Haydon-Jones
(10) Pancho Segura
(11) Gordon Forbes

(a) France
(b) Egypt
(c) Spain
(d) Germany
(e) Czechoslovakia
(f) U.S.A.
(g) Great Britain
(h) Australia
(i) Chile
(j) South Africa
(k) Ecuador

(1) Ken Rosewall played for (h) Australia; (2) Suzanne Lenglen, (a) France; (3) Bob Falkenburg, (f) U.S.A.; (4) Jaroslav Drobny, (b) Egypt; (5) Cilly Aussem, (d) Germany; (6) Manuel Santana, (c) Spain; (7) Jan Kodes, (e) Czechoslovakia; (8) Anita Lizana, (i) Chile; (9) Ann Haydon-Jones, (g) Great Britain; (10) Pancho Segura, (k) Ecuador; and (11) Gordon Forbes, (j) South Africa.

Pam Shriver, tennis' 16-year-old sensation, advanced to the finals of the 1978 Women's U.S. Open Tennis Championship by upsetting one of the best female tennis players in the world today. Who did she beat?

Young Pam Shriver upset the heavily favored Martina Navratilova, the 1978 Wimbledon Women's Singles Champion, to advance to the finals of the U.S. Open.

The $500,000 won by Jimmy Connors in a 1975 challenge match is the most money earned by any tennis player for a single match. Who did Connors beat to win that record prize?

Jimmy Connors of the United States won his $500,000 by defeating Australia's John Newcombe in a challenge match at Caesar's Palace Hotel in Las Vegas, Nevada, on April 26, 1975.

Tennis star Rod Laver is ambidextrous — he can play with either hand. True or false?

False. Australia's Rod Laver is a left-handed tennis player.

What is a *let ball*?

A *let ball* is a serve that hits the net and lands within the service court. A let ball does not count and the player must serve again.

Jimmy Connors was favored to win the 1975 Men's Singles at Wimbledon, but he lost in a surprising upset. Who beat Connors? Was it Arthur Ashe, Rod Laver, or Bjorn Borg?

Arthur Ashe upset heavily favored Jimmy Connors to win the Wimbledon Men's Singles crown in 1975.

Can you name the World Team Tennis Champions of 1977? Was it the Los Angeles Strings, the Indiana Loves, or the New York Apples?

The New York Apples were the World Team Tennis Champions in 1977, defeating the Phoenix Racquets in the playoff finals, 2-0.

True or false? The Davis Cup tennis matches were started in 1920.

False. The Davis Cup matches were first played in 1900, when Dwight F. Davis, an American tennis player at Harvard University, donated the silver bowl to the winners of singles and doubles matches, pitching the top players of Great Britain against those of the United States. Several years later, the competition was opened to players from all countries of the world.

True or false? Martina Navratilova, the Czech-born American star, won the 1978 Virginia Slims Tennis Championship.

True. Navratilova beat Australia's Evonne Goolagong, 7-6, 6-4, to win first place in the $150,000 1978 Virginia Slims Pro Tournament.

When was the first United States Men's Singles Championship tennis match played? Was it 1915, 1917, or 1920?

The first U.S. Men's Singles Championship was played in 1915, and the first champion it produced was William M. Johnston of the United States.

True or false? A singles court is wider than a doubles court.

False. A doubles court, at 36 feet, is wider than a singles court, which is 27 feet wide. Sidelines for a singles court are usually marked *within* a doubles court, thus permitting the court to be used for either singles or doubles play.

Who won the Men's Singles Championship at Wimbledon in 1976? Was it Jimmy Connors, Ilie Nastase, or Bjorn Borg?

Sweden's Bjorn Borg took the 1976 Wimbledon Singles crown by beating Ilie Nastase of Romania, 6-4, 6-2, 9-7.

Who was the youngest tennis player to win a championship at Wimbledon? Was it Chris Evert, Charlotte Dod, or Maureen Connolly?

Charlotte Dod was the youngest Wimbledon Champion. She was only fifteen years old when she won her championship in 1887. Evert was twenty when she won her first Wimbledon title in 1974, and Connolly, the 1952-54 Wimbledon winner, was eighteen when she captured her first Wimbledon crown.

True or false? Tennis was once played with the palm of the hand batting the ball over the net.

Absolutely true. The first known players of tennis, the French in the 1100s and 1200s, called their game *jeu de paume*, which means "game of the palm." Players *did* bat the ball back and forth over a net with the palm of their hands.

Two teams in World Team Tennis dropped their franchise in 1978. Can you name them?

Because of their failure to sign top players to contracts, the New York Apples and the Boston Lobsters dropped out of WTT in 1978.

Althea Gibson of the United States won the Wimbledon Women's Singles Championship and the U.S. Singles Championship for two successive years. Can you remember those years?

American star Althea Gibson won both the Wimbledon and the U.S. Women's Singles Championships in 1957 and again in 1958. In addition to her singles titles, Althea was also a member of the Wimbledon Women's Doubles Champions, teaming up with Darlene Hard of the U.S. in 1957 and with Maria Bueno of Brazil in 1958.

Who was the first Grand Slam winner in the history of tennis?

J. Donald Budge of the United States was the first man to simultaneously hold the four titles that make up the Grand Slam of Tennis. In 1937-38, Budge won the Wimbledon Championship, along with the Championships of the United States, Australia, and France. That same year, the undefeated Budge led the U.S. team in the recapture of the Davis Cup before he switched from amateur to professional tennis.

What is a net ball?

A ball that touches the net during play after a serve and lands fair is a *net ball.* Net balls count and must be played.

True or false? Chuck McKinley of the United States was never a Wimbledon Men's Singles Champion.

False. Chuck McKinley was the Wimbledon Men's Singles Champion in 1963.

Even though the Davis Cup Tennis Competition is now open to players from all countries, originally only four countries competed for the coveted trophy. Can you name those original four countries?

Until 1927, only the United States, England, Australia, and New Zealand competed for the Davis Cup. But in that year, the tournament was opened for the best tennis players from *all* countries to compete for the trophy.

In 1976, Freddy McNair and Sherwood Stewart were the number-2 ranked U.S. Doubles team. Can you name the doubles team that was ranked number-1?

Stan Smith and Bob Lutz were the number-1 ranked U.S. Doubles team in 1976.

When did Wimbledon first allow professional tennis players to compete in its tournament?

The year 1968 marked the first time that professional tennis players were allowed to play against amateurs at Wimbledon.

The net across a tennis court stands at different heights. It is forty-two inches high at the sides. How high is it in the center?

A tennis court net is thirty-two inches high at the center.

Martina Navratilova of Dallas, Texas, played against Chris Evert of Fort Lauderdale, Florida, for the 1978 Women's Singles Championship at Wimbledon. Who won?

Martina Navratilova was the Wimbledon Women's Singles Champion in 1978. She beat Chris Evert, 2-6, 6-4, 7-5, to win the world's most coveted tennis title.

Which country has won the Davis Cup the most times? Is it the United States, Great Britain, or Australia?

Australia's 1977 Davis Cup win tied her with the United States for the most victories, 24 apiece, since the competition began in 1900. Great Britain is second with 9 wins.

True or false? No tennis player has ever served a ball over 150 mph.

False. In 1963, Michael Sangster of Great Britain established a record for the fastest tennis serve ever recorded when he fired a tennis ball 154 mph.

In 1978, Roscoe Tanner and Jimmy Connors met in the finals of the U.S. Pro Indoor Championship in Philadelphia. Who won the first prize?

Jimmy Connors beat Roscoe Tanner, 6-2, 6-4, 6-3, to win the first prize in the $225,000 1978 U.S. Pro Indoor Championship.

Which tennis player was the leading money winner in 1976? Was it Bjorn Borg, Jimmy Connors, or Ilie Nastase?

Jimmy Connors earned $687,335 in prize money in 1976, to become the year's top money winner in tennis. Nastase was second highest with $576,705.

Which tennis tournament is considered to be the unofficial world championship for men's and women's singles and doubles?

The Wimbledon Championship, which is the oldest lawn tennis championship in the world, is considered to be the unofficial world title.

Bjorn Borg finished first in the Grand Prix of Denver in 1977. Who did he beat to collect the first-place prize?

Bjorn Borg beat Brain Gottfried, 7-5, 6-2, to win the 1977 Grand Prix prize of $20,000.

Only one woman in tennis history has ever won the Wimbledon Singles Championship eight times. Can you name her?

If you remember back to 1927, 1928, 1929, 1930, 1932, 1933, 1935, and 1938, you'll know that the correct answer is Helen Wills Moody. The American tennis star was the only woman to win the Wimbledon Singles title an amazing eight times.

On a tennis court, how far are the service lines from the net? Are they seventeen, twenty-one, or twenty-five feet away?

The service lines are twenty-one feet from the net and are parallel to it.

Who won the Swiss International Tennis Championship in 1978? Was it Guillermo Vilas or Jose Luis Clerc?

Argentina's Guillermo Vilas defeated his fellow-countryman, Jose Luis Clerc, 6-3, 7-6, 6-4, to take the Swiss International Tennis Championship in 1978. The Swiss International had previously been the scene of Vilas' first major international victory in 1974.

Was Bobby Riggs ever a Wimbledon Singles Champion?

Yes. Riggs won the Men's Singles at Wimbledon in 1939, the same year he won the U.S. Singles Championship at Forest Hills. Riggs repeated his U.S. win in 1941.

What is a *fault* in tennis?

When a player serves the ball and the serve fails to clear the net or lands outside the service court, a *fault* is called, and the player gets a second chance to serve. If the player's second attempt to serve is also unsuccessful, this is called a *double fault*, and a point is scored by his or her opponent.

The January, 1978, Grand Prix Masters saw closely matched Jimmy Connors, Bjorn Borg, and Guillermo Vilas face each other. Which tennis superstar won the $400,000 tournament?

The double-elimination tournament saw Jimmy Connors as the victor before sellout crowds at New York's Madison Square Garden. According to Connors, his performance in the 1978 Grand Prix Masters was "the best tennis I have ever played."

Who won the Independent Players Association Tournament in Virginia Beach in 1977? Was it Guillermo Vilas, Ilie Nastase, or Corrado Brazzotti?

Guillermo Vilas beat Ilie Nastase, 6-2, 4-6, 6-2, to win the 1977 Independent Players Association Tournament.

Before Bobby Riggs lost to Billie Jean King in their $100,000 "Battle of the Sexes" in 1973, he had defeated the woman who went on to win the U.S. Women's Singles Championship that year. Who was that woman?

Bobby Riggs defeated Australian champion Margaret Smith Court in a $10,000 winner-take-all match, before losing to Billie Jean King.

How many sets does a tennis match consist of?

A tennis match usually consists of five sets. Sometimes, if prearranged, a match may consist of only three sets.

Who won the French Open Tennis Tournament in 1976? Was it Brian Gottfried, Raul Ramirez, or Adriano Panatta?

Italy's Adriano Panatta defeated Harold Solomon of the U.S. to win the French Open Championship in 1976. Panatta also took the Italian Open that same year.

Only one man has ever won the United States Singles Championship at Forest Hills seven times? Can you remember who he was?

Bill Tilden, considered by many to be tennis' finest player, holds the distinction of seven U.S. Singles Championships. He captured six of these consecutively from 1920 to 1925, and won again in 1929.

In what year were the first lawn tennis championship matches held at Wimbledon? Was it 1877, 1887, or 1900?

The Old Wimbledon Grounds near London was the site of the first lawn tennis championship matches in 1887. Under the sponsorship of the All-England Croquet and Lawn Tennis Club, the matches were open to amateur tennis players who paid an entrance fee of one shilling. The tournament offered two prizes — one gold and one silver — to the first- and second-place winners.

True or false? Women were permitted to compete at Wimbledon when competition began in 1877.

False. The Wimbledon Championships were only for men for the first seven years of its existence. It wasn't until 1884 that female players were permitted to compete.

Arthur W. Gore of Great Britain was the oldest tennis player to win the Men's Singles Championship at Wimbledon. How old was Gore when he won the 1909 title?

Arthur W. Gore was 41 years old when he won the Men's Singles Championship at Wimbledon in 1909.

Can you name the trophy that is considered the premier prize in Women's International Tennis Competition?

The Wightman Cup, donated by American tennis champion and socialite Mrs. Hazel Hotchkiss Wightman, is the most sought-after and honored prize in women's international tennis. Mrs. Wightman presented the cup in 1923 as a trophy for competition between British and American women's teams.

Who were tennis' leading money winners in 1977?

Jimmy Connors led the male tennis players with a 1977 earnings total of $922,657. Chris Evert outdistanced all female challengers with a 1977 total of $503,134.

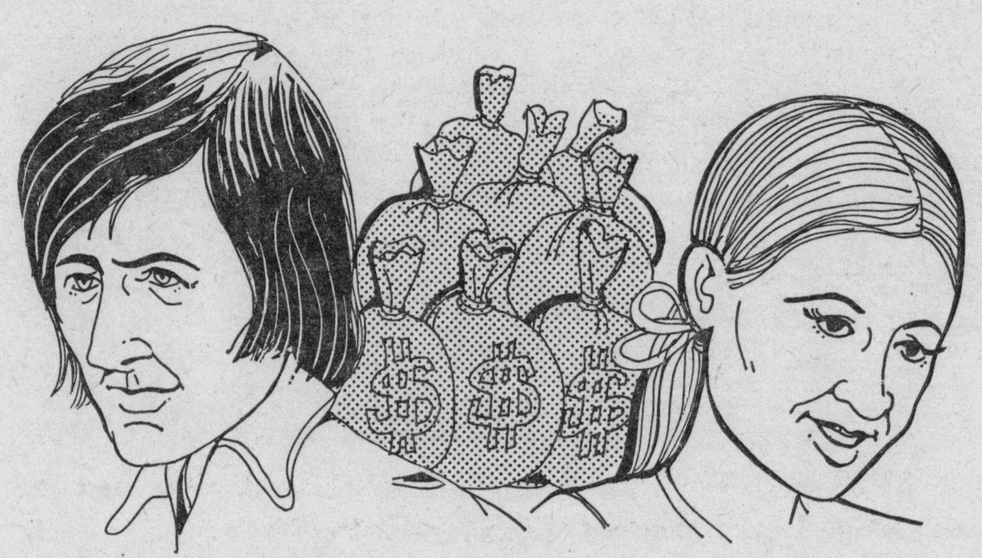

True or false? A standard tennis ball measures about 4½ inches in diameter. Can you guess its weight? Is it 2 ounces, 3 ounces, or 4 ounces?

A standard tennis ball's inner layer of rubber plus its woven covering of dacron, nylon, and wool add up to a total weight of about 2 ounces.

Which tennis star was nicknamed "Little Mo"?

Maureen Connolly, who at the age of 15 was ranked tenth among all women tennis players, was nicknamed "Little Mo." At 16, she won the Women's Singles at Forest Hills, a championship she repeated for the next two years, along with three Wimbledon Championships. At age 19, "Little Mo" became the first woman tennis player in history to win the Grand Slam of Tennis.

The largest crowd ever to watch a tennis match was at the Wimbledon Championship in 1977. True or false?

False. On September 20, 1973, a crowd of 30,472 — the largest crowd ever to attend a tennis match — gathered at the Houston Astrodome to watch 30-year-old Billie Jean King play against Bobby Riggs, 25 years her senior, in the so-called "Tennis Match of the Century." Millions more viewed the match on TV and saw King defeat Riggs in straight sets.

Who won the U.S. Men's Singles Championship and the U.S. Women's Singles Championship at Forest Hills in 1976?

Jimmy Connors took the 1976 U.S. Men's Singles Championship at Forest Hills, and Chris Evert won the U.S. Women's Singles title.

Regulation tennis rackets have to be made of wood. True or false?

False. Tennis rackets can be made of wood, aluminum, or steel. They can weigh from 12 to 16 ounces and are 26 to 27 inches long.

Only two women have ever captured the Grand Slam of Tennis. One was Maureen Connolly of the United States, who won it in 1953. Who was the other?

Margaret Court Smith of Australia was the only other woman to capture the Grand Slam of Tennis. She did it in 1970, by winning the singles titles at Forest Hills, Wimbledon, Australia, and France.

Who won the Virginia Slims Tennis Championship in 1976? Was it Chris Evert, Rosemary Casals, or Evonne Goolagong?

Australian star Evonne Goolagong defeated Chris Evert in the finals to win the 1976 Virginia Slims Championship.

Which tennis stars authored the following books: *A Tennis Memoir, The Education of a Tennis Player,* and *Court Hustler*?

A Tennis Memoir was written by Don Budge. *The Education of a Tennis Player* was Rod Laver's story. And *Court Hustler* came from the pen of Bobby Riggs.

Vitas Gerulaitis faced Ilie Nastase in the 1978 Invitational at Forest Hills. Who won?

Vitas Gerulaitis won the Championship of the Forest Hills Invitational by beating Ilie Nastase, 6-2, 6-0. The $300,000 Invitational was a new WCT event inaugurated in 1978.

How many times did the great Pancho Gonzales win the United States Men's Singles Championship?

Pancho Gonzales won the U.S. Men's Singles Championship twice: first in 1948, and then in 1949.

Who was Ilie Nastase's partner when he won the Wimbledon Mixed Doubles Championships in 1970 and 1972?

Ilie Nastase of Romania teamed up with Rosemary Casals of the United States to take the Wimbledon Mixed Doubles Championships in 1970 and 1972.

How long is a tennis court? Is it 70 feet, 78 feet, or 80 feet long?

A tennis court is 78 feet long.

Where is the annual Davis Cup Challenge Round held?

The country of the defending Davis Cup Champion hosts the Challenge Round.

In June, 1977, in Eastbourne, England, the United States team of Chris Evert, Billie Jean King, and Rosemary Casals met the Australian team of Kerry Reid, Dianne Fromholtz, and Wendy Turnball in singles and doubles matches for the Federation Cup. Which team won?

The United States team defeated Australia, 2-1, to win the 1977 Federation Cup.

Who is credited with inventing the game of lawn tennis?

Major Walter Clopton Wingfield, an Englishman, introduced the game of lawn tennis to Great Britain in 1873, and is considered the "Father of Modern Tennis." In 1874, Wingfield, set down rules for playing on grass courts and patented his tennis equipment, which consisted of a spoon-shaped racquet with a long handle and a hollow rubber ball. His original name for the game, *sphairistike* — Greek for "playing ball," was soon replaced by "lawn tennis."

When Billie Jean King of the United States won the Wimbledon Mixed Doubles in 1967, 1972, and 1973, her partner was an Australian. Can you name him?

Owen Davidson of Australia teamed up with Billie Jean King of the U.S. to win the Wimbledon Mixed Doubles Championships in 1967, 1971, and 1973.

On what type of surface is the Wimbledon Tennis Championship played? Is it clay, grass, or artificial turf?

The Wimbledon Tennis Tournament is played on real grass.

Which World Team Tennis teams did Billie Jean King, Chris Evert, and Martina Navratilova play for in 1978?

Billie Jean King played for the New York Apples, Martina Navratilova sparked the Boston Lobsters, and Chris Evert starred for the Los Angeles Strings in the 1978 season.

How did the word *love* come to be used as a tennis term meaning a score of zero?

The most widely held theory attributes *love* to the French word *l'oeuf,* meaning "egg." American slang often refers to a score of zero as a "goose egg," and *love,* meaning zero, is nothing more than our bad pronounciation of the French *l'oeuf.*

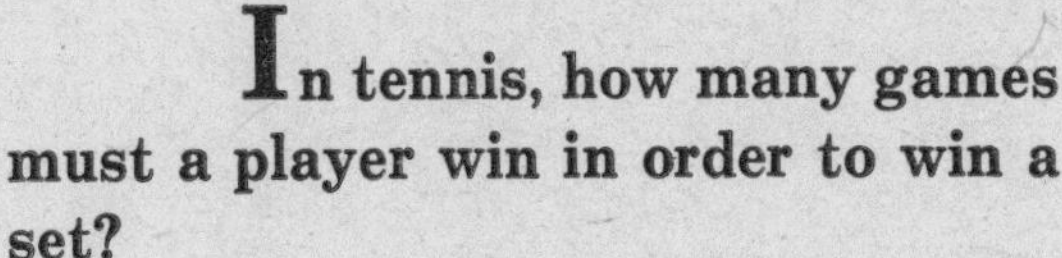

In tennis, how many games must a player win in order to win a set?

Six games ordinarily constitute the winning of a set. However, this is provided that the player's opponent has won four games or less, for a set must always be won by a margin of two games. If this margin is only one game, the set is extended until a two-game margin exists.

Evonne Goolagong, the tennis champion, has an interesting last name. Do you know what kind of name it is?

Goolagong is an Australian aborigine name and Evonne is a descendant of these original settlers of the continent. The aborigine name Goolagong means "tall trees by still waters."

In tennis, what is a *drop shot*?

A *drop shot* is a ball hit very lightly so it just drops over the net.

In 1976, Chris Evert won the Wimbledon Women's Singles Championship. Who did she beat in the finals? Was it Rosemary Casals, Martina Navratilova, or Evonne Goolagong?

Chris Evert beat Evonne Goolagong to become the 1976 Wimbledon Women's Singles Champion.

How is the serve decided in a tennis game?

Most players decide who serves by a racquet "toss." One player stands the racquet upright on the ground and spins it. The opponent calls "heads" or "tails," usually using the manufacturer's markings on one side as "heads." If the call is correct, that player may choose to serve or receive first.

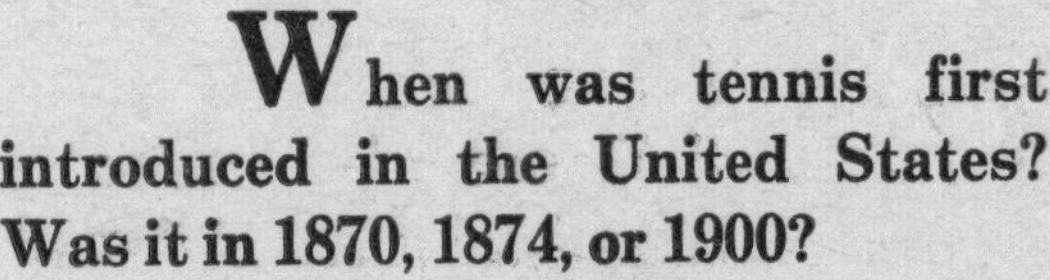

When was tennis first introduced in the United States? Was it in 1870, 1874, or 1900?

The game of tennis was introduced in the United States in 1874 by sportswoman Mary Ewing Outerbridge, a Staten Island, New York, socialite. While on a vacation in Bermuda, Miss Outerbridge bought tennis racquets, balls, and a net from some British army officers. With the help of her two brothers, Miss Outerbridge obtained permission from the Staten Island Cricket and Baseball Club to lay out a tennis court on their grounds, and played the first lawn tennis game in the United States in the spring of 1874.

What type of stroke is the pictured tennis player using?

The tennis player in the picture is using a *forehand* stroke. The forehand is usually a player's best and most powerful stroke.

The big serve combined with the big volley became known as "The Big Game" in the 1940s. Who popularized this style of tennis?

Jack Kramer popularized his "Big Game" style of tennis in the late 1940s. He combined a strong attack with geometrical theories to plan the placement of the hit ball.

AUTO & MOTORCYCLE RACING

True or false? The winner of the 1977 Long Beach Grand Prix was Graham Hill.

False. In 1977, Mario Andretti won the Long Beach classic in his Lotus-Ford, averaging 86.889 mph.

In 1895, J. Frank Duryea, a pioneer automobile maker, won the first automobile race ever held in the United States. Was that race held in New York, California, or Illinois?

The very first automobile race in America took place on Thanksgiving Day, 1895, between Chicago and Evanston, Illinois. The average speed of Duryea's car, which he had built himself, was a "speedy" 7.5 mph.

Who won the Indianapolis 500 in 1973? Was it Graham Hill or Gordon Johncock?

Gordon Johncock won at Indy in 1973. Graham Hill's victory came seven years earlier, in 1966.

Who won the United States Automobile Club Stock-Car Race at Mosport, Ontario, in 1978?

A.J. Foyt, driving a Chevrolet, was the winner of the 1978 USAC Stock-Car Race. Joe Ruttman finished second in a Pontiac Ventura, and Terry Ryan in a Chevelle finished third.

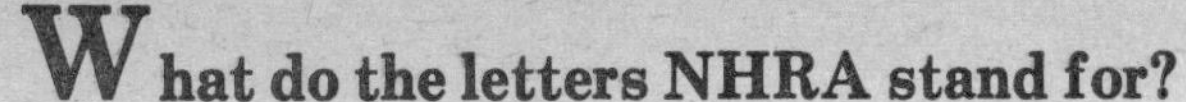

What do the letters NHRA stand for?

The letters stand for the National Hot Rod Association, one of the four major racing organizations in the United States.

Who was the United States Auto Club Rookie of the Year in 1977?

The USAC Rookie of the Year Award went to Danny Ongais in 1977. Ongais was the winner of the 1977 Michigan 200-Mile Race and also set the record as the fastest rookie qualifier at the Indianapolis 500, with a 4-lap average of 193.040 mph.

In order to win a *drag race*, a dragster must complete a predetermined number of laps around an oval track. True or false?

False. *Drag races* are high-speed events run on short, straight pieces of track called *drag strips*. Racing two at a time, the cars accelerate from a standing start and attempt to reach the highest possible speed. A record is kept of the time it takes each car to move down the track. The car that moves down the track in the least amount of time is declared the winner.

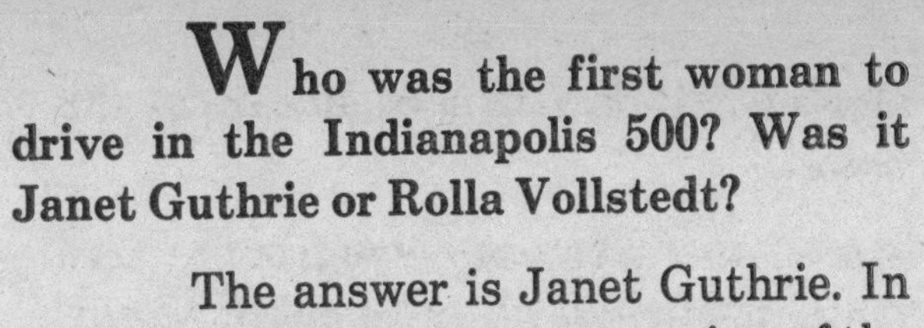

Who was the first woman to drive in the Indianapolis 500? Was it Janet Guthrie or Rolla Vollstedt?

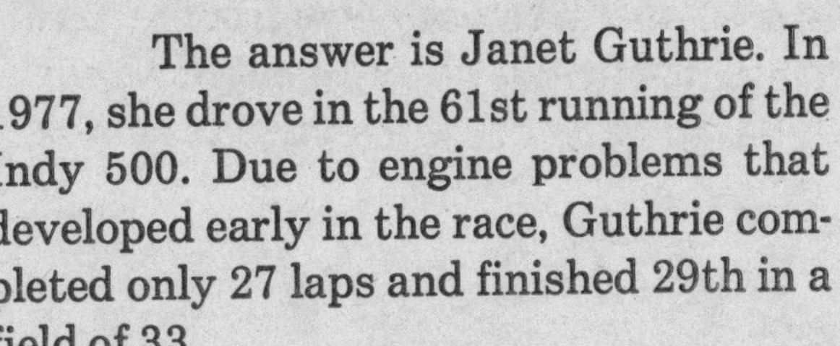

The answer is Janet Guthrie. In 1977, she drove in the 61st running of the Indy 500. Due to engine problems that developed early in the race, Guthrie completed only 27 laps and finished 29th in a field of 33.

Peter DePaulo was the first driver to break the 100 mph average speed in the Indianapolis 500. Did he do it in 1925, 1930, or 1935?

In 1925, Peter DePaulo and his relief driver, Norman Batten, shattered the 100 mph average by maintaining an average speed of 101.13 mph. DePaulo was also the first driver to cover the 500 miles in under five hours.

In 1965, Mario Andretti became the youngest driver to ever win the USAC National Championship. How old was he when he won that prestigious award?

Mario Andretti was only 25 years old when he won the 1965 United States Auto Club National Championship.

True or false? A driver once started 28th in a field of 40 cars at the Indianapolis 500 and went on to win the race.

True. In 1911, Ray Harroun scored the greatest come-from-behind victory in Indy history when he started 28th in a field of 40 and went on to win the 500-mile race. Finishing second was Ralph Mulford, who started the race in the 29th position.

Can you name the driver who had the fastest single lap ever recorded in the Indianapolis 500?

In 1977, rookie driver Danny Ongais set the single-lap Indy 500 speed record by going 192.678 miles per hour.

What is a *stock-car* race?

Stock-car races, which are extremely popular in the United States, are run with production- or factory-made cars, rather than cars built especially for racing. However, stock cars usually have rebuilt engines and a few additional safety devices.

Who won the 1974 Schaefer Pocono 500? Was it Tom Sneva, Johnny Rutherford, or Mario Andretti?

Johnny Rutherford won the 1974 Schaefer Pocono 500 in a McLaren-Offy, traveling at an average speed of 156.701 mph.

One of the most famous race courses in the world for attempts at establishing land speed records is found in the United States. In which state is that straight-mile course located?

The Bonneville Speedway, on the Bonneville Salt Flats in western Utah, is the site each August of the speed trials. The 100 square miles of flat salt beds, as hard as cement, attract racing drivers from all over the world.

What is the world's record for the fastest pit stop? Is it 4, 6, or 10 seconds?

It's 4 seconds. On May 30, 1976, on lap 10 of the Indianapolis 500, American Bobby Unser took a mere 4 seconds to refuel his car in the pits.

Which vast automotive empire was built on earnings from an automobile race?

A 10-mile auto race at Grosse Point, Michigan, in 1901 attracted a young man named Henry Ford. Ford entered the race, using the gasoline-powered automobile he had built five years earlier. He won that race with an average speed of 44.8 mph. His winnings and the publicity that followed helped him organize the Ford Motor Company — one of today's automotive giants.

What do the letters SCCA stand for?

SCCA stands for the Sports Car Club of America — an organization which governs professional and amateur sports car racing.

Sam Hanks has the distinction of being the oldest man to win the Indianapolis 500. How old was he when he won that race in 1957?

Sam Hanks was a few weeks shy of his 43rd birthday when he won at Indy in 1957.

Jackie Stewart of Scotland holds the world record for the most Grand Prix victories. How many races did he win to establish the record?

Between September 12, 1965 and August 5, 1973, Jackie Stewart had a total of 27 Grand Prix victories. In 1969, 1971, and 1973, Stewart was the Grand Prix Formula-One Driving Champion: in 1969, in a Matra-Ford; in 1971, in a Tyrrell-Ford; and in 1973, the year he retired, also in a Tyrrell-Ford.

In what year did a car first travel over 500 mph to establish a land speed record? Was it in 1962, 1964, or 1966?

In 1964, Craig Breedlove, in his jet-powered *Spirit of America*, went over 500 mph for the first time. Breedlove's record speed of 526.277 mph was topped later that same year when Art Arfons, in his jet-powered *Green Monster*, went 536.71 mph.

True or false? World War I fighter pilot Eddie Rickenbacker was once a race-car driver.

True. The automobile-mechanic-turned-racing-driver won fame in international auto racing before World War I. Rickenbacker later owned and ran the Indianapolis Motor Speedway.

As of 1978, who was the winningest driver in National Hot Rod Association history? Was it Don Prudhomme, Don Nicholson, or Dave Settles?

The answer is Don Prudhomme of Granada Hills, California, with 26 national event titles. From 1974 to 1978, Prudhomme won 89 of 97 funny-car heats and three consecutive world championships. During that four-year period, he captured 18 national event titles, which is more than any other driver has racked up in an entire career.

Who was the youngest driver to ever win the 500-mile race at the Indianapolis Motor Speedway? Was it Wilbur Shaw, Troy Ruttman, or Al Unser?

The youngest Indy winner was Troy Ruttman, who was only 22 years old when he took the 500-mile classic in 1952. Wilbur Shaw's first win in 1937 came when he was 35, and Al Unser was 31 when he was the Indy Champion in 1970.

Can you match the following drivers with the races they won in 1972?

(1) Joe Leonard, averaging 154.781 mph in a Parnelli-Offy

(2) Roger McCluskey, averaging 151.540 mph in a McLaren-Offy

(3) Mark Donohue, averaging 162.962 mph in a McLaren-Offenhauser

(a) Won the 1972 California 500 at the Ontario, California, Motor Speedway

(b) Won the 1972 Indianapolis 500 at the Indianapolis Motor Speedway

(c) Won the 1972 Schaefer Pocono 500 at Pocono International Speedway, Long Pond, Pennsylvania

The correct match ups are (1) c. Joe Leonard, averaging 154.781 mph in a Parnelli-Offy, won the 1972 Schaefer Pocono 500. (2) a. Roger McCluskey, averaging 151.540 mph in a McLaren-Offy, won the 1972 California 500. And (3) b. Mark Donohue, averaging 162.962 mph in a McLaren-Offenhauser, won the 1972 Indianapolis 500.

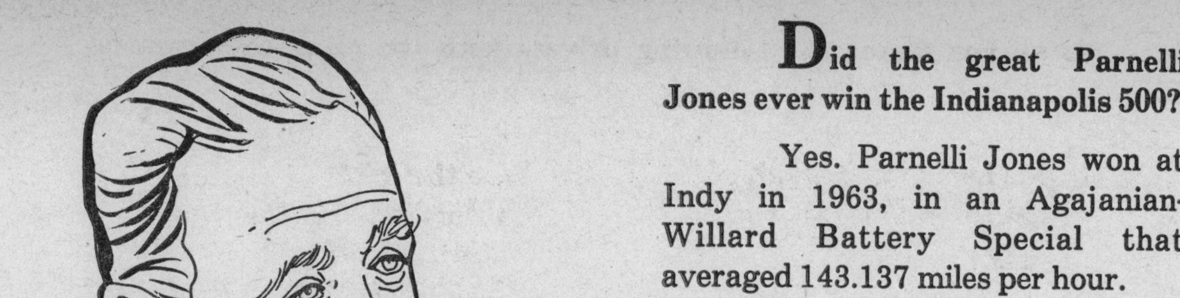

Did the great Parnelli Jones ever win the Indianapolis 500?

Yes. Parnelli Jones won at Indy in 1963, in an Agajanian-Willard Battery Special that averaged 143.137 miles per hour.

How is the United States Champion of Auto Racing determined?

Each year, a series of about twenty track races, ranging from 100 to 500 miles long and including the Indy 500, are sponsored by USAC. These races constitute the "Championship Trail." The winner and runners-up in each race receive points. The driver accumulating the most points during the year is named the United States Champion.

Emerson Fittipaldi of Brazil was the youngest man ever to become the World Grand Prix Driver Champion. How old was he when he won his first World Championship?

Fittipaldi was only 25 years old when he won his first World Championship on September 10, 1972.

True or false? A racing car driver once *pushed* his car across the finish line to win the Indianapolis 500.

Unbelievable as it seems, it's true. In 1915, Ralph DePalma pushed his Mercedes the final 1½ miles to win the Indy 500.

Who supplies the prize money for the Indianapolis 500 and other big-car races?

Auto manufacturers spend millions of dollars each year as prize money for major racing purses.

The oldest auto race in the world still being run regularly is the French Grand Prix. True or false?

False. The oldest auto race in the world still run regularly is the R.A.C. Tourist Trophy, which was staged for the first time on September 14, 1905, on the Isle of Man, in the Irish Sea between England and Ireland. The French Grand Prix was started the following year, in 1906.

What famous words spoken by the announcer signal the start of the Indianapolis 500?

The famous words are "Gentlemen, start your engines."

How are *track races* different from *road races*?

Track races are high-speed races run on oval tracks with long straightaways and curves, which are sometimes banked. *Road races* are slower races run on ordinary roads or on special road courses which have a number of curves, sharp corners, and sometimes hills.

Juan-Manuel Fangio was the oldest racing car driver to ever become the World Grand Prix Driver Champion. How old was he when he won the title for the last time?

Juan-Manuel Fangio of Argentina was 46 years old when he became the World Champion in 1957. Fangio had also been the Grand Prix winner in 1951, 1955, and 1956.

Who won the Indianapolis 500 in 1978?

The winner of the 1978 Indy 500 was Al Unser. Driving a Lola-Cosworth and starting from the 10th position, Unser covered the 500-mile course in 3 hours, 5 minutes, 54.99 seconds. His average speed was 161.363 mph — the second fastest in Indy history.

Racing car drivers Jim Clark of Scotland and Graham Hill of England have both won the Indianapolis 500 and the World Grand Prix Driver Championships. True or false?

True. Jim Clark won at Indy in 1965 and was the World Grand Prix Driver Champion in 1963 and 1965. Graham Hill won the Indianapolis 500 in 1966 and was the World Grand Prix Driver Champion in 1962 and 1968.

Who was the first driver to break the 200 mph barrier?

In 1977, while running a practice lap before the qualifying sessions of the Indianapolis 500, Mario Andretti became the first driver ever to break the 200 mph barrier.

Who captured the pole position at the 1978 Indianapolis 500? Was it A.J. Foyt, Roger Penske, or Tom Sneva?

Tom Sneva captured the pole position at the 1978 Indy 500 for the second year in a row. To earn the coveted starting position, Sneva had set a new one-lap record of 203.620 miles per hour in his Norton Spirit Penske-Cosworth. This shattered his own record of 200.535 mph, which he had set in 1977.

How many times has Bobby Unser won the Pike's Peak Auto Hill Climb?

The Pike's Peak Auto Hill Climb, which was instituted in 1916, was won 13 times by Bobby Unser between 1956 and 1974. This 12.42-mile course rises from 9,402 to 14,110 feet up the Colorado peak, requiring the driver to maneuver through 157 curves.

Who won the 1978 $165,000 Rebel 500 in Darlington, South Carolina? Was it Benny Parsons or Darrell Waltrip?

Benny Parsons led for the final 52 laps of the 1978 Rebel 500 by averaging 127.544 mph, and finished 1.9 seconds in front of second-place Darrell Waltrip.

What is the length range of Grand Prix races? Is it from 150 to 250 miles, 275 to 300 miles, or 300 to 375 miles?

Grand Prix races range from 150 to 250 miles (241 to 402 kilometers) in length.

Can you name the man who was the USAC National Driving Champion in 1976? Was it Roger McCluskey, Gordon Johncock, or Joe Leonard?

Gordon Johncock was the 1976 United States Auto Club National Driving Champion. McCluskey won the title in 1973, and Leonard in 1971 and 1972.

True or false? A dragster uses regular brakes to stop at the end of its run.

False. Due to the high speeds a dragster attains, regular braking is impossible. In order to stop at the end of its run, a dragster uses a drag parachute, which is ejected from the rear of the automobile.

As of 1978, the highest speed ever recorded by a wheeled vehicle was achieved by Californian Gary Gabelich at the Bonneville Salt Flats on October 23, 1970. How fast did he go to set the record? Was it about 600 mph, 622 mph, or 630 mph?

Gary Gabelich, in his 37-foot-long, 4950-pound rocket-engined *The Blue Flame*, averaged 622.407 mph to set the land speed record. His peak speed during the trials was 650 mph.

How many Grand Prix races did Austrian racer Niki Lauda win in 1975?

Enroute to being named the World Grand Prix Driver Champion in 1975, Niki Lauda had a total of 5 Grand Prix wins, capturing the titles in Monaco, Belgium, Sweden, France, and the United States.

As of 1978, how many times has the Indianapolis 500 been run?

May 28, 1978 marked the 62nd time that the annual 500-mile race at the Indianapolis Motor Speedway has been run.

What do the letters NASCAR stand for?

They stand for the National Association for Stock-Car Auto Racing. NASCAR, one of the major racing organizations in the United States, sponsors Grand National Championship races for late-model stock cars.

True or false? Grand Prix cars are also called Formula-One cars.

True. Grand Prix cars are called Formula-One cars because they are built according to a *formula*, or certain set of specifications drawn up by the *Federation Internationale de l'Automobile*. Formula-One cars are small, low, single-seat cars with no fenders.

Shirley Muldowney and Don Prudhomme are two of the top drivers in drag racing. What are their nicknames?

Shirley is known as "Cha Cha" Muldowney, and Prudhomme has been nicknamed Don "The Snake" Prudhomme.

Between 1960 and 1965, how many times was A.J. Foyt the United States Auto Club National Champion? Was two, three, or four times?

A.J. Foyt was the USAC National Champion four times in the five-year period between 1960 and 1965. He won the title in 1960, 1961, 1963, and 1964, then came up with two additional wins — in 1967 and 1975.

As of 1977, only one American has ever won the World Grand Prix Formula-One Driving Championship. Can you name him?

The answer is Phil Hill. Driving a Ferrari in the 1961 Grand Prix circuit, the American racer won the World Championship.

What are *pit* areas?

The *pits* are special areas along the race track where drivers stop to refuel their cars and change their tires. This is usually done in less than 30 seconds. Skilled mechanics, capable of making emergency repairs to a driver's car during the race, make up the pit crew.

Most fans know racing driver A.J. Foyt simply by his initials. Do you know what A.J. stands for?

Foyt's full name is Anthony Joseph.

The record for the lowest elapsed time recorded by a piston engined dragster, 5.637 seconds, is held by Donald Glenn Garlits. Garlits is better known to most racing fans by his nickname. Do you know it?

Most drag racing fans know Don as "Big Daddy" Garlits.

Championship cars are extremely different types of racing cars from Grand Prix cars. True or false?

False. Championship cars are very much like Grand Prix cars. Both are small, low fenderless cars with a single seat.

The $100,800 Old Dominion 500 was won by the same man in 1976 and 1977. Was it Cale Yarborough, Benny Parsons, or Richard Petty?

The answer is Cale Yarborough. He won the Martinsville, Virginia, Old Dominion 500 in 1976 and again in 1977.

Who was the first stock-car driver to go over the $1 million mark in career earnings? Was it Richard Petty, Ned Jarrett, or Dave Pearson?

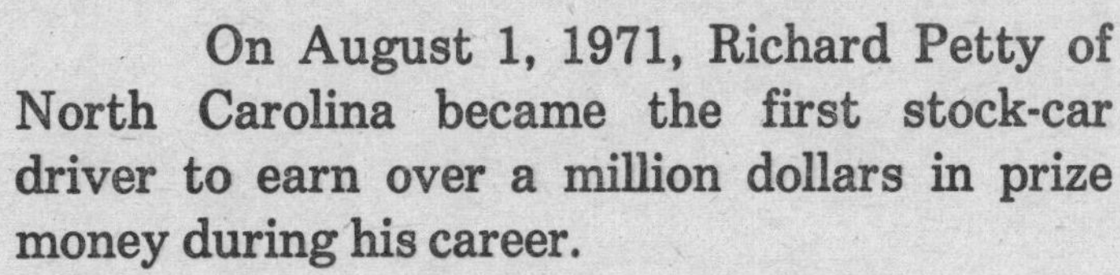
On August 1, 1971, Richard Petty of North Carolina became the first stock-car driver to earn over a million dollars in prize money during his career.

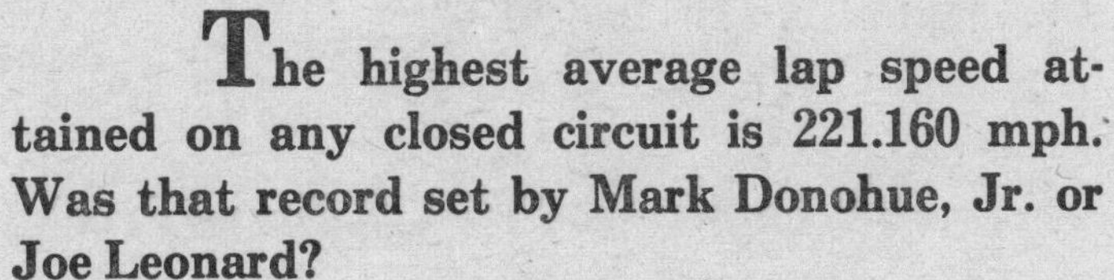
The highest average lap speed attained on any closed circuit is 221.160 mph. Was that record set by Mark Donohue, Jr. or Joe Leonard?

Driving a 5.374cc turbocharged Porsche 917-30 Cam-Am, Mark Donohue, Jr. lapped the 2.66-mile banked tri-oval at Alabama International Motor Speedway at Talladega, Alabama, on August 9, 1975. His time of 43.299 seconds gave him the highest average lap speed on a closed circuit.

Only four men have won the Indianapolis 500 three times. Can you name them?

Louis Meyer won the Indianapolis 500 in 1928, 1933, and 1936; Wilbur Shaw did it in 1937, 1939, and 1940; Mauri Rose was victorious at Indy in 1941, 1947, and 1948; and Al Unser duplicated that feat in 1970, 1971, and 1978.

Who is the only driver to win the Indianapolis 500 four times?

The answer is the great A.J. Foyt. As of 1978, Foyt was the only man to win the Indy 500 a record four times. He took the championship in 1961, 1964, 1967, and 1977.

Who won the 1977 U.S. Grand Prix?

James Hunt, in his McLaren-Ford, was the U.S. Grand Prix winner in 1977. Averaging 100.98 miles per hour, Hunt finished a mere 100 yards in front of second-place Mario Andretti.

Who won the 500-Mile Grand National Stock Car Race at Pocono International Speedway in 1977? Was it Benny Parsons or Richard Petty?

Benny Parsons, in a Chevrolet, averaged a record-breaking 128.379 mph to win the race, crossing the finish line less than half a second in front of Richard Petty's Dodge.

Until 1971, the Indianapolis 500 was always held on a certain holiday. Can you name that holiday?

The Indy 500 was held *on* Memorial Day until 1971, when it was changed to the Sunday of the Memorial Day weekend. It was in 1971 that the Federal Government legislated the last Monday in May to be the official Memorial Day, giving the nation a three-day holiday weekend.

True or false? The *Federation Internationale de L'Automobile* regulates all organized automobile racing.

True. The *FIA* regulates auto racing throughout the world from its headquarters in Paris, France.

When racing car experts talk about a car's *cornering ability*, what are they referring to?

Cornering ability refers to the automobile's ability to maneuver turns.

Can you name the first woman licensed to drive racing's 250 mile-per-hour top-fuel dragsters in the United States?

Shirley Muldowney of Mt. Clemens, Michigan, the third winningest driver in top-fuel history, was the first woman licensed to drive top-fuel dragsters in the U.S.

True or false? Al Unser has won the Indy 500, but his brother, Bobby, has never been victorious at Indianapolis.

False. Bobby Unser won the 1968 Indianapolis 500 in an Eagle-Offenhauser, with an average 152.88 miles per hour.

Can you name the fastest auto race in the world?

The NASCAR Grand National 125-Mile Race, which is held on the 2½-mile, 31-degree banked tri-oval at Daytona International Speedway, is the fastest race in the world. The record time for the event, 40 minutes 55 seconds, was set by William Caleb "Cale" Yarborough on February 19, 1970, when he averaged 183.295 mph in a 1969 Mercury V8.

When was the Daytona Beach Speedway built? Was it in 1948, 1955, or 1959?

The Daytona Beach Speedway was constructed in 1959 and almost immediately became the hub of stock-car racing in the United States. Daytona Beach was a likely choice for the Speedway site because large numbers of stock cars had been racing on the sands of Daytona since the early 1900s.

One man — a Belgian — won the LeMans 24-hour race in 1975, 1976, and 1977. Can you name him?

Belgium's pride is racing car driver Jacky Ickx. Jacky, who had won at LeMans in 1969, repeated as the winner of that world-famous race in 1975, 1976, and 1977. His 1977 win set a record for one 8.3-mile lap with a time of 141.36 miles per hour.

What was the original reason for building the Indianapolis Motor Speedway?

In 1909, when the track was built, Indianapolis was the fourth largest producer of automobiles in the country, but it had no testing facilities. Carl Fisher, the industrialist responsible for the track's construction, thought that erecting the speedway would make Indianapolis the number-one automobile producer in the country.

True or false? Dragsters and stock cars both use the same kind of rear tires for racing.

False. Stock cars use a modified version of regular tires. Dragsters, however, use extra wide tires made of a special kind of soft, sticky rubber that helps them grip the track.

Who won the 1978 South African Grand Prix? Was it Ronnie Peterson or Patrick Depailler?

Ronnie Peterson, in his Lotus-Ford, crossed the finish line .4 of a second in front of Patrick Depailler, in his Tyrrell-Ford, to win the 1978 South African Grand Prix. Peterson's average speed for the 78 laps of the 2.5-mile course at Kyalami, South Africa, was 117.4 mph.

Can you name the winner of the Daytona 500 in 1976? Here's a hint. He's one of NASCAR's all-time winning drivers.

Richard Petty, considered by many to be the "King of Stock-Car Racing," won the Daytona 500 in 1976.

In 1977, at the National Hot Rod Association's Summernationals at Englishtown, New Jersey, both the Funny-Car and Top-Fuel titles were won by default. True or false?

True. Shirley Muldowney won in the Top-Fuel division when the other finalist found he was unable to start his car because of a faulty battery, and Don Prudhomme won the Funny-Car division when his opponent broke down at the starting line.

Where is the U.S. Grand Prix held?

Watkins Glen, New York, is the site of the U.S. Grand Prix. The course has 12 corners to be negotiated on each lap, requiring the driver to shift through five different gears more than 2,000 times during the race.

In qualifying for the Indianapolis-car portion of the 1978 Twin 200-Mile U.S. Auto Club Races at Cambridge Junction, Michigan, Tom Sneva set a track record by going a blazing 209.059 mph — only to have the record shattered the very next day. True or false?

True. Tom Sneva's day-old record *was* broken at Cambridge Junction, Michigan, during the early part of the 1978 season, but it was Sneva, himself, who did it. His scorching 211.392 mph qualifying lap won him his fourth pole position in nine races.

True or false? Mechanics once rode along with drivers during the Indianapolis 500.

Although it sounds crazy, it's absolutely true. Mechanics rode with the racing drivers, on and off, at Indy until 1937, when the procedure was permanently discontinued.

As of 1978, only four men have ever won the Indianapolis 500 two consecutive times. Can you name those four drivers?

Wilbur Shaw won at Indy in 1939 and 1940; Mauri Rose took top 500 honors in 1947 and 1948; Bill Vukovich led the 500 in 1953 and 1954; and Al Unser chalked up his two consecutive wins in 1970 and 1971.

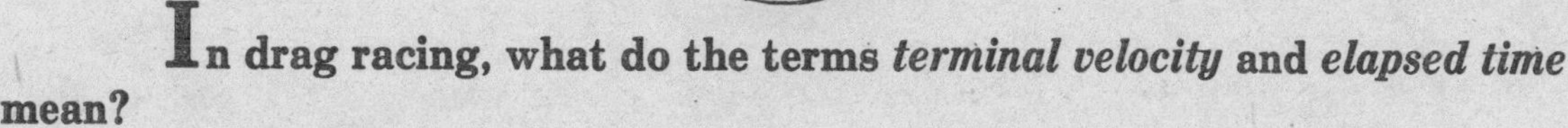

In drag racing, what do the terms *terminal velocity* and *elapsed time* mean?

Terminal velocity is the speed attained by the end of a 440-yard run made from a standing start, and *elapsed time* is the time taken for the run.

Who won the $205,800 Atlanta 500 at Hampton, Georgia, in 1978? Was it Bobby Allison, Dave-Marcis, or David Pearson?

Bobby Allison, in a Thunderbird, won the Atlanta 500 in 1978 by averaging 142.520 miles per hour. He finished one lap ahead of Dave Marcis, who took second place in a Chevrolet.

In 1974, Johnny Rutherford won two of the biggest races on the American circuit. Can you name them?

Johnny Rutherford won the 1974 Indianapolis 500 and Schaefer Pocono 500.

Mario Andretti won the Argentine Grand Prix in 1978. Who came in second?

Andretti, who started at the pole position in his Lotus, easily defeated Niki Lauda, who finished 13.21 seconds behind him in the 1978 Argentine Grand Prix.

Only two men, both Belgians, have ever won at LeMans more than three times. One is Jacky Ickx, whose LeMans' victories took place in 1969, 1975, 1976, and 1977. Who is the other? A tip of the hat to you if you know the answer.

The answer is Oliver Gendebien. He won at LeMans in 1958, 1960, 1961, and 1962.

In 1978, Carlos Reutemann, in a Ferrari, won the Brazilian Grand Prix. In what city is that race held?

The Brazilian Grand Prix is held in Rio de Janeiro.

True or false? Lenny Pond won the $80,000 Richmond 400 in 1978.

False. Benny Parsons, in a Chevy, won the 1978 Richmond 400. He averaged 80.304 mph on the .542-mile oval course and lapped every car in the field except Lenny Pond's Chevy, which finished second.

Who is the winningest driver in racing history? Is it Richard Petty, David Pearson, or Bobby Isaac?

The answer is Richard Petty of Randleman, North Carolina. From 1960 to February, 1977, Petty chalked up 180 NASCAR Grand National wins. Of these victories, 27 were amassed in 1967.

Teammates Wally Dallenbach and Gordon Johncock ran neck and neck down the final stretch of the 1977 Trentonian 200 for Indy-type cars. Who won the race?

Wally Dallenbach edged teammate Gordon Johncock by the slim margin of 8 seconds to win the 1977 Trentonian 200 for Indy-type cars.

The Austrian Grand Prix was won by an Australian racing car driver in 1977. Can you name him?

Alan Jones of Australia averaged 123.020 mph in his Shadow over 54 laps to win the Austrian Grand Prix in 1977. It was his first Formula-One victory.

Who was the NASCAR Champion in 1977? Was it Cale Yarborough, Buddy Baker, or Benny Parsons?

Cale Yarborough was the 1977 National Association for Stock-Car Auto Racing Champion.

True or false? Stock-car driver Benny Parsons has won over a million dollars in prize money during his racing career.

True. With the winning of the $250,000 Charlotte National 500 in 1977, Parsons passed the million-dollar mark in career earnings.

Can you name the men who finished first and second in the 1978 Daytona 500?

Bobby Allison, in a Thunderbird, finished first in the 1978 Daytona 500, and Cale Yarborough, in an Oldsmobile, finished second. Allison's victory came after 18 unsuccessful attempts to win the famed Florida race.

What is the distance over which most drag strips are timed? Is it a quarter of a mile, a half-mile, or a mile?

Most drag strips are timed over a distance of a quarter of a mile. The car that travels a quarter-mile in the shortest elapsed time wins the drag meet.

In what year was the Monaco Grand Prix run for the first time? Was it in 1929, 1935, or 1938?

The Monaco Grand Prix, which is run through the streets and around the harbor of Monte Carlo, was run for the first time on April 14, 1929. This race is generally considered to be the most difficult on the Grand Prix circuit because of its 11 pronounced corners and sharp grade changes. Its 2.058-mile length is run over 78 laps, totaling 160.522 miles.

How many starting positions are there in the Indianapolis 500? Are there 30, 33, or 35 starting positions?

There are 33 starting positions in the Indy 500. To earn one of those positions, drivers must compete in qualification trials, which are held prior to the race. The 33 fastest cars in those trials are then allowed to compete in the race.

Which famous stock-car driver is nicknamed "The Silver Fox"?

David Pearson, the racing grandfather from Spartanburg, North Carolina, is known as "The Silver Fox." Pearson, who won the Firecracker 400 at Daytona in 1978, is one of NASCAR's all-time winning drivers.

Who holds the all-time USAC money-earning record for a single season? Is it Mario Andretti, A.J. Foyt, or Al Unser?

Al Unser is the record holder. In 1970, he won $494,149, to set the money-earning mark for a season. Unser's earnings of $397,583 in early 1978 may enable him to top his own record.

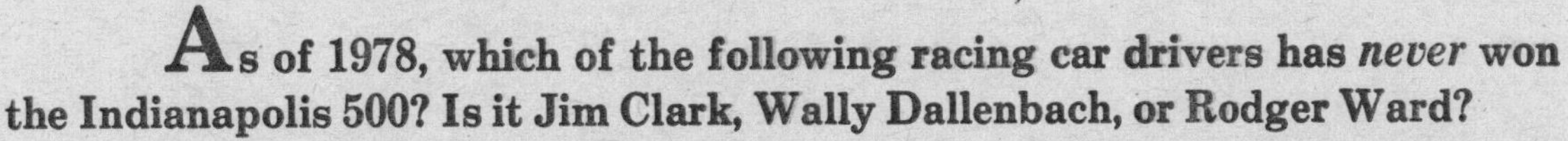

As of 1978, which of the following racing car drivers has *never* won the Indianapolis 500? Is it Jim Clark, Wally Dallenbach, or Rodger Ward?

Wally Dallenbach has never won the Indy 500. Jim Clark was victorious at Indianapolis in 1965, and Rodger Ward won the 500-mile race twice, in 1959 and again in 1962.

In which country were the first automobile races held? Was it France, the United States, or Great Britain?

The first important auto race was held in France, from Paris to Rouen, in 1894. It was won by a steam car with an average speed of 11 miles per hour. The following year, a round-trip race between Paris and Bordeaux saw the average speed climb to a "mighty" 15.01 miles per hour with the addition of a 3½ hp engine.

True or false? No major American city has ever allowed an auto race to be run through its downtown streets.

False. The Long Beach Grand Prix, an annual event since 1976, is run on the city streets of Long Beach, California. In this 200-mile race, Formula-One cars race over a 2.02-mile course through the center of town, which has been cleared of normal traffic.

Can you match the following "firsts" with their appropriate dates in auto racing history?

(1) The first Grand Prix race was held on a small, closed road course at LeMans, France	**(a) 1896**
(2) The first automobile track race was held at Providence, Rhode Island	**(b) 1911**
(3) The first Indianapolis 500 took place	**(c) 1906**

The correct answers are: (1) c. The first Grand Prix race was held on a small, closed road course at LeMans, France, in 1906. (2) a. The first automobile track race was held at Providence, Rhode Island, in 1896. And (3) b. The first Indianapolis 500 took place in 1911.

The first Long Beach Grand Prix was run in 1976. Was the winner Mario Andretti, Clay Regazzoni, or Dan Gurney?

Swiss racer Clay Regazzoni won the 1976 Long Beach Grand Prix, averaging over 85.5 mph. Mario Andretti took top honors the following year in 1977. Dan Gurney, however, was not the driver, but rather the designer of the course used in the Long Beach Grand Prix.

What was the world's longest rally race?

The 1977 Singapore Airlines London to Sydney Rally, which covered a distance of 19,329 miles, was the world's longest rally event. It started on August 14, 1977, passed through 17 countries, and ended on September 28. The winners were Michael Broad, Andrew Cowan, and Colin Malkin, driving a Mercedes 280E.

Who was the American Motorcycle Association's Grand Champion in 1975? Was it Gary Scott or Joe Smith?

Gary Scott of Springfield, Ohio, was motorcycle racing's 1975 Grand Champion. Joe Smith of West Covina, California, was the National Drag Racing Champion in the Pro Bike Class that same year.

The first motorcycle race was held on an oval track at Sheen House, Richmond, Surrey, England. Was it held in 1887, 1897, or 1905?

The first motorcycle race was held on November 29, 1897. It was won by Charles Jarrott on a Fournier.

What is the highest speed ever achieved by a motorcycle? Is it 298.692 mph, 307.692 mph, or 311.692 mph?

Riding his 21-foot-long *Silver Bird* Streamliner, powered by two 750cc Yamaha TZ750 4-cylinder engines, Don Vesco of California set the motorcycle speed record on September 28, 1975. Vesco covered a flying quarter mile at the Bonneville Salt Falts in Utah in 2.925 seconds, which is a speed of 307.692 mph.

In 1977, an American took the World Formula 750 Road Race Championship for the first time in forty years. Who was that driver?

Young Steve Baker of Bellingham, Washington, powered his big, sleek Formula-750 Yamaha into 7 wins, 2 seconds, and 1 third in 11 international races in Europe, the U.S.A., and Canada in 1977. He thus became the first American champ in forty years and earned $150,000 in purse money for the year.

Mike Hailwood and Giacomo Agostini share the record for winning the most championship races in one year. How many races did they win to set the record?

The answer is 19. Mike Hailwood of England won 19 championship races in 1966 to set the record, and Giacomo Agostini of Italy equaled that record in 1970.

Who was the 1977 winner of the AMA Grand National (Camel Pro) Series? Was it Gary Scott, Jay Springsteen, or Ted Boody?

Jay Springsteen of Lapeer, Michigan, drove his Harley-Davidson for 260 points, to take the 1977 AMA Grand National title.

The record for the highest average lap speed attained in any closed circuit is held by Yvon du Hamel of Canada. How fast did he go to set the record? Was it 150.288 mph, 160.288 mph, or 170.288 mph?

In March, 1973, at Daytona International Speedway, Yvon du Hamel went 160.288 mph to set the record. He was riding a 903cc four-cyclinder Kawasaki 21, and his lap time for the 2.5-mile course was 56.149 seconds.

Hermann-Peter Muller of West Germany was the oldest man to ever win a motorcycling world championship title. Can you guess how old he was when he accomplished that feat?

Hermann-Peter Muller was 46 years old when he won the 250cc title in 1955.

Giacomo Agostini of Italy is one of the most famous motorcyclists in world competition. How many World Championships did he win as of 1977?

Giacomo Agostini set a world's record by winning 15 World Championship titles up to 1977. He won the 350cc Class title every year from 1968 to 1974, and the 500cc Class title consecutively from 1966 to 1972, and again in 1975.

True or false? The only time Joe Leonard was the Grand National Champion of Motorcycling was in 1954.

False. Joe Leonard won the Grand National Championship in 1954 and repeated as the Grand National Champion in 1956 and 1957.

How is the Grand National Champion of Motorcycle Racing chosen?

The American Motorcycle Association sponsors a number of races annually. Points are awarded for official races for first- to sixth-place finishes. The racer with the most points at the end of the year is named the Grand National Champion.

In order to get to motorcycle racing's big leagues, a driver must make it through three levels. What are these levels?

A pro driver is classified a Novice during his first year. When he accumulates 40 points, he reaches the Junior level. Another 40 points qualifies him as an Expert — the level at which he is eligible to enter the toughest and most important races.

True or false? In motorcylcling, *official* world speed records are set by a single run over a measured distance within a time limit.

False. *Official* world speed records must be set with *two* runs over a measured distance within a time limit. That time limit is one hour for *Federation Internationale Motorcyclist* records and two hours for American Motorcycle Association records.

Who was the youngest driver to win a World Championship?

Alberto "Johnny" Cecotto of Caracas, Venezuela, holds that honor. He was only 19 when he won the 350cc title in 1975.

Although flat-track racing is the most popular type of motorcyle racing today, *motocross* is steadily gaining favor with many racers. What is motocross?

Motocross is racing over natural terrain.

BASEBALL

What is a *shoe-string* catch?

A *shoe-string* catch is made when a fielder bends very low to snare a ball on the fly before it touches the ground. Usually shoe-string catches are made on line drives hit to the outfield.

The major league's single-game attendance record was set on April 18, 1958 at Dodger Stadium in Los Angeles. Who did the Dodgers play that day?

A total of 78,672 fans came to Dodger Stadium that April day to watch their team play the San Francisco Giants in the game which set the single-game major league attendance record.

Are the Seattle Mariners in the National League or the American League?

The Seattle Mariners are in the West Division of the American League, along with the Texas Rangers, the California Angels, the Kansas City Royals, the Chicago White Sox, the Minnesota Twins, and the Oakland Athletics.

Which player holds the New York Mets' record for hitting the most home runs in a season? Is it Dave Kingman, Willie Mays, or Cleon Jones?

Dave Kingman, currently with the Chicago Cubs, holds the Mets' record for homers in a single season. Kingman hit 37 round-trippers in 1976 to establish the mark.

If a player is said to have *rabbit ears,* what does that mean in baseball jargon?

Having *rabbit ears* is baseball slang for a player who listens to what fans or opposing players shout at him while he is playing. This can destroy a player's concentration, disturb him, and sometimes make him angry — thus distracting him from playing his best.

Can you name the managers of the two teams that played in the 1977 World Series?

The Los Angeles Dodgers, Champions of the National League in 1977, were managed by Tom Lasorda. The New York Yankees, the winners of the American League Pennant and the World Series, were managed by Billy Martin.

Roger Maris of the New York Yankees hit 61 homers to establish a baseball record for the most round-trippers in a single season. How many times did Maris lead the AL in home runs?

Roger Maris was the American League home-run king only once — in 1961, the year in which he belted his record-breaking 61 home runs.

How did Larry Berra get nicknamed "Yogi"?

Because of his short, squat build, Berra has been the butt of teasing for many years. But it was in grade school in St. Louis that a classmate said he walked a *yogi*—someone who practiced yoga, though it is almost certain that none of the kids, childhood friend Joe Garagiola included, had any idea how a yogi walked, or, for that matter, even what a yogi was. Still, the name stuck, and Berra even used it on his marriage license!

Babe Ruth is one of the most famous men to ever play the game of baseball. What was Babe's full name?

Babe Ruth's full name was George Herman Ruth.

Who won the 1978 one-game playoff for the championship of the AL's East Division between the New York Yankees and the Boston Red Sox?

The New York Yankees won the playoff game for the American League Pennant by beating the Red Sox by the slim margin of 5 to 4.

The 1979 publication of *The Bronx Zoo* ruffled many feathers in the New York Yankee organization. Who wrote that exposé of the behind-the-scene happenings of the Bronx Bombers?

Sparky Lyle, currently a Texas Ranger, caused a sensation with the March, 1979, publication of his book, in which he "told all" about his former Bronx teammates and bosses.

True or false? Stan "The Man" Musial began his professional baseball career in the minor leagues as a southpaw pitcher.

True. Musial pitched in the minor leagues from 1938 to 1940 and did well on the mound as well as at the plate. But in August, 1940, with a batting average of .369 and 17 wins as a pitcher, Musial injured his shoulder making a diving catch and was never able to pitch again. He was moved into the outfield, and in late 1941 brought up to the parent club, the St. Louis Cardinals, where he hit .426 for the remainder of the season. In only his second season with the Cards, Musial led the National League with a BA of .357, and quickly established himself as one of the greatest hitters in the history of baseball.

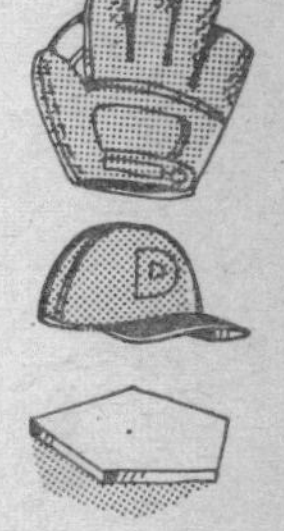

If some baseball players are having a *pepper game*, what are they doing?

They are having an informal hitting and fielding drill. *Pepper*, a fun way to practice, is used by major league and amateur ball players alike. In a pepper game, several fielders line up relatively close to one batter and face him. One of the fielders throws a ball to the batter, who hits it gently so it can be fielded by one of the players in the game. After the ball is caught, it's thrown back to the batter and the process is repeated again and again.

Who was the 1978 Commissioner of Baseball?

Bowie Kuhn was the Baseball Commissioner in 1978. As Commissioner, he oversees all teams in the National and American Leagues, enforces all rules and regulations, and remedies any disputes. The former lawyer was appointed to the job in 1969.

Joltin' Joe DiMaggio holds the major league record for hitting safely in the most consecutive games — 56. Did DiMaggio set that record in 1938, 1941, or 1943?

Joe DiMaggio of the New York Yankees hit safely in 56 straight games in 1941, to set a record which may never be broken.

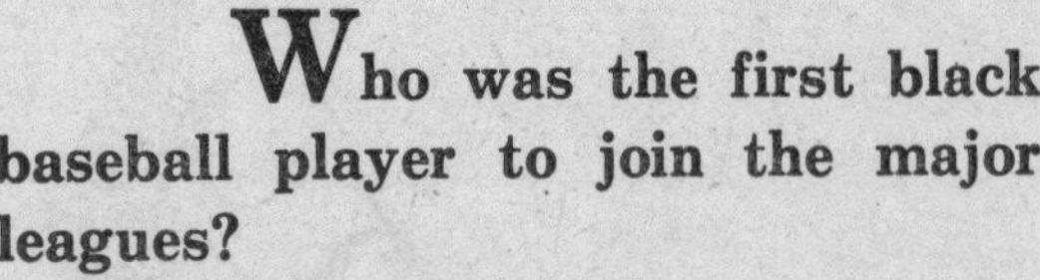

Who was the first black baseball player to join the major leagues?

The first black baseball player to break the color barrier and play in the major leagues was Jackie Robinson. A former UCLA star, Robbie had been signed to play in the Brooklyn farm system in 1945 in a shrewd and visionary move by Dodger boss Branch Rickey. After sparking Montreal of the International League to a pennant in 1946, the 28-year-old Robinson was brought up to the Dodgers in 1947, where he soon established himself as a big-league great. Versatile at first, second, and third bases and the outfield, Robbie won Rookie of the Year honors that year and later went on to win an NL batting championship (1949), a berth on many All-Star teams, and the MVP Award (1949).

If there is a runner on first base and a coach tells the next hitter to *sacrifice*, what is he telling that batter to do?

He is telling him to bunt the ball to the infield in order to advance the runner on first base to second. By *sacrificing* himself, permitting himself to be thrown out, he is placing the runner in a better scoring position.

Are you a baseball fan who understands baseball slang? What does it mean if someone says a player *pulled a rock*?

In baseball slang, *pulling a rock* means that the player has made a stupid play.

Rod Carew's .388 batting average in 1977 made him the American League's leading hitter. Which team did Carew play for?

The Minnesota Twins benefited from Rod Carew's 239 hits in 616 times at bat, giving him an amazing .388 batting average.

In what year were pitchers allowed to use a resin bag for the first time? Was it 1890, 1925, or 1930?

The resin bag was first legalized for baseball pitchers in 1925. It dries the pitcher's hand, making his palm sticky and allowing him to get a good grip on the ball.

When Lou Gehrig entered the Yankee line-up on June 2, 1925, he replaced a veteran first baseman who was ill. Can you name that Yankee first baseman?

Lou Gehrig replaced veteran Yankee first baseman Wally Pipp, who had led the American League in home runs in 1916 and 1917. When Pipp complained of a headache before the game that day, Yankee manager Miller Huggins gave him the afternoon off and inserted the young rookie, Lou Gehrig, in Pipp's place in the line-up — a place Gehrig held for a record 2,130 consecutive games.

Try your baseball slang on this one. What do baseball players call the hand on which they *don't* wear a glove?

Baseball players refer to it as *the meat hand.*

Who was the first man to assemble an all-professional baseball team? Was it Alexander Cartwright, Abner Doubleday, or Harry Wright? Here's a hint. The team was known as the Cincinnati Red Stockings.

The answer is Harry Wright, who organized the Cincinnati Red Stockings in 1869. It was the first time anyone had ever paid an entire team of baseball players just to play the game. That year, the Red Stockings won 80 games in a row before losing one.

Where is the Baseball Hall of Fame located?

The National Baseball Hall of Fame and Museum, the shrine of organized baseball, is located in Cooperstown, New York — the town where the game is believed to have been invented by Abner Doubleday. Early balls, bats, and gloves are displayed in the museum, as well as photographs and famous paintings of baseball scenes. The Hall of Fame is hung with plaques of the players immortalized there, as well as with uniforms and equipment of these stars.

True or false? Babe Ruth began his major league baseball career as a pitcher for the Boston Red Sox.

True. Babe Ruth joined the Red Sox in 1914 after a brief stint in the minor leagues. He was a successful pitcher for Boston, and in 1916 was the best left-handed hurler in the major leagues, with a 23-12 record. He later moved into the outfield in 1919.

In which National League stadium is it easier to hit a home run — Atlanta Stadium, the home of the Atlanta Braves, or Jarry Park, the home of the Montreal Expos?

Atlanta Stadium is the easier of the two fields for home-run hitters. Both the right- and left-field fences are 10' shorter in Atlanta than in Montreal (330' as opposed to 340'), and the centerfield fence is 18' shorter as well (402' as compared to 420').

The St. Louis Cardinals and the Philadelphia Phillies played the longest night game in the history of baseball. True or false?

False. The longest night game in the history of baseball, a 25-inning contest, was between the St. Louis Cardinals and the New York Mets at Shea Stadium in New York on September 11, 1974. After 7 hours and 4 minutes, the Cardinals beat the Mets by the score of 4 to 3.

Only two sluggers have ever received more than 2,000 bases on balls. Can you name them?

The mighty Babe Ruth drew 2,056 walks and Ted Williams, 2,018.

Jimmy Piersall, a great but zany outfielder for the Boston Red Sox and the Cleveland Indians, had his life story made into a motion picture. Do you remember the name of that movie?

The 1957 movie was *Fear Strikes Out*, starring Anthony Perkins as Jimmy Piersall. The movie dealt with the emotional pressure Piersall experienced as he tried to make it in the major leagues and his eventual mental breakdown and recovery.

In order to win baseball's Triple Crown, what must a player do?

A Triple Crown winner in baseball has to lead his league for the season in runs batted in and home runs, and must have the highest batting average.

Who holds the National League record for the highest season batting average? Is it Hugh Duffy, Rogers Hornsby, or Stan Musial?

Hugh Duffy of the old Boston Red Stockings holds the NL record. In 1894, Duffy batted a hefty .438 — a BA that has never been topped. Rogers Hornsby of the St. Louis Cardinals had the second highest BA ever, hitting a resounding .424 in 1924. Stan Musial's highest season average was .376 in 1948.

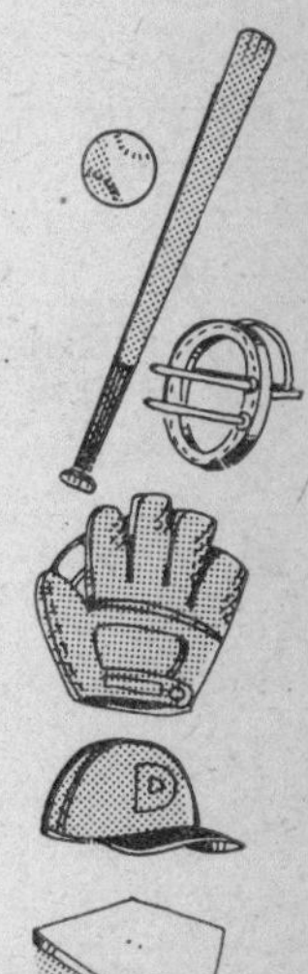

Did any 1978 major league team have more than one 20-game winner?

Yes. The only team in either league with more than one 20-game winner in 1978 was the New York Yankees, who had two: Ron Guidry, with a 24-3 record, and Ed Figueroa, with a 20-9 record.

Tinkers to Evers to Chance were a famous double-play combination. For which team did they play?

Shortstop Joe Tinkers, second baseman Johnny Evers, and first baseman Frank Chance played for the National League's Chicago Cubs in the early 1900s. They were probably the hottest double-play combination in the history of baseball.

Home-run king Babe Ruth led the American League in batting five times. True or false?

False. Babe Ruth led the American League in batting only once. During his 1924 season with the New York Yankees, Ruth had a .378 average, which was tops in the league, and also won the home-run title with 46 round-trippers that year.

Can you name the fabulous old-time baseball brothers who were nicknamed "Big Poison" and "Little Poison"?

Outfielders Paul and Lloyd Waner of the 1920s' Pittsburgh Pirates were nicknamed "Big Poison" and "Little Poison" because they were such good hitters that they were "poison" to opposing pitchers. "Big Poison" Paul Waner was more of a long-ball threat, while "Little Poison" Lloyd Waner consistently sprayed hits all over the field.

Only one man in the history of baseball has ever pitched two no-hitters in a row. Can you name that famous hurler?

The answer is Johnny Vander Meer of the Cincinnati Reds, who no-hit the Boston Braves and the Brooklyn Dodgers back to back on June 11 and June 15, 1938.

The Philadelphia Phillies and the Los Angeles Dodgers, champions of their respective divisions in 1978, met in a best-of-5 playoff for the National League Pennant. Which team won it?

The Los Angeles Dodgers won the 1978 National League Pennant for the second year in a row. They beat the Philadelphia Phillies, 3 games to 1, in the playoffs.

Who was the youngest player to ever put on a major league uniform?

Pitcher Joe Nuxhall holds that record. When he joined the Cincinnati Reds in June, 1944, Nuxhall was only 15 years, 10 months, and 11 days old.

Can you name the pitcher who holds the record for getting the most consecutive hits? No hints on this one, baseball buffs.

It's Don Larsen, the Yankee pitcher who also has a World Series no-hitter to his credit. Larsen was an excellent hitter for a pitcher and once got 7 consecutive hits — a major league record for a pitcher.

True or false? Babe Ruth never spent a season in the major leagues without hitting at least 10 home runs.

False. During his first four years with the Boston Red Sox as a pitcher, Babe Ruth hit a *total* of only 9 home runs: none in 1914, 4 in 1915, 3 in 1916, and 2 in 1917.

In marking a baseball score card, what does a "K" stand for?

"K" is a baseball symbol that means a strikeout.

Which award is given annually to the best pitcher in the major leagues?

The answer is the Cy Young Award, named after Denton T. "Cyclone" Young, one of baseball's all-time great pitchers who chalked up more winning seasons than any other pitcher in the history of baseball. From 1956, when the Award was established, until 1966, the Cy Young Award was given to the best pitcher in all baseball. But from 1967 on, two Cy Young Awards have been given: one to the best pitcher in the National League and one to the top hurler in the American League.

From 1965 to 1969, three second basemen were voted the National League's Rookie of the Year. Can you name those three?

In 1965, second baseman Jim Lefebvre of the Los Angeles Dodgers won the Rookie of the Year Award. In 1966, Tommy Helms, who starred at second for the Cincinnati Reds, took top rookie honors. Then in 1969, second sacker Ted Sizemore of the Los Angeles Dodgers was named the best rookie in the National League.

Which slugger belted more home runs in World Series play — Babe Ruth or Mickey Mantle?

It's Mickey Mantle of the New York Yankees. Mantle hit a record-setting total of 18 homers in World Series play. Babe Ruth is second, with 15 World Series homers as a Red Sox and Yankee.

True or false? No pitcher has ever won Cy Young Awards in both the National and American Leagues.

False. That feat was accomplished for the first time in 1978 when Gaylord Perry of the San Diego Padres won the National League's Cy Young Award. Perry had previously won the American League's Cy Young Award in 1972, while pitching for the Cleveland Indians.

A New York Yankee pitcher holds the World Series record for the most victories. Can you name him?

That record holder is Edward C. "Whitey" Ford. The left-hander chalked up 10 World Series victories (1 in 1950, 2 in 1955, 1 in 1956, 1 in 1957, 2 in 1960, 2 in 1961, and 1 in 1962) to establish that record.

Who was the Most Valuable Player of the 1978 World Series between the Los Angeles Dodgers and the New York Yankees? Was it Reggie Jackson, Jim "Catfish" Hunter, or Bucky Dent?

The Baseball Writers and *Sport Magazine* named Yankee shortstop Bucky Dent the MVP of the 1978 World Series. Dent got 10 hits in 24 at bats for a .417 average, scored 3 runs, and batted in 7 runs.

Why is a baseball field called a *diamond*?

A baseball field is called a *diamond* because the four bases are laid out in a tilted square which, when viewed from above or from a distance, does, indeed, resemble a diamond.

The cry of "Ya' gotta believe!" was the slogan of a National League team that went on to win the pennant after being in last place in their division in mid-July. Which team was it?

"Ya' gotta believe!" was the slogan of the 1973 New York Mets. It was coined by Met star relief pitcher Tug McGraw in mid-July, when the team was in last place, but still within striking distance of the pennant. Once McGraw uttered the phrase, it was immediately adopted by loyal Met fans. During the next four weeks, the Mets "believed" and went on to win 21 out of 29 games on their way to their division title. The "Amazing Mets" later defeated the Cincinnati Reds in the playoffs to win the National League Pennant.

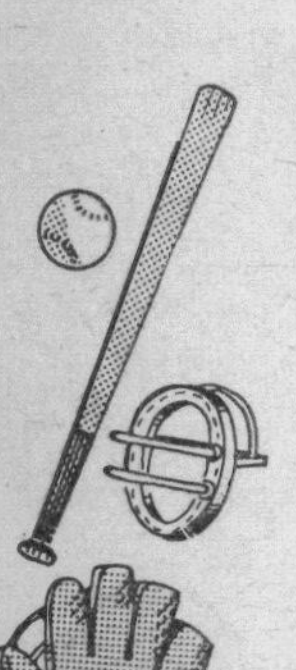

Cy Young was one of baseball's greatest pitchers, but "Cy" was only a nickname. Do you know how he got it?

Born Denton Tecumseh Young on an Ohio farm, pitcher Young made his first start for the Cleveland Indians on August 6, 1890. He threw the ball so hard and so fast that he soon earned himself the nickname of "Cyclone." Eventually, "Cyclone" was shortened to "Cy," and that's how Denton T. Young became known as Cy Young.

Former singing cowboy star Gene Autry owns a major league baseball team. Do you know which one?

Gene Autry traded his horse for a baseball team when he became the principal owner of the American League's California Angels.

Was there ever a major league game in which each player on one team had the same batting average after the game as he had before it?

The answer is yes. Here's how it happened. On the opening day of the 1940 season, pitcher Bob Feller of the Cleveland Indians threw a no-hitter against the Chicago White Sox. It was the only opening day no-hitter in the history of baseball. Since all of the players on the White Sox had a .000 batting average before the game and got no hits during the game, their averages after the game were still .000.

Ralph Kiner, the play-by-play announcer for the New York Mets, holds the Pittsburgh Pirates' team record for home runs in a single season. True or false?

True. Ralph Kiner, a powerful slugger, knocked 54 balls over the fence in 1949, to set the Pirates' record for homers in a single season.

Third baseman Graig Nettles has played for three American League teams during his twelve-year major league career. Can you name those teams?

Graig Nettles, the number-4 draft pick of the Minnesota Twins in 1965, played for the Twins from 1967 to 1969. From 1970 to 1972, he played for the Cleveland Indians, and in November, 1972, he was traded to the New York Yankees, where he was still playing as of 1978. Nettles took the American League's Home Run Championship in 1976, with 39 round-trippers.

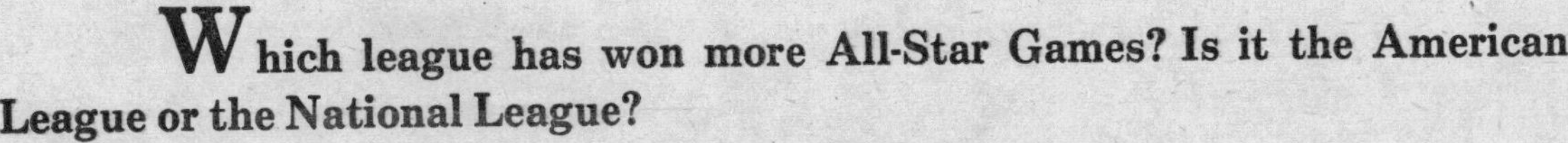

Which league has won more All-Star Games? Is it the American League or the National League?

The National League has won more All-Star Games, with 30 victories to the American League's 18. From 1963 to 1978, the NL has been victorious in 15 out of 16 contests. Of the 49 games played, only one, the 1961 All-Star Game, ended in a tie when rain stopped play.

In which state was the first game of team baseball, as we know it, played? Was it New York, New Jersey, or California?

The first game of team baseball, as we know it, was played at Elysian Field in Hoboken, New Jersey, on June 19, 1846. The game was between the Knickerbockers and the New York Nine. The Knickerbockers lost the game by the score of 23 to 1, in four innings.

Pitcher Jim Hunter of the New York Yankees is known to most baseball fans by his nickname. Do you know it?

Hunter is known to most baseball fans as "Catfish," a nickname given him by Charles Finley, owner of the Oakland Athletics — the team Hunter played for from 1964 to 1973.

Can you name the baseball immortal who was nicknamed "The Iron Horse"?

Lou Gehrig of the New York Yankees was nicknamed "The Iron Horse," because as a steady player he seemed indestructible. During 14 major league seasons from June 1, 1925 to April 30, 1939, Gehrig played in 2,130 consecutive games, making nearly 8,000 appearances at the plate. At last, on May 2, 1939, Lou Gehrig removed himself from the Yankee line-up because of the rare and incurable nerve disease that was creeping up on him. A little more than two years later, at the age of thirty-eight, Gehrig tragically died of that disease.

Can you name the colorful American League pitcher who is nicknamed "The Bird"? Here's a little help. He's a member of the Detroit Tigers.

Pitcher Mark Fidrych of the Detroit Tigers is known as "The Bird" to most baseball buffs. His eccentric antics on the mound, like getting down on his hands and knees to smooth out the dirt around the pitcher's rubber or occasionally chirping like a bird, delight fans all across the country. He got his nickname because of his slight resemblance to the "Big Bird" character on TV's *Sesame Street*.

Outfielder Al Kaline of the Detroit Tigers spent two years in the minor leagues before moving up to the majors, where he stayed for two decades. True or false?

False. Al Kaline *never* played baseball in the minors. He was signed by the Tigers in 1953 and was good enough to play for the parent club even though he was still a teen-ager. In his first year with Detroit, the 6-foot 1-inch, 185-pound slugger hit only .250, but his 20-year career average is over .300.

Can you name the first black manager in major league baseball? Here's a hint. He managed the Cleveland Indians.

In 1975, Frank Robinson, a former Cincinnati Red and Baltimore Oriole, became the first black manager in major league baseball when he joined the Cleveland Indians.

For which manager did the New York Yankees win the most games in a single season? Was it Miller Huggins, Casey Stengel, or Ralph Houk?

The 1927 Yankees gave manager Miller Huggins a record 110 wins and only 44 losses. Under Casey Stengel, the Yankees' best year was 1953, when they were 99 and 52. Ralph Houk's best year as manager was in 1961, when the Bronx Bombers had a record of 109 and 53.

Which National League baseball team did Sparky Anderson manage in 1978?

In 1978, Sparky Anderson was the manager of the Cincinnati Reds.

What is a *change-of-pace* pitch?

A *change of pace*, or *change-up*, is a slow pitch intended to upset the hitter's timing. It is generally much slower than the pitcher's normal speed and is usually thrown after several fast pitches.

True or false? Jose Cardenal of the Chicago Cubs and Bert Campaneris of the Oakland A's are related.

True. Jose Cardenal and Bert Campaneris are cousins.

BASEBALL

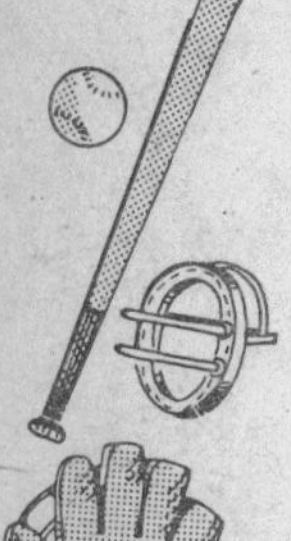

One of the most extraordinary fiascos to occur during a World Series game took place during the 1934 Series when a St. Louis Cardinal player was bombarded by Detroit fans with garbage and bottles as he took the field at Tiger Stadium. Who was that Cardinal?

It was Joe "Ducky" Medwick. Before taking the field, Medwick had hit a triple and as he flew into third base, he knocked over Tiger third sacker Marv Owen. A long heated argument followed, almost resulting in a fight between Medwick and Owen. Later, when Medwick took the field, the Tiger fans showed their displeasure with garbage and bottles, and Medwick had to be removed from the game for his own safety.

How close was the balloting among Gaylord Perry, Vida Blue, and Burt Hooton for the National League's Cy Young Award in 1978?

With a season record of 21 wins and only 6 losses, Gaylord Perry of the San Diego Padres was voted the 1978 Cy Young Award by the Baseball Writers Association by a landslide total of 116 points. Burt Hooton of the Los Angeles Dodgers, who won 19 games and lost 10, was second with 38 points, and Vida Blue of the San Francisco Giants, with an 18 and 10 record, finished third with 17 points.

Who was the National League's Most Valuable Player in 1977?

Left fielder George Foster of the Cincinnati Reds was named the senior league's 1977 MVP by the Baseball Writers Association of America. Foster hit 52 home runs, batted .320, and led the league in RBIs, with 149, and in runs scored, with 124.

Who holds the major league record for stealing the most bases in a single season? Is it Maury Wills, Lou Brock, or Ty Cobb?

Lou Brock of the St. Louis Cardinals stole more bases in a single season than any other baseball player. His 118 bases, stolen in 153 games in 1974, set the record. Brock also established a new lifetime record for stolen bases with 900. This record, which he set between 1961 and 1977 while a Chicago Cub and St. Louis Cardinal, broke Ty Cobb's old record of 892.

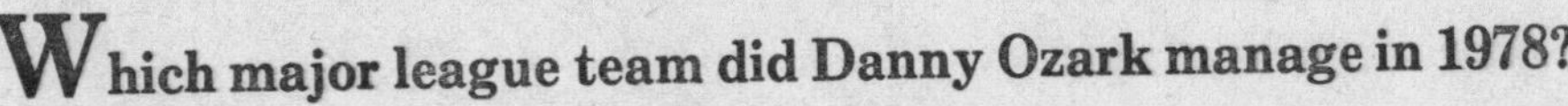
Which major league team did Danny Ozark manage in 1978?

Danny Ozark was the 1978 manager of the National League East's Philadelphia Phillies, the team he led to three consecutive division titles in 1976, 1977, and 1978.

True or false? The New York Mets have always played all of their home games at Shea Stadium.

False. In 1962 and 1963, the newborn New York Mets played their home games at the old Polo Grounds in New York, the former home of the New York Giants. In 1964, when demolition started on the Polo Grounds, the Mets moved to the newly built Shea Stadium.

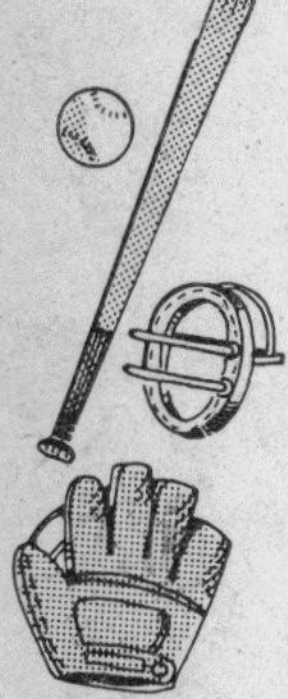

Only two players in the history of baseball ever got 7 hits in a regular 9-inning game. One was Wilbert Robinson of the old NL Baltimore Orioles, who did it in 1892 with 6 singles and 1 double. Who was the other?

Rennie Stennett of the 1975 Pittsburgh Pirates duplicated Robinson's feat with 4 singles, 2 doubles, and 1 triple, for a 7-hit total in a 9-inning game. The record for an extra-inning game is held by John Burnett of the 1932 Cleveland Indians. In an 18-inning game, Burnett banged out 7 singles and 2 doubles, for a total of 9 hits.

Has any major league manager had pennant-winning teams in both leagues?

The only manager to accomplish this was Joe McCarthy, who had a pennant-winner with the NL's Chicago Cubs in 1929 and then went on to win 8 pennants (1932, 1936-1939, and 1941-1943) piloting the AL's New York Yankees.

Eddie Collins batted .300 or better sixteen times during his 19-year major league career. What position did Collins play?

Edward Trowbridge Collins was a second baseman for the Chicago White Sox and the old Philadelphia Athletics.

Every baseball fan has heard the story of how Babe Ruth pointed to a spot in the right-field stands during the 1932 World Series and then belted a home run that landed in that exact spot. But are you one of the few baseball fans who can name the Chicago Cub pitcher who threw Ruth's famous "called shot"?

That Cub pitcher was right-hander Charlie Root. Babe's homer came in the 5th inning of the 3rd game of the 1932 Series, which the Yankees won in four straight games.

What is the difference between a *wild pitch* and a *passed ball*?

Both terms refer to a pitched ball that gets away from the catcher, allowing a runner to advance to the next base. The difference is in *who* gets blamed for the advance. A *wild pitch* is considered to be the pitcher's fault, and he is charged with an error on his throw. However, if the pitch is good and the ball gets away from the catcher, it is scored a *passed ball*, and the catcher gets the error, since he should have caught the ball that he allowed to get past him.

Which modern-day team holds the major league record for the most losses in a season?

During their first season as a club, 1962, the New York Mets piled up a disastrous 120 losses and only 40 wins.

Which baseball manager once said, "Nice guys finish last!"?

The brash, quick tongue of Leo Durocher, famed Dodger manager, spoke those "immortal" words.

Did the New York Yankees ever win an American League Pennant while Yogi Berra was their manager?

Yes. Under Yogi Berra, the Yankees won the AL pennant in 1964 with a record of 99 wins and 64 losses. However, they lost the World Series to the St. Louis Cardinals that year, 4 games to 3.

Which American League baseball stadium has the deepest outfield fences?

Comiskey Park, the home field of the Chicago White Sox, has the deepest outfield fences. The distance from home to the left-field and right-field fences is 352 feet, and from home to the centerfield fence, the distance is 440 feet.

Only one active player on the 1978 Mets' roster was a member of the original Mets when they were formed in 1962. Can you name that player?

Reserve first baseman Ed Kranepool has been a member of the Mets since their formation in 1962. Kranepool, a native New Yorker who was born in the Bronx, was only 18 years old when he first put on a Met uniform.

Where did Little League Baseball begin? Was it in New Jersey, New York, or Pennsylvania?

Little League Baseball began in Williamsport, Pennsylvania, in 1939 to govern baseball teams for players 8 to 12 years old from the U.S., Canada, Europe, Latin America, and the Far East. Today, over 2½ million children play on the more than 60,000 teams throughout the world.

Which great New York baseball player was nicknamed "The Yankee Clipper"?

Center fielder Joe DiMaggio of the New York Yankees, who glided through the outfield like a sleek sailing ship, was nicknamed "The Yankee Clipper." In his fifteen years with the Yankees, DiMag collected 2,214 hits, 361 HRs, and a lifetime BA of .325.

The only rookie ever to be named the American League's Most Valuable Player won the Award in 1975 when he joined the Boston Red Sox. Do you remember who he was?

Red Sox rookie outfielder Fred Lynn, who finished the 1975 season with 105 RBIs, 21 homers, and a .331 batting average, earned the AL's MVP Award and Rookie of the Year honors.

What is the distance between the bases on a baseball field? Is it 60 feet, 75 feet, or 90 feet?

A distance of 90 feet separates the bases.

On May 1, 1920, the Brooklyn Dodgers and the Boston Braves played the longest game in baseball history in terms of innings. How many innings did that record-breaking game last and which team finally won?

That historic 1920 game lasted 26 innings and ended with the score tied, 1 to 1. The game was played at Braves Field in Boston and was finally called because of darkness 3 hours and 50 minutes after it had started. When it ended, the starting pitchers for both clubs were still in the game: Leon Cadore for Brooklyn and Joe Oeschger for the Braves.

Who was the youngest player to ever win an American League batting title?

The correct answer is Al Kaline of the Detroit Tigers. Kaline was only 20 years old in 1955 when he won the AL batting title with a BA of .340. This was only the star outfielder's third year with the Tigers, having joined the team in 1953 at age 18.

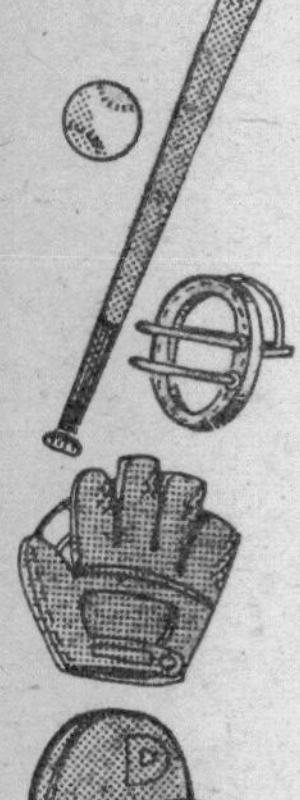

How did the New York Yankees obtain Babe Ruth from the Boston Red Sox? Did Ruth play out his option with Boston and sign with the Yanks? Did the Yanks trade other players for Babe? Or did the Yankees buy his contract?

The Yankees bought Babe Ruth's contract from the Red Sox on December 26, 1919, paying the financially troubled Boston Red Sox $100,000, plus a loan of $385,000. At Ruth's insistence, his first-year salary with the Yankees was $20,000, twice what Boston had paid him the previous year.

Who holds the Braves' team record for hitting the most home runs in a season? Is it Eddie Mathews or Hank Aaron?

Eddie Mathews and Hank Aaron share the Braves' team record for homers. Mathews hit 47 home runs in 1953 while the team was still in Milwaukee, and Aaron matched his record in Atlanta in 1971. Mathews' 47 HRs also earned him the NL home-run crown in 1953.

True or false? Infielder-outfielder Ike Brown of the Detroit Tigers hit a home run in his first at bat in a major league game.

True. On June 17, 1969, in a game against the New York Yankees, Ike Brown came to the plate for the Tigers and homered in his first major league turn at bat.

True or false? Catcher Thurman Munson has never played for any other major league baseball team except the Yankees.

True. Thurman Lee "Squatty" Munson has worn a Yankee uniform every year of his ten-year major league career. In 1970, the Baseball Writers of America named the Yankee catcher the American League's Rookie of the Year, and in 1970 and '71, he led all AL catchers in assists and fielding.

Black players were always allowed to play in the major leagues. True or false?

False. Until 1947, racial prejudice kept black players out of major league baseball. However, many black baseball stars played professional ball in the Negro Baseball League, a poor country cousin of the American and National Leagues. The caliber of play in the Negro League was excellent, but the pay and playing conditions were far from good. Still, it produced such stars as outfielder Cool Papa Bell, catcher Josh Gibson, and pitcher Satchel Paige.

Chris Chambliss, the 1978 New York Yankees' first baseman, was originally a New York Met. True or false?

False. Chris Chambliss, a 6'1", 212-pound first baseman, was originally a member of the Cleveland Indians and their Rookie of the Year in 1971. A native New Yorker, Chambliss came to the Yankees via a trade with the Indians in April, 1974.

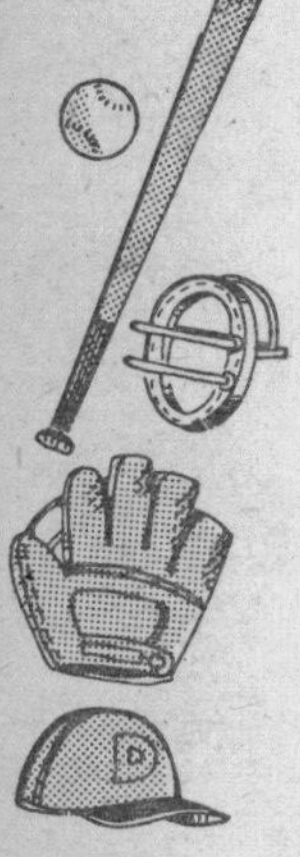

Which baseball team won the National League Pennant in 1977? Was it the Cincinnati Reds, the Los Angeles Dodgers, or the Philadelphia Phillies?

The Los Angeles Dodgers finished first in the National League's West Division and played the East Division Champion Philadelphia Phillies for the 1977 pennant. The Dodgers 3-game-to-1 win over the Phillies gave them the pennant.

As of 1978, can you guess how many times a major league baseball team from New York has won the World Championship? (That includes wins by the Giants, the Yankees, the Mets, and the Brooklyn Dodgers.)

New York baseball teams have won the World Series a total of 29 times as of 1978. Brooklyn won it once; the Mets, once; the Giants, 5 times; and the Yankees, 22 times.

On-deck batters sometimes use a *doughnut* to loosen up. What is a doughnut?

A *doughnut* is a rubber coated circular metal weight that slips onto a bat, making it heavier. Swinging a weighted bat while awaiting his turn at the plate makes the player's bat seem lighter and easier to handle when he's facing the pitcher. Before the invention of the doughnut, players used a hollow bat filled with lead or a lead bat to loosen up. The doughnut gives a batter the advantage of loosening up with the bat he plans to use when he's at the plate.

What is a *squeeze play*?

A *squeeze play* occurs only when there is a runner on third base. As soon as the pitcher starts his delivery toward the plate, the runner breaks for home at top speed. It is the batter's job to bunt the ball far enough away from the catcher to allow the runner to score safely. It is called a *squeeze play*, or a *suicide squeeze*, because if the batter misses the ball, the runner will most likely be tagged out.

Can you name the only baseball player to win the Most Valuable Player Award in both the American and National Leagues?

The answer is the great Frank Robinson, who later became the first black manager in the major leagues. In 1961, the Baseball Writers of America named Frank Robinson of the Cincinnati Reds the MVP of the National League. Five years later, while he was a member of the 1966 Baltimore Orioles, Robinson was voted the Most Valuable Player of the American League.

What position did Bill Mazeroski of the Pittsburgh Pirates play?

Bill Mazeroski, a dangerous hitter and a slick fielder, was a second baseman for the Pittsburgh Pirates for almost 20 years. Many fans consider him one of the best second sackers to ever play the game of baseball.

True or false? Jim Derrington was the youngest player to ever get a base hit in the American League.

True. In 1956, Jim Derrington of the Chicago White Sox became the youngest American Leaguer to ever get a base hit in a major league game. He was only sixteen years old.

Pete Rose, the former Cincinnati Reds' star infielder-outfielder, is a consistent .300 hitter and one of the brightest stars in major league baseball. What is his nickname?

Pete Rose's nickname is "Charlie Hustle." He got this nickname because he gives his team 100% while on the field, always hustling on every play.

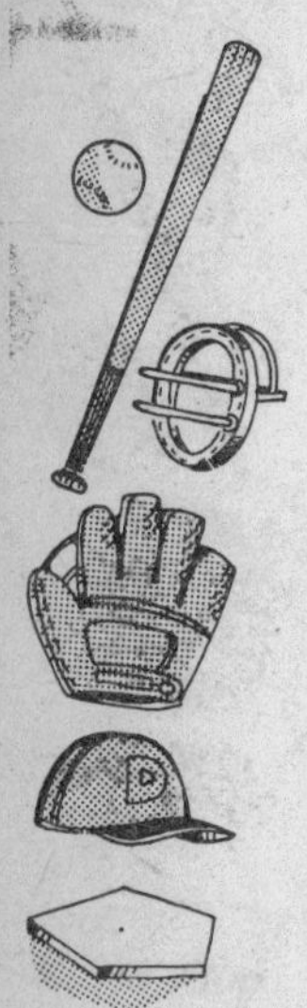

What is the highest batting average Willie Mays ever had? Is it .319, .333, or .347?

Willie Mays' highest average was .347. As a member of the New York Giants when they moved to San Francisco in 1958, Willie connected with 208 hits in 600 at bats, to notch the highest BA of his career. In all, Mays hit over .300 ten times and had a better than .300 average for seven consecutive years from 1957 through 1963. With 409 out of a possible 432 votes, Mays was voted into the Baseball Hall of Fame in 1979.

Which slugger hit more home runs in his career — "Boog" Powell of the Baltimore Orioles or Frank Howard of the Washington Senators?

Frank Howard's total of 382 career homers tops "Boog" Powell's 339.

Which President of the United States was the first to attend a baseball game? Was it Theodore Roosevelt, William Howard Taft, or Calvin Coolidge?

It was William Howard Taft. On April 19, 1909, President Taft attended a game between the Washington Senators and the Boston Red Sox. The following year, Taft showed up again at the stadium, this time to toss out the first ball of the season.

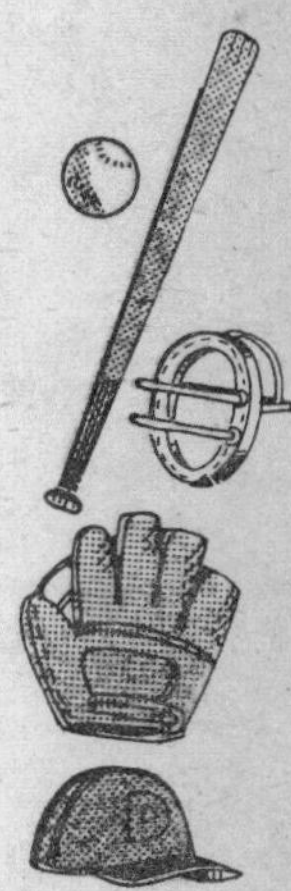

True or false? All major league scoreboards are now electronically operated.

False. As of 1978, there were still two hand-operated baseball scoreboards in use in the major leagues. One was at Wrigley Field in Chicago, the home stadium of the National League's Chicago Cubs. The other was at Fenway Park, the home of the Boston Red Sox of the American League.

Can you name the only man who is enshrined in both the Baseball Hall of Fame *and* the Pro Football Hall of Fame?

That man is Cal Hubbard. Hubbard played tackle for the Green Bay Packers for nine years and is a charter member of the Pro Football Hall of Fame. He was elected to the Baseball Hall of Fame for having served sixteen years as an American League umpire and seventeen more as the AL supervisor of umpires.

Here's another baseball slang question to tease your brain. What is a *goat*?

In baseball slang, a *goat* is a player who makes an error very costly to his team. It can be a mental or physical error, and very often causes his team to lose the game.

Which New York or San Francisco Giant holds more team records? Is it Willie Mays or Bill Terry?

Bill Terry holds more Giants' team records than Willie Mays. Terry's six records include the most hits in a season, 254, set in 1930, and the highest batting average, .401, also set in 1930. Mays owns two team records: the most homers in a season, 52, set in 1965, and the most doubles, 43, set in 1953. This record tied Bill Terry's record of 43 doubles, set in 1930.

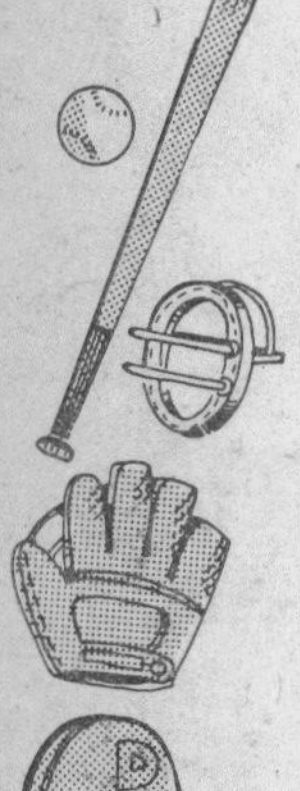

Which baseball team was the first to fly to an away game? Was it the New York Yankees, the Boston Red Sox, or the Cleveland Indians?

The Boston Red Sox were the first team to travel by air. On July 30, 1936, they flew from a game in St. Louis to a game in Chicago. Never before had a baseball team used air transportation. Until then, most teams traveled to away games by bus or train. Today, all major sports teams fly to away games.

In what year was the first legitimate professional baseball league organized? Was it 1865, 1868, or 1871?

In the spring of 1871, representatives of ten professional baseball teams met in New York and formed the National Association of Professional Baseball Players, the first pro baseball league. The original teams in the league were the Philadelphia Athletics, the Forest Cities of Rockford, the Chicago White Stockings, the Forest Cities of Cleveland, the Boston Red Stockings, the Troy Unions, the New York Mutuals, the Washington Olympics, the Washington Nationals, and the Kekiongas of Fort Wayne, Indiana. The National Association provided for a series of games between the member teams, resulting in crowning one team as the Baseball Champion of America.

Which two major league teams played the longest game by time in the history of baseball? Here's a clue. The teams are in the National League.

The longest baseball game ever played, time-wise, was between the San Francisco Giants and the New York Mets at Shea Stadium in New York on May 31, 1964. The game lasted a record 7 hours and 23 minutes, and was won by the Giants in the 23rd inning by the score of 8 to 6.

True or false? Carl Yastrzemski began his major league career as a member of the Pittsburgh Pirates in the National League.

Absolutely false. Carl "Yaz" Yastrzemski has worn a Boston Red Sox uniform for every one of the eighteen seasons he's spent in the American League. Carl signed with the Boston organization in 1958 and joined the parent club in 1961. The 5'11", 188-pound outfielder, who bats left and throws right, hits consistently around .300, and is usually one of the team leaders in home runs and RBIs.

True or false? Nolan Ryan is the fastest baseball pitcher in the world.

True. Nolan Ryan, who played for the California Angels in 1978, threw a fast ball at the speed of 100.9 mph, as timed by an electric clock at Anaheim Stadium in California, on August 20, 1974. No other pitcher has ever topped that speed.

In what year was the spit ball ruled illegal in the major leagues? Was it in 1921, 1931, or 1941?

Because the spit ball provides an artificial aid to pitchers, its use was ruled illegal in 1921. By moistening the covering of the ball with saliva or perspiration, a pitcher was able to make it break, or curve sharply, away from the batter.

How many innings must be played in a baseball game in order for the game to be considered official?

If a ball game goes 5 innings (4½ if the home team is ahead) and then has to be called due to rain, darkness, fog, or some other reason, it is considered official and counts in the standings.

BASEBALL

Has an infielder played a double-header without *ever* having a chance to touch the ball?

Yes. That amazing "do-nothing" record is held by Toby Harrah of the American League's Texas Rangers. On June 26, 1976, Harrah played an entire double-header at shortstop without making any fielding plays, assists, or putouts.

There was once a major league baseball player who had one arm. True or false?

It's true. The man was Pete Gray, a one-armed outfielder who played for the St. Louis Browns of the American League in 1945. During his career of 77 major league games, Gray proved that a determined athlete could make it to the majors despite a physical handicap.

Can you name the colorful major league player and manager who was nicknamed "The Lip"?

Leo Durocher, who played shortstop for the New York Yankees, the Cincinnati Reds, and the St. Louis Cardinals, and managed four National League teams, was nicknamed "The Lip" because of the many loud, bullying arguments he had with umpires and opposing players.

How far is the pitcher's rubber from home plate? Is it 50' 5", 60' 6", or 70' 7"?

The pitcher's rubber sits in an 18-foot circle 60' 6" from home plate.

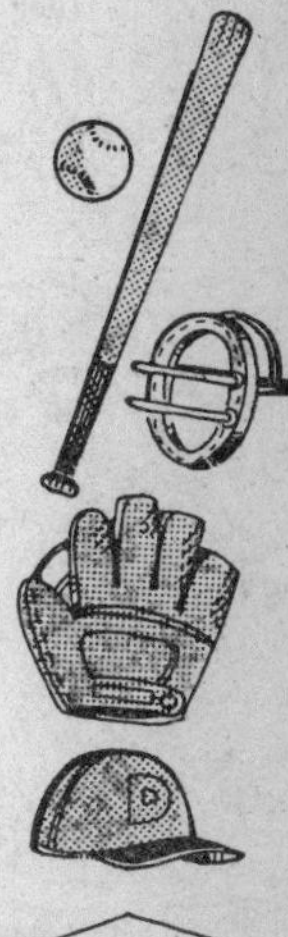

Abner Doubleday drew up the first set of rules for the game of baseball. True or false?

False. Alexander Cartwright, a New York sportsman, drew up the first rules for the game of baseball in 1845, when he organized the first baseball club, the Knickerbocker Base Ball Club of New York. Cartwright's rules established foul lines, the strikeout, three-out innings, nine-man teams, and a distance of 90 feet between bases.

True or false? The National League is the oldest baseball league still in operation.

True. The National League was organized in 1875-76 from the National Association of Baseball Players, which was formed in 1871. The new league was structured by William A. Hulbert, a part-owner of the Chicago White Stockings, and became a league of clubs instead of an association of players. A president was elected, and a 70-game schedule was worked out for all member teams. This was the forefather of the National League, still in existence today.

Almost every fan has heard about the wild antics of baseball's funniest pitchers — two brothers named Jerome and Paul. Do you know the nicknames by which these two were known?

Jerome and Paul — the Dean brothers — were fondly called "Dizzy" and "Daffy" by baseball fans. Although the Dean brothers sometimes acted looney, they were both skillful pitchers for the St. Louis Cardinals. In 1934 alone, the two combined to win 49 games for St. Louis and give them the National League Pennant. Their 4 wins in the World Series gave the Cards the Championship as well. Dizzy Dean, who became a baseball announcer after his retirement, is a member of the Baseball Hall of Fame.

BASEBALL

Which major-leaguer and Hall-of-Famer used the smallest bat ever used by a ball player? Was it Willie Keeler of the Baltimore Orioles, Bud Harrelson of the New York Mets, or Fred Patek of the Kansas City Royals?

The answer is "Wee" Willie Keeler. The bat that he used was only 21½ inches long, but even with a tiny bat, Keeler was a dangerous hitter. He set the major league record for the most singles in a season (199) in 1897.

Grover Cleveland Alexander has a no-hit game in the record books. True or false?

False. Although Alexander doesn't have any no-hitters to his credit, he did pitch 4 one-hitters during the 1915 season, to set a major league record.

True or false? Ron Hunt, who played for several National League teams, holds the major league record for being hit by the most pitched balls in a career.

True. Ron Hunt took more lumps from pitchers than any other major league baseball player. He led the major leagues in getting hit by pitched balls for seven consecutive years. Over all, from 1963 to 1974, Hunt was hit 243 times — a major league record.

In 1956, Edwin "Duke" Snider hit 43 home runs to establish a season record for his team. What team was Snider on in 1956?

Duke Snider was a centerfielder for the 1956 Brooklyn Dodgers — the team for which he starred from 1950 to 1959. Snider's 43HRs in 1956 also gave him the NL home-run title that year.

True or false? Experts calculate that the odds against an unassisted triple play in baseball are 50,000 to 1.

True. An unassisted triple play is the rarest play in baseball, and the odds are somewhere around 50,000 to 1 that you'll ever see it made.

True or false? Little League diamonds have the same distances between bases as major league diamonds.

False. There is 90 feet between major league bases and only 60 feet between Little League bases. In the majors, the pitching distance is 60 feet 6 inches from the mound to home plate, while in Little League it's only 46 feet.

Who holds the American League record for the most runs batted in during a single game? Here's a hint. The record was set by a New York Yankee in 1936.

The answer is Tony Lazzeri, who set the AL record in 1936 by getting 11 RBIs in one game.

In 1927, two unassisted triple plays occurred in major league baseball on successive days. True or false?

True. On May 30 and 31, 1927, shortstop Jim Cooney of the Chicago Cubs and first baseman Johnny Neun of the Detroit Tigers pulled off unassisted triple plays on successive days. Cooney's triple play came with men on first and second. The batter lined to Cooney, who caught the drive for one out. Catching the runner off second base, he touched second for the next out, then tagged the runner coming from first for the third out. Nuen's play came with men on first and second. The batter hit a line drive, which Neun caught. Catching the base runners moving, Nuen tagged one man between first and second, then sped to second, touching it before the runner could return.

True or false? According to most baseball historians, the first pitcher to throw a curve ball was Grover Cleveland Alexander in 1915.

False. The first curve-ball pitcher was Arthur "Candy" Cummings, who played baseball around 1860.

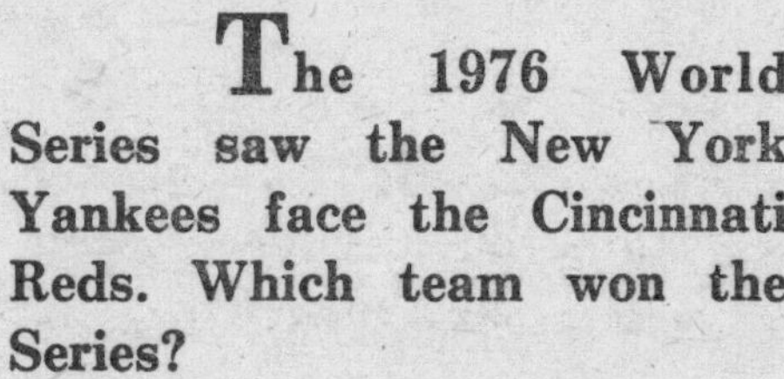

The 1976 World Series saw the New York Yankees face the Cincinnati Reds. Which team won the Series?

The National League's Cincinnati Reds walloped the American League's New York Yankees in four straight games, 5-1, 4-3, 6-2, and 7-2, to take the World Series crown in 1976.

Who is often referred to as the "Father of Baseball"?

Alexander Cartwright, Jr., a member of one of the first baseball teams in the early 1800s — the New York Knickerbockers, is considered by many sports experts to be the "Father of Baseball." Cartwright is credited with formulating the first baseball rules and getting them published in 1845.

True or false? Ty Cobb, who many people believe to be the best player of all time, was an orphan and so poor that he didn't own a pair of shoes until he was 15 years old.

Absolutely false. Tyrus Raymond Cobb, who is often called the "Georgia Peach," came from a well-to-do Georgia family. Cobb's father, a state senator in Georgia and later a county superintendent of schools, was bitterly opposed to Ty playing baseball because he didn't consider it a reputable profession.

How many times did Babe Ruth lead the American League in home runs? Was it eight, twelve, or sixteen times?

Babe Ruth was the American League's home-run champion twelve times between 1918 and 1931. His greatest and best-remembered year was 1927, when he hit 60 HRs for the New York Yankees.

If a baseball announcer says that "*a batter has been caught looking,*" what does it mean?

In baseball slang, it means that the batter has been called out on strikes, having taken a third strike without swinging at the ball.

Years ago, the spit ball, which is illegal in baseball today, was called something else by most players and fans. Do you know what it used to be called?

Originally, the spit ball was nicknamed the "cuspidor curve."

Can you name the infielder who played more games at shortstop than any other player in the history of baseball?

The answer is Luis Aparicio of the Chicago Cubs, the American League's Rookie of the Year in 1966. Aparicio played in 2,581 games, which is more than any other shortstop in baseball history.

True or false? A major league pitcher once struck out ten men in a row?

True. On April 22, 1970, Tom Seaver of the New York Mets struck out ten consecutive batters in a game against the San Diego Padres. This set a major league record for consecutive strikeouts.

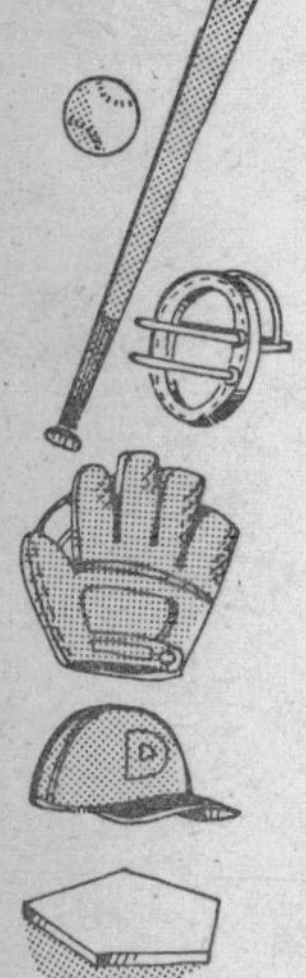

True or false? Carl Yastrzemski holds Boston Red Sox team records for the highest batting average in a season and for the most home runs in a season.

False. The great Ted Williams is the holder of the Red Sox team record for the highest batting average. His .406 BA in 1941 is still tops. The immortal Jimmy Foxx is the team record holder for the most home runs in a single season. Foxx smashed 50 homers in 1938.

In baseball, what is a *balk*?

The baseball rules state that a pitcher's front foot must step toward the base when he attempts to pick a runner off first base or third base. If he steps toward home plate and then throws to a base, a *balk* — a kind of penalty, is called against him, and the runner is automatically allowed to advance to the next base.

Which two teams played in the 1977 World Series, and which team won the Series that year?

The NL's Champion Los Angeles Dodgers played the New York Yankees, the AL Champions, in the 1977 World Series. The Yankees won the Series, beating the Dodgers, 4 games to 1.

In which year were baseball cards issued for the first time? Was it 1884, 1910, or 1935?

Believe it or not, baseball cards are nearly 100 years old, with the first ones issued around 1884. They were packed as prizes in cigar boxes and tobacco tins. They weren't packaged with bubble gum until the 1930s. Today, one early Honus Wagner card sells for as much as $4,800!

True or false? The San Diego Padres entered the National League in 1967 and were followed by the Montreal Expos in 1968.

False. The San Diego Padres and the Montreal Expos both joined the National League in 1969, when the senior circuit expanded from 10 to 12 teams.

Which American-Leaguer won the 1977 Rookie of the Year Award?

The Baseball Writers Association selected Eddie Murray, a designated hitter for the Baltimore Orioles, as the 1977 American League Rookie of the Year. Murray had a .283 batting average, belted 27 home runs, and had 88 runs batted in.

Who was voted the Most Valuable Player of the 1978 All-Star Game? Was it Fred Lynn of the Boston Red Sox, Pete Rose of the Cincinnati Reds, or Steve Garvey of the Los Angeles Dodgers?

First baseman Steve Garvey was named the MVP of the 49th All-Star Game in 1978. Garvey tied the game with a bases-loaded single in the third inning and sparked the National League's winning rally with a triple in the eighth. The 1978 All-Star MVP trophy was Garvey's second, his first coming in 1974.

Who is generally credited with inventing the game of baseball?

Most people believe that Abner Doubleday invented the game of baseball in 1839, but stick-and-ball games date as far back in history as the ancient Egyptians. Researchers have also shown that similar games were played in England and America before that date. The English game of *rounders* was played in Great Britain in the 1600s and in the New England colonies in the 1700s. To play rounders, a ball was hit with a bat, and the runner ran around posts in the ground, which were used as bases. Fielded balls were then thrown at the runners to get them out. So although Doubleday is credited with inventing baseball, there is no actual proof that he did.

Casey Stengel, the colorful manager of the New York Yankees and the New York Mets, never played major league baseball. True or false?

False. Casey Stengel played major league baseball for thirteen seasons through the 1920s and the early 1930s. He was an outfielder for the Brooklyn Dodgers, the Milwaukee Braves, the Philadelphia Phillies, and the New York Giants, and had a .284 lifetime batting average.

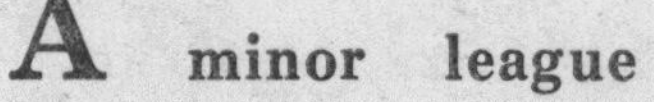

A minor league player was once traded to another team in return for 20 uniforms. True or false?

Strange but true. A class D pitcher, Lindy Chappoten, was traded by the Shawnee Hawks of the Sooner State League to the Texarkana Bears of the Big State League for 20 uniforms. Chappoten went on to win 20 games for the Bears—1 for each uniform.

Baseball players are remembered for the numbers on their uniforms as well as for their batting averages. Do you know which New York Yankee numbers were worn by Babe Ruth, Joe DiMaggio, and Mickey Mantle?

Babe Ruth, the best home-run hitter of all time, wore number 3. Joe DiMaggio, "The Yankee Clipper," made number 5 famous. And Mickey Mantle, the mighty switch-hitter, sported number 7. As a tribute to these immortals when their playing days were over, the numbers 3, 5, and 7 were retired so that no future Yankee would ever wear them.

There are six teams in the National League's West Division. Can you name them?

The six teams in the National League West are the Los Angeles Dodgers, the Cincinnati Reds, the Houston Astros, the San Diego Padres, the San Francisco Giants, and the Atlanta Braves.

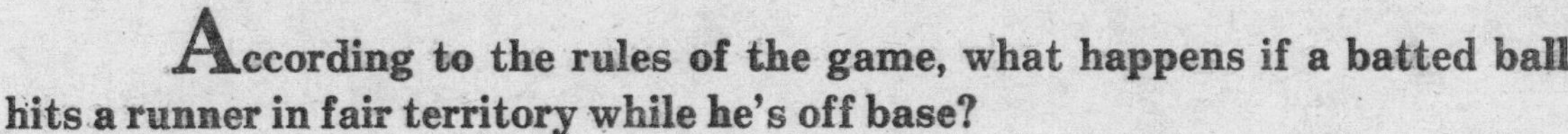

According to the rules of the game, what happens if a batted ball hits a runner in fair territory while he's off base?

When a batted ball hits a base runner in fair territory, he is automatically out.

What is the distance from home plate to second base? Is it 90 feet, 127 feet, or 132 feet?

From home plate through the pitcher's mound to second base, the distance is 127 feet, 3 3/8 inches.

What was Willie Mays' famous nickname?

Willie Mays, who played centerfield for the New York Giants, the San Francisco Giants, and the New York Mets, was known as "The Say Hey Kid." Willie had a habit of calling to the other players and beginning each sentence with "Say, hey. . . ." The fans picked this up and dubbed him "The Say Hey Kid."

What kind of base hit is a *Texas Leaguer*?

A *Texas Leaguer* is a softly hit ball that drops between the reach of the infielders and the outfielders. Texas Leaguers are generally considered to be "lucky" hits.

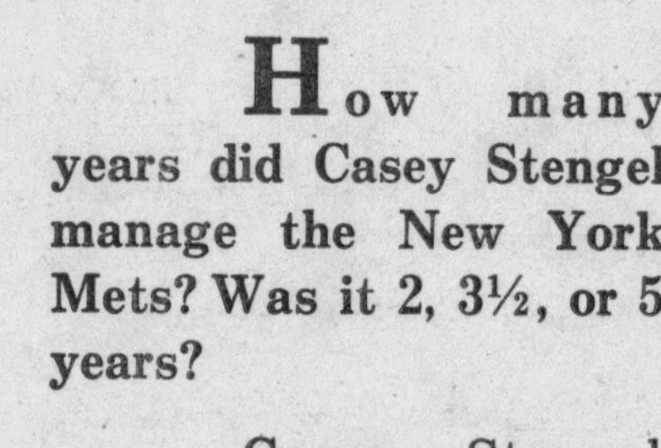

How many years did Casey Stengel manage the New York Mets? Was it 2, 3½, or 5 years?

Casey Stengel managed the New York Mets from their formation in 1962 until the middle of the 1965 season, a total of 3½ years. During that time, the Mets never finished higher than 10th in NL standings.

Who was the team captain of the 1977 World Champion New York Yankees? Was it Thurman Munson, Reggie Jackson, or Lou Piniella?

The team captain of the 1977 New York Yankees was catcher Thurman Munson, who remained the captain in 1978. Munson, who is steady and skilled behind the plate, is a dangerous hitter whose batting average is always around or just below .300.

Did Ty Cobb ever win the home-run title of the American League?

Yes. Ty Cobb of the Detroit Tigers was the AL's home-run king in 1909 — with an "amazing" total of 9 homers!

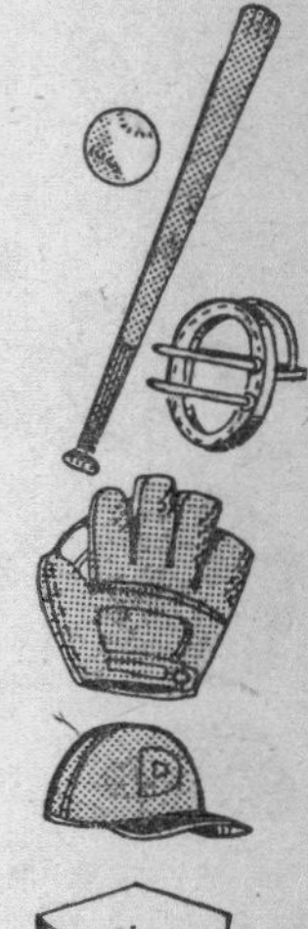

True or false? In 1978, Arizona State University won the NCAA College World Series.

False. The University of Southern California was the winner of the 1978 National Collegiate Athletic Association's College World Series. Arizona State University finished second.

Who is the smallest player in the major leagues? Here's a hint. He's in the American League.

Fred Patek, the shortstop for the Kansas City Royals, is the smallest player in the majors. The slick infielder is only 5 feet 4 inches tall and weighs 140 pounds.

Yogi Berra played on more World Championship baseball teams than any other man in baseball history. True or false?

True. Yogi Berra, as a catcher for the New York Yankees, played in 14 World Series, of which 10 were Championships for the Yanks. Of Berra's 71 Series hits, 49 were singles — a record he still holds. No other player is close to Berra's 10-Championships record.

True or false? Tris Speaker, a centerfielder for the Boston Red Sox, once made two unassisted double-plays in one month.

True. The unassisted double-plays were a result of Speaker's habit of playing extremely shallow in centerfield in order to catch line drives and Texas-Leaguers. Sometimes, when a runner was on second base, Speaker would snare a line drive and race to second before the runner could return, to make an unassisted double-play. In April, 1918, he managed to pull off that trick twice.

On May 4, 1975, the one millionth run in baseball history was scored. Who scored it and who drove him in?

Houston Astro Bob Watson scored that famous one millionth run on a 3-run homer hit by catcher Milt May in a game against the San Francisco Giants.

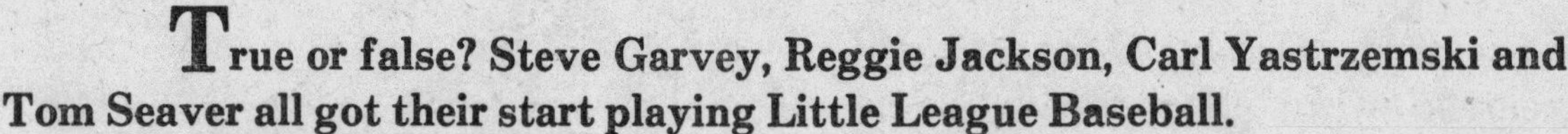

True or false? Steve Garvey, Reggie Jackson, Carl Yastrzemski and Tom Seaver all got their start playing Little League Baseball.

True. Garvey of the Los Angeles Dodgers, Jackson of the New York Yankees, Yastrzemski of the Boston Red Sox, and Seaver of the Cincinnati Reds all played Little League Baseball. In fact, of the 2,500 men in organized baseball who played Little League, 65% of them are in the majors. Other former Little Leaguers include Thurman Munson of the New York Yankees, Steve Carlton of the Philadelphia Phillies, and Nolan Ryan of the California Angels.

How many times did the great Jimmy Foxx hit over 30 home runs and bat over .300 in the same season? Was it three, five, or nine times?

Jimmy Foxx belted over 30 homers and hit over .300 in the same season nine times during his 21-year career. His best year at bat was 1939, when his season average was .360. His top year in home runs was 1932, when he had 58 round-trippers.

In what year was the first World Series played? Was it 1891, 1900, or 1905?

World Series competition between the Champions of the National and American Leagues was officially inaugurated in 1905. In that first game, the NL's New York Giants defeated the AL's Philadelphia Athletics, 4 games to 1. The star of the Series was Giant pitcher Christy Mathewson, who won 3 games, all of them shutouts, and struck out 18 Philadelphia batters.

Which of the following New York Yankees did *not* win the American League's Rookie of the Year Award? Was it Gil McDougald, Tony Kubek, Tom Tresh, or Mickey Mantle?

Surprisingly enough, outfielder Mickey Mantle, the greatest switch-hitter in the history of baseball, did not win the Rookie of the Year Award. Gil McDougald won the Award in 1951 as a rookie third baseman. Tony Kubek, an infielder-outfielder, was the AL's Rookie of the Year in 1957. And Tom Tresh won it in 1962 as a shortstop-outfielder.

Who won more consecutive National League batting championships — Willie Keeler of the Baltimore Orioles or Rogers Hornsby of the St. Louis Cardinals?

The answer is Rogers Hornsby, who won six consecutive NL batting titles from 1920 to 1925 — more than any other player in baseball history. Willie Keeler held consecutive National League batting titles only twice: in 1897 and 1898.

True or false? A baseball team once scored in all nine innings of a game.

True. The New York Giants did it in a game against the Philadelphia Phillies on June 1, 1923. The final score of the game was the Giants, 22, and the Phillies, 5.

What is a *grand-slam* home run?

A *grand-slammer* is a home run hit when the bases are loaded.

The 1921 World Series saw the AL Champion New York Yankees play the NL Champion New York Giants. Who won the Series that year?

The New York Giants took the 1921 Series, 5 games to 3. Many fans and baseball experts believed that the absence of the injured Babe Ruth accounted for the Yankees' loss.

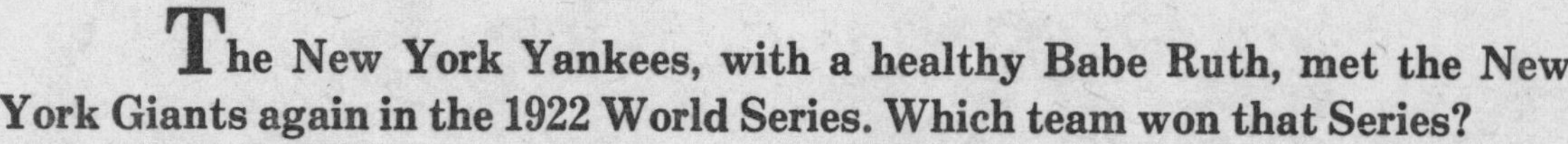

The New York Yankees, with a healthy Babe Ruth, met the New York Giants again in the 1922 World Series. Which team won that Series?

The 1922 World Series saw the Giants again defeating the Yankees, this time winning 4 out of 5 games, with one game ending in a tie. As for Babe Ruth, he had his poorest World Series ever, managing to get only 2 hits in 17 trips to the plate.

In baseball, what determines which team bats first?

The visiting team always bats first while the home team takes the field. This polite ritual, however, allows the home team the advantage of batting last and, if necessary, catching up if they are behind.

Is it legal for a batter to swing at the same pitch twice?

Yes, it is legal. A batter can swing at the same pitch twice as long as he misses it the first time. If he misses twice, it still only counts as one strike.

The pattern of the New York Yankees' home uniforms is well known to all baseball fans. What do the Yankee home uniforms look like?

The Yankee uniforms are white with pinstripes.

How many major league pitchers have pitched 3 or more no-hit games during their career?

Only four pitchers have pitched 3 or more career no-hitters. Cy Young of the Boston Red Sox did it in 1897, 1904, and 1908. Bob Feller of the Cleveland Indians equaled that mark in 1940, 1946, and 1951. But Sandy Koufax of the Los Angeles Dodgers and Nolan Ryan of the California Angels went one better and pitched 4 no-hitters each. Koufax pitched his in 1962, 1963, 1964, and 1965, and Ryan hurled his in 1973 (2 no-hitters), 1974, and 1975.

A National League team has only nine players in its line-up, but an American League team has ten. True or false?

True. Although both leagues played with a nine-man line-up for many years, in 1973 the AL introduced the "*designated-hitter*" into its line-up. This is a hitter who bats in the pitcher's position in the line-up, but who remains on the bench while his team is in the field.

No baseball player has ever been able to hit a ball high enough to touch the roof of the Houston Astrodome. True or false?

False. In 1974, slugging third baseman Mike Schmidt of the Philadelphia Phillies socked a ball in Houston so hard that it soared skyward like a rocket and actually touched the roof of the 208-foot-high Astrodome.

True or false? Lou Gehrig was playing baseball for Columbia University when he was first spotted by a scout for the New York Yankees.

True. Lou Gehrig, a pitcher and outfielder for New York's Columbia University in the early 1920s, was first spotted by Yankee scout Paul Krichell in a 1923 game between Columbia University and Rutgers University of New Jersey. During the course of the game, Gehrig belted two homers that sailed out of the field and into the nearby woods. At the end of that school term, Lou Gehrig was signed by the Yankees to a $3,000 contract, which included a $1,500 bonus.

How many times was Babe Ruth the American League's home-run champion while playing for the Boston Red Sox?

While playing for Boston, Babe Ruth won the home-run crown twice. He shared it with Clarence Walker of the Philadelphia Athletics in 1918, when both men hit 11 homers. In 1919, Ruth's last year at Boston, he won the home-run title with a league-leading total of 29 round-trippers.

In what place did the New York Mets finish in the East Division of the National League in 1978?

The Mets' season record of 66 wins and 96 losses in 1978 placed them 6th, or last, in the NL East.

True or false? The New York Yankees were originally called the New York Highlanders.

True. In the early 1900s, the American League's New York team was known as the Highlanders, and played their home games at the Polo Grounds. After the team was purchased by Jacob Ruppert and Tillinghast L'Hommedieu Huston in 1916, the name was changed to the Yankees.

Richard "Rube" Marquard and Timothy Keefe of the old New York Giants in the National League were two of the greatest hitters in the early days of pro baseball. True or false?

Absolutely false. They were both sensational Giant pitchers and share the record for winning the most consecutive games. In 1888, Keefe won 19 consecutive games, and in 1912, Marquard duplicated that amazing feat by also winning 19.

Which major league greats were nicknamed "King Kong," "The Flying Dutchman," and "The Fireman"?

Left fielder Charlie Keller of the New York Yankees was "King Kong." Shortstop Honus Wagner of the Pittsburgh Pirates was "The Flying Dutchman." And Yankee reliever Joe Page was "The Fireman."

What was the highest official batting average ever recorded in the American League? Was it .410, .422, or .498?

Nap Lajoie of the Philadelphia Athletics had the highest AL batting average in history. In 1901, he won the batting title with an amazing .422.

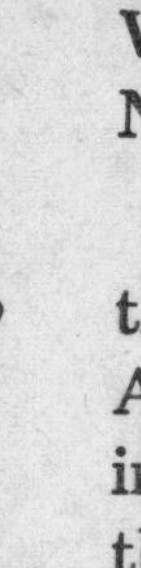

Which pitcher struck out the most batters in a single season? Was it Rube Waddell, Bob Feller, or Nolan Ryan?

Right-hander Nolan Ryan of the American League's California Angels struck out the most batters in a single season. In 1973, Ryan set the record by striking out 383 batters, breaking Cleveland Indian Bob Feller's 1946 record of 348. Feller, in turn, had topped by 5 Rube Waddell's record of 343, set in 1904 when he was a Philadelphia Athletic.

Which National League team has won the most World Series Championships?

The record is held by the St. Louis Cardinals, who were World Champions seven times: in 1926, 1931, 1934, 1942, 1944, 1946, and 1964.

True or false? The Detroit Tigers once played a game against the Philadelphia Athletics using a team of coaches and college players.

True. In 1912, Detroit Tiger star Ty Cobb was suspended by the baseball commissioner because he'd jumped into the stands to fight with a fan a week earlier. The entire Detroit squad staged a walk-out in protest and refused to play. The commissioner warned the Detroit management that the team would be fined $5,000 for each game not played. To avoid the fine, the Tigers fielded a team of retired coaches and college ball players for a game against the Philadelphia Athletics — a game the Tigers lost 24 to 2. After a 10-day suspension, Cobb returned to the team and the Tiger squad returned with him.

Who was the first player elected to the National Baseball Hall of Fame? Was it George "Rube" Waddell of the Philadelphia Athletics, Ty Cobb of the Detroit Tigers, or Tris Speaker of the Boston Red Sox and Cleveland Indians?

Outfielder Ty Cobb was the first player elected to the Hall of Fame by the Baseball Writers Association in 1936. When the Museum, itself, opened in 1939, Cobb was among the baseball personalities on hand to participate in the dedication and to see momentos, from his uniform to his sliding pads, enshrined there. Centerfielder Tris Speaker entered the Hall of Fame in 1937, and Rube Waddell, eleven years later in 1946.

Norm Cash won the American League batting title in 1961 with a hearty average of .360. Which team did Cash play for?

Norm Cash was a first baseman for the Detroit Tigers.

Who was voted the Most Valuable Player of the 1977 World Series between the Los Angeles Dodgers and the New York Yankees?

New York Yankee rightfielder Reggie Jackson was voted the MVP of the 1977 World Series. Jackson's five home runs during the 6-game Series spurred the Yankees to their 4 wins and the championship. Three of those runs came in game 6 and tied Babe Ruth's World Series record for homers in one game. Ruth had set that Series record twice, once in the 1926 Series and then again in the 1928 Series, both against the St. Louis Cardinals.

How many times did the New York Yankees win the American League Pennant with Casey Stengel as their manager? Was it six, ten, or twelve times?

Under Casey Stengel, the Yankees won the AL Pennant ten times. They held the league championship from 1949 to 1953, from 1955 to 1958, and in 1960.

In 1978, Pete Rose of the Cincinnati Reds made a valiant attempt to establish a new major league record for hitting safely in consecutive games. In how many games did Rose hit safely before his streak was snapped?

Pete Rose hit safely in 44 consecutive games before he was stopped by rookie left-hander Larry McWilliams and veteran hurler Gene Barber in a game against the Atlanta Braves on August 1, 1978. However, Rose's 44-game streak tied him for the NL consecutive-game hitting record set by Willie Keeler in 1897.

Is there any way that a batter with two strikes can be called out if he hits a foul ball?

With a two-strike count on him, a batter can be called out if he bunts the ball and it goes foul, or if he hits a foul tip that is caught and held by the catcher. In either case, the batter is out, and the pitcher is credited with a strikeout.

Did the great National League slugger Stan Musial ever put together a consecutive hitting streak of more than 20 games?

Yes. In 1930, Stan "The Man" Musial of the St. Louis Cardinals hit safely in 30 consecutive games.

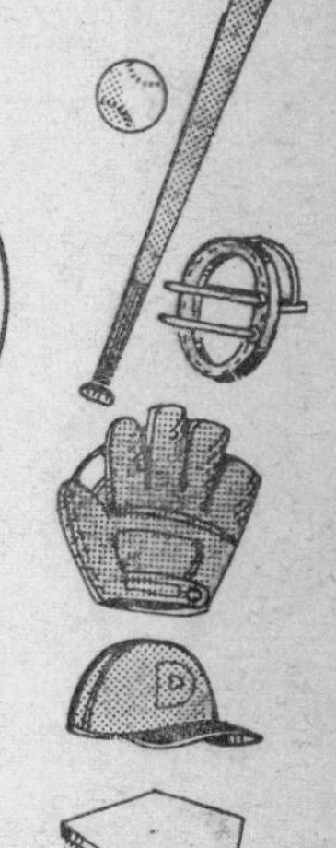

Who won the American League home-run title more times — Lou Gehrig or Jimmy Foxx?

Jimmy Foxx, who played for the Philadelphia Athletics and the Boston Red Sox, won the AL homerun title four times, as compared to New York Yankee Lou Gehrig's three. Foxx took the home-run title in 1932, with 58 round-trippers; in 1933, with 48; in 1935, with 36; and in 1939, with 35. Gehrig led the AL in homers in 1931, with 46; in 1934, with 49; and in 1936, with 49. Both sluggers were also Triple Crown winners.

Who had more runs batted in during his career — Babe Ruth or Hank Aaron?

Hank Aaron holds the National League and the major league records for career RBIs. From 1954 to 1976, Aaron batted in a total of 2,297 runs. Babe Ruth, the holder of the American League record for RBIs, sent a total of 2,197 runners home during his 1914-1934 career.

What is the major league record for the most triples by a player in a single season? Is it 20, 27, or 36 triples?

The record is 36 triples in a single season, and it's held by Owen Wilson of the Pittsburgh Pirates, who established it way back in 1912.

What famous hard-throwing right-hander was known as "The Big Train"?

Walter P. Johnson, who pitched for the Washington Senators in the early 1900s, was nicknamed "The Big Train." During his 21 seasons with the Senators, Johnson won 413 games.

In 1960, two American League baseball managers traded teams in mid-season. Manager Joe Gordon took over manager Jimmy Dykes' team and Dykes took over Gordon's team. Can you name the teams involved in that trade?

Joe Gordon, manager of the Cleveland Indians, traded jobs with Jimmy Dykes, manager of the Detroit Tigers, in the middle of the 1960 season. Unfortunately, the swap didn't help either team. Cleveland finished in fourth place and Detroit finished in sixth — the exact positions they were in at the time of the trade.

The 1978 president of an American League team once won the home-run title (43), the RBI crown (145), and missed the batting lead by just one percentage point. Can you name this former star?

It's Al Rosen, who had this outstanding year in 1953 with the Cleveland Indians. Rosen joined the New York Yankee as Executive Vice-President in December, 1977, and was named President in March, 1978. For his 1953 accomplishments, Al Rosen was named the AL's Most Valuable Player that year.

What famous New York Yankee infielder was nicknamed "The Scooter"? Here's a hint. He's now a play-by-play announcer for his former teammates.

The answer is New York Yankee shortstop Phil Rizzuto, who now calls the plays for his former team on radio and TV.

Joe "Ducky" Medwick won baseball's Triple Crown in 1937. What team did Medwick play for that year?

Ducky Medwick was a member of the NL's St. Louis Cardinals when he won the Triple Crown with 31 home runs, a .374 batting average, and 154 runs batted in.

How many times did Babe Ruth hit 50 or more home runs in a single season? Was it two, three, or four times?

Babe Ruth hit 50 or more home runs in a season four different times: 54, in 1920; 59, in 1921; 60, in 1927; and 54, in 1928.

Which two of these great hitters batted over .400 for two consecutive years: Ty Cobb, Rogers Hornsby, George Sisler, or Ted Williams?

Ty Cobb of the Detroit Tigers and Rogers Hornsby of the St. Louis Cardinals are the only two men to ever hit .400 or better two years in a row. Cobb hit .420 in 1911 and .410 in 1912. Hornsby batted .424 in 1924 and .403 in 1925.

In the 1978 season, only two major league baseball players got over 200 hits. Can you name them?

Steve Garvey of the NL's Los Angeles Dodgers got 202 hits in 1978 while batting .316. Jim Rice of the AL's Boston Red Sox led both leagues in hits by smashing 212 safeties, giving him a solid season average of .315.

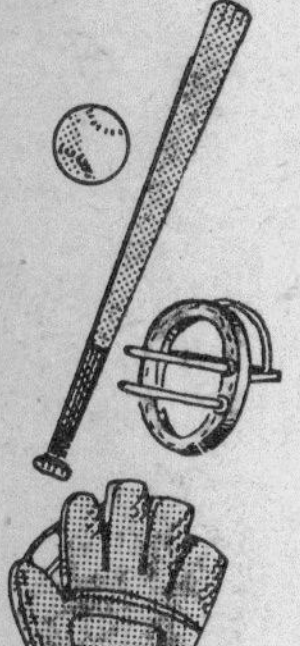

How many trips to the mound can a baseball manager make in an inning before he is required to remove the pitcher?

A manager is allowed only one trip to the pitcher's mound during an inning. If he goes to the mound a second time, he is required to remove his pitcher from the game and substitute a new one.

In 1961, Roger Maris of the New York Yankees hit 61 home runs playing in a 162-season. In 1927, Babe Ruth hit 60 home runs playing in a 154-game season. How close did Maris come to breaking Ruth's record in 154 games?

In 1961, Roger Maris missed breaking Babe Ruth's 154-game home-run record by only 2 homers. Maris hit his 59th four-bagger in the 154th game of the season, but didn't tie Ruth's record of 60 homers until the 158th game. Then, in the final game of the season before a sell-out crowd at Yankee Stadium, Maris belted record-breaking homer number 61.

How many times did Stan Musial of the St. Louis Cardinals win the National League batting title? Was it three, five, or seven times?

Stan "The Man" Musial was the batting champion of the National League seven times between 1943 and 1957. He led the league with .357 in 1943, .365 in 1946, .376 in 1948, .346 in 1950, .355 in 1951, .336 in 1952, and .351 in 1957.

Sandy Koufax of the Los Angeles Dodgers holds the National League record for the most strike-outs in a season. How many batters did he fan to set that record?

Sandy Koufax, the great Dodger left-hander, struck out 382 batters in 1965 to set the record.

Ernie Banks of the National League and Jim Gentile of the American League hold their respective league records for hitting the most grand-slam home runs in a single season. Which man hit more grand-slammers? Be careful on this one, baseball buffs.

Banks and Gentile are *tied*, with 5 grand-slammers apiece. Banks, of the Chicago Cubs, hit his 5 in 1955 to set the NL record. Gentile, of the Baltimore Orioles, tied Banks' grand-slam record in 1961, setting the AL record at the same time.

Two pitchers, who are brothers, both won Cy Young Awards in the 1970s. Can you name them?

Jim Perry, pitching for the Minnesota Twins, won the 1970 Cy Young Award as the American League's Outstanding Pitcher. In 1972, Jim's brother Gaylord won the Award while pitching for the American League's Cleveland Indians, then repeated in 1978 as a San Diego Padre in the National League.

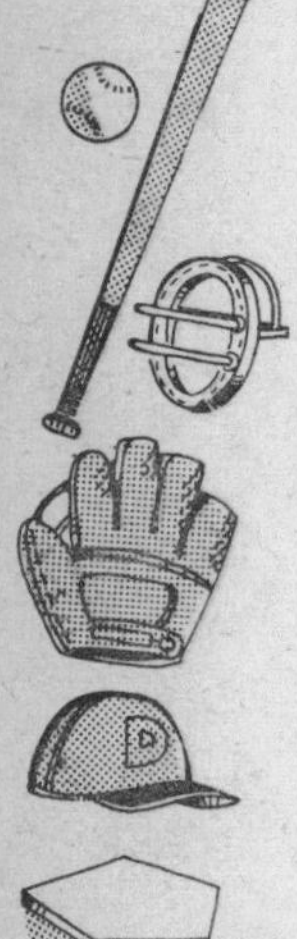

Who had a higher career batting average — Lloyd Waner or his brother, Paul?

Paul Waner's career average of .333 is higher than Lloyd's .316. Both Waners starred for the 1920s Pittsburgh Pirates and were later voted into Baseball's Hall of Fame.

How many years in a row did Ralph Kiner of the Pittsburgh Pirates win or share the National League's home-run crown?

Ralph Kiner was the top home-run hitter in the National League for seven consecutive years, from 1946 to 1952. Of a total of 294 homers, 54 were hit in 1949, his best year, and 51 in 1947, when he tied with Johnny Mize of the New York Giants.

In baseball what is a *ground rule double*?

A *ground rule double* is a ball which, when hit into the outfield, bounces over a fence or wall and goes out of play. The batter is automatically awarded a two-base hit.

The lowest average to ever win the batting title in the American League was a .301 in 1968. Who won the AL batting crown that year?

Carl Yastrzemski of the Boston Red Sox took the 1968 AL batting crown with his modest .301 BA.

Who was the most recent winner of baseball's Triple Crown?

Carl Yastrzemski of the Boston Red Sox was the last man to win the Triple Crown. In 1967, he led the American League with 44 home runs, 121 runs batted in, and a league-leading batting average of .326.

True or false? A major league team once scored 9 runs with two out in the bottom of the ninth inning to win a game, 14 to 13.

True. It happened on May 23, 1901, in a game between the Cleveland Indians (then called the Blues) and the Washington Senators. With the score 13 to 5 in favor of Washington, Cleveland scored 9 runs with 2 out in the bottom of the ninth inning, to notch a 14-to-13 victory.

Who hit more home runs in 1978? Was it George Foster of the National League's Cincinnati Reds or Jim Rice of the American League's Boston Red Sox?

Jim Rice's total of 46 home runs was tops in both leagues in 1978. George Foster led the National League with 40 homers.

Which pitcher spent the most years on major league mounds — Allie Reynolds, Bob Feller, or Early Wynn?

That record is held by Early Wynn, who pitched 23 years for the Washington Senators, the Cleveland Indians, and the Chicago White Sox. Wynn finished his career with 300 wins and 244 losses, but also holds the dubious honor of walking the most batters in a lifetime — 1,775!

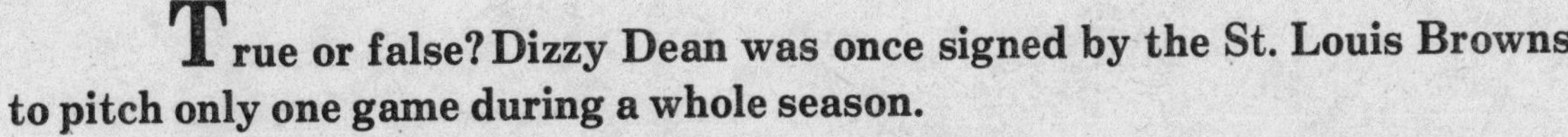

True or false? Dizzy Dean was once signed by the St. Louis Browns to pitch only one game during a whole season.

True. It happened in 1947. The St. Louis Browns of the American League signed Dizzy Dean, then a popular baseball broadcaster, to pitch the final game of the 1947 season simply to lure fans to the ball park. Dean pitched 4 innings of the game, gave up 3 hits, no runs and walked one batter. He also got one hit in one time at bat and was credited with having a 1.000 batting average in his only American League appearance. Until then, Dean had spent all of his ten major league seasons with the St. Louis Cardinals and the Chicago Cubs of the National League.

The National League, the oldest pro baseball league, was formed in 1875-76. When was the American League organized?

The American League wasn't truly born until 1900-1901, when a minor league known as the Western Association was reorganized by Connie Mack and Charles Comiskey to compete against the National League.

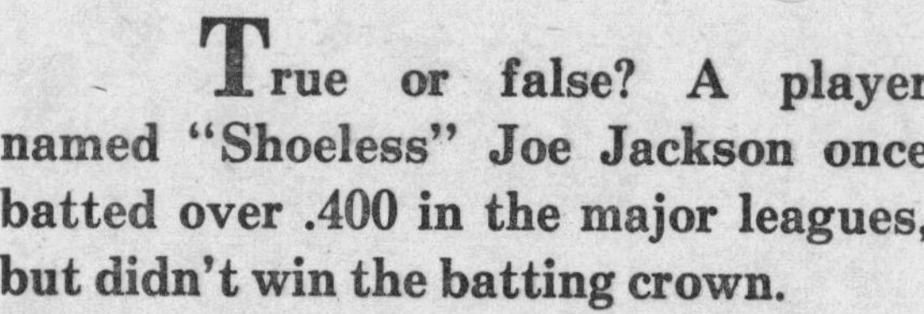

True or false? A player named "Shoeless" Joe Jackson once batted over .400 in the major leagues, but didn't win the batting crown.

True. "Shoeless" Joe Jackson of the Cleveland Indians batted .408 in 1911, but didn't win the AL batting crown because Ty Cobb of the Detroit Tigers batted .420 that year.

Which famous baseball team of the 1930s was known as the "Gas House Gang"?

The St. Louis Cardinals of the National League were known as the "Gas House Gang" because of their rough-and-tumble type of play. Members of the Gas House Gang were Pepper Martin, Dizzy Dean and his brother Daffy, Joe Medwick, and Leo Durocher.

Which slugger *scored* more runs in his career — Ty Cobb or Willie Mays?

Ty Cobb scored more runs and holds the AL and major league records in that category. Playing for the Detroit Tigers and the Philadelphia Athletics, Cobb crossed home plate with a total of 2,244 runs. Willie Mays holds the National League record, scoring 2,062 times while playing for the New York Giants, the San Francisco Giants, and the New York Mets.

Which baseball team holds the all-time season record for major league attendance? Here's a hint. It's a National League team.

The Los Angeles Dodgers set the all-time season attendance record in 1962, when 2,755,184 fans attended their home games.

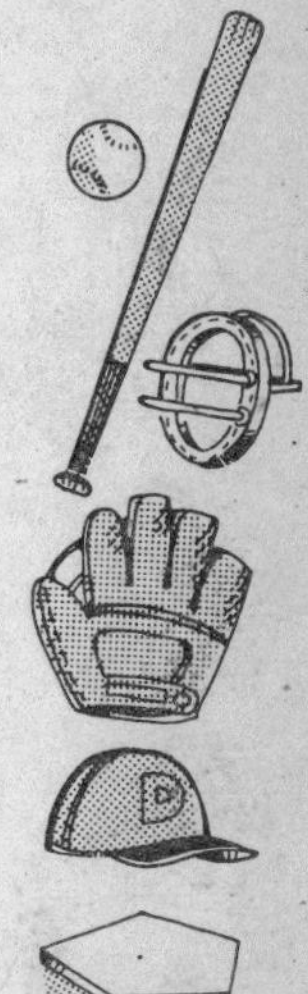

Who is the oldest player to ever appear in a major league game?

Leroy "Satchel" Paige holds that honor. He was 59 in 1965 when he played for Kansas City. When Paige joined the Cleveland Indians in 1948, he became the first black pitcher in the major leagues. Prior to that, he had spent 25 years barnstorming and with the Negro League, where he pitched 3,000 games, of which 300 were shutouts and 50 were no-hitters.

Only one man in the history of major league baseball — a Philadelphia Athletics' star in the early 1900s — has ever been given the nickname "Home Run." Can you name that player?

The man was Frank "Home Run" Baker, who got this nickname during the course of the 1911 World Series between the Philadelphia Athletics and the New York Giants. Baker hit tremendous homers off Giant pitchers Christy Mathewson and Rube Marquard to help the Athletics defeat the Giants, 4 games to 2. Baker also led the American League in home runs every year from 1911 to 1914.

What is the longest bat a major-leaguer is permitted to swing?

A 42-inch bat is the longest permissible in the majors.

Honus Wagner, who was elected to baseball's Hall of Fame in 1936, spent 18 years playing for the National League club he later coached. Which team was that?

Honus Wagner, who was a shortstop for the Pittsburgh Pirates from 1900 to 1917, was hired as a Pirate coach in 1933.

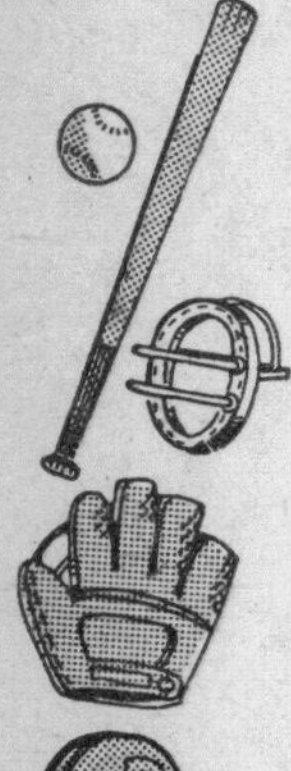

Pitcher Jack Chesbro holds the major league record for winning the most games in a season. What National League team did Chesbro play for in 1904 when he set that record?

Jack Chesbro was with the 1904 New York Giants when he won 41 games. This major league record for the most wins by a pitcher in a single season still stands today.

What is the most runs ever scored in a single inning by a modern major league baseball team? Is it 14, 17, or 22 runs?

The most runs scored by one team in a single inning of a modern major league contest is 17. The Boston Red Sox set the record on June 18, 1953, in the seventh inning of a game over the hapless St. Louis Browns, in which 23 Boston batters came to the plate.

How many times did Harmon Killebrew lead the American League in home runs? Was it three, four, or six times?

Slugger Harmon Killebrew, as a Washington Senator and a Minnesota Twin, led the American League in home runs six times. He belted 42 round-trippers in 1959, 48 in 1962, 45 in 1963, 49 in 1964, 44 in 1967, and 49 in 1969.

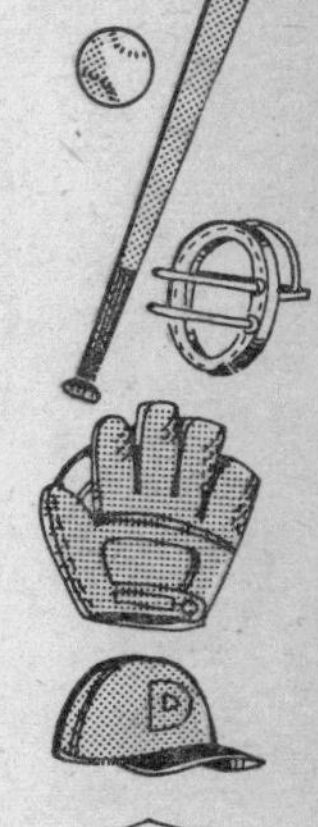

Pitcher Grover Cleveland Alexander spent 20 years in the National League playing for the Philadelphia Phillies, the Chicago Cubs, and the St. Louis Cardinals. How many losing seasons did Alexander have during those 20 years? Was it one, two, or five?

During his 20 years as a National League pitcher, Grover Cleveland Alexander had only one losing season. It was in 1930, his last year in the major leagues. As a Philadelphia Phillie that year, Alexander had an 0-3 record. His best year was with Philadelphia in 1916, when he won 33 games and lost 12.

The best relief pitcher in each league receives the Fireman of the Year Award. Who won it in the American League in 1978?

Rich "Goose" Gossage, the ace relief pitcher of the New York Yankees, won the 1978 Fireman of the Year Award, with a league-leading record of 27 saves.

True or false? Mickey Mantle is the only New York Yankee to ever win baseball's Triple Crown.

False. "The Iron Horse," Lou Gehrig, won baseball's Triple Crown while playing first base for the Yankees in 1934. Gehrig's league-leading totals that year were 49 home runs, 165 runs batted in, and a hefty batting average of .363.

Pitcher Whitey Ford holds the major league record for the most World Series strikeouts. How many batters did Ford fan between 1950 and 1964?

New York Yankee Whitey Ford, a left-handed pitcher, struck out 94 batters in World Series play to set the major league record.

There are seven teams in the American League's East Division. Can you name them?

The teams in the American League's East Division are the New York Yankees, the Boston Red Sox, the Baltimore Orioles, the Cleveland Indians, the Milwaukee Brewers, the Detroit Tigers, and the Toronto Blue Jays.

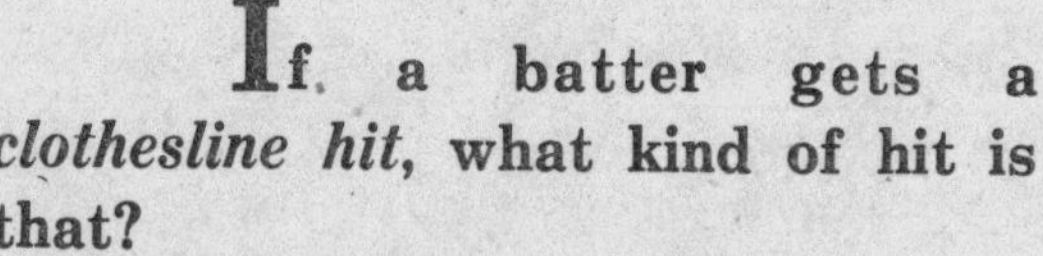

If a batter gets a *clothesline hit*, what kind of hit is that?

A *clothesline hit* is a very well-hit line drive.

A tip of the baseball cap to you if you can answer this question. Who was the first player to hit home runs in 6 straight games?

Frank Hurst, who played for the 1929 Philadelphia Phillies, was the first man to hit 6 homers in 6 consecutive games. Since then, several modern players have duplicated that feat. The record for the most consecutive games hitting home runs is held by R. Dale Long of the Pittsburgh Pirates, who hit 8 home runs in 8 straight games from May 19 to May 28, 1956.

Can you name the manager of the New York Mets in 1978?

Joe Torre managed the New York Mets in 1978. The former catcher and third baseman, and 1971 Most Valuable Player in the National League played for the Milwaukee Braves, the Atlanta Braves, the St. Louis Cardinals, and the Mets during his 17-year career before becoming the Mets' manager in 1977. The team, unfortunately, finished in last place in the National League's Eastern Division that year.

Who won the National League's Cy Young Award in 1977? Was it Steve Carlton or Tommy John?

The Baseball Writers Association of America voted Philadelphia Phillie Steve Carlton the NL's Cy Young Award in 1977. Carlton had 23 wins, 17 complete games, and an earned run average of 2.64. This was the second win for Carlton, who had earned the Award in 1972, when he had a 27-10 record. Tommy John of the Los Angeles Dodgers finished second to Carlton in the 1977 voting.

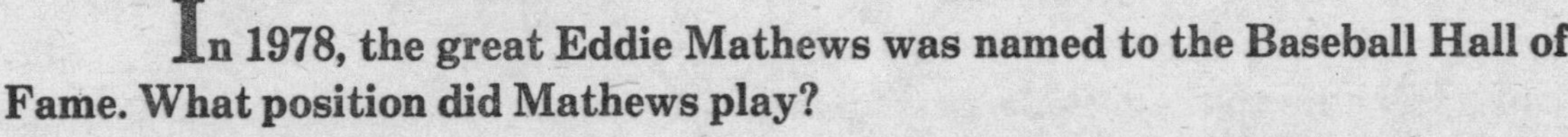

In 1978, the great Eddie Mathews was named to the Baseball Hall of Fame. What position did Mathews play?

Eddie Mathews was a major league third baseman for seventeen years. He spent fifteen of those years as a member of the Braves, as they moved from Boston to Milwaukee to Atlanta. During his career, Mathews hit 572 home runs, placing him ninth on the all-time home-run list.

Joe Medwick of the St. Louis Cardinals holds the NL record for the most doubles in a season, and Earl Webb of the Boston Red Sox holds the AL record for doubles. Which man hit more two-baggers?

Earl Webb's record tops Joe Medwick's. Webb set the American League record by banging out 67 two-base hits in 1931, while Medwick's National League record, set in 1936, is 64.

A Los Angeles Dodger pitcher set a National League record in 1968 by pitching 58 consecutive scoreless innings. Can you name him?

Don Drysdale is that record-setting pitcher. From May 14 to June 8, 1968, he pitched 58 consecutive scoreless innings and won six consecutive shutout games — also a record. Drysdale had been the National League's Cy Young Award winner six years earlier, in 1962.

The 1960 World Series between the New York Yankees and the Pittsburgh Pirates is rated as one of the most thrilling ever. With the Series tied at three games apiece and the score tied, 9 to 9, in the bottom of the ninth inning of the seventh game, a Pittsburgh hitter came to bat. With one swing, this Pirate hitter drove the ball over the wall for a Series-winning homer for Pittsburgh. Who hit that home run that won the 1960 World Series for the Pirates?

Pittsburgh's second baseman Bill Mazeroski hit Yankee hurler Ralph Terry's pitch over the left field wall to give the Pirates a 10-to-9 victory in the seventh and deciding game of the 1960 World Series.

Billy Martin, who managed the New York Yankees to the 1977 World Series Championship, resigned his job in July, 1978. Who replaced Martin as Yankee manager?

Bob Lemon, a former pitcher for the Cleveland Indians and the former manager of the Chicago White Sox, was hired to replace Billy Martin. With Lemon at the helm, the Yankees came from 14 games behind the division-leading Boston Red Sox in July to win their Division Championship, the AL Pennant, and the World Series.

Only one of the following players collected more than 3,500 hits during his career. Was it Babe Ruth, Tris Speaker, or Rogers Hornsby?

The correct answer is Tris Speaker, the slugging outfielder for the Boston Red Sox, the Cleveland Indians, the Washington Senators, and the Philadelphia Athletics. Speakers collected 3,515 hits during his 21-year career. Babe Ruth had a total of 2,873 hits, and Rogers Hornsby, 2,930.

Who holds the major league record for the most runs batted in during a single season? Is it Lou Gehrig of the New York Yankees or Lewis "Hack" Wilson of the Chicago Cubs?

Hack Wilson holds the major league and the National League records for RBIs in a single season. In 1930, he drove 190 men across the plate. Lou Gehrig set the American League record in 1931, when he drove home 184 runners.

In what stadium did Babe Ruth hit his first major league home run?

Babe Ruth, as a rookie pitcher for the Boston Red Sox, hit his first major league home run at the Polo Grounds in New York on May 6, 1915.

Did the Brooklyn Dodgers ever win a World Series?

Yes. In 1955, the Brooklyn Dodgers won the World Series by beating the New York Yankees, 4 games to 3. In all, the Brooklyn team played in the World Series a total of nine times (1916, 1920, 1941, 1947, 1949, 1952, 1953, 1955, 1956), but managed to win the championship only once.

In 1955, Gil Hodges, Roy Campanella, Carl Furillo, and Duke Snider were stars on which National League team? Was it the Brooklyn Dodgers, the New York Giants, or the St. Louis Cardinals?

Hodges, Campanella, Furillo, and Snider were all members of the 1955 Brooklyn Dodgers and led the team to the National League Pennant.

True or false? There is no such pitch as a *fork ball*.

False. There is a pitch called a *fork ball*. The pitcher wedges the ball between two fingers, and as it travels through the air, it resembles a knuckle ball.

The great pitcher Christy Mathewson was also a fine football player, and won varsity letters in football and baseball at college. Do you know which college Mathewson attended?

Christy Mathewson went to Bucknell College in Pennsylvania, where he was a pitcher on the varsity baseball team and an excellent kicker on the varsity football team.

Besides New York's Babe Ruth and Roger Maris, only two other hitters have cracked 58 home runs in one season. Can you name them?

The only two men other than Ruth and Maris who have ever hit 58 homers in a season are Jimmy Foxx of the Philadelphia Athletics, who hit 58 in 1932, and Hank Greenburg of the Detroit Tigers, who smacked 58 in 1938.

What is a *sacrifice fly*?

A *sacrifice fly* is a long fly ball to the outfield which is caught for an out. It is a strategy usually attempted when a runner is on third base with less than two outs. The runner *tags up*, or stays on third until the ball is caught, at which time he leaves the base and heads for home. Meanwhile, the ball is usually enroute to the infield, and if the runner crosses home before the catcher gets the ball and tags him, a run is scored. This play is called a sacrifice fly because the batter gives himself up as an out in order to drive home a run. He is credited with a run batted in and his time at bat is not counted as part of his official average.

True or false? First baseman Steve Garvey was the leading hitter for the Los Angeles Dodgers in the 1978 World Series.

False. Shortstop Bill Russell led the Dodgers, with 11 hits in 26 at bats for a .423 average. Superstar Steve Garvey had a poor Series, getting only 5 hits in 24 at bats for a .208 average.

During the Brooklyn-New York "Subway" World Series in the 1950s, the Dodgers' "Reading Rifle" often came up to bat against the Yankees' "Springfield Rifle." Who were those two players?

Brooklyn rightfielder Carl Furillo was the "Reading Rifle," and New York righthander Vic Raschi was the "Springfield Rifle."

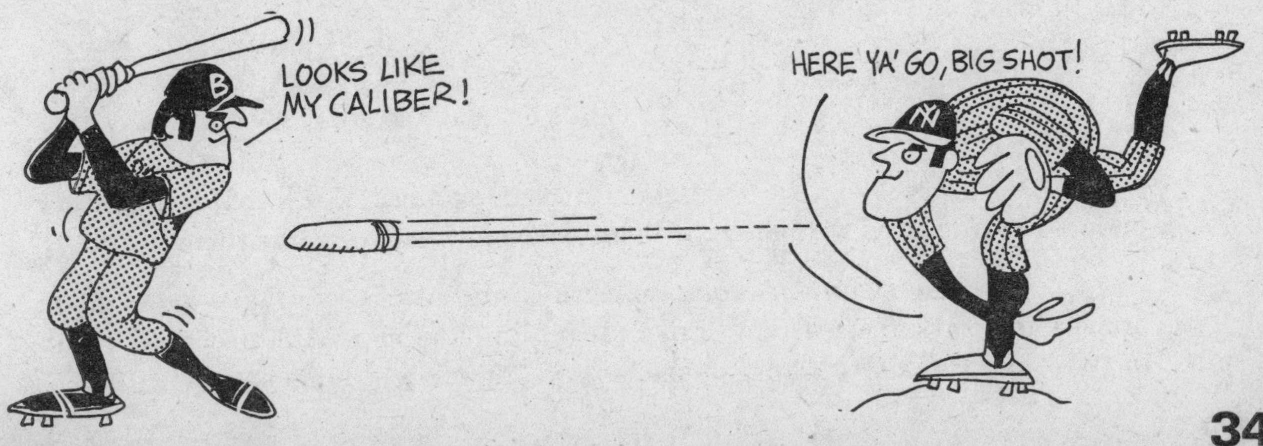

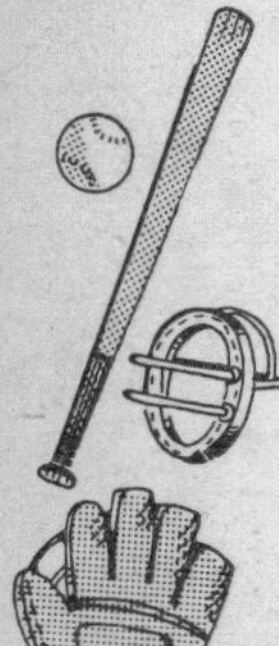

Which pitcher has won more Cy Young Awards — Tom Seaver or Sandy Koufax?

Seaver and Koufax each won the Cy Young Award three times. Seaver won it as a New York Met in 1969, 1973, and 1975. Koufax won it as a Los Angeles Dodger in 1963, 1965, and 1966 — each time as the unanimous choice of the Baseball Writers Association.

How many times have two New York teams competed against each other in the World Series? Is it seven, nine, or thirteen times?

The World Series has been played between two New York teams on thirteen different occasions. The AL's New York Yankees met the NL's old New York Giants in the World Series six times: in 1921, 1922, 1923, 1936, 1937, and 1951. The Yanks played the old Brooklyn Dodgers for the World Championship in 1941, 1947, 1949, 1952, 1953 and 1956, a total of seven times.

The NL Champion Los Angeles Dodgers met the AL Champion New York Yankees in the 1978 World Series. Which club had the highest team batting average and which hit more team home runs during the regular season?

The 1978 New York Yankees' team batting average of .267 topped by a slim margin the Los Angeles Dodgers' .264. However, the Dodgers hit more home runs as a team, with 149 homers as compared to the Yankees' 125.

True or false? A huge player nicknamed "Moose" once played for the New York Yankees.

True. Bill "Moose" Skowron was a star first baseman for the Yankees from the middle 1950s to the early 1960s. In 1955, Skowron led all Yankee batters in hitting, with a hardy .319 BA. Skowron later played for the Los Angeles Dodgers in the National League.

Carl Hubbell of the New York Giants was one of the greatest left-handed pitchers in baseball history. Was he best known for his pick-off move, his fast ball, or his ball control?

Carl Hubbell was famous for his fantastic control — his ability to get the ball over the plate time and time again. In 16 years with the Giants, Hubbell averaged fewer than two bases on balls per nine-inning game.

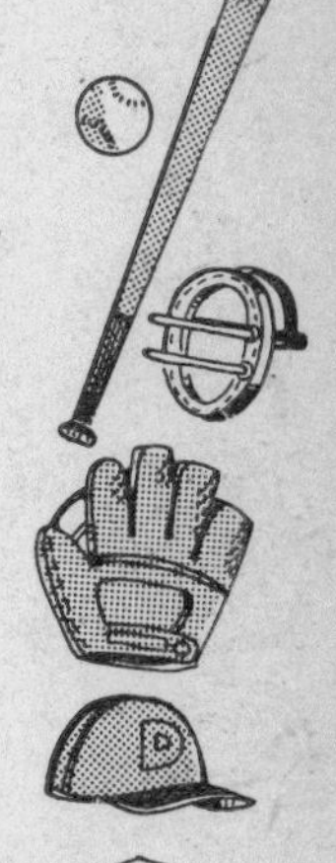

Who holds the major league record for the most career base hits?

The major league record of 4,191 base hits is held by Ty Cobb, who played in the American League for the Detroit Tigers from 1905 to 1926 and for the Philadelphia Athletics from 1927 to 1928.

Only three men in the history of baseball have hit 4 consecutive home runs in one game. One was Robert L. Lowe of the Boston Braves, who did it on May 30, 1894. Can you name the other two?

Lou Gehrig of the N.Y. Yankees hit 4 consecutive homers on June 3, 1932, and Rocky Colavito of the Cleveland Indians duplicated that feat on June 10, 1959.

Most baseball historians and fans agreed on one man when they selected "the greatest third baseman in the history of baseball." Was that third baseman Pepper Martin, Pie Traynor, or Al Rosen?

The choice was Harold "Pie" Traynor, a star third baseman for the Pittsburgh Pirates during the 1920s. Traynor spent 17 years in the major leagues and had a career batting average of .320.

Which New York Yankee team holds the record for getting the most hits in the World Series? Is it the 1936 or the 1978 Yankees?

The 1978 Yankees, led by Reggie Jackson and Thurman Munson, blasted 68 hits and broke the old record of 65 hits held by the 1936 Yankees, led by Joe DiMaggio and Lou Gehrig.

Connie Mack and John J. McGraw were famous major league baseball managers. Can you name the teams they managed?

Connie Mack managed the Philadelphia Athletics of the American League from 1900 to 1931, and John J. McGraw managed the New York Giants of the National League from 1902 to 1932.

With today's baseball stars paid millions of dollars for their services, can you guess how much the Detroit Tigers paid Ty Cobb when they signed him? Was it $700, $1,700, or $7,000?

In 1905, the Detroit Tigers bought Tyrus Raymond Cobb, the man considered to be the best player in the history of the game, for the bargain price of $700.

If a batter gets on base on a *fielder's choice*, what does that mean?

A *fielder's choice* can only occur with less than two out and with a runner or runners on base. It happens when the batter hits the ball to a fielder who has an opportunity to put out the lead runner or the hitter. If the fielder chooses to put out the lead runner, allowing the hitter to reach base safely, that is a fielder's choice. Simply, it means that the fielder chose to put out the runner instead of the hitter.

Who hit more regular-season home runs during his major league baseball career? Was it Babe Ruth or Henry Aaron?

Henry "Hank" Aaron of the Milwaukee Braves, the Atlanta Braves, and the Milwaukee Brewers is the all-time career home-run leader. In 22 major league seasons, Aaron belted a total of 755 homers during regular-season play. Babe Ruth, in 22 years with the Boston Red Sox and New York Yankees, clubbed 714 homers.

Which American League team has played in more World Series games — the Chicago White Sox or the Detroit Tigers?

The answer is the Detroit Tigers, who played in eight World Series and won three. The White Sox played in the Series four times and won it twice.

New York's Lou Gehrig holds both the AL and major league records for consecutive games played, with a total of 2,130 games. Who holds that record in the National League?

Billy Williams of the Chicago Cubs tops the NL in consecutive games played, with 1,117, which he accomplished from 1963 to 1970.

In the 1978 World Series between the Dodgers and the Yankees, Lou Gehrig's record of 5 home runs in four World Series games was broken. Who broke it?

New York's Reggie Jackson broke the record of 5 home runs set by Lou Gehrig in the 1928 and 1932 classics. Jackson hit 6 homers in four World Series games spanning the 1977 and 1978 Championship Series.

True or false? Earl Williams of the Atlanta Braves, the Rookie of the Year in 1971, was the only National League catcher to ever win that Award.

False. One other catcher won Rookie of the Year honors in the National League. That catcher was Johnny Bench of the Cincinnati Reds, who won the Award in 1968.

Who won more batting titles — Rogers Hornsby or Ty Cobb?

Ty Cobb of the Detroit Tigers won more batting titles than any other baseball player. He led the American League in hitting twelve times between 1907 and 1919. During that span, he batted over .400 twice and over .350 nine times. His best year was in 1911, when he batted .420. Rogers Hornsby of the St. Louis Cardinals led the National League in batting seven times.

In 1978, did any major league baseball team in either league win 100 games?

Yes. Only one team won 100 games. The New York Yankees won the AL's East Division with a record of 100 wins and 63 losses. Their regular season wins totaled 99, but they won the playoff against the Boston Red Sox, thus giving them 100 wins.

How many times did Bob Feller, one of the fastest right-handed pitchers in baseball history, lead the American League in games won?

Bob Feller, who spent all of his 14 major league seasons with the Cleveland Indians, led the American League in pitching five times, each time winning 20 or more games. He did it in 1939, with a record of 24 and 9; in 1940, with a 27-and-11 record; in 1941, with 25 wins and 13 losses, in 1946, with a 26-and-15 record, and in 1947, with a record of 20 wins and 11 losses.

BASEBALL

True or false? A major league baseball team once won 17 straight games and then put together another streak of 26 victories in a row, but ended up finishing in fourth place.

True. It happened to the National League's New York Giants in 1916. Even though they won 43 games during those two streaks, their season record was 86 wins and 66 losses, which put them in fourth place, 8 games behind the pennant-winning Brooklyn Dodgers.

John "Pepper" Martin was one of the fieriest players to ever compete in the major leagues. What team did he play for?

Pepper Martin played for the National League's St. Louis Cardinals and was a star performer at third base in the 1931 World Series against the Philadelphia Athletics. The gutsy infielder-outfielder hit, ran, and performed dazzling fielding plays as he led St. Louis to a 4-games-to-3 victory over Philadelphia.

How many catchers have been named the American League's Rookie of the Year?

Only two catchers have ever won the Rookie of the Year Award in the American League. One was New York Yankee Thurman Munson, who won it in 1970. The other was Carlton Fisk of the Boston Red Sox, the 1972 AL Rookie of the Year.

Who hit more singles during his major league career — Stan Musial or Tris Speaker?

The answer is Tris Speaker of the Boston Braves. During his 22-year career, Speaker banged out 5,101 singles. Stan Musial of the St. Louis Cardinals had 2,253 singles during his 23-year career.

Although Joe DiMaggio has baseball's longest hitting streak, do you known who had the longest consecutive-game hitting streak among Stan Musial, Willie Davis, and Dom DiMaggio?

Dom DiMaggio, who like his brother Joe played the outfield, had the longest hitting streak of the three. In 1949, Dom hit safely in 34 straight games for the Boston Red Sox. Willie Davis, the star outfielder for the Los Angeles Dodgers, had a hitting streak of 31 games in 1969, topping Stan Musial, the great St. Louis Cardinal outfielder, who hit in 30 consecutive games in 1950.

What is the score of a forfeited game?

It's 9-0.

True or false? Ted Kluszewski of the Cincinnati Reds was best known for his ability as a defensive ball player.

That is absolutely false. Kluszewski was best known for his power hitting. In 1954, he led the AL in homers with 49, and during his career, he belted a total of 279.

True of false? In the 1968 World Series between the St. Louis Cardinals and the Detroit Tigers, an average of more than eight Tiger batters a game were struck out.

It's amazing, but true . . . and a Series record, besides. In the 1968 World Series, Cardinal pitchers set a record by fanning 59 Tiger batters in seven games — an average of more than eight batters per game, or almost one batter every inning.

The World Champion 1934 St. Louis Cardinals were nicknamed the "Gas House Gang." Who was the manger of the "Gas House Gang"?

Hall-of-Famer Frankie Frisch managed the "Gas House Gang," after piling up 2,880 career hits and a lifetime BA of .316.

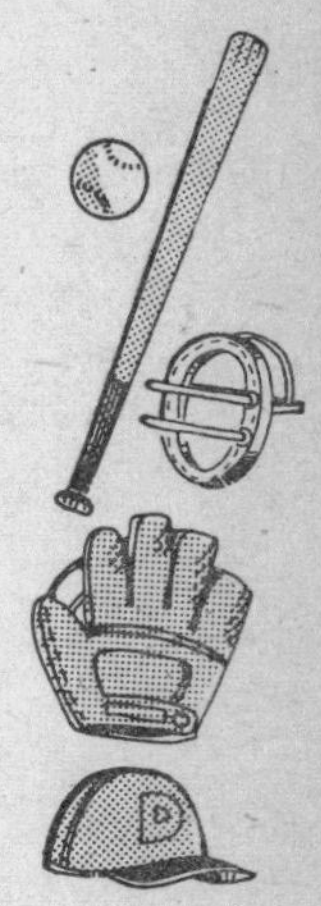

Who won the American League batting crown in 1978? Was it Rod Carew of the Minnesota Twins, Lou Piniella of the New York Yankees, or Fred Lynn of the Boston Red Sox.

Minnesota's Rod Carew won the 1978 AL batting crown with a .333 average. The Yankee's Lou Piniella finished fourth, with a .314 BA, and Boston's Fred Lynn was seventh, with a .298 BA.

What is a *hit-and-run play*?

A *hit-and-run play* is a prearranged play that occurs with a runner on first base. The success of the play depends on the batter, who must hit the ball no matter where it is thrown. On that predetermined pitch, the runner breaks for second just as the pitcher starts to deliver the ball to the plate. The batter attempts to hit the ball to the right side of the diamond, pulling the second baseman away from the bag. If the batter is successful, the runner can easily continue on to third base, where he will be in excellent scoring position.

Actor William Bendix starred in a 1948 movie based on the life of the famous New York Yankee baseball player who is often referred to as the "Sultan of Swat." Do you know the name of that movie?

The movie was *The Babe Ruth Story*. In the film, William Bendix played George Herman "Babe" Ruth.

The opening of the Houston Astrodome, with its artificial turf, revolutionalized the game of baseball by eliminating weather problems. In what year did the Astrodome open?

The $20,500,000 Houston Astrodome opened on April 9, 1965.

Who was the last member of the old Brooklyn Dodgers to win the National League batting title? Was it Carl Furillo, Jackie Robinson, or Dixie Walker?

Carl Furillo was the last of the old Brooklyn Dodgers to win the National League batting title. His average of .344 led the league in 1953. Jackie Robinson had won the NL batting crown with an average of .342 in 1949, and Dixie Walker earned it in 1944 with a .357.

Between 1957 and 1977, only one major league pitcher has had a year with an earned run average of less than 1.50. Can you name him?

The only pitcher in the past two decades with an ERA of less than 1.50 is Bob Gibson of the St. Louis Cardinals. In 1968, Gibson's earned run average was 1.12, the lowest in the major leagues since Ferdinand M. Schupp's ERA of 0.90 for the 1916 New York Giants.

Can you name the stadiums that were the home fields of the old Brooklyn Dodgers and the old New York Giants?

Ebbets Field was the home stadium of the old Brooklyn Dodgers, and the Polo Grounds was the home of the old New York Giants. Neither stadium is now standing.

With a seven-game lead and only two weeks left in the season, a National League team once lost the pennant. Which team was it?

Those losers were the 1964 Philadelphia Phillies.

The cry of "Wait til next year!" was the popular slogan of which old National League team?

"Wait til next year!" was the cry of the old Brooklyn Dodgers. They were the "wait-til-next-year" team because, after winning the NL pennant in 1916, 1920, 1941, 1947, 1949, 1952, and 1953 — a total of seven times, they always ended up losing the World Series. Their fans looked forward to each "next year" with great expectations. That long-awaited "next year" finally came in 1955, when the Dodgers beat the Yankees in the World Series, 4 games to 3, to win their first World Championship.

True or false? Vic Davalillo, who played for the 1978 Los Angeles Dodgers, is one of the best pinch-hitters in baseball.

True. Davalillo shares the major league record for the most pinch-hits in a season with Dave Philley of the Baltimore Orioles, who established the mark of 24 pinch-hits in 1961. Davalillo tied Philley's record while playing for the St. Louis Cardinals in 1970.

How many times did Hank Aaron, the all-time leader in career home runs, hit 50 homers in a single season?

During his 22-year career, Hank Aaron *never* hit 50 home runs in a single season. His highest was 47, in 1971.

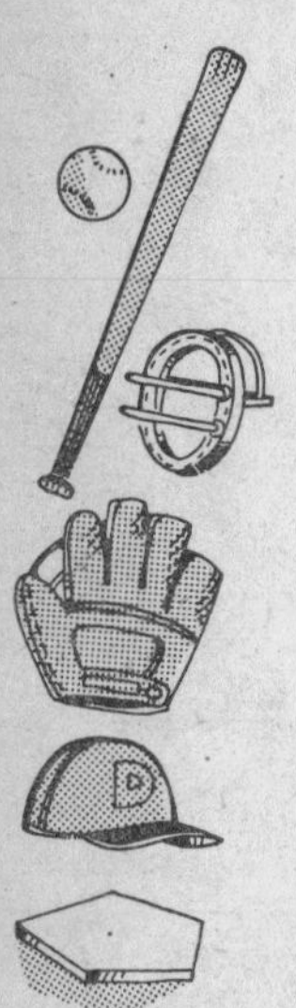

True or false? Lou Piniella, Thurman Munson, and Chris Chambliss — members of the 1978 Yankees, were all former American League Rookies of the Year.

It's true. Lou Piniella, the Yankee leftfielder, won Rookie of the Year honors in 1969 while playing for the Kansas City Royals. Yankee catcher Thurman Munson won the Award as a Yankee rookie in 1970. And Chris Chambliss, the New York first baseman, was named Rookie of the Year in 1971, his first year with the Cleveland Indians.

Who did the Baseball Writers Association select as the Rookie of the Year in the National League in 1977?

Centerfielder Andre Dawson of the Montreal Expos was the National League's Rookie of the Year in 1977. Dawson had 19 homers, batted .282, had 65 runs batted in, and stole 21 bases.

How many times did Tony Oliva of the Minnesota Twins win the American League batting title? Was it once, twice, or three times?

Tony Oliva won the AL batting title three times. His first title was in 1964, when his batting average was .323. He repeated in 1965 with a .321, and in 1971 with a .377.

In 1969, who did the Baseball Writers Association of America select as "the greatest living second baseman" and "the greatest living catcher"?

The Baseball Writers of America selected Charley Gehringer of the Detroit Tigers as "the greatest living second baseman" and Bill Dickey of the New York Yankees as "the greatest living catcher."

Can you name the Baltimore Oriole who was famous for his ability to "hit 'em where they ain't"?

The player was "Wee" Willie Keeler, an outfielder with the Baltimore Orioles from 1892 to 1910. Keeler, a magician with a bat, had the uncanny ability to hit the ball into the open areas between fielders. He led the National League in batting in 1897 and 1898, had a career average of .345, and was elected to the Hall of Fame in 1939.

Who did the *Sporting News* name as baseball's "Player of the Year" in 1978?

The *Sporting News*, a reowned sports newspaper, named pitcher Ron Guidry of the New York Yankees as their 1978 "Player of the Year." Guidry was the winningest pitcher in major league baseball in 1978, with a phenomenal record of 24 wins and only 3 losses. He struck out 243 batters and had a league-leading earned run average of 1.72.

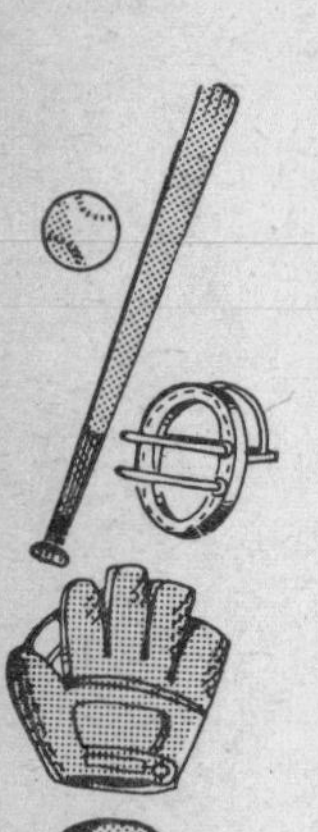

Jim Gilliam, the coach to whom the Los Angeles Dodgers dedicated the 1978 World Series, played baseball for the old Brooklyn Dodgers. What position did he play?

Jim "Junior" Gilliam was a talented second baseman and later a coach for the Dodgers, and the National League's Rookie of the Year in 1953. After his death in October, 1978, the Dodgers retired his number 19.

There have been only two playoffs in American League history. One was between the New York Yankees and the Boston Red Sox in 1978. When was the other and which two teams played in that game?

The first playoff in American League history occurred in 1948, when the Cleveland Indians and the Boston Red Sox ended the regular season in a tie. The Indians won the playoff and the pennant, then went on to beat the NL's Boston Braves, 4 games to 2, in the World Series.

Who was responsible for instituting the tradition of the two major leagues competing in All-Star Games?

Arch Ward, the sports editor of the *Chicago Tribune,* got the idea for the game because attendance had been slipping badly at most major league parks. That first game was played in 1933 in Chicago, the site of the World's Fair that year. The AL beat the NL, 4 to 2.

Hank Aaron broke Babe Ruth's career home-run record (714) in 1974. Against which pitcher and team did Hank Aaron hit his record-breaking 715th home run?

Hank Aaron of the Atlanta Braves hit his 715th career homer off Al Downing in a game against the Los Angeles Dodgers in April of 1974. Aaron then went on to add to that total, finishing his career in 1976 with 755 home runs.

How many times did Mickey Mantle bat .300 or more during his 18-year major league career? Was it five, seven, or ten times?

Mickey Mantle of the New York Yankees hit .300 or better ten times during his major league baseball career, including five consecutive years from 1954 to 1958. His highest average was .365, which he hit in 1957.

In 1969, when the Baseball Writers of America came up with "the greatest living baseball team," who did they name to the outfield positions?

The selections for "the greastest living team's outfield" were centerfielder Joe DiMaggio of the New York Yankees, leftfielder Ted Williams of the Boston Red Sox, and rightfielder Willie Mays of the New York and San Francisco Giants.

Graig Nettles led the American League in home runs in 1976. What team was he on that year?

Graig Nettles played third base for the New York Yankees in 1976, when he belted 32 HRs.

Hank Aaron, major league baseball's home-run prince, was never named the Most Valuable Player of the National League. True or false?

False. Hank Aaron won the MVP award in 1957 while playing for the Milwaukee Braves. That year, Aaron belted out a league-leading total of 44 home runs.

True or false? A major league pitcher once hit two homers in a game while hurling a no-hitter.

True. On June 23, 1971, Rick Wise of the Philadelphia Phillies smacked out 2 home runs while pitching a no-hitter against the Cincinnati Reds.

Why are pitchers Tom Zachary, Guy Bush, and Tracy Stallard in baseball record books?

Each of these three pitchers gave up record-breaking hits. In 1927, it was Tom Zachary's pitch off which Babe Ruth hit his 60th homer. In 1935, Guy Busch had his pitch hit by Ruth for his 714th career homer. And in 1961, Tracy Stallard pitched the ball that gave Roger Maris his 61st home run.

True or false? Bill Terry of the 1930 New York Giants set the major league record for the most hits in a season.

False. The major league record — 257 hits — is held by American-Leaguer George Sisler of the 1920 St. Louis Browns. New York's Bill Terry had 254 hits in 1930 and shares the National League record with Frank J. O'Doul of the 1929 Philadelphia Phillies.

Which team won the American League's West Division title in 1978? Was it the Kansas City Royals, the California Angels, or the Texas Rangers?

The Kansas City Royals were the AL's West Division Champions in 1978. They finished in front of the California Angels in second place and the Texas Rangers, who finished third.

Who had a higher lifetime batting average — Joe DiMaggio or Stan Musial?

Stan "The Man" Musial of the St. Louis Cardinals had a higher lifetime average than New York's "Yankee Clipper," Joe DiMaggio. Musial's career average is .331, just .006 points higher than DiMaggio's .325.

BASEBALL

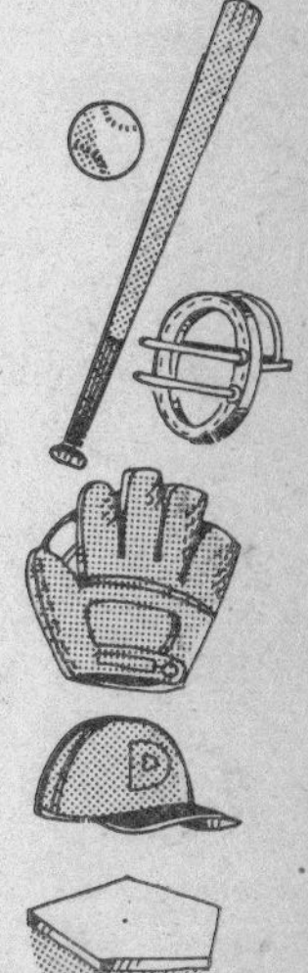

In what year did the Boston Braves of the National League move to a new city and what city did they move to?

After a meager season attendance of 281,278 in 1952, the Boston Braves moved to Milwaukee in 1953, in an attempt to improve their home-game support. In their first year at Milwaukee, the Braves' attendance jumped to 1,826,397.

A 1978 TV movie, *One in a Million: The Ron LeFlore Story*, was based on the true story of a young athlete who at age 19 learned to play baseball while serving a prison sentence and who later became a major league ball player after his release. Which American League team did Ron LeFlore play for?

Ron LeFlore played center-field for the Detroit Tigers. In the early 1970s, LeFlore was a model prisoner at Michigan State Prison, where he played on the prison baseball team. Billy Martin, then the manager of the Detroit Tigers, noticed LeFlore and offered him a tryout after his release. Young LeFlore made the Detroit Team and later went on to star for the Tigers. In the 1978 movie, LeVar Burton, the star of *Roots*, played Ron LeFlore.

Who ranks higher on the all-time home-run list? — Frank Robinson or Harmon Killebrew?

Frank Robinson of the Baltimore Orioles and the Cincinnati Reds ranks fourth on the all-time list, with 586 homers, while Killebrew of the Minnesota Twins is fifth, with 573 homers.

True or false? Mickey Mantle hit over 30 home runs in a season nine times.

True. Nine times during his 18-year career as a New York Yankee, Mickey Mantle smacked 30 or more homers. His biggest year was in 1961, when he belted 54.

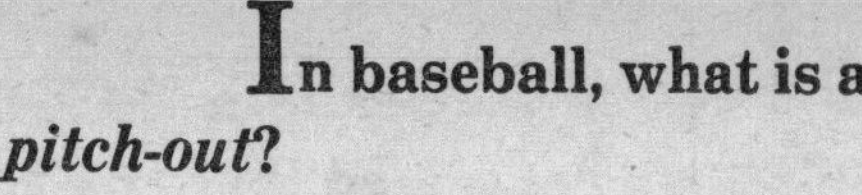

In baseball, what is a *pitch-out*?

A *pitch-out* is a play prearranged by the pitcher and catcher when a base runner is expected to steal. Instead of throwing the ball over the plate where the batter can swing at it and block the catcher's view of the runner, the pitcher throws the ball wide, but straight at the catcher who has stepped away from the plate.

The following men are in early baseball record books for performing an amazing feat: Addie Joss of the Cleveland Indians, Ernie Shore of the Boston Red Sox, and Charles Robertson of the Chicago White Sox. What did they do?

Addie Joss, Ernie Shore, and Charles Robertson are all pitchers with perfect games to their credit. Joss' perfect game was in 1908 against the Chicago White Sox; Shore's was in 1917 against the Washington Senators; and Robertson's was in 1922 against the Detroit Tigers.

In 1951, when New York Yankee centerfielder Joe DiMaggio was injured, manager Casey Stengel called up a young speedster from a Yankee farm team to replace him. Can you name that young replacement who soon became a Yankee superstar?

The man Casey Stengel called up from the minors in 1951 to replace the injured Joe DiMaggio was Mickey Mantle.

When the National Baseball Hall of Fame was opened in 1936 at Cooperstown, New York, five baseball immortals were enshrined there by the Baseball Writers Association. The first player elected was Ty Cobb. Can you name the other four players voted into the Baseball Hall of Fame that first year?

Christy Mathewson, Honus Wager, Babe Ruth, and Walter Johnson followed Ty Cobb into Baseball's Hall of Fame in 1936.

Only one baseball team has ever lost the first two games of the World Series and then won the next four to take the Championship. Can you name the team that did it?

The only team in the history of major league baseball to accomplish that is the New York Yankees. In the 1978 World Series against the Los Angeles Dodgers, the Yanks lost the first two games in Los Angeles, then came back to win the next three games in New York and the sixth game at Los Angeles.

Denny McLain of the Detroit Tigers was a great pitcher in the late 1960s. Did he ever win the Cy Young Award?

Yes. Denny McLain was voted the AL's Cy Young Award twice. He won it in 1968 and shared it with Mike Cuellar of the Baltimore Orioles in 1969. McLain's 1968 Award came as the unanimous choice of the Baseball Writers Association.

At the Baseball Hall of Fame in Cooperstown, New York, the adjective "graceful" is inscribed on only one plaque honoring the great players enshrined there. Can you name the only ball player described as the "most graceful and efficient second baseman of his era"?

It's Napoleon "Nap" Lajoie, the great hitting second sacker of the Philadelphia Athletics, who played major league ball from 1896 to 1916, collecting 3,251 hits and earning a .339 lifetime batting average.

True or false? Willie Mays and Pete Rose never won Rookie of the Year Awards.

Absolutely false. Willie Mays, an outfielder for the New York Giants, was the NL's Rookie of the Year in 1951, and Pete Rose, as a second baseman for the Cincinnati Reds, was the National League's top rookie in 1963.

Who had a higher lifetime batting average — Rogers Horsby or Pie Traynor?

Second baseman Rogers Horsby of the St. Louis Cardinals and the Chicago Cubs had a higher lifetime average than third baseman Pie Traynor of the Pittsburgh Pirates. Hornsby's lifetime average was .358, topping Traynor's .320 by .038.

Which of these sluggers hit the most home runs during his career — Ron Santo, Yogi Berra, or Gil Hodges?

Gil Hodges hit 370 homers, which is more than Berra's total of 358 or Santo's 342.

True or false? Between 1967 and 1976, no team from the United States won the Little League World Series.

False. One U.S. team won the Little League World Series during that ten-year span. A team from Wayne, New Jersey captured the Little League title in 1970. Except for that year, teams from Japan and Nationalist China have won the Little League Championship every year from 1967 to date.

Leo Durocher was a colorful baseball player and an even more colorful manager. Can you name the first major league team that Durocher managed?

The first major league team Leo Durocher managed was the Brooklyn Dodgers, where he stayed from 1939 to 1948. From 1949 to 1954, Durocher crossed the river to manage the New York Giants. After a break of 18 years, Durocher returned to the majors in 1972 to pilot the Chicago Cubs, then switched to the Houston Astros for the balance of the 1972 season and stayed there in 1973.

Which immortal New York Giant pitcher won more consecutive games during one season — Carl Hubbell or Rube Marquard?

Rube Marquard won more consecutive games in a season than Hubbell. Marquard's 19 in a row set a National League record in 1912. In 1936, Carl Hubbell won 16 in a row, but the season ended before he could continue his streak. Then in 1937, he won 8 more consecutive games to run his streak to 24 games over two seasons, which is another major league record.

Only one man has played in 3,298 major league baseball games — a record number. Can you name him?

The record holder is Hank Aaron of the Milwaukee Braves, the Atlanta Braves, and the Milwaukee Brewers. Aaron also holds major league records for the most times at bat (12,093), the most total bases (6,856), the most RBIs (2,297), the most extra-base hits (1,459), and the most career home runs (755).

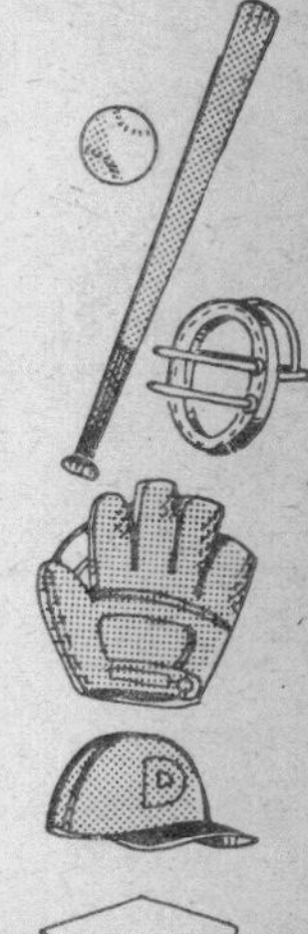

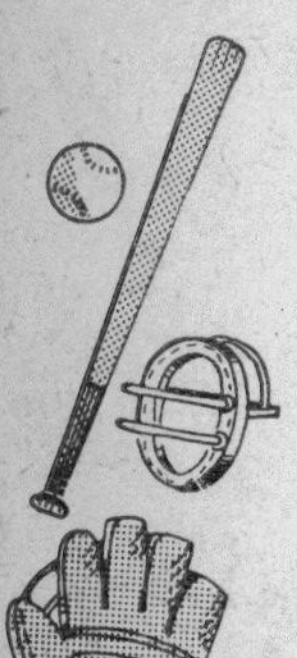

How many times did Willie McCovey of the San Francisco Giants win the NL home-run crown?

Willie McCovey, a first baseman for the Giants, won the home-run title three times. He won it in 1963 (44 HRs), in 1968 (36 HRs), and in 1969 (45 HRs).

True or false? Experts have determined that a major league batter has actually about 1/50th of a second to get his bat around and meet the ball in the right place.

It's amazing, but true. Scientific testing has shown that most pitchers can throw the ball up to 90 mph. Therefore, a batter has less than half a second to decide if he will swing at the ball. After deciding, he has about 1/50th of a second to get the bat around quickly enough to make solid contact.

Although they're not related, Brooks Robinson and Frank Robinson were both stars for the Baltimore Orioles during the mid 1960s. Which Robinson was a third baseman?

Brooks Robinson was a third baseman and is considered one of the best third basemen of all time. Frank Robinson was a good outfielder and a great hitter.

In 1969, when the Baseball Writers of America picked "the greatest baseball team in history," who did they pick as "the greatest right handed and greatest left-handed pitchers"?

Walter Johnson of the Washington Senators, who won 416 games and lost 279 from 1907 to 1927, was voted "the greatest right-handed pitcher," and Bob "Lefty" Grove of the Boston Red Sox, who won 300 games and lost 140 from 1925 to 1941, was picked as "the greatest left-hander."

True or false? The Baltimore Orioles were formerly called the St. Louis Browns.

True. The American League's St. Louis Browns moved to Baltimore in 1954 and changed their name to the Orioles. Poor home attendance was the cause of the franchise shift. In 1953 in St. Louis, they drew a season crowd of only 297,238, while in 1954 in Baltimore, they were supported by 1,060,910 fans.

How many World Series team batting records did the New York Yankees set in 1978 when they beat the Los Angeles Dodgers, 4 games to 2? Was it two, three, or four records?

In the 1978 World Series, the Yankees set four new team batting records for a six-game Series — records previously held by the 1936 New York Yankee team. The 1978 Yanks got 68 hits, bettering the old mark of 65. They also collected 57 singles, shattering the old Series record of 49. Their team batting average was .306, which beat the old record average of .302, and they had a total of 222 at bats, erasing the old World Series record of 215.

Which pitcher struck out more batters in a single game? Was it Sandy Koufax or Tom Seaver?

The answer is Tom Seaver. On April 22, 1970, pitching for the New York Mets, Tom Seaver struck out 19 San Diego Padres to tie the major league record for strikeouts set by Steve Carlton of the St. Louis Cardinals in 1961. Nolan Ryan of the California Angels joined the elite duo with his 19 strikeouts in 1974. Sandy Koufax is in second place, with 18 strikeouts in a single game — a feat he accomplished twice.

Whose hit has been called "the shot heard around the world"?

New York Giant slugger Bobby Thompson belted a 3-run homer off Brooklyn Dodger relief pitcher Ralph Branca in the 1951 playoffs for the National League Pennant. That home run has been called "the shot heard around the world," for it came with the three-game playoff series tied at one game apiece and the Dodgers leading, 4 to 2, with the Giants up in the bottom of the ninth inning. Thompson's 3-run homer, one of the most thrilling in baseball history, gave the Giants the NL Pennant.

True or false? A major league baseball player once got 12 hits in a row.

True. Two men have done it. Mike Higgins of the Boston Red Sox did it over a span of four games in 1938, and Walt Dropo of the Detroit Tigers did it in three games in 1952.

One of Babe Ruth's dreams was to manage the New York Yankees. Did his dream ever come true?

No. Babe Ruth never got the chance to manage the New York Yankees or any other major league baseball team. However, Ruth did coach the Brooklyn Dodgers from June 18, 1938 to the end of the 1938 baseball season.

The New York Yankees played the Los Angeles Dodgers in the 1977 and the 1978 World Series. Which Series had the higher gate receipts?

The gate receipts in the 1978 World Series were $4,667,542.57, which broke the old record of $3,978,825.33, set by the Dodgers and Yankees in 1977.

True or false? The great Ty Cobb had hitting streaks of more than 30 consecutive games twice during his career.

True. In 1911, Ty Cobb of the AL's Detroit Tigers hit safely in 40 straight games. Then in 1917, Cobb put together a consecutive-game hitting streak of 35 games.

Which pitcher holds the record for the most career strikeouts — Walter Johnson or Cy Young?

Walter Johnson holds the record with a career total of 3,497 strikeouts. Cy Young, on the other hand, won more games than any other pitcher in baseball history. Young had 511 wins during his career.

A St. Louis Cardinal pitcher set a World Series record in 1968 by striking out 17 batters in a single game. Can you name that pitcher?

In the opening game of the 1968 World Series, Bob Gibson of the St. Louis Cardinals struck out 17 Detroit Tiger batters to set the record.

True or false? In 1978, the Pittsburgh Pirates topped the East Division of the National League.

False. The Philadelphia Phillies won the NL's East Division title in 1978. It was the third straight Divisional Championship for the Phillies. The Pirates finished in second place.

Who holds the major league record for hitting the most grand-slam home runs during his career? Here's a clue. He's a former first baseman for the New York Yankees.

The answer is "The Iron Horse," Lou Gehrig. The great Yankee first sacker belted 23 bases-loaded homers to set the career mark for grand-slam home runs.

In the 1934 All-Star Game, the starting pitcher for the National League struck out in consecutive order five of the most dangerous hitters in baseball history: Babe Ruth, Lou Gehrig, Jimmy Foxx, Al Simmons and Joe Cronin. Who was that National League All-Star pitcher?

Carl Hubbell, a southpaw for the New York Giants, was the 1934 All-Star pitcher who fanned Ruth, Gehrig, Foxx, Simmons, and Cronin all in a row. That 1934 All-Star Game was to become one of the most famous baseball contests of all time, since eighteen of the players who participated in it were later to be enshrined in the Baseball's Hall of Fame.

The pitching rotation for the 1948 Boston Braves was chanted by fans with the words, "___________and___________, and 2 days of rain." Who were those pitchers who led the Braves to the National League Pennant?

The chant was "Spahn and Sain, and 2 days of rain." Warren Spahn and Johnny Sain were the aces who practically alternated pitching rotations (with 2 days of rain) to carry the Braves to the NL Pennant.

Randy Moffitt, a pitcher for the San Francisco Giants in 1977, has a famous tennis star for a sister. Do you know who she is?

Billy Jean Moffitt King, one of the best female tennis players in the world, is the sister of San Francisco Giants' hurler Randy Moffitt.

Brooks Robinson and Frank Robinson have each received a Most Valuable Player Award. Which man was the first to win it?

Frank Robinson won the NL's MVP award as a Cincinnati Red in 1961. Brooks Robinson was the AL's Most Valuable Player in 1964, while playing for the Baltimore Orioles. Then in 1967, Frank Robinson repeated as the AL's MVP as a member of the Baltimore Orioles.

According to a 1969 poll of the Baseball Writers of America, who was "the greatest catcher" in the history of major league baseball? Was it Bill Dickey, Yogi Berra, or Mickey Cochrane?

The Baseball Writers of America voted Mickey Cochrane of the old Philadelphia Athletics and Detroit Tigers "the greatest catcher" in baseball history. Cochrane was also the American League's MVP in 1934.

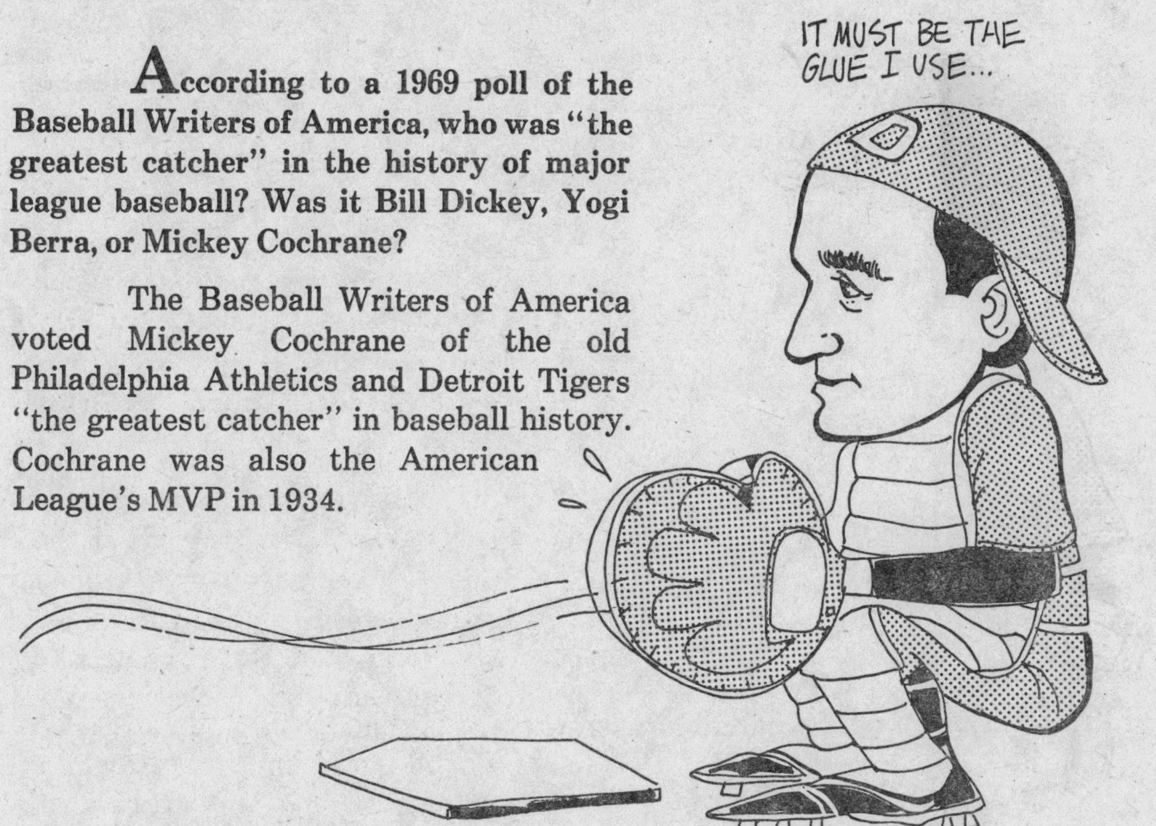

True or false? In 1941, Ted Williams of the Boston Red Sox ended the season with a .406 BA by getting six hits on the final day.

True. Ted Williams' average was .399 going into the final day of the 1941 season when the Red Sox met the Philadelphia Athletics for a Sunday double-header. Williams went 4 for 5 in the first game and 2 for 3 in the final game, to boost his average to .406. Williams was the first major-leaguer to hit .400 or better since 1930. No major league player has hit .400 since then.

In which baseball season were the most no-hitters thrown? Was it in 1961, 1966, or 1971?

More no-hitters were thrown in 1971 than in 1961 or 1966. In 1971, three pitchers hurled no-hitters: Ken Holtzman of the Chicago Cubs, Bob Gibson of the St. Louis Cardinals, and Rick Wise of the Philadelphia Phillies. In 1961, Warren Spahn of the Milwaukee Braves pitched the season's only no-hitter, and in 1966, Sonny Siebert of the Cleveland Indians did the same.

True or false? In a special election in 1974, Roberto Clemente, the slugging outfielder for the Pittsburgh Pirates, was elected to Baseball's Hall of Fame.

True. On New Year's Eve, 1973, Roberto Clemente died in a plane crash while on a mercy mission to aid earthquake victims in Nicaragua. Shortly afterward, in 1974, he was voted into Baseball's Hall of Fame in a special election. Clemente, the National League's Most Valuable Player in 1966, had one of the strongest arms of any right fielder in baseball history, and had collected over 3,000 hits during his career.

Which New York Yankee had the highest batting average in the 1978 World Series? Was it outfielder Lou Piniella, catcher Thurman Munson, or second baseman Brian Doyle?

Brian Doyle, a young infielder who got the chance to play in the 1978 World Series only because regular Yankee second baseman Willie Randolph was injured, had the highest batting average of any player on either team. Doyle got 7 hits in 16 at bats for a .438 batting average. Piniella was 7 for 25 and had a .280 average. Munson was 8 for 25, giving him a .320 batting average. The highest BA in baseball history for one Series is held by Babe Ruth, who batted a resounding .625 in 1928.

In 1976, Walter Matthau and Tatum O'Neal starred in a hilarious movie based on the exploits of a fictional Little League team. Can you name that film?

The movie was *The Bad News Bears*. The hapless Bears were truly "bad news" until their beer-guzzling manager, Matthau, brought in a star pitcher — a girl!

Only two American League players have won batting titles at different times while playing for two different teams. Can you name them?

The two sluggers are Nap Lajoie and Jimmy Foxx. Lajoie first won the AL batting crown in 1901, with an average of .422, while playing for the Philadelphia Athletics. Then in 1904 and 1905, Lajoie, as a member of the Cleveland Indians, won the title again, with averages of .355 and .381. Jimmy Foxx was the best hitter in the American League as a Philadelphia Athletic in 1933, with a batting average of .356. Later, while playing for the Boston Red Sox in 1938, Jimmy again won the batting crown, with an average of .349.

Since the Rookie of the Year Award began in 1947, which team has had the most winners — the Dodgers or the Yankees?

The Dodgers have had the most Rookies of the Year, with seven. Jackie Robinson was their first winner in 1947; Don Newcombe followed in 1949; Joe Black, in 1951; Jim "Junior" Gilliam, in 1953; Frank Howard, in 1960; Jim Lefebve, in 1965; and Ted Sizemore, in 1969. The Yankees are second with six: Gil McDougald, in 1951; Bob Grim, in 1954; Tony Kubek, in 1957; Tom Tresh, in 1962; Stan Bahnsen, in 1968, and Thurman Munson, in 1970.

True or false? Rod Carew of the Minnesota Twins once stole home ten times in one season.

False. In 1969, Carew set an American League record by stealing home seven times in one season. No one in either league has ever stolen home more than seven times in one season.

Which team has played in the most World Series? Here's a hint. It's an American League team.

The New York Yankees have played in more World Series competitions than any other major league baseball team. From 1903 — when Series play began — to 1978, the Bronx Bombers have been in 30 World Series, winning 20, losing 9, and tying 1.

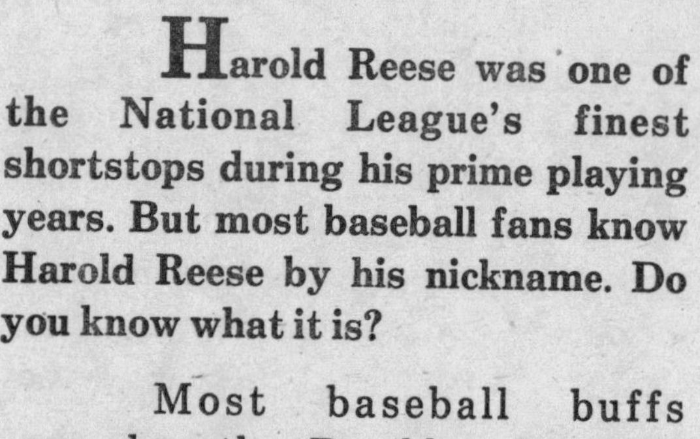

Harold Reese was one of the National League's finest shortstops during his prime playing years. But most baseball fans know Harold Reese by his nickname. Do you know what it is?

Most baseball buffs remember the Brooklyn Dodgers' diminuitive shortstop as "Pee Wee" Reese.

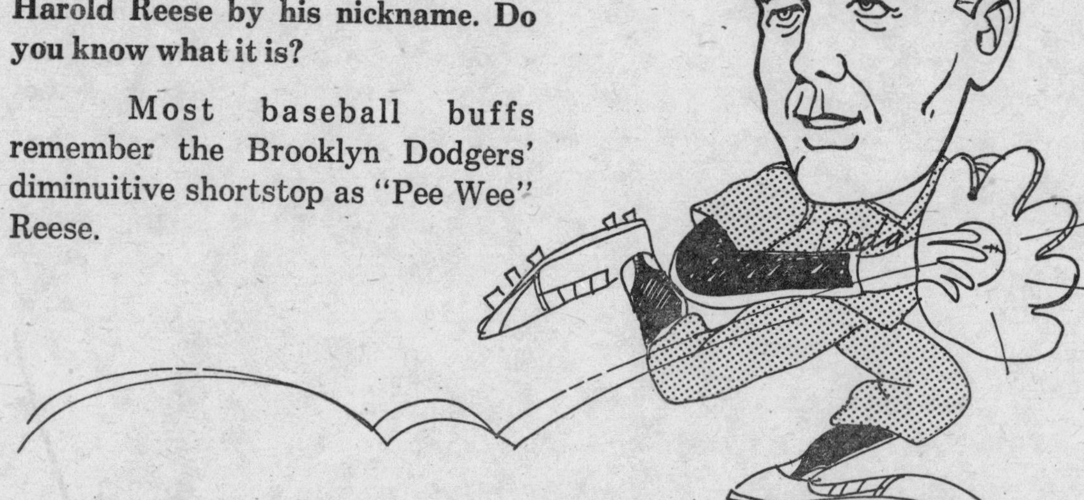

Which National League baseball teams play at the following stadiums: Shea Stadium, Wrigley Field, and Riverfront Stadium?

Shea Stadium is the home of the NL's New York Mets; Wrigley Field hosts the home games of the Chicago Cubs; and Riverfront Stadium is home to the Cincinnati Reds.

Jim Bunning pitched 2 no-hitters, one — a perfect game, during his major league career. True or false?

True. Bunning pitched his first no-hitter as a Detroit Tiger on July 20, 1958. His second no-hitter — and perfect game — came on June 21, 1964 as a Philadelphia Phillie.

How many hits did Stan Musial of the St. Louis Cardinals get during his major league career? Was it 1,630, 2,630, or 3,630 hits?

Musial got 3,630 hits during his 21-year, 3026-game career. Of these 3,630 hits, 475 were home runs.

True or false? Four different pitchers once combined to pitch a no-hitter.

True. It happened on September 28, 1975, in a game between the Oakland A's and the California Angels. Oakland pitchers Vida Blue, Glenn Abbot, Paul Lindblad, and Rollie Fingers combined to no-hit California. Oakland won, 5 to 0, and Vida Blue, who pitched five of the game's nine innings was the winning pitcher. It was the first time a no-hitter was thrown by more than two pitchers.

Have the San Francisco Giants ever won a World Series?

No. The Giants have played in the World Series only once since they moved to San Francisco. That was in 1962, when they lost to the New York Yankees, 4 games to 3. Prior to the move west, as the New York Giants, they won the World Series five times: in 1905, 1921, 1922, 1933, and 1954.

A professional baseball player in Japan has hit more home runs than Hank Aaron. True or false?

True. Sadaharu Oh, who plays for Tokyo's Yomiuri Giants, has hit more home runs than Hank Aaron. On September 3, 1977, Oh hit his 756th homer, and is still adding to his total.

True or false? The Houston Astros of the National League were formerly known as the Houston Colt 45s.

True. When Houston was granted a National League franchise in 1962, the team was named the Colt 45s. Shortly afterward, they were renamed the Houston Astros.

Has a fair ball ever been hit out of Yankee Stadium?

No player has succeeded in accomplishing that feat, but several, including Mickey Mantle, have come mighty close.

True or false? A minor league baseball player once hit over 80 home runs in a single season.

True. The man is Josh Gibson, a great early baseball player who never made it to the major leagues because of the color barrier. Gibson, who played for the Homestead Grays of the Negro League from 1911 to 1947, is reported to have clouted 84 homers in a single season. In addition to that great feat, Gibson's total of 800 career home runs is claimed to be an all-league record. For these accomplishments, Josh Gibson was elected to the Baseball Hall of Fame in 1972.

True or false? Pitcher Nolan Ryan of the California Angels once pitched two no-hitters in a single season.

True. In 1973, Nolan Ryan became the fourth pitcher in baseball history to pitch two no-hitters in one season. He joined Redleg Johnny Vander Meer, Yankee Allie Reynolds, and Tiger Virgil Trucks in the baseball record books.

Can you name the year that Roy Campanella, the great Brooklyn Dodger catcher, was named the Most Valuable Player in the National League?

Catcher Roy Campanella of the Dodgers was named the MVP of the National League *three* times: first in 1951, and again in 1953 and 1955. The playing career of this great catcher was ended in 1958 when an auto accident injured his spine and confined him to a wheelchair.

In 1949, Stan Musial of the St. Louis Cardinals finished second in the balloting for the Most Valuable Player of the National League. Who beat Musial and won the MVP Award that year?

Jackie Robinson of the Brooklyn Dodgers became the first black player to win the NL's Most Valuable Player Award when he beat Stan Musial in the 1949 balloting. Robinson took the honor with 264 votes, while Musial finished second with 226.

Who won the National League batting title in 1978? Was it Pete Rose of the Cincinnati Reds, Steve Garvey of the Los Angeles Dodgers, or Dave Parker of the Pittsburgh Pirates?

The Pirates' Dave Parker won the 1978 NL batting crown. His 194 hits in 581 at bats gave him a league-leading average of .334. Steve Garvey took second place with 202 hits in 639 at bats for a .316 average. Pete Rose finished in seventh place with 198 hits in 655 at bats for a .302 average.

How many times did Mel Ott of the New York Giants lead the National League in home runs? Was it once, twice, or six times?

Mel Ott, with his odd habit of lifting his front foot into the air before swinging at a pitch, was the home-run king of the National League six times. He won the HR crown in 1932, 1934, 1936, 1937, 1938, and 1942, for a total of 203 round-trippers.

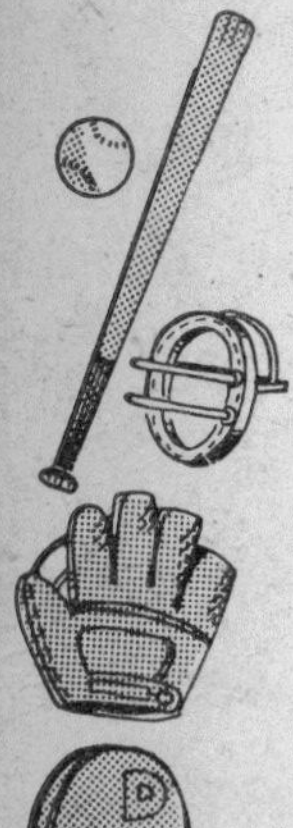

True or false? A pitcher once pitched a perfect game for 12 innings and ended up losing the game.

True. It happened to lefthander Harvey Haddix of the NL's Pittsburgh Pirates on May 26, 1959. In a game against the Milwaukee Braves, Haddix did not allow a single runner to reach base for 12 innings, but his team could not score any runs, and the score remained tied, 0 to 0, going into the 13th inning. Then disaster struck in the last half of the 13th. A Milwaukee Brave reached base on an error. A home run followed, giving the Braves the win over the Pirates and Haddix.

Only one pitcher has ever been voted the Most Valuable Player of the National League more than once. See if this hint will help you name him — he pitched for a New York team.

The answer is Hall-of-Famer Carl Hubbell of the New York Giants. Hubbell was the MVP of the National League in 1933 and 1936.

Has Jim "Catfish" Hunter of the New York Yankees ever pitched a perfect game?

Yes, but that perfect game came when Hunter was an Oakland Athletic in 1968.

How many times did Ted Williams win baseball's coveted Triple Crown?

Ted Williams of the Boston Red Sox won the Triple Crown twice. In 1942, his 137 runs batted in, 36 home runs, and a batting average of .356 earned him the Triple Crown. In 1947, he captured it again with 114 RBIs, 32 HRs, and a .343 BA.

Between 1969 and 1978, which team won the National League's East Division the most times — the New York Mets, the Pittsburgh Pirates, or the Philadelphia Phillies?

It's the Pittsburgh Pirates, with a total of five East Division titles, which they won in 1970, 1971, 1972, 1974, and 1975. The Phillies won it 3 times: in 1976, 1977, and 1978. The Mets won it twice: in 1969 and 1973.

Can you name the baseball player who received more walks than any other player in history?

Surprisingly, the answer is Babe Ruth. He received 2,056 bases on balls during his career — a major league record. Ruth's 170 walks in 1923 also established a season record.

A 1942 movie was based on the life of baseball's "Iron Horse," Lou Gehrig. Do you remember the name of that movie?

The movie was *Pride of the Yankees*, and starred Gary Cooper as Lou Gehrig, along with Walter Brennan, Teresa Wright, and Babe Ruth, who played himself.

In baseball, what is an *intentional pass*?

An *intentional pass* is a walk, or base on balls, given to a dangerous hitter to set up a double play or to bring up the next man in the batting order who may not be quite as dangerous as the hitter walked. Usually, the pitcher throws four consecutive balls so far away from the plate that the batter cannot reach them.

BASEBALL

Was an unassisted triple play ever made in a World Series?

Yes. It happened on October 10, 1920, in the fifth game of the World Series between the AL's Cleveland Indians and the NL's Brooklyn Dodgers. In the top of the 5th inning, with Dodger runners on first and second, slugger Clarence Mitchell slammed a hot liner, which Cleveland second baseman William Wambsganss managed to snare on the fly. Catching the runner at second off base, Wambsganss stepped on the bag for a double play. Then noticing the Dodger runner off first and scrambling madly to get back to base, Wambsganss ran him down and tagged him, making the only unassisted triple play in World Series competition.

Only one National League club has been in the same city and in the league since it was formed. Can you name the club?

It's the Chicago Cubs. Even though the Braves were also in the league since its formation, its franchise moved from Boston to Milwaukee to Atlanta.

When Babe Ruth hit his 60 home runs in 1927, he seemed to have a favorite inning for those four-baggers. Do you know which it was?

Of the Babe's 60 homers, 16 came in the first inning of the game.

Which team has the best World Series percentage record — the New York Yankees, the Oakland Athletics, or the Los Angeles Dodgers?

The answer is the Oakland Athletics, who were in the World Series three times, winning the title three times. They took the Series in 1972, beating the Cincinnati Reds, 4 games to 3; in 1973, defeating the New York Mets, 4 games to 3; and in 1974, beating the Los Angeles Dodgers, 4 games to 1.

What is an *Iron Mike*?

An *Iron Mike* is a machine used in spring training to pitch batting practice.

A passed-ball third strike once helped the New York Yankees defeat the Brooklyn Dodgers in the World Series. True or false?

True. It happened during the 1941 World Series between the Dodgers and the Yanks. New York was leading, 2 games to 1, when the teams met in the fourth game at Brooklyn's Ebbets Field. In the ninth inning, the Dodgers were leading, 4 to 3, with 2 out. The final Yankee batter was Tommy Henrich. Dodger pitcher Hugh Carey ran to a full count on Henrich, who swung at the next pitch and missed. The ball glanced off catcher Mickey Owens' glove. It was a third strike, but since the catcher had dropped the ball, Henrich raced to first and was safe. The Yankees then exploded and went on to win, 7 to 5. The next day, they wrapped up the Series by beating the Dodgers once again. If Owens hadn't dropped that ball and if the Dodgers had tied the Series at 2 games apiece, would the outcome have been different? . . . Who knows!

Grover Cleveland Alexander was a 20-game winner several times during his 19-year major league career. Did he win 20 or more games eight times, ten times, or twelve times?

Grover Cleveland Alexander, the great right-handed hurler for the Philadelphia Phillies, the Chicago Cubs, and the St. Louis Cardinals, won 20 games or more ten times during his career, including three seasons (1915-1917) with 30 wins.

Has any pitcher ever hurled a no-hitter in his first major league start?

Yes. "Bobo" Holloman pitched a no-hitter for the St. Louis Browns against the Philadelphia Athletics on May 6, 1953 — the day of Holloman's first start in the majors.

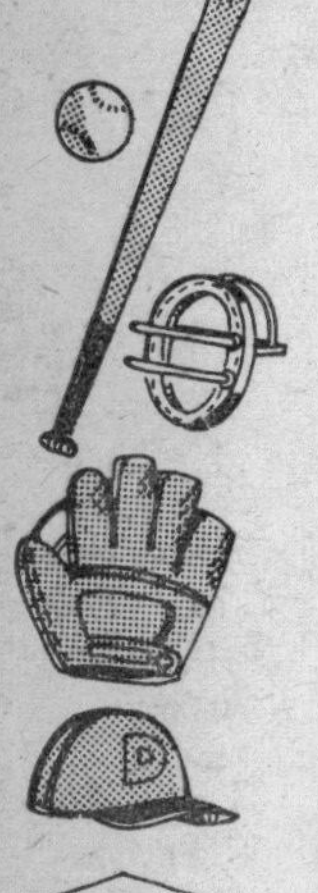

Is there a rule in major league baseball requiring players to run the bases facing frontwards?

There is now, but there wasn't one in 1963. The rule was a result of the zany antics of New York Met Jimmy Piersall. On June 23, 1963, while playing against the Philadelphia Phillies, Piersall cracked his 100th major league homer. He was so happy that he circled the bases facing backwards, much to the delight of the crowd. Soon afterwards, however, major league officials passed a law outlawing running the bases backwards.

True or false? Mickey Mantle holds the record for the most World Series career hits.

False. Yankee catcher Yogi Berra collected the most hits in World Series competition during his playing career. Between 1947 and 1961, Yogi banged out 71 hits in World Series play. Mantle, on the other hand, holds the World Series record for the most runs batted in, with 40, from 1951 to 1964.

Who was the *first* man to ever receive the American League's MVP Award three times?

The answer is Jimmy Foxx, the only American-Leaguer other than a New York Yankee to win that Award three times. Foxx took MVP honors in 1932 and 1933 as a Philadelphia Athletic, then again in 1938 as a Boston Red Sox.

Bob Feller, the fire-balling right-hander for the Cleveland Indians, pitched 3 no-hitters during his career. How many one-hitters did he hurl?

Feller, who pitched for the Indians from 1936 to 1956, had a total of 12 one-hitters in addition to his 3 no-hitters, among his 266 career wins. The fire-baller was elected to the Baseball Hall of Fame in 1962.

Which famous pitcher won more games during his baseball career? Was it Grover Cleveland Alexander or Christy Mathewson? Be careful, sports fans. This is a tricky one.

Both Alexander and Mathewson won exactly the same number of games. Alexander, who pitched from 1911 to 1930, won 373 games and lost 208. Christy Mathewson, who pitched from 1900 to 1916, won 373, but lost only 188.

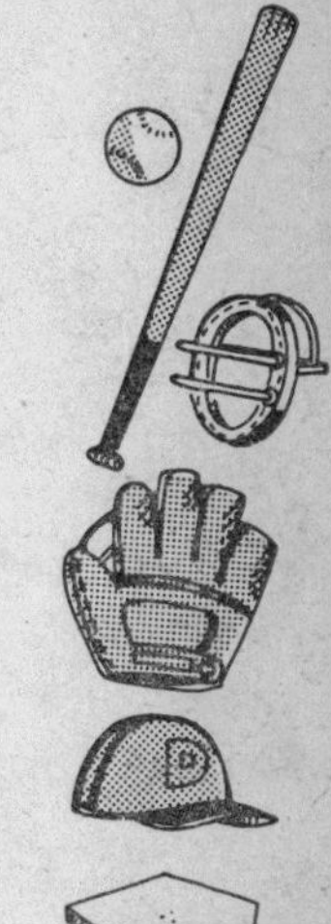

True or false? A relief pitcher once won a game without throwing a single pitch to home plate.

Incredible, but absolutely true. Relief pitcher Nick Altrock of the American League's Chicago White Sox did it in 1906. He entered a game with 2 out, a runner on first, and his team losing by 1 run in the top of the ninth inning. Altrock picked the runner off first base to end the inning. Then, in the bottom of the ninth, his team scored 2 runs to make him the winning pitcher. Altrock won the game without throwing one pitch to home plate!

Only one man has ever pitched a perfect game in World Series competition. Can you name him?

Don Larsen, a right-handed pitcher for the New York Yankees, hurled that perfect game against the Brooklyn Dodgers in the fifth game of the 1956 World Series, to become the only no-hit, no-run pitcher in World Series history. A crowd of 64,519 fans at Yankee Stadium watched in awe as Larsen retired 27 batters in a row on only 97 pitches — the last, a called third strike against pinch-hitter Dale Mitchell, to give the Yanks a 2-to-0 win.

What is a *screwball*?

A *screwball* is a special pitch usually thrown by left-handed pitchers. It breaks away from left-handed batters and breaks in toward right-handed batters.

Can you name the 1958 movie about a Washington Senator baseball fan who was so tired of the powerful New York Yankees always winning the pennant that he agreed to trade his soul to the Devil in return for a Washington win?

The movie was *Damn Yankees!* and was based on the 1955 Broadway play of the same name. The movie starred Tab Hunter as an old man turned into the young superstar to defeat the Yankees. Ray Walston repeated his stage role as the Devil.

How many players have collected 3,000 or more hits during their major league career?

Only 12 major league ball players have totaled 3,000 or more hits during their career. They are Ty Cobb, Hank Aaron, Stan Musial, Tris Speaker, Honus Wagner, Eddie Collins, Willie Mays, Nap Lajoie, Paul Waner, Cap Anson, Al Kaline, and Roberto Clemente.

What is an *inside-the-park home run*?

It is, in fact, just what it sounds like — a home run without the batter hitting the ball out of the park or into the stands. These days, an *inside-the-park homer* is very rare in major league baseball. To get one, the batter must be an exceptionally fast runner, and the ball must hit the outfield wall and roll away from the fielders.

The Minnesota Twins were known by another name before 1961. What was that name?

The Minnesota Twins were formerly the Washington Senators. In 1961, the Senators moved to Minnesota because of poor attendance in Washington. Their last year in Washington, 1960, the Senators drew only 743,404 fans, while their first year in Minnesota, as the Twins, they had 1,256,722 paid supporters at their home games.

Only two men have won baseball's elusive Triple Crown more than once. Ted Williams did it in 1942 and 1947. Who is the other?

The answer is Rogers Hornsby of the St. Louis Cardinals. Hornsby won the Triple Crown in 1922 with 42 homers, a batting average of .401 and 152 runs batted in. In 1925, Hornsby took the crown again, with league-leading totals of 39 home runs, a .403 BA, and 143 RBIs.

Three members of the New York Yankees were voted the Most Valuable Player in the American League three times each. Can you name those three Yankee stars?

The answer is Joe DiMaggio, Yogi Berra, and Mickey Mantle. DiMaggio was the MVP in 1939, 1941, and 1947. Berra won the Award in 1951, 1954, and 1955, and Mantle, in 1956, 1957, and 1962.

Has a relief pitcher ever won the MVP Award?

Yes. Jim Konstanty of the Philadelphia Phillies was voted that honor in 1950. His 22 saves in 74 relief appearances helped insure the Phillie "Whiz Kids" of the National League Pennant that year.

Although Ty Cobb was one of the greatest hitters and base runners in the history of baseball, he was not much of a home-run hitter. What is the most homers he ever hit in one season? Is it 12, 16, or 27?

The most home runs Ty Cobb ever hit in one season during his 25-career was 12, which he slammed out in 1921 and again in 1925.

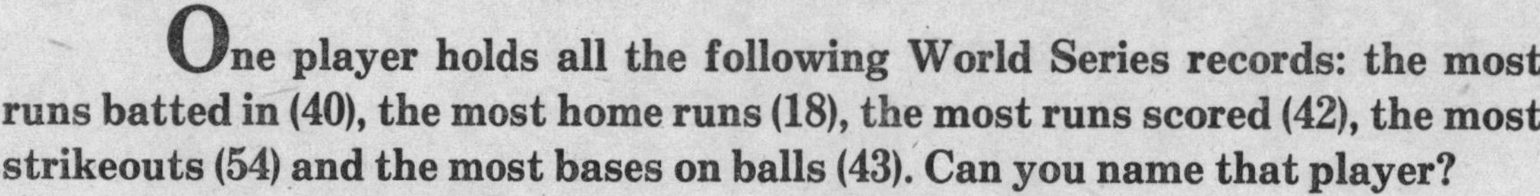

One player holds all the following World Series records: the most runs batted in (40), the most home runs (18), the most runs scored (42), the most strikeouts (54) and the most bases on balls (43). Can you name that player?

Mickey Mantle of the New York Yankees is the holder of all of those World Series records.

Did Jimmy Foxx of the Philadelphia Athletics ever win baseball's Triple Crown?

Yes. Jimmy Foxx won the Triple Crown in 1933, with his league-leading 48 homers, 163 RBIs, and a .356 batting average.

The New York Mets played the Oakland Athletics in the 1973 World Series. Who won?

The Athletics beat the Mets, 4 games to 3, to win the 1973 World Series.

Dick Groat won the National League batting title and the Most Valuable Player Award in 1960. What team did Dick Groat play for that year?

Dick Groat was a shortstop for the Pittsburgh Pirates in 1960 when he won the National League's MVP Award and the NL batting crown with a .325 average.

True or false? No team has ever scored 20 runs in a single World Series game.

False. A team total of 20 runs was scored in a single World Series game on two occasions. The New York Yankees scored 20 runs against the New York Giants in a 1921 World Series game, and the St. Louis Cardinals did it against the Boston Red Sox during the 1946 World Series.

Cy Young is the winningest pitcher in baseball history, with 511 wins and 315 losses. Can you name the second- and third-place hurlers behind Young?

Walter Johnson is second behind Young, with 416 wins and 279 losses. Grover Cleveland Alexander, with 373 wins and 208 losses, and Christy Mathewson, with 373 wins and 188 losses, are tied for third place.

In the 1978 World Series, the New York Yankees set a new record for hitting the most singles in one Series game. How many singles did they hit to set that record?

In game five of the 1978 World Series between the New York Yankees and the Los Angeles Dodgers, the Yanks set a record by banging out 16 singles in their 12-to-2 triumph. In that game, every starter in the Yankee line-up produced at least one single.

Which left-handed pitcher holds the American League record for the most shutouts in a single season? Is it Ron Guidry or Babe Ruth?

Ron Guidry and Babe Ruth *both* hold the record. As a pitcher for the Boston Red Sox, Ruth set the record with 9 shutouts in the 1916 season. Guidry of the New York Yankees tied that record in 1978.

Who was the last National League player to hit .400 or better and in what year did he do it?

Bill Terry of the New York Giants was the last NL player to hit over .400. He did it in 1930, with an average of .401.

What is a *double steal*?

A *double steal* occurs with two runners on base, usually on first and second. On a set signal, both runners attempt to advance to the next base. Usually the man on second steals third, and while the catcher throws to third, the man on first steals second.

Which baseball immortal wrote his autobiography, *My Turn at Bat*?

My Turn at Bat is the autobiography of Ted Williams.

In 1978, Gaylord Perry of the San Diego Padres became the oldest pitcher to ever receive the Cy Young Award. Was he 38, 40, or 41 years old when he won it?

Gaylord Perry was 40 years old when he won the National League's Cy Young Award in 1978. The oldest previous winner was Early Wynn of the AL's Chicago White Sox. Wynn was 39 years old when he won the Award in 1959.

True or false? Gil Hodges and Willie Mays each hit 4 home runs in one game.

True. Gil Hodges of the Brooklyn Dodgers hit his 4 round-trippers in a game on July 18, 1948, and Willie Mays of the N.Y. Giants collected his 4 homers in a game on April 30, 1961.

What is a *pinch hitter*?

A *pinch hitter* is a substitute who comes into the game to bat for another player.

Are girls permitted to participate in Little League Baseball?

Although girls were barred from Little League for many years, a 1974 change in the rules permitted them to play on teams.

Lefties Whitey Ford of the New York Yankees and Warren Spahn of the Milwaukee Braves were both voted into the Hall of Fame in the 1970s. Which pitcher received that honor first?

Warren Spahn became a Hall-of-Famer in 1973 and was followed by Ford in 1974.

True or false? A major league team once *lost* 134 games and won only 20 during a season.

True. The old Cleveland Spiders of the National League lost 134 games and won only 20 contests during the 1899 season.

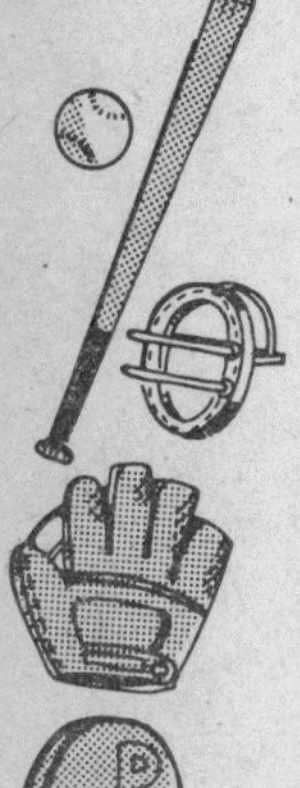

Who was the first professional baseball player to become a sports announcer?

The answer is Jack Graney, who retired from baseball in 1921 after playing for the Cleveland Indians for twelve years. In 1933, he returned to the Indians as a play-by-play broadcaster and announced their games until 1954.

Only two National League ball players have ever won the NL batting crown playing for more than one team. Which two of these three are they: Lefty O'Doul, Hack Wilson, or Ernie Lombardi?

Lefty O'Doul and Ernie Lombardi are the only two National-Leaguers who have won batting titles playing for more than one club. In 1921, O'Doul, of the Philadelphia Phillies, won the batting crown with an average of .398. Then in 1932, O'Doul hit .368 as a Brooklyn Dodger, to capture the title again. Ernie Lombardi won the batting championship with a .342 while playing for the Cincinnati Reds in 1938. Four years later, as a member of the 1942 Boston Braves, Lombardi hit .330, to win the title a second time.

True or false? From 1921 to 1925, Rogers Hornsby, one of baseball's greatest hitters, never batted below .380 for the season.

True. In 1921, Hornsby's average was .397; in 1922, .401; in 1923, .384; in 1924, .424; and in 1925, .403.

Who won the American League batting crown in 1949? Was it George Kell of the Detroit Tigers or Ted Williams of the Boston Red Sox?

George Kell edged out Ted Williams for the 1949 AL batting crown by the slim margin of .0002. Kell's average was .3429, and Williams' was .3427.

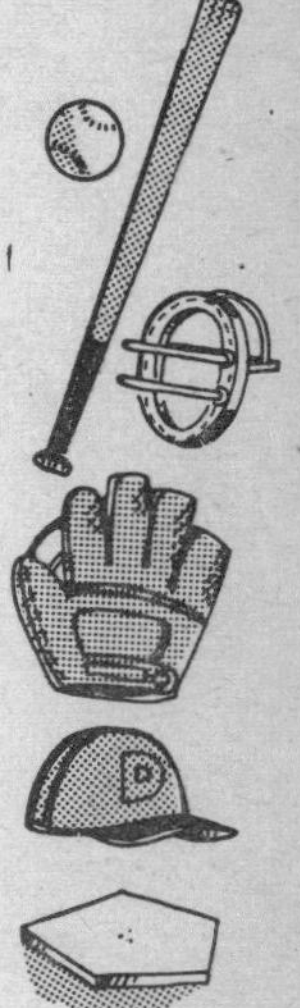

True or false? Ty Cobb was a great major league baseball player, but never managed a major league baseball team.

False. Tyrus Raymond Cobb served as the player-manager of the Detroit Tigers in the American League from December, 1920, to November, 1926.

What is the *Grapefruit Circuit?*

The games played by major league teams during their spring training in Florida, where grapefruits grow in abundance, make up the *Grapefruit Circuit.*

In what year did the Brooklyn Dodger franchise move to Los Angeles? Was it 1950, 1955, or 1958?

The Dodgers moved from New York to California in 1958.

How many times did Roy Campanella, the great catcher of the Brooklyn Dodgers, hit more than 30 home runs in a single season?

During his ten years with the Dodgers, from 1948 to 1958, Roy Campanella belted a total of 242 home runs. He had four seasons in which his HR total went over 30: in 1950, when he hit 31; in 1951, 33; in 1953, 41; and in 1955, 32.

True or false? Catcher Forrest "Smokey" Burgess is best known for his uncanny ability to pick runners off first base.

False. Smokey Burgess was probably the best pinch-hitter of all time and holds the record for the most career pinch-hits. Burgess collected 144 pinch-hits while playing for almost a half-dozen NL and AL teams from 1949 to 1967.

True or false? Rogers Hornsby smoked a corncob pipe and enjoyed drinking homemade moonshine.

Absolutely false. Rogers Hornsby never smoked or drank and, as a manager, advised his players to follow his example. Hornsby believed that smoking and drinking alcoholic beverages deteriorated a player's physical ability, so he abstained from both. He did, however, have a secret passion for charcoal broiled steak, which was his favorite meal.

Did Rogers Hornsby, the great hitting infielder, ever lead the National League in home runs?

Yes. Hornsby led the National League in homers twice while playing for the St. Louis Cardinals. He took the NL home-run crown in 1922 with 42 home runs, and in 1925, with 39. Hornsby's lifetime total was 302 round-trippers.

Nelson "Nellie" Fox once played in 98 straight games without striking out. True or false?

True. Nellie Fox, a great hitter for the Chicago White Sox, set an American League record in 1958 by playing in 98 consecutive games without striking out a single time.

Can you name the former Dodger (1949) and Cub (1951) first baseman who went on to become a famous TV and movie star when he left the game?

That former major league first baseman is Chuck Connors, star of the TV series *The Rifleman* and of many movies, including *Flipper, Old Yeller, Target Zero,* and *Good Morning, Miss Dove*.

Who was the first Commissioner of Baseball? Take a bow if you get this answer right.

Judge Kenesaw Mountain Landis was the first Commissioner of Baseball and is a member of the Baseball Hall of Fame.

Can you name the three baseball stars who were voted to All-Star teams in the 1930s, 1940s, 1950s, *and* 1960s?

That honored distinction is shared by Ted Williams, Early Wynn, and Mickey Vernon.

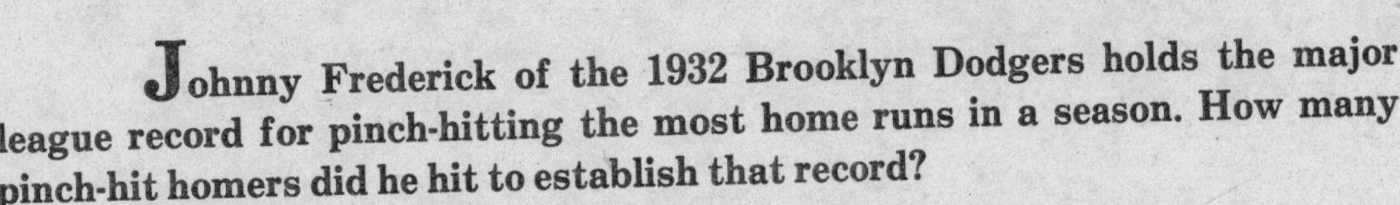

Johnny Frederick of the 1932 Brooklyn Dodgers holds the major league record for pinch-hitting the most home runs in a season. How many pinch-hit homers did he hit to establish that record?

Frederick hit 5 pinch-hit homers in 1932 to set the record.

True or false? The World Series has always been a best-of-seven competition.

False. The World Series was a best-of-eight competition in the early 1900s, but in 1922 the best-of-seven format was established.

Managers Casey Stengel and Joe McCarthy share an honored record. Do you know what that record is?

Both men managed seven World Championship teams — all the New York Yankees! McCarthy's Yanks brought him the Series in 1932, from 1936 to 1939, and in 1941 and 1943. Stengel's Yanks won the crown from 1949 to 1953, and in 1956 and 1958.

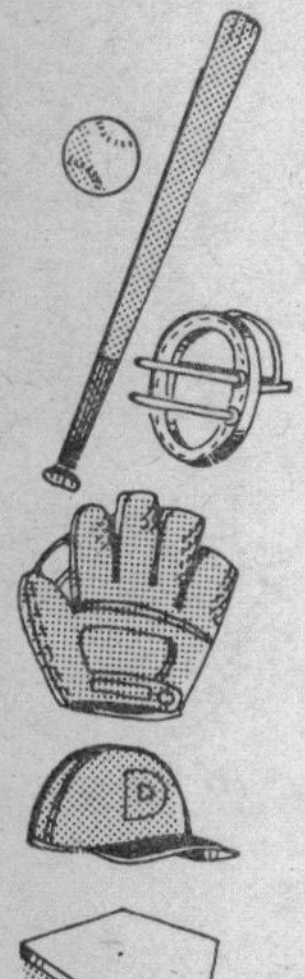

Can you remember who these famous nicknames belonged to — "The Kitten," "Old Reliable," and "The Barber"?

Loyal baseball buffs will remember that Harvey Haddix of the Pittsburgh Pirates was "The Kitten." New York Yankee Tommy Henrich was "Old Reliable." And Sal Maglie of the old New York Giants and Brooklyn Dodgers was "The Barber."

How many times did Ty Cobb get 200 or more hits in a single season? Was it five, nine, or eleven times?

Ty Cobb, who played major league baseball from 1905 to 1928, got 200 or more hits in a single season nine times, with his most productive season in 1911, when ge got 248 hits.

Between 1956 and 1966, how many times did Dodger pitchers win the Cy Young Award?

Dodger pitchers won five Cy Young Awards between 1956 and 1966. Don Newcombe started off capturing the Award in 1956. He was followed by Don Drysdale in 1962, and Sandy Koufax in 1963, 1965, and 1966.

True or false? The batting title of the National League was once decided by .0003 percentage points.

True. In 1931, Chick Hafey of the St. Louis Cardinals won the batting crown with a .3489 batting average, just nosing out Bill Terry of the New York Giants, who finished second with a .3486.

Has any major-leaguer ever driven in 200 runs during a single season?

No. The record for the most RBIs in a single season is 190, and it's held by Lewis "Hack" Wilson, who set it while playing for the Chicago Cubs in 1930.

Only six players in the history of baseball have won the Most Valuable Player Award three times. Can you name them?

Those six immortals are Joe DiMaggio (1939, '41, '47), Yogi Berra (1951, '54, '55), Roy Campanella (1951, '53, '55), Stan Musial (1943, '46, '48), Jimmie Foxx (1932, '33, '38), and Mickey Mantle (1956, '57, '62).

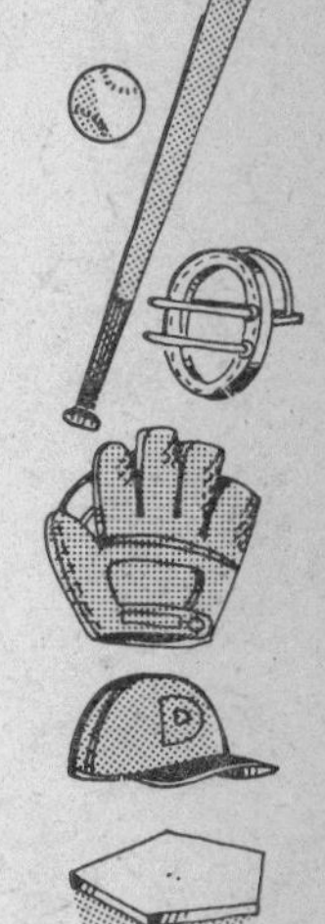

Catcher Johnny Bench of the Cincinnati Reds won the National League home-run crown in 1970 and 1972. In which year did he hit more homers?

Bench hit more home runs — 45 — in 1970, as compared to his 40 round-trippers in 1972.

In 1969, the Baseball Writers of America selected "the greatest baseball player in history" and "the greatest living baseball player." Can you name the men who won those honors?

George Herman "Babe" Ruth, the New York Yankee home-run king, was selected as "the greatest baseball player in history," and Joe DiMaggio, "The Yankee Clipper," was voted "the greatest living baseball player."

Name the baseball teams that play in the following stadiums: Three Rivers Stadium, Candlestick Park, Fenway Park, and Arlington Stadium.

Three Rivers Stadium is the home field of the National League's Pittsburgh Pirates. The San Francisco Giants of the National League play in Candlestick Park. Fenway Park is the home stadium of the American League's Boston Red Sox. The AL's Texas Rangers play their home games at Arlington Stadium in the Dallas-Fort Worth area.

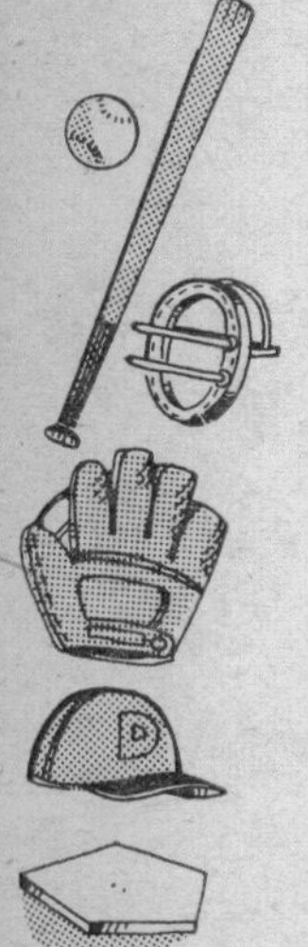

Which of the following men was *not* the MVP of the National League two times — Dizzy Dean, Willie Mays, or Ernie Banks?

The answer is Dizzy Dean of the St. Louis Cardinals. He was voted the Most Valuable Player of the National League only once, in 1934. Mays won the Award twice — as a New York Giant in 1954 and as a San Francisco Giant in 1965. Ernie Banks of the Chicago Cubs was also the NL's Most-Valuable Player two times — in 1958 and in 1959.

Which baseball star among these three had the highest career batting average: Jimmy Foxx, Lou Gehrig, or Jackie Robinson?

Of the three baseball greats, Lou Gehrig had the highest career batting average. For his 2,130 games, Gehrig had a .340 average. Jimmy Foxx played in 2,317 games and had a .325 average. Jackie Robinson's 894 games earned him a .318 career batting average.

True or false? A noted television and movie star once had a clause written into all of his contracts stating that he didn't have to work while the World Series was being played.

True. The actor was William Frawley, a veteran of hundreds of movies and the co-star of the successful TV programs *I Love Lucy* and *My Three Sons*. Frawley, an ardent baseball fan, refused to miss the World Series and never worked if he could help it while the Series was in progress.

A major league baseball game was once delayed because of bright sunshine. True or false?

It's funny, but true. It occurred on September 7, 1973 during a twilight game between the New York Mets and the Montreal Expos at Montreal's Jarry Park. The game was delayed 11 minutes because the sun setting over the rim of the stadium was shining directly in the eyes of the first baseman, nearly blinding him. Rather than risk any injuries, the umpires delayed the game.

According to most baseball historians, who hit the longest home run ever hit?

It is generally accepted that Babe Ruth hit the longest home run ever hit. It was on April 4, 1919 in an exhibition game at Tampa, Florida. Ruth, playing left field for the Boston Red Sox, came to bat for the first time in the second inning and smashed a deep drive to center off New York Giant pitcher George Smith. The drive easily cleared the fence, much to the astonishment of everyone present. After the game, sportswriters attempted to estimate how far Ruth's homer had traveled. With the help of the Giant centerfielder, they agreed that the ball had traveled 579 feet, making it the longest homer ever hit.

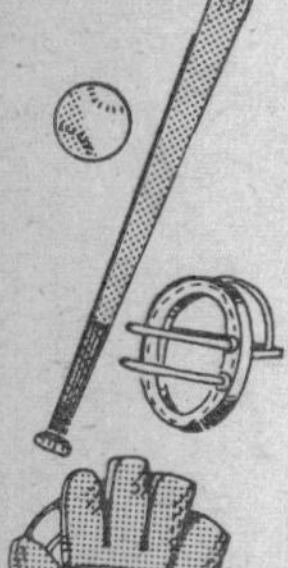

Which team hit more home runs in the 1978 World Series — the New York Yankees or the Los Angeles Dodgers?

The Dodgers hit twice as many home runs as the Yankees in the 1978 World Series even though they lost the Championship to the Yankees in six games. The Dodgers clouted 6 homers (3 by Dave Lopes and 1 each by Reggie Smith, Ron Cey, and Dusty Baker), while the Yanks belted only 3 (2 by Reggie Jackson and 1 by Roy White).

Four teams have reached the World Series, but have never won the Series even once. Can you name those four teams?

The four teams are the St. Louis Browns and the Minnesota Twins of the American League and the San Francisco Giants and the Philadelphia Phillies of the National League. The Phillies played in the World Series twice without winning. The other teams played in the fall classic only once.

Which of these three sluggers hit the most home runs in his career — Stan Musial, Mickey Mantle, or Ted Williams?

Mickey Mantle of the New York Yankees hit the most homers of the three. His total of 536 HRs puts him 6th on the all-time home-run list. Ted Williams of the Boston Red Sox is 8th on the list, with a total of 521 home runs, and Stan Musial of the St. Louis Cardinals is 13th, with 475 round-trippers.

A player named Heinie Zimmerman once won baseball's Triple Crown. True or false?

True. Heinie Zimmerman of the Chicago Cubs won the Triple Crown way back in 1912.

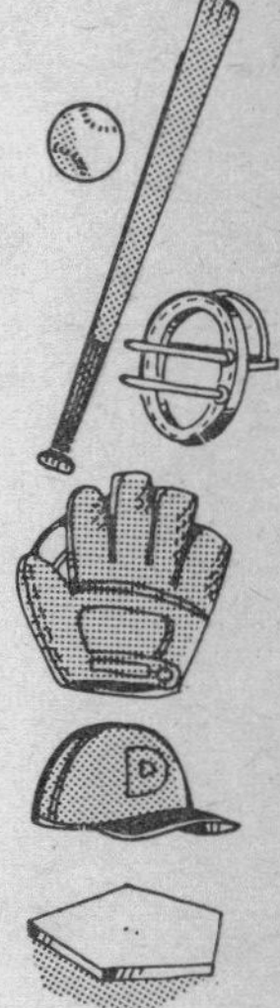

Which great baseball player was known as the "Sultan of Swat"?

Babe Ruth was known as the "Sultan of Swat" because he was the greatest home-run hitter in the history of baseball. In addition to hitting 60 homers in a 154-game season in 1927, Babe clouted 2 home runs in a single game *72 times,* to set a record which may never be broken.

Who is third on the all-time home-run list behind Hank Aaron and Babe Ruth?

Willie Mays ranks behind Hank Aaron and Babe Ruth on the all-time home run list, with a total of 660 homers.

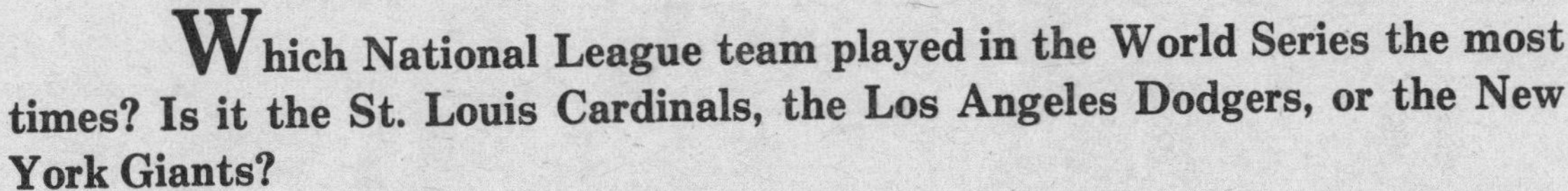

Which National League team played in the World Series the most times? Is it the St. Louis Cardinals, the Los Angeles Dodgers, or the New York Giants?

The old New York Giants played in the most World Series games — fourteen, and won the Championship five times. The Cardinals were in twelve World Series, winning eight, and the Los Angeles Dodgers played in seven and won three.

True or false? A midget, who wore the number 1/8, once played major league baseball.

True. On August 19, 1951, Bill Veeck, the publicity-seeking owner of the St. Louis Browns, inserted a 3'7" midget named Eddie Gaedel into the line-up as a stunt. Gaedel wore the number 1/8 and batted one time against Detroit Tiger pitcher Bob Cain. Gaedel's strike zone was so small that he was walked on four pitches, after which a runner was sent in for him. Soon afterward, major league club owners passed a rule banning the use of midgets as players.

Two of the most famous hitters of all time hold the National and American League records for striking out the most times during their careers. Can you name the owners of those infamous records?

Mickey Mantle of the New York Yankees holds the American League record with 1,710 strikeouts, and Willie Mays of the New York Giants, the San Francisco Giants, and the New York Mets holds the National League record with 1,526.

The 1960 Baltimore Orioles had five pitchers who were fondly nicknamed the "Diaper Squad." Do you know why?

The five pitchers of the "Diaper Squad" — Chuck Estrada, Jack Fisher, Jerry Walker, Milt Pappas, and Steve Barber — were given that nickname because they were all 22 or younger.

Which New York Yankee won the most American League batting titles? Was it Lou Gehrig, Mickey Mantle, or Joe DiMaggio?

Joe DiMaggio led the American League in batting twice: in 1939, with an average of .381, and in 1940, with a .352. Lou Gehrig won the batting crown only once, with a .363 in 1934. Mickey Mantle also took the title only once, with a .353 average in 1956.

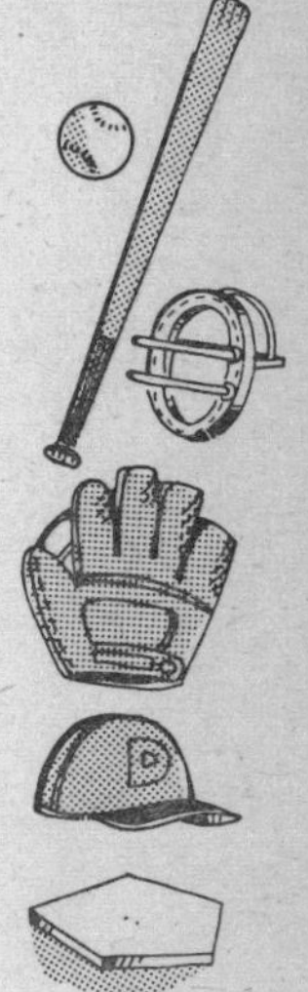

True or false? During his career, Ty Cobb stole home more than 20 times.

True. Fleet-footed, hard-hitting Ty Cobb stole home 27 times during his career to set the major league record. No other player has stolen home even *half* as many times as Cobb.

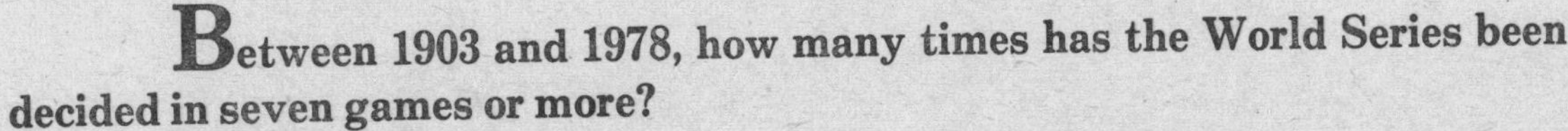

Between 1903 and 1978, how many times has the World Series been decided in seven games or more?

The World Series has been decided in seven games or more thirty times from 1903 to 1978.

Which of these men did *not* hit 4 home runs in one game — Joe Adcock of the Milwaukee Braves, Gil Hodges of the Brooklyn Dodgers, or Deron Johnson of the Philadelphia Phillies?

The Phillies' Deron Johnson did not hit 4 homers in one game, but he did hit 4 home runs in succession in two consecutive games in 1971. Adcock hit his 4 homers in a game on July 31, 1951, and Hodges clubbed 4 round-trippers in a single game on August 31, 1950.

Whitey Ford of the New York Yankees holds the World Series record for pitching the most consecutive scoreless innings. How many scoreless innings did he pitch to set that record? Was it 20 2/3, 28 2/3, or 33 2/3 innings?

Lefty Whitey Ford pitched 33 2/3 consecutive scoreless innings in 1960, 1961, and 1962 World Series play to set the record. He also pitched the most innings in World Series competition — 146.

Which Philadelphia Phillie pitcher holds the team record for the most shutouts in a season? Is it Grover Cleveland Alexander or Steve Carlton?

Grover Cleveland Alexander had 16 shutouts in 1916, which is the Phillies' team record. Alexander also holds team records for complete games (38, in 1916), most innings pitched (389, in 1916), most wins (33, in 1916), and the lowest ERA (1.22, in 1915). Steve Carlton holds the Phillies' record for strikeouts, with 310 in 1972.

In 1927, the New York Yankees had some of the game's most dangerous hitters in their line-up: Babe Ruth, Lou Gehrig, Earle Combs, Bob Meusel, and Tony Lazzeri. What was the famous nickname given to that line-up of Yankee sluggers?

The hitting of those five sluggers in 1927 was so fearsome that they were known as "Murderers' Row." Ruth hit 60 homers, had 164 RBIs, and a BA of .356. Gehrig hit 47 homers, had 174 RBIs, and an average of .373. Combs batted a strong .356 and led the league in singles. Meusel's average was a healthy .336, and Lazzeri clubbed 18 homers while hitting a solid .309. Those totals certainly explain why that line-up was referred to as "Murderers' Row".

Which member of the Cincinnati Reds was named the MVP of the 1976 World Series? Was it Pete Rose, Johnny Bench, or George Foster?

Catcher Johnny Bench was the Most Valuable Player of the 1976 World Series. In the four-game Series in which the Reds trounced the Yankees, Bench hit .533, smashed 2 homers, a double, and a triple, while driving in six runs.

Where must a ball be pitched in order for it to be called a strike?

The ball must be pitched over home plate, higher than the batter's knees and lower than his shoulders. Since batters differ in height and physical makeup, the strike zone varies from batter to batter.

Baseball catchers always had special gloves and always wore face masks and chest protectors. True or false?

False. The catcher's mask was first worn in 1875; the chest protector was introduced in 1885; and padded gloves became standard equipment in 1891.

Once Jackie Robinson broke the color barrier in the majors, who became the first black player in the American League?

Larry Doby became the first black American-Leaguer when he joined the Cleveland Indians in 1948 as an outfielder and helped them win the pennant that year.

Can you name the team that won the World Series in 1973? Here's a hint. It was an American League club.

The Oakland Athletics, managed by Dick Williams, won the 1973 World Series by defeating Yogi Berra's New York Mets, 4 games to 3.

Lefty Grove was a famous American League pitcher and is a member of the Baseball Hall of Fame. What is Lefty Grove's real name?

The former Philadelphia Athletics' hurler was born Robert Moses Grove. Since he was a southpaw, he was quickly nicknamed "Lefty."

Can you name the star outfielder who established five team records when he played for the Kansas City Royals in 1969? Here's a hint. He was on the World Championship New York Yankees in 1977 and 1978.

Lou Piniella, the left fielder on the New York Yankees World Championship teams in 1977 and 1978, established these five team records for the Kansas City Royals in 1969: the most hits (139), the most doubles (21), the most triples (6), the most total bases (205), and the highest batting average (.282).

Mike Torrez pitched for the Boston Red Sox in 1978. For which team did he play in 1977?

Mike Torrez was with the New York Yankees in 1977. His 17-13 record helped the Yanks gain the AL Pennant, and his 2 World Series victories led the Yankees to the World Championship.

To pitcher Floyd "Bill" Bevens, the name Cookie Lavagetto spelled crushing heartbreak. Do you remember why?

It was the fourth game of the 1947 World Series between the New York Yankees and Brooklyn Dodgers, and Yankee pitcher Bill Bevens had a no-hitter going in the last of the ninth inning at Ebbets Field, with New York leading, 2 to 1. The first batter up for Brooklyn, Carl Furillo, walked and Al Gionfriddo, running for Furillo, stole second. Yankeee manager Bucky Harris had Bevens walk Pete Reiser. Dodger manager Burt Shotton then sent Cookie Lavagetto in to pinch-hit for Eddie Stanky, and hit he did — a crashing double to the right field scoreboard. With that blow, two runs scored, and Bevens lost his World Series no-hitter and the ball game.

OLYMPIC GAMES

Sixten Jernberg of Sweden has won more medals in the Winter Olympics than any other athlete. How many medals did he win in all?

Sixten Jernberg, a Nordic skier, has a grand total of 9 medals in cross-country individual and team relay events in Winter Olympic competition. In 1956, 1960, and 1964, Jernberg won 4 gold, 3 silver, and 2 bronze medals.

Which country won the most medals at the Summer Olympics in Montreal?

The Soviet Union won the most medals at the Montreal Games, with a total of 125 (47 gold, 43 silver, and 35 bronze).

Only one athlete from the United States has ever won an Olympic gold medal in the javelin throw. Is that athlete Cyrus Young, Steve Seymour, or Bill Schmidt?

The answer is Cyrus Young, who won the gold medal in the javelin throw at the 1952 Olympics. Steve Seymour took a silver medal at the 1948 Games, and Bill Schmidt, a bronze in 1972.

Who was the youngest athlete to compete in the 1976 Winter Olympic Games at Innsbruck, Austria? Was it an Alpine skier from Finland, a figure skater from the Soviet Union, or a speed skater from the U.S.?

Elena Vodorezova, a Russian figure skater, was the youngest competitor in the 1976 Winter Olympics. At the time of the Games, Vodorezova was only 12 years old. She did not win a medal at Innsbruck, but is expected to be a contender in 1980.

True or false? At the 1904 St. Louis Olympics, the United States took every gold medal in the boxing competition.

It's amazing, but true. There were seven weight classifications in the 1904 Olympic boxing competition, and American boxers won all 7 gold medals: flyweight, George Finnegan; bantamweight, Oliver Kirk; featherweight, Oliver Kirk; lightweight, H.J. Spangler; welterweight, Albert Young; middleweight, Charles Mayer; and heavyweight, Sammy Berger.

How are Olympic boxing matches decided?

An Olympic boxing match is won in one of three ways: by a knockout, by a referee stopping the fight for the safety of the loser, or by a point decision. Boxers are awarded 20 points by the judges for each round they win. The boxer with the most points at the end of the contest is declared the winner.

The Winter Games were not always a part of Olympic competition. Were the Winter Games instituted in 1900, 1908, or 1924?

The Winter Olympic Games were started in 1924, and were held in Chamonix, France, that first year.

Where were the first Olympic Games held? Was it in Ancient Greece, Ancient Rome, or Ancient Egypt?

The first Olympic games were held in Ancient Greece. According to written evidence, the first Olympiad was in 776 B.C., but many historians

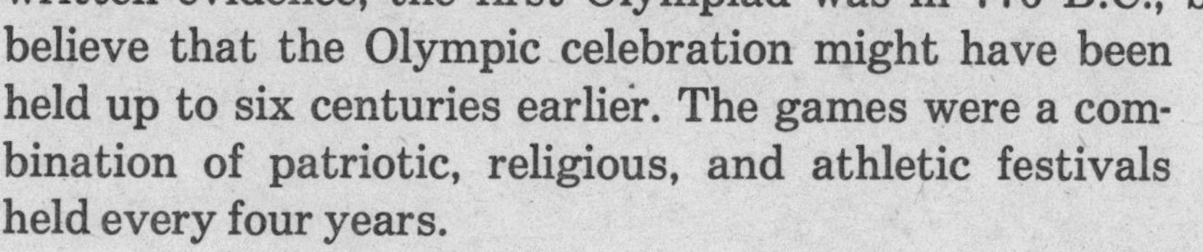

believe that the Olympic celebration might have been held up to six centuries earlier. The games were a combination of patriotic, religious, and athletic festivals held every four years.

The winner of which Olympic event is considered to be "The World's Greatest Athlete"?

The winner of the Olympic decathlon is considered to be "The World's Greatest Athlete" because the event consists of ten varied competitions that test everything from an athlete's speed and agility to his coordination and strength. The events in the Olympic decathlon are: the 100-meter run, the long jump, the shot put, the high jump, the 400-meter run, the 110-meter hurdles, the discus, the pole vault, the javelin throw, and the 1500-meter run. These ten events are run over a period of two days, with points being awarded to the top finishers. The athlete with the most points at the end of the competition is the winner.

How long has cycling been a part of the Olympics? Is it since 1896, since 1928, or since 1948?

Cycling has been on the Olympic program since the Games were revived in 1896.

Exactly how much money is an Olympic gold medal worth? Is it $110, $250, or $565?

An Olympic gold medal is basically silver, and is coated with about six grams of gold, for a total worth of $110.

Archie Hahn is the only man to win the 100-meter dash at two successive Olympic Games. What country was Archie Hahn from?

Archie Hahn, who won the 100-meter dash at the 1904 and 1906 Olympics, was from the United States.

Peter Mueller won the men's 1000-meter speed skating event at Innsbruck in 1976. Is Mueller from the United States, West Germany, or East Germany?

Gold medalist skater Peter Mueller, who set an Olympic record of 1:19.32 for the 1,000 meters, is from the United States.

True or false? Since the modern Olympics began, the U.S.S.R. has won more gold medals than any other country.

False. The United States has won more gold medals than the U.S.S.R. Americans have brought home 630 gold medals, which is more than any other country, as compared to the Russian total of 271.

Little Olga Korbut, the uncontested starlet of the 1972 Olympics in Munich, won 2 individual gold medals and 1 team gold medal. In what events did she earn those medals?

Olga Korbut, the pride of the Russian gymnastics team in 1972, won her individual gold medals on the balance beam and in floor exercise, and her team gold medal in the combined exercises.

Ray Ewry of the United States was a famous Olympian who won 10 individual gold medals at several Games. Can you name the three events Ewry competed in?

Ray Ewry competed in the standing broad jump, the standing high jump, and the standing hop, step, and jump. In 1900 and 1904, he took gold medals in all three events. In 1906 and 1908, he won gold medals in the standing broad jump and the standing high jump.

Is there an Olympic event known as *walking*?

Yes. There are two walking events: a 20-kilometer walk and a 50-kilometer walk. The competitors in these events walk the course as quickly as possible, staying within the Olympic rule book definition of walking: "a progression by steps so taken that unbroken contact with the ground is maintained." The walker's leg must be straightened, not bent at the knee, for at least one moment while progressing step by step. Competitors can be cautioned only once during the race for not walking; after that, they are disqualified.

Edoardo Mangiarotti holds the record for winning the most Olympic medals in fencing. How many medals did he win to set that record?

Edoardo Mangiarotti of Italy won a record total of 13 Olympic medals in fencing with foil and epée. Between 1936 and 1960, he won 6 gold medals, 5 silver, and 2 bronze.

True or false? NBA superstars Jerry West, Walt Bellamy, Jerry Lucas, and Oscar Robertson were all former Olympic basketball players.

True. In fact, West, Bellamy, Lucas, and Robertson were all members of the 1960 Olympic squad that won a gold medal at Rome, Italy.

For which event did Bob Mathias win a gold medal at the 1948 Olympics in London?

In 1948, 17-year-old Bob Mathias took first place in the Olympic decathlon. The 6', 190 lb. football, basketball, and track star was one of California's top high school athletes, but he had never pole vaulted, broad jumped, run a distance, or thrown a javelin before his coach started a 3-week workout before the Olympic trials. There, Mathias beat out older and more experienced college stars, and he also went on to do the same in London.

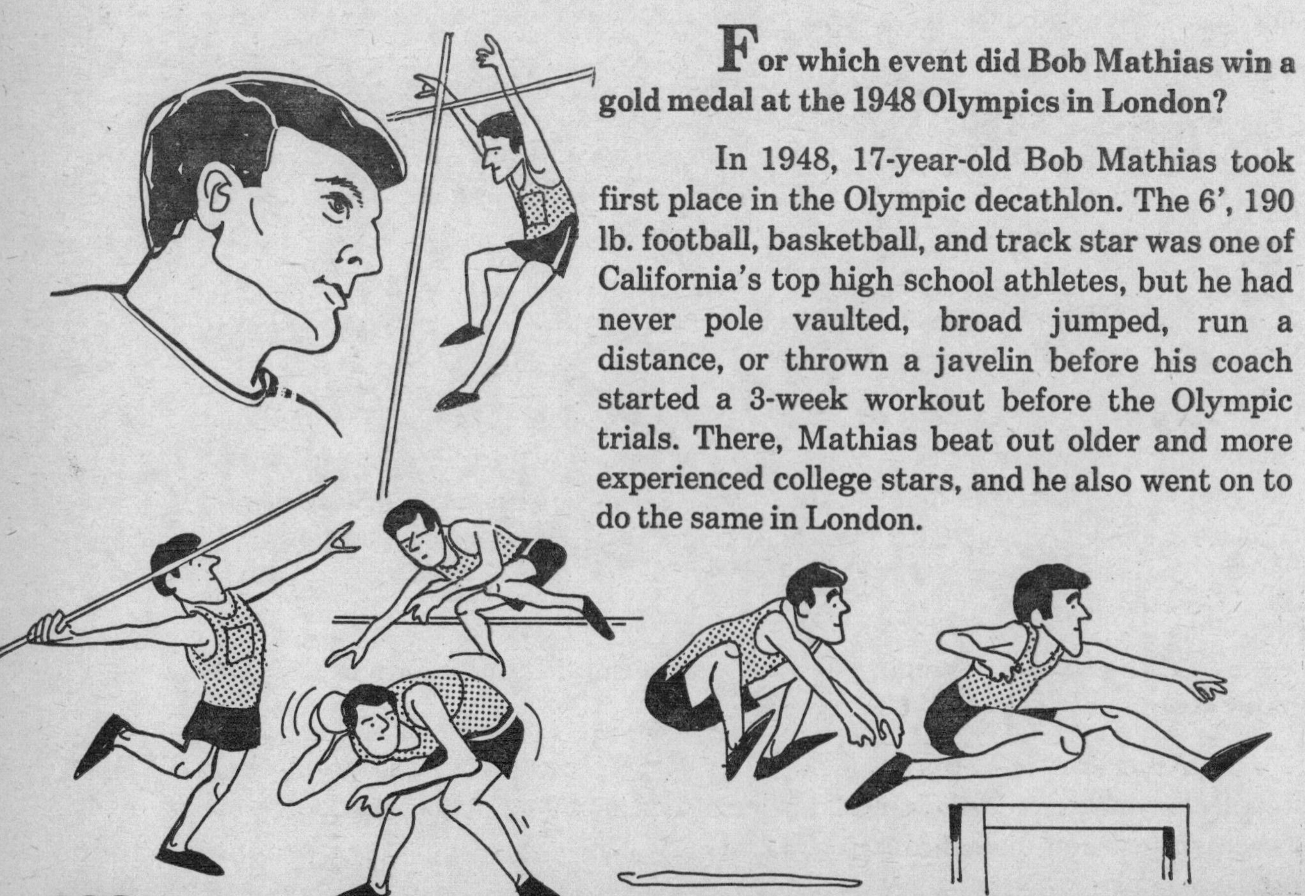

Peggy Fleming and Dorothy Hamill both won Olympic gold medals for the United States in figure skating. Which one won hers first?

The answer is Peggy Fleming, who was the gold medalist at the 1968 Winter Olympic Games. Dorothy Hamill won her gold medal in 1976.

True or false? At the 1956 and 1960 Olympics, American athletes won every gold, silver, and bronze medal in the 400-meter hurdles events.

True. Glenn A. Davis of the U.S. won the gold medal in the 400-meter hurdles at both the 1956 and 1960 Olympics, and 4 other American hurdlers won the silver and bronze medals, sweeping every medal in that event for two Olympiads.

One of the equestrian sports at the Olympics is *dressage*. What is dressage?

Dressage is the performance of predetermined movements which test the harmonious development of the horse's physique and ability, and which display the degree of understanding between horse and rider. The tests include a variety of paces, halts, changes of direction, movements, and figures.

How many Olympic medals has the United States won in the 3000-meter steeplechase? Is it 2, 4, or 8 medals?

American athletes have won 4 Olympic medals in the 3000-meter steeplechase: 1 gold, 1 silver, and 2 bronze. The only gold medalist was Horace Ashenfelter, who finished first in 1952.

True or false? The Olympic Games were once banned by an ancient Roman Emperor.

True. Emperor Theodosius I of Rome banned the Olympic Games in 394 A.D. because after Rome conquered Greece, the Olympics deteriorated under the Roman emperors and became nothing more than professional carnivals and circuses, with contestants interested only in winning money. The Olympic Torch was extinguished for over 1,500 years.

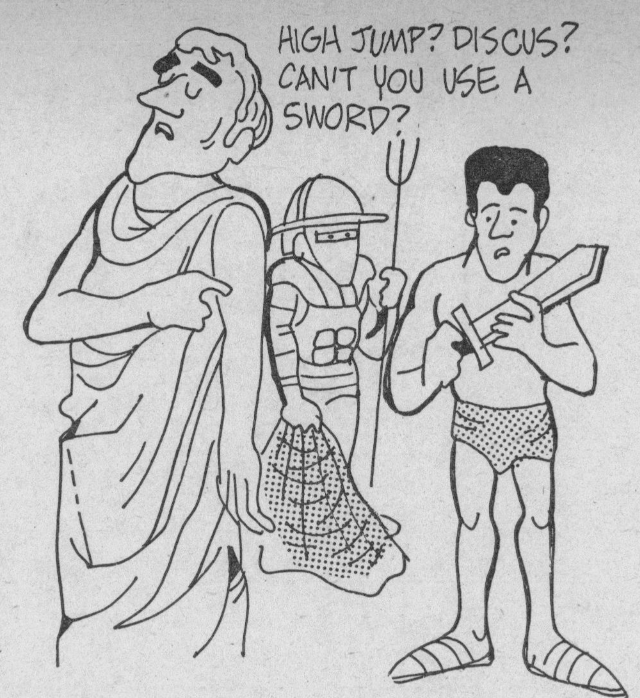

There are five events in the modern Olympic pentathlon. Can you name them in the order in which they are held?

The five pentathlon events, in the order held, are: horseback riding (800-meter course), fencing (with epée), pistol shooting (at 25 meters), swimming (300-meter freestyle), and cross-country running (4,000 meters).

NBA stars K.C. Jones and Bill Russell were on the U.S. Olympic basketball team in 1956. True or false?

True. Jones and Russell were on the 1956 Olympic basketball team which finished in first place, giving the U.S. a gold medal.

Which American Olympic decathlon champion scored the most points in the event? Was it Jim Thorpe in the 1912 Olympics or Bruce Jenner in the 1976 Olympics?

The answer is Bruce Jenner. He scored a total of 8,618 points in the 1976 decathlon to set an Olympic record, breaking the 1972 Olympic point record of 8,454 set by Nikolai Avilov of the Soviet Union. At the 1912 Olympics, Jim Thorpe won the decathlon, under the original scoring system, with a total of 6,845 points.

Swimmer Mark Spitz of the United States holds the record for winning the most gold medals in a single Olympiad. How many medals did he win to set that record?

Mark Spitz won 7 gold medals at the 1972 Olympics at Munich to set that record. His 4 individual gold medals were earned in the 100-meter freestyle, the 200-meter freestyle, the 100-meter butterfly, and the 200-meter butterfly. The other 3 were as a member of relay teams: the 4 X 100-meter freestyle relay, the 4 X 200-meter freestyle relay, and the 4 X 100-meter medley relay.

Oliver L. Kirk, a United States Olympic boxer, did something in 1904 that no other Olympic boxer will probably ever duplicate. What did he do?

Kirk won gold medals in boxing in two *different* weight classifications at the same Olympic competition: bantamweight and featherweight.

True or false? The U.S.S.R. has won the most Olympic team titles in men's gymnastics.

False. The Japanese have won the most men's gymnastic team titles, taking five consecutive Olympics between 1960 and 1976. The Russians took the team title twice: in 1952 and 1956.

When the National Track and Field Hall of Fame was opened in Winfield, West Virginia, in 1978, a former Olympic gold medal winner was selected as its first member. Can you name him?

Jessie Owens, the winner of 4 gold medals at the 1936 Berlin Olympics, was that man.

How many medals did the United States win in freestyle wrestling at the Montreal Olympics? Was it 1, 3, or 6 medals?

The U.S. won 6 medals in freestyle wrestling at Montreal in 1976, but the only gold medal went to John Peterson in the middleweight division. American wrestlers won silver medals in the lightweight, light heavyweight, and heavyweight divisions, and bronze medals in the featherweight and welterweight divisions.

Originally, the ancient Olympic Games were celebrated over a two-day period. True or false?

False. The ancient Olympic Games lasted five days. The first day was spent in religious observances. On the second day, foot races, wrestling, horse riding, boxing, and the pentathlon contests were held for boys. Running, jumping, and wrestling contests for men were scheduled for the third day. The men's pentathlon, chariot racing, and horse racing were the fourth day's events. And the fifth and last day was set aside for the ritual garlanding of the victors.

What is the distance of the Olympic marathon race?

The Olympic marathon is now run over a 26-mile, 385-yard course. This distance was standardized in 1924 after several years of varying lengths.

Which country won the gold medal in soccer at the 1976 Olympics? Was it East Germany, Poland, or the U.S.S.R.?

East Germany was the gold medalist in soccer in 1976. Poland took the silver medal and the U.S.S.R., the bronze.

True or false? No gymnast has ever achieved a perfect score of 10 in Olympic competition.

False. A perfect score of 10 was achieved for the first time at the 1976 Olympics at Montreal by gymnasts Nadia Comaneci of Romania and Nelli Kim of the U.S.S.R. Comaneci tallied seven perfect scores of 10: four on the uneven parallel bars and three on the balance beam. Kim's two perfect scores of 10 came in the individual apparatus competition and in the floor exercise.

Where and when were the first modern Olympic Games held? Was it in Rome, Italy, in 1900; in Athens, Greece, in 1896; or in Paris, France, in 1892?

The first modern Olympic Games were held in Athens, Greece, in 1896. Thirteen nations sent athletes to the first modern Olympics. The United States was the unofficial winner of the Games, taking 9 out of the 12 track and field events.

How many gold medals did track star Wilma Rudolph win at the Rome Olympics in 1960? Was it 1, 2, or 3?

Wilma Rudolph won 3 gold medals at the 1960 Olympic Games: the 100 meters, the 200 meters, and as a member of the winning 4 X 100-meter relay team that also included Martha Hudson, Lucinda Williams, and Barbara Jones.

Which of the following events is no longer on the Olympic program — the 10,000-meter run, the 3000-meter steeplechase, or the 200-meter hurdles?

The answer is the 200-meter hurdles, which was an Olympic event in 1900 and 1904, but not since. In 1900, the event was won by Alvin Kraenzlein and in 1904, by Harry Hillman — both Americans.

Dick Button won 2 Olympic gold medals for the United States. Can you remember the years he won them?

Dick Button won his gold medals in the men's singles figure skating competition at the 1948 and 1952 Olympics.

Who won the long jump event at the 1976 Montreal Olympics? Was it Arnie Robinson of the United States, Frank Wartenberg of East Germany, or Randy Williams of the United States?

Arnie Robinson's jump of 27' 4¾" earned him the gold medal in the long jump at the Montreal Olympics in 1976 after winning the bronze medal in the same event at the 1974 Munich Games. Randy Williams was second and Frank Wartenberg was third in the 1976 Games.

Carol Heiss, Peggy Fleming, and Tenley Albright are all Olympic gold medal figure skaters. Which of the three was the first to bring an Olympic gold medal in figure skating to the United States?

Tenley Albright, the figure skating gold medalist of the 1956 Winter Olympics at Cortina, Italy, was the first female figure skater to win the award for the United States. Albright, a pre-medical student from Boston, Massachusetts, won the competition despite a painful skate-blade gash in her right ankle suffered during a practice session. Heiss won her gold medal in 1960 and Fleming, in 1968.

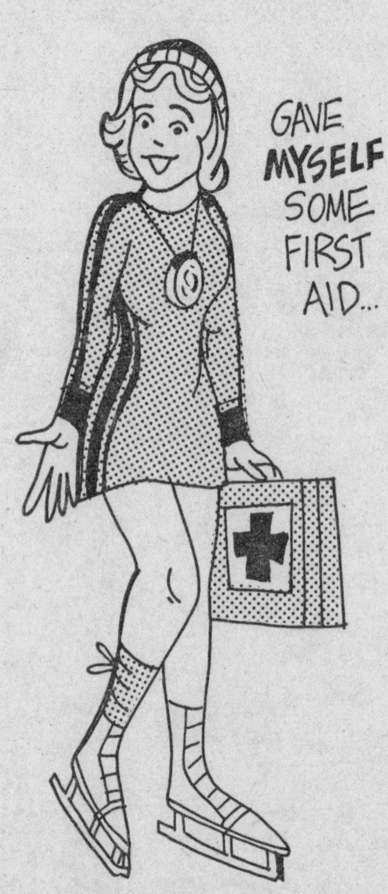

True or false? The United States did not win any medals in fencing at the 1976 Olympics.

True. American fencers, both male and female, did not win any medals at the 1976 Games.

Only one man has ever won the Olympic decathlon event two consecutive times. Is it Bob Mathias of the United States, Nikolai Avilov of the U.S.S.R., or Wili Holdorf of Germany?

Bob Mathias is the only man to successfully retain an Olympic crown in the decathlon event. He won his first decathlon at London in 1948 and repeated as decathlon champion at Helsinki in 1952. Avilov, the 1972 gold medalist, and Holdorf, the 1964 winner, each were one-time decathlon champions.

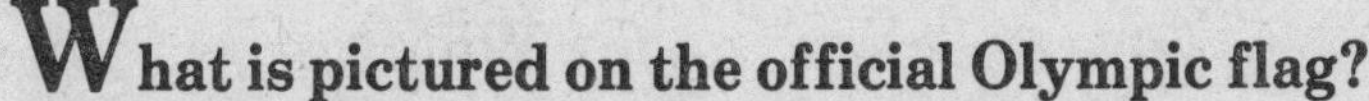

What is pictured on the official Olympic flag?

Five interlocking circles (blue, yellow, black, green, and red) are on the white background of the Olympic flag. The five circles represent the five continents, and their interlocking design signifies the sporting friendship of all people.

Is water polo an Olympic event?

Yes. Water polo has been played at the Olympics since 1908. Although water polo teams competed in the 1900 and 1904 Olympics, these were clubs and not international teams. Since 1908, Hungary has won 6 gold medals in water polo, followed by Great Britain with 3, and Italy with 2.

Cathy Rigby was one of the best-known American gymnasts. Did she ever win an Olympic medal?

No. Although Cathy Rigby was a member of the U.S. Olympic team in 1972, she did not do well enough to win a medal, for Russian gymnasts Olga Korbut and Ludmila Turischeva overshadowed all competitors. However, Rigby did win a silver medal on the balance beam at the 1970 World Games.

Three female speed skaters from the United States won silver medals in the same event at the 1968 Olympic Games at Grenoble, France. True or false?

It's very unusual, but true. Jennifer Fish, Dianne Holum, and Mary Meyers, all of the United States, turned in identical times of 46.3 seconds in the 500-meter speed skating event at the 1968 Winter Olympics and shared silver medals for second place. The gold medal winner was Ludmila Titova of the U.S.S.R.

Lydia Skoblikova set an astounding Winter Olympic record in 1964 when she won a gold medal in every one of the four speed skating races open to women. Is Skoblikova from the U.S.S.R., Austria, or Sweden?

Sloblikova is from the Soviet Union, and the only woman speed skater to accomplish the amazing feat of winning the 500 meters, the 1,000 meters, the 1,500 meters, and the 3,000 meters at one Olympiad — the 1964 Olympiad at Innsbruck, Austria.

In what year were women's events in track and field introduced in the Olympic Games? Was it in 1924, 1928, or 1932?

Track and field events for women were introduced in the 1928 Olympics, at Amsterdam, The Netherlands.

Boxers Howard Davis and Ray Leonard both won gold medals for the United States at the 1976 Olympics. In which weight classes did they fight?

Davis won a gold medal in the lightweight division, and Leonard was the gold medal winner in the light welterweight division.

There are two types of canoeing events in the Olympics — kayak and Canadian. What is the difference between the two?

The basic difference between kayak and Canadian canoeing is in the kind of paddle used. In kayak canoeing, the paddle has a blade at both ends. When paddling, the canoeist uses the left blade on the left side of the canoe and the right blade on the right side of the canoe. The Canadian paddle has only one blade, which is used on both sides of the canoe.

True or false? Ski jumping is part of the Alpine skiing division at the Winter Olympics.

False. Ski jumping is part of the Nordic skiing division.

Can you name the man directly responsible for founding the modern Olympic Games?

The modern Olympics were the result of the efforts of Baron Pierre de Coubertin, a French educator. Inspired by the discovery of the ruins of the original stadium of Olympia, in Greece, de Coubertin conceived the idea of organizing modern international Olympics. His idea was not only to use athletics to mold a person's character, but also to use the competition to further world peace. De Coubertin presented his idea to an international committee on amateur sports, which then established the International Olympic Committee.

Which athlete holds the Olympic record for winning the most total gold medals? Is it an American track star, a Russian gymnast, or an Australian swimmer?

American track star Raymond Ewry holds the unequaled record of 10 Olympic gold medals, which he won in the standing high jump, the standing broad jump, and the standing hop, step, and jump events. What is amazing about Ewry's performance is that they spanned four Olympiads, from 1900 to 1908, with Ewry taking his first 3 medals when he was 27 years old. But even more amazing is the fact that Ray Ewry was a wheelchair invalid as a child and took up jumping to build up his body.

The gold medalist in the heavyweight division at the 1964 Olympics in Tokyo went on to become a pro fighter with smoking fast fists. Can you name him?

The answer is Smokin' Joe Frazier, the 1968 heavyweight champion of the world. As an amateur in 1964, Frazier won the gold medal in heavyweight boxing at the Tokyo Olympics.

How many riders take part in the 400-meter individual pursuit cycling event at the Olympics?

There are two riders in the 400-meter individual pursuit event. Starting at opposite sides of the track and heading in the same direction, each rider tries to catch the other within a specified time limit. The one caught is eliminated from the competition. If one rider fails to catch the other, the rider with the fastest time around the course wins.

In the moving target event of the Olympic shooting competition, what is the shape of the target? Is it shaped like a running boar, a running rabbit, or a charging wolf?

The target in the moving target event is in the shape of a running boar.

In 1960, a boxer from the United States was the Olympic light heavyweight boxing champion. Can you name him?

Cassius Clay, who later changed his name to Muhammad Ali, won a gold medal in boxing in the light heavyweight division at the 1960 Olympic Games.

Can you name the first female Olympian from the United States to win a gold medal in track and field? Was it Elizabeth Robinson, Jean Shiley, or Helen Stephens?

In 1928, when women were allowed to compete in track and field events at the Olympics for the first time, Elizabeth Robinson won the 100 meters with a time of 12.2 seconds. She was the only gold medalist for the U.S. in women's track and field that year. Jean Shiley and Helen Stephens were later gold medal winners for the U.S. in track and field, with Shiley taking the high jump in 1932 and Stephens, the 100 meters in 1936.

Rosi Mittermaier of West Germany won 2 gold medals and 1 silver medal at the 1976 Winter Olympics at Innsbruck, Austria. In which skiing events did she win them?

Rosi Mittermaier is the skier who finished first in the women's downhill and the women's slalom, and took second in the women's giant slalom, just missing a grand slam, by 12/100 of a second. An Olympic grand slam has never been achieved by a woman skier.

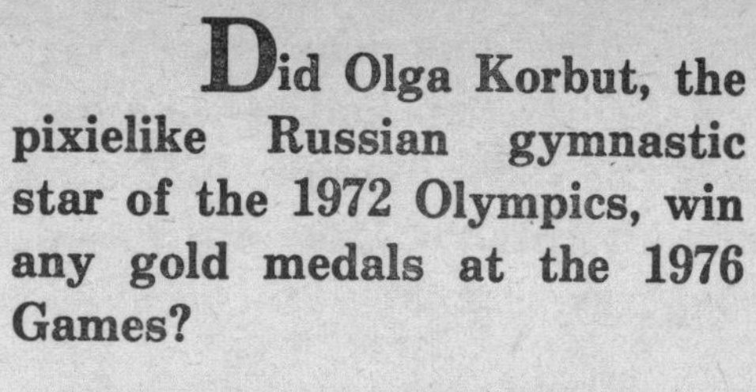

Did Olga Korbut, the pixielike Russian gymnastic star of the 1972 Olympics, win any gold medals at the 1976 Games?

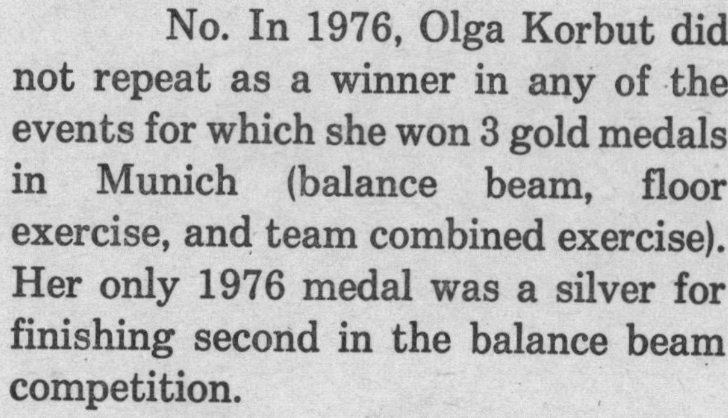

No. In 1976, Olga Korbut did not repeat as a winner in any of the events for which she won 3 gold medals in Munich (balance beam, floor exercise, and team combined exercise). Her only 1976 medal was a silver for finishing second in the balance beam competition.

Jean Claude Killy of France accomplished an amazing feat at the 1968 Winter Games. What was that feat?

Killy won all three Alpine skiing events. By taking gold medals in the downhill, the slalom, and the giant slalom, Killy duplicated the record set by Toni Sailer of Italy at the 1956 Games.

Which country won more gold medals at the 1976 Summer Olympics — the United States or East Germany?

East German athletes captured 40 gold medals at the 1976 Games, while American athletes won 34. However, the U.S. won 35 silver and 25 bronze medals for a grand total of 94, which beat the East German total of 90 (25 silver and 25 bronze).

An American track star won 4 gold medals and became the hero of the 1936 Olympic Games at Berlin, Germany. Can you name him?

That track star was Jessie Owens. At the 1936 Games, "The Tan Cyclone" from Ohio State University won individual gold medals for the 100 meters, the 200 meters, and the long jump, and was a team medalist in the 4 X 100-meter relay. Owens won more gold medals at the Berlin Olympics than any other athlete.

Who holds the Olympic record for winning the marathon in the least amount of time? Is it Abebe Bikila of Ethopia, Frank Shorter of the United States, or Waldemer Cierpinski of East Germany?

The answer is Waldemer Cierpinski, who set the Olympic marathon record in 1976 at Montreal when he ran the 26 miles, 385 yards in 2 hours, 9 minutes, and 55 seconds. Cierpinski broke Bikila's 1964 record of 2 hours, 12 minutes, and 11.2 seconds.

If a runner unintentionally knocks down a hurdle in an Olympic hurdle event, he is automatically disqualified. True or false?

False. According to the official Olympic rules, knocking down a hurdle unintentionally does not automatically disqualify a competitor. Because the hurdles are weighted, hitting them causes a disadvantage to the runner. His timing is upset and he is slowed.

Willie Davenport won a gold medal in the pole vault event at the 1968 Olympics at Mexico City. True or false?

False. Willie Davenport was the 1968 gold medalist in the 110-meter hurdles.

In 1960, the Winter Olympics at Squaw Valley, California, were officially declared open by the Vice President of the United States. Can you name him?

Vice President Richard M. Nixon officially declared the VIIth Winter Olympic Games open.

Was America's first gold medal winner in the Winter Olympics a male or female athlete?

America's first gold medalist in the Winter Olympics was a male athlete, Charley Jewtraw, a speed skater from Lake Placid, New York. Jewtraw won the 500-meter race in 1924 at the first Winter Games, held at Chamonix, France.

Which country has won the most Olympic gold medals in rowing the eight-oared-shells-with-coxswain event? Is it the United States, Great Britain, or New Zealand?

The United States holds the record with 11 gold medals in the eight-oared-shells-with-coxswain event. Americans won this event in 1900 and 1904, then in eight consecutive Olympics from 1920 to 1956. The last U.S. victory came in 1964. Great Britain has won this rowing event twice (1908 and 1912) and New Zealand, once (1972).

True or false? Suzy Chaffee, the famous *hot dog* skier, was once a member of the U.S. Olympic skiing team.

True. Suzy Chaffee was the captain of the U.S. ski team that competed at the Grenoble, France, Games in 1968. Suzy did not win any medals in her downhill event and turned to *hot dog*, or *freestyle*, skiing as a professional soon afterward. No American woman has ever won the downhill.

Ralph Boston, Parry O'Brien, and Rafer Johnson are all famous U.S. Olympic medalists. In which events did they win their medals?

Ralph Boston won an Olympic gold medal in the long jump event in 1960. Parry O'Brien, the first man to throw the 16-pound shot put more than 60 feet, won gold medals in the shot put at the 1952 and 1956 Games and a silver in 1960. Rafer Johnson was the Olympic decathlon silver medalist in 1956 and the gold medalist in 1960.

At the 1972 Olympic Games at Munich, Germany, Maxine "Micki" King won a gold medal in springboard diving. At the time, was King a captain in the U.S. Army, the U.S. Navy, or the U.S. Air Force?

Micki King was a captain in the United States Air Force when she won her Olympic gold medal in diving at Munich in 1972.

True or false? The Soviet Union's Olympic team in 1976 included a 66-pound athlete and a 7' 2" tall woman.

True. The 66-pound athlete was Maria Filatova, a 15-year-old gymnast. The 7' 2" tall woman was Yuliana Semyonova, a member of the women's basketball team that won a gold medal.

Who is the only Olympian to win four consecutive individual titles in the same event? Here's a clue. He did it in the discus throw.

That record holder is Al Oerter of the United States, who won the discus throw in 1956, 1960, 1964, and 1968. The 6'4", 251 lb. Oerter took the field in 1964 with ripped cartilages in his rib cage, yet set a new Olympic discus record distance of 200' 1½".

True or false? Baron Pierre de Coubertin, the man who was responsible for the birth of the modern Olympic Games, was also a key figure in organizing the Winter Olympic Games.

False. Baron Pierre de Coubertin was originally opposed to the creation of the Winter Olympics and voted against the proposal, but a majority of other Olympic Committee members overruled the baron and passed the proposal. The Winter Olympics was mainly the brainchild of France's Marquis de Polignac.

How many medals did the United States win in weight lifting at the 1976 Olympics?

The United States won only 1 medal in weight lifting at the 1976 Games — a silver, won by Lee James in the middle heavyweight division.

Which female gymnast won the gold medal in the floor exercise at the 1976 Montreal Olympics? Was it Nadia Comaneci of Romania, Nelli Kim of the U.S.S.R., or Ludmila Turischeva of the U.S.S.R.?

Nelli Kim, the 18-year-old daughter of a Korean, won the gold medal in the floor exercise for the U.S.S.R. in 1976. Ludmila Turischeva won the silver medal and Nadia Comaneci, the bronze.

Two American athletes were the stars of the 1912 Olympic Games at Stockholm, Sweden. One of them was an American Indian and the other was a Polynesian. Can you name those two famous American athletes?

The American Indian was the immortal Jim Thorpe, who won gold medals in the pentathlon and the decathlon. The Polynesian was Duke Kahanamoku, whose gold medal was for the 100-meter freestyle swimming event.

Thomas Hicks, John H. Hayes, and Frank Shorter all won gold medals for the United States in the same Olympic event. Was it the 60-meter run, the 3000-meter steeplechase, or the marathon?

Hicks, Hayes, and Shorter all won gold medals in Olympic marathon events: Hicks, in 1904; Hayes, in 1908; and Shorter, in 1972.

True or false? A runner in the 400 meters once won a gold medal by default because he was the only competitor in the event.

It's strange, but true. It happened at the 1908 Olympic Games in England. In the finals of the 400-meter event, a U.S. runner was disqualified for obstruction. In protest, two other U.S. runners withdrew from the race, leaving a lone runner from Great Britain, Wyndham Hallswelle, to compete. Hallswelle ran in the event, all alone, and won a gold medal.

Has the United States ever won an Olympic medal in cycling?

Yes, but only one. That medal in cycling was a bronze, and it was won by Carl Shutte in the individual road race event at the 1912 Olympics.

Which country has won the most Olympic gold medals in weightlifting?

The U.S.S.R. has won 28 Olympic gold medals in weightlifting, which is the record. The U.S. is second with 15, and France is third with 9. Although the Russians have dominated all weight divisions, their 5 consecutive gold medals in the heavyweight division is a record.

TV sports commentator Donna de Varona is a former Olympic track and field star. True or false?

False. Donna de Varona was an Olympic swimmer. She competed in her first Olympic Games in 1960 when she was only 13 years old, but didn't win a gold medal until 1964 at the Tokyo Games. She earned 1 gold medal in the 400-meter individual medley and another as a member of the winning 4 X 100-meter freestyle relay team.

Match the following U.S. Olympic gold medal winners with the events they won at the 1976 Games at Montreal.

(1) Matt Vogel	**(a) Springboard diving**
(2) Edwin Moses	**(b) 100-meter butterfly**
(3) Phil Boggs	**(c) 400-meter hurdles**

The correct match-ups are (1) b. Matt Vogel won the 100-meter butterfly; (2) c. Edwin Moses won the 400-meter hurdles; (3) a. Phil Boggs won the springboard diving. Incidentally, Edwin Moses' time of 47.64 set an Olympic record.

True or false? An Olympic runner once caused a scandal when he used a car to travel 10 miles of the marathon course.

True, it happened at the third modern Olympics in 1904. Fred Lorz, an American marathon runner who was leading, suddenly got a cramp and hitched a 10-mile ride in one of the cars chugging along with the runners. When the car broke down, Lorz returned to the stadium on foot. Thinking him the winner, the crowds cheered his entrance and prepared to crown him the winner. Then the hoax was revealed, and the gold medal was awarded to Thomas Hicks, also an American.

True or false? "Buster" Crabbe, who played Flash Gordon and Buck Rogers in the movies, was a former Olympic gold medal winner.

True. Clarence "Buster" Crabbe won the 400-meter freestyle at the 1932 Games, becoming the first Olympic champion to swim the 400 meters in less than 5 minutes (4:48.4). Crabbe also set five world records during his swimming career — records which have since been broken.

At the Melbourne, Australia, 1956 Olympic Games, Australian swimmers came out with a total of 2 gold medals. True or false?

Absolutely false. The Australians completely dominated the swimming events, winning 8 out of 13. The biggest winners for Australia were Betty Dawn Fraser, who took gold medals in the 100-meter freestyle and the 4 X 100-meter freestyle relay, and Murray Rose, the gold medalist in the 400- and 1500-meter freestyle.

These famous lines — "The important thing in life is not the triumph but the struggle. The essential thing is not to have conquered but to have fought well." — are part of the world famous Olympic Creed. Do you know who wrote them?

Pierre de Coubertin of France, the man responsible for reviving the Olympic Games, authored the Olympic Creed.

The 110-meter hurdles event has been held at the Olympics 18 times. How many times has that event been won by the United States?

Athletes from the U.S. have won the 110-meter hurdles at the Olympics 15 out of 18 times. From 1896 to 1912, Americans had 5 consecutive wins and from 1932 to 1972, 9 consecutive wins. In all, the U.S. has won 41 gold, silver, and bronze medals in this event, and has never ever failed to win at least one medal at each Olympic competition.

Can you name the American woman who, although paralyzed by polio as a child, went on to win 3 Olympic gold medals in track and field?

The answer is Wilma Rudolph, who won 3 gold medals at the 1960 Olympic Games in the 100 meters, the 200 meters, and 4 X 100-meter relay. Wilma, who was one of 19 children, had a form of polio that paralyzed her legs and kept her a cripple between the ages of 4 and 8. After years of medical treatment, Wilma learned to walk and later blossomed into a graceful, fleet-footed runner.

True or false? Originally, the Greeks used stones and rough pieces of metal for the weight-throwing contests.

True. Stones and rough pieces of metal called *hateres* were used for the weight-throwing contests at the early Olympic Games. Later, the Greeks used a rounded shot and the discus for those events.

In 1960, the Olympics were held in Tokyo, Japan. True or false?

False. The 1960 Olympic Games were held in Rome, Italy. Tokyo hosted the 1964 Games.

Who is the only American female skier to ever win more than one Olympic gold medal in Alpine skiing?

Andrea "Andy" Mead Lawrence was the American skier who won the women's slalom and the women's giant slalom at the 1952 Winter Olympics at Oslo, Norway. The 19-year-old wizard on skis outclassed 44 female skiers from fifteen countries.

How many times did Sonja Henie of Norway win the gold medal in women's singles figure skating competition? Was it two, three, or four times?

Sonja Henie won the gold medal in women's singles figure skating at three Games: 1928, 1932, and 1936. After winning her 3 gold medals, Miss Henie became a well-known Hollywood celebrity and starred in many motion pictures, including *Sun Valley Serenade, Wintertime,* and *Iceland.*

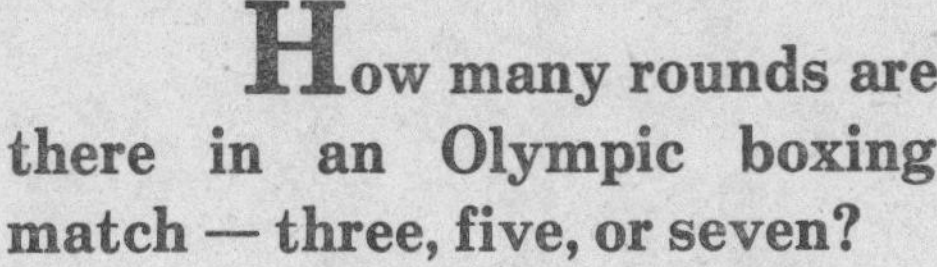

How many rounds are there in an Olympic boxing match — three, five, or seven?

In an Olympic boxing match there are three 3-minute rounds.

Shirley Babashoff, John Naber, Jenni Chandler, and Mike Spinks all won medals for the United States at the 1976 Olympics. Which of them won gold medals and which, silver?

Swimmer Shirley Babashoff won 3 silver medals; swimmer John Naber won 4 gold medals and 1 silver medal; diver Jenni Chandler won a gold medal; and middleweight boxer Mike Spinks won a gold medal.

Which one of the following Olympians medalists is *not* a gold medalist? Is it long jumper Bob Beamon, decathlon competitor Bruce Jenner, hurdler Willie Davenport, or high jumper Dwight Stones?

The answer is high jumper Dwight Stones, who won bronze medals at the 1972 and 1976 Olympics. Beamon, Jenner, and Davenport are all Olympic gold medal winners.

True or false? In the ski jumping events at the Olympics, winners are determined by distance only.

False. Olympic winners in the ski jumping events are judged by distance and form. Form includes the take-off position, the position in the air, and the landing.

In the Nordic skiing division of the Winter Olympics, there is an event called the *biathlon*. What do the competitors in the biathlon have to do?

In the *biathlon*, the competitors ski cross-country over a 20-kilometer course, carrying rifles with them. They fire at targets along the way, with time penalties assessed for target bullseyes that are missed. At the 1968 Olympics, a 40-kilometer biathlon relay was introduced as a continuing event.

Spiridon Loues was the only Greek athlete to win a gold medal at the first modern Olympics at Athens, Greece, in 1896. What event did he compete in?

Spiridon Loues, a 25-year-old shepherd, became the hero of his native country when he took the only gold medal for Greece in the marathon in 1896, covering the 24 miles, 1,500 yards from Marathon to Athens in 2 hours, 55 minutes, and 20 seconds.

True or false? Volleyball has been played at the Olympics since 1948.

False. There was no volleyball competition at the Olympic Games from 1896 through 1960. In 1964, the first volleyball competition was held, and the U.S.S.R. won the gold medal in the men's competition, with Japan taking the women's.

How many medals did the United States win in equestrian events at the 1976 Olympics? Was it 2, 4, or 6?

The United States won 4 medals in equestrian events in 1976. Tad Coffin took the gold medal and John Plumb, the silver medal in the 3-day individual event. First place in the 3-day team event added another gold medal for the Americans, and a third place in team dressage earned a bronze.

Which country has had the most gold medalists in the Olympic shot put event? Is it the United States, the U.S.S.R., or East Germany?

The United States has won the most gold medals for the shot put. Of the 18 times that the event has been held, American shot putters have won it 14 times. Two of these shot putters have been two-time gold medalists. They are Ralph Rose (in 1904 and 1908) and Parry O'Brien (in 1952 and 1956).

Which American athlete won the 100-meter freestyle swimming event at the 1976 Montreal Olympics? Was it Jim Montgomery or Don Schollander?

The 100-meter freestyle gold medalist was Jim Montgomery, who set an Olympic record in 1976 with his time of 49.99. Don Schollander was the 1964 winner of the event.

The Olympic featherweight weightlifting gold medal has been won only twice by Americans. The first winner was Anthony Terlazzo, who took his gold medal in 1936. Can you name the other?

Isaac Berger of New York won the gold medal for the United States in 1956 at the Melbourne, Australia, Games with his lift of 776.500 pounds.

How are the Olympic Games officially started?

The Olympic Games are officially started with the lighting of the Olympic Flame by a runner who has carried the torch from the site of the original Games at Olympia, Greece. The flame in the torch is kindled by the morning rays of the sun striking a concave mirror in the ancient stadium at Olympia. Then 370 relay runners light torch after torch and journey to the site of the Olympic Games, wherever they may be. The flame at the stadium is kindled, and the Games are officially started.

Are the standing high jump and standing broad jump still Olympic events?

The standing broad jump and the standing high jump are no longer recognized Olympic events. They were performed for the last time in 1912.

Norbert Schemansky, a middle heavyweight, holds the record for winning the most Olympic medals in weightlifting. Is Schemansky from Poland, the United States, or Hungary?

Norbert Schemansky, who set a record with 4 Olympic weightlifting medals, is from the United States. He won 1 gold medal (1952), 1 silver (1943), and 2 bronze (1960 and 1964).

There were no Olympic Games in 1916, 1940, or 1944. True or false?

True. Due to World Wars I and II, the Games were canceled by the International Olympic Committee.

Janet Lynn is one of America's best-known figure skaters. Did she ever win an Olympic gold medal?

No. Although Janet Lynn was a member of the 1968 and 1972 U.S. Olympic teams, she never won an Olympic gold medal. However, in the 1972 Games at Sapporo, Japan, she finished third in the women's singles figure skating event and won a bronze medal.

Dr. Sammy Lee and Robert Webster both brought 2 consecutive gold medals home to the United States. In which event did they both win their medals?

Platform diving was Lee's and Webster's event. Lee won his gold medals at two consecutive Olympiads, 1948 and 1952, and Webster did the same in 1960 and 1964.

True or false? Men compete against women in the Olympic shooting events.

True. Male and female marksmen may compete against each other.

Only one American woman has ever won the Olympic javelin throw. Can you name that famous all-around athlete?

Mildred "Babe" Didrikson of the U.S. won the gold medal in the javelin throw at the 1932 Olympics.

Tenley Albright, the winner of the women's singles figure skating competition, was one of only two American athletes to win a gold medal at the 1956 Winter Olympic Games. Who was the other?

Hayes Alan Jenkins won America's only other gold medal at the 1956 Winter Games, taking it for the men's singles figure skating competition.

What are the three positions used in the miniature rifle event?

The three positions in the miniature rifle event are standing, kneeling, and prone. The contestants get 40 shots in each of the three positions, and the shots are fired in four groups of ten at a target similar to the one used for archery.

How are the Olympic Games officially ended?

The Games are officially ended when the Olympic flag is lowered and presented to the chairman of the Olympic Council for safekeeping.

True or false? An ice hockey team once scored 85 goals in three games in Olympic competition.

True. It happened at the first Winter Olympics in 1924. The Canadian hockey team scored 85 goals in three games, to win the gold medal in hockey for the second straight time.

Which country has produced the most Olympic decathlon champions? Is it Germany, the United States, or the U.S.S.R.?

The United States has won the decathlon more than any other country. Of the 14 times that the decathlon has been held, Americans have won it 9 times, starting with Harold Osborn at the 1924 Games, and followed by James Bausch in 1932, Glenn Morris in 1936, Bob Mathias in 1948 and 1952, Milton Campbell in 1956, Rafer Johnson in 1960, Bill Toomey in 1968, and Bruce Jenner in 1976.

Which country won the most medals at the 1976 Winter Olympics at Innsbruck, Austria? Was it the Soviet Union, East Germany, or the U.S.?

The Soviet Union won the most medals. Russian athletes collected 13 gold, 6 silver, and 8 bronze medals for a total of 27 in all. The East Germans won 7 gold, 5 silver, and 7 bronze for a total of 19, which was the second highest total. The U.S. won a total of 10 medals: 3 gold, 3 silver, and 4 bronze.

How many times have the Winter Olympics been held in the United States?

The United States has hosted the Winter Olympics twice. In 1932, the Games were held at Lake Placid, New York and in 1960, at Squaw Valley, California. The 1980 Winter Olympics are again scheduled at Lake Placid.

Has any country other than the United States ever won all 3 medals in the high jump competition at one Olympic celebration?

The answer is no. The United States is the only country to ever win all 3 medals in the high jump at a single Olympiad. In fact, the United States did it twice: in 1896 and in 1936.

Earlene Brown was the first female medalist from the United States in an Olympic track and field event. Was that event the 100 meters, the high jump, or the shot put?

The answer is the shot put. Earlene Brown became the first American woman to win an Olympic medal in the shot put event when she took a bronze medal at the 1960 Games at Rome, Italy.

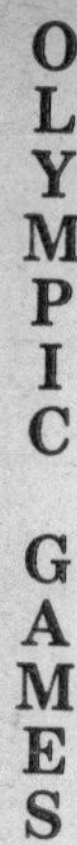

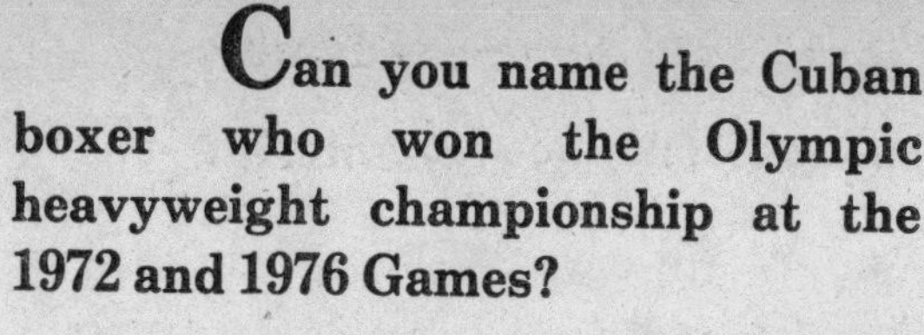

Can you name the Cuban boxer who won the Olympic heavyweight championship at the 1972 and 1976 Games?

That Cuban boxer is Teofilio Stevenson, who, with 2 Olympic gold medals in boxing, is considered the next potential heavyweight champion of the world if he decides to become a professional fighter.

How many Olympic medals did U.S. wrestlers win in Greco-Roman wrestling at the 1976 Games?

American wrestlers didn't win a single medal in Greco-Roman wrestling at the 1976 Games. The U.S.S.R. dominated the field, winning 7 gold, 2 silver, and 1 bronze medal.

True or false? Winter athletic events were not part of the Olympic program until the Winter Olympic Games were inaugurated in 1924.

False. Ice rink events were part of the IVth Olympic Games in 1908. Then, at the VIIth Olympic Games in 1920, four ice skating events were on the program: men's figure skating, women's figure skating, figure skating pairs, and ice hockey.

How many of the seven shooting events at the Olympics can you name?

The seven shooting events are: (1) free pistol; (2) small-bore rifle prone; (3) free rifle — 3 positions; (4) rapid fire pistol; (5) moving target; (6) trap shooting; and (7) skeet shooting.

How many countries competed in the 1976 Summer Olympics?

Forty-one countries took part in the 1976 Games at Montreal.

The United States did not win any medals in yachting at the Montreal Olympics. True or false?

False. The U.S. won 3 medals in yachting at Montreal. The 2 silver medals were won in the Soling and Tornado events, and the bronze, in the Tempest.

How many weight divisions are there in Olympic boxing competition?

There are 11 weight divisions in Olympic boxing competition: light flyweight, flyweight, bantamweight, featherweight, light welterweight, welterweight, light middleweight, middleweight, light heavyweight, and heavyweight.

True or false? Many of the U.S. athletes who competed in the first modern Olympics at Athens in 1896 paid their own way to Greece.

True. In 1896, there was no U.S. Olympic Committee and no money to send athletes to Greece. Members of the Boston Athletic Association paid the expenses for nine of their amateur sportsmen to travel to Greece, but the rest of the athletes on the U.S. team paid all of their own expenses.

Only one man in the history of the Olympics has ever won the marathon twice. Do you know who that man is?

It's Abebe Bikila of Ethiopia, the Olympic marathon winner at the Rome Games in 1960 and at the Tokyo Games in 1964.

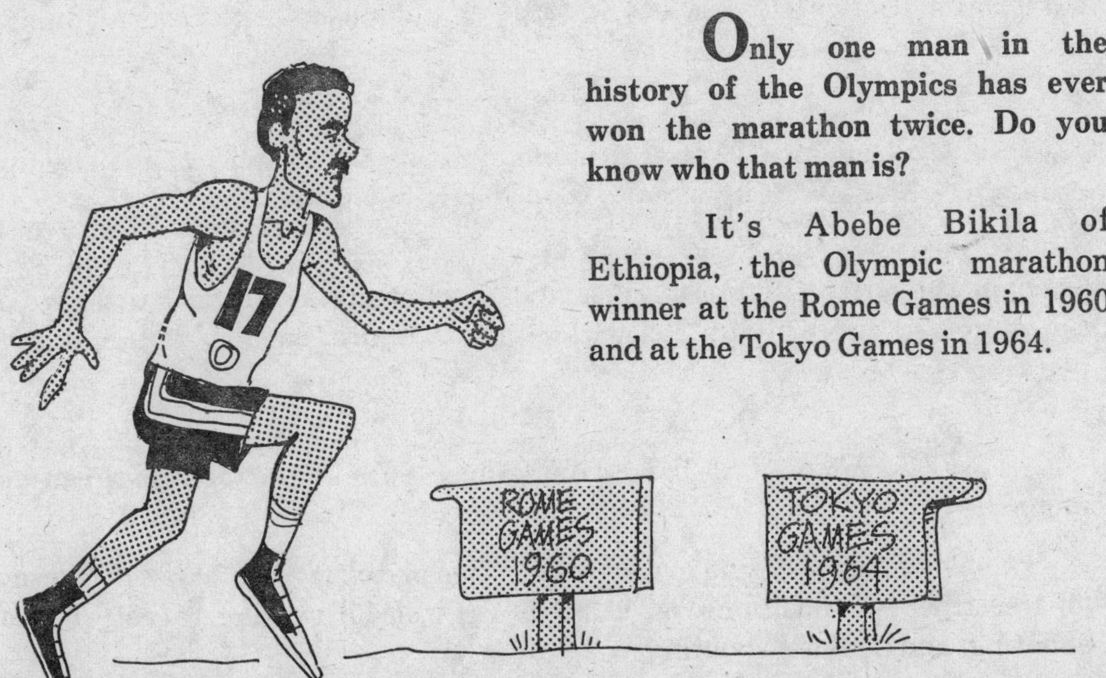

True or false? In 1976, a Russian athlete competing in the modern pentathlon was expelled from the Olympics for having an electronic cheating device in his epée.

Although it sounds far-fetched, it's true. Boris Onishchenko of the U.S.S.R. was caught with an electronic cheating device in his sword and was expelled from the 1976 Games. Since fencing is scored electronically, every "touch" of a sword on an opponent's chest shield automatically registers on the scoreboard. Onishchenko's sword had a transmitter in it that recorded hits when he pressed a button in the handle regardless of whether he scored an actual hit against his opponent or not.

As of 1978, how many times have the Olympic Games been held in North America? Is it once, three times, or four times?

The Olympics have been held on the North American continent four times: in 1904, at St. Louis, Missouri; in 1932, at Los Angeles, California; in 1968, at Mexico City, Mexico; and in 1976, at Montreal, Canada.

A swimmer once lost an Olympic gold medal by a distance of less than 1/8th of an inch. True or false?

It's true. On August 30, 1972, at the Olympic Games in Munich, Gunnar Larsson of Sweden beat Tim McKee of the United States in the 400-meter individual medley final by 2/1000ths of a second, or by a distance of less than 1/8th of an inch.

How many sleds can each country enter in the 2-man bobsled competition at the Winter Olympics? Is it one, two, or three sleds?

Each country is allowed to enter two sleds in the 2-man competition and two sleds in the 4-man competition. The course on which the sleds compete is 1,220 meters long, and has 14 curves and a vertical drop of 97 meters.

Equestrian events were not held at the XVIth Olympic Games at Melbourne, Australia. True or false?

True. Due to Australia's rigid horse quarantine laws, the equestrian events had to be held separately at Stockholm, Sweden.

When were the Winter Olympics televised for the first time? Was it in 1956, 1960, or 1964?

The 1956 Winter Olympics at Cortina, d'Ampezzo, Italy, were the first Games televised.

A gymnast once broke his leg during one Olympic event and refused to withdraw from the other event in which he was entered .... And he ended up winning a gold medal! Can you name him?

The man was Japanese gymnast Shun Fujimoto, and it happened at the 1976 Olympic Games. Fujimoto fractured his leg during his floor exercises, but refused to withdraw from the ring competition. He was fitted with a plastic cast from hip to toe and in it, he entered the ring competition, achieving the highest score of his life, and earning a gold medal. Fujimoto even ended his routine with a triple somersault. Although the landing caused him excruciating pain, he maintained his balance and did not reveal his agony. Olympic doctors later commented that they were amazed that he didn't collapse in pain as soon as his feet touched the floor.

Frank C. Wykoff of the United States won a gold medal at three consecutive Olympic celebrations. Can you name the years and the events in which he won them?

Frank C. Wykoff won his 3 gold medals at the 1928, 1932, and 1936 Olympic Games as a member of the 4 X 100-meter relay team. Wykoff is the only man in Olympic history to be a member of three different winning relay teams, and for this unique accomplishment, he was voted into the National Track and Field Hall of Fame in 1977.

Can you name the events in the Nordic skiing competition at the Winter Olympics?

Olympic Nordic skiing competition includes cross-country skiing for men (15, 30, and 50 kilometers) and for women (5 and 10 kilometers), ski jumping for men (70 and 90 meters), Nordic combined for men only, and Nordic biathlon for men only.

How long is an Olympic swimming pool?

An Olympic swimming pool is 54.68 yards long and is divided into eight lanes.

How much is an Olympic bronze medal worth? Is it $16, $20, or $28?

The pure bronze medal has a metal value of $16.

A man once ran from New Orleans, Louisiana, to St. Louis, Missouri, to compete in the 1904 Olympics and reached his destination just in time to run in the marathon. True or false?

True. This is one of the most unique stories in Olympic history. In 1904, Felix Carvajal of Cuba paid his own way to the United States in order to compete in the Olympic Games at St. Louis, Missouri. At a stopover in New Orleans, gamblers suckered him out of all of his money. Broke, but determined to compete in the Olympics, Carvajal ran all the way from New Orleans to St. Louis. Begging food along the way, he reached St. Louis in just enough time to run in the marathon — which he did, in a long-sleeve shirt, long trousers, and heavy walking shoes. Carvajal was one of the fourteen men to eventually finish the race, just missing a bronze medal by finishing fourth.

At the ancient Olympic Games, the entrants had to meet certain requirements. Which one of the following was *not* one of those requirements: (a) they had to take an oath to compete fairly; (b) they had to have been in training for 10 months before the Olympic Games; or (c) they had to pay a registration fee of about two dollars?

The answer is c. The ancient athletes did not have to pay a registration fee in order to compete in the Olympic Games. However, they did have to meet all of the following requirements: they had to be Greek; they had to take an oath to compete fairly; they had to have been in training for 10 months prior to the Games; they had to have never committed a crime; and they had to have spent the month before the Games at the Greek city of Olympia (where the Games were held).

In what year was Alpine skiing introduced into the Olympics? Was it 1928, 1932, or 1936?

Alpine skiing was introduced into the Olympic Games in 1936. At that time, downhill racing was a combined event with the giant slalom. It wasn't until 1948 that the two were made into separate events.

How long is the course for Olympic rowing events? Is it 1 mile 427 yards, 1 mile 500 yards, or 1 mile 525 yards?

In earlier years the course size varied, but today the standard Olympic rowing course is firmly established at 1 mile 427 yards.

Five countries have competed in all 21 of the modern Olympic Games. Can you name those countries?

Australia, Greece, Great Britain, Switzerland, and the United States have been represented at all 21 celebrations of the Olympic Games.

Which individual athlete holds the Olympic record for winning the most total medals?

A Soviet gymnast named Larisa Semyonovna Latynina holds that record with a grand total of 18 medals (9 gold, 5 silver, and 4 bronze). Latynina is currently the coach of the Soviet women's gymnastics team.

True or false? The United States has won the Olympic gold medal in the discus throw 10 out of 18 times.

False. The U.S. has had 13 wins in the discus throw. These 13 wins out of 18 tries far surpasses every other country. Finland won it twice (1912 and 1920), and Hungary (1900), Italy (1948), and Czechoslovakia (1972), once each. The last American to win the discus throw was Mac Wilkins, the gold medalist in 1976.

Mildred "Babe" Didrikson of the U.S. won both a gold and silver medal at the 1932 Olympics. For which events did she win them?

Babe Didrikson won her gold medal in the javelin throw and her silver medal in the high jump.

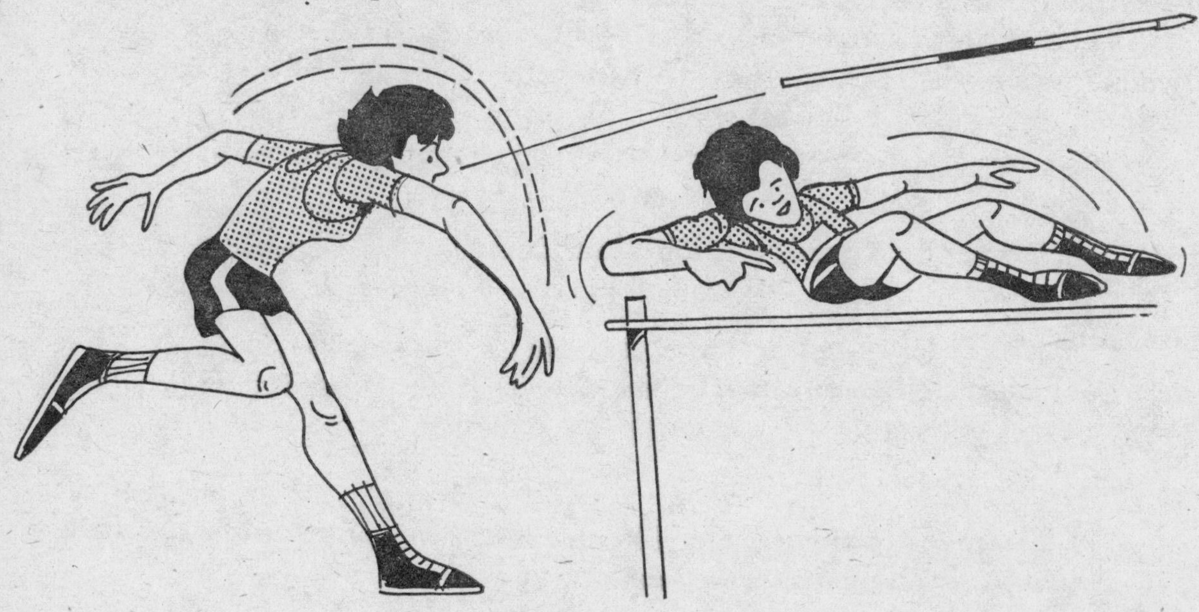

At the Winter Olympics there is a *luge* event. Do you know what a luge is?

A *luge* is a small, wooden toboggan with a canvas or braided plastic seat. A racer lies on his back and steers the luge with his feet. At the Olympic Games, there is a single-seater luge event for men and one for women. There is also a two-seater event for men. The course used for luge events is the same one used for the bobsled races, with the luges reaching speeds of 70 mph traveling down the course.

Wyomia Tyus of the United States won gold medals at the Olympics in 1964 and 1968. Was she a swimmer, a sprinter, or a gymnast?

Wyomia Tyus was a sprinter. She won the 100-meter dash at the 1964 Games at Tokyo and at the 1968 Games at Mexico City, thus becoming the only woman to ever win 2 consecutive medals in that event.

Has the United States ever won an Olympic gold medal in canoeing?

No. The United States has never won a gold medal in men's or women's canoeing in the history of Olympic competition. However, Stephen Lysak and Stephen Macknowski won silver medals in the 1000-meter Canadian pairs in 1948, and Marcia Jones won a bronze medal in the women's 500-meter kayak singles in 1964.

True or false? The sport of polo was never part of Olympic competition.

False. Polo was played at the Olympics five times: in 1900, 1908, 1920, 1924, and 1936.

Kathy McMillian of the United States won a silver medal in a field event at the 1976 Olympics. Which field event was it?

Kathy McMillian won the silver medal in the long jump behind Angela Voigt of East Germany, who won the gold.

Laszlo Papp of Hungary holds an Olympic record that no other boxer has been able to duplicate. Can you guess what that record is?

Laszlo Papp is the only boxer to win 3 Olympic gold medals in boxing. He took the middleweight championship in 1948 and the light middleweight in 1952 and 1956.

Between 1924 and 1976, Canada and the U.S.S.R. dominated ice hockey at the Olympics with 5 gold medals each. Can you name the only other countries that have taken gold medals in ice hockey?

Great Britain and the United States are the only countries to interrupt the Russian-Canadian streaks. Great Britain won a gold medal in ice hockey in 1936, and the U.S., in 1960.

True or false? In 1960, a runner competed in the Olympic marathon barefooted and won the race.

True. The man was Abebe Bikila, an Ethopian solider in the Palace Guard of Emperor Haile Selassie. Bikila, who is the only man to ever win two consecutive Olympic marathons (1960 and 1964), never wore shoes while racing.

A 29-year-old housewife with two children won 4 gold medals at the 1948 Olympic Games. True or false?

It's true. The woman was Francina Blankers-Koen, Holland's track and field "Flying Housewife." Coached by her husband, Blankers-Koen was the sensation of the 1948 London Games, winning the 100 meters, the 80-meter hurdles, the 200 meters, and anchoring the winning 4 X 100-meter relay team.

How many Olympic medals have been won by Kornelia Ender, the teen-age swimming star from East Germany? Is it 3, 7, or 10 medals?

Kornelia Ender holds 7 Olympic medals. She won 3 silver medals at Munich in 1972, when she was only 13 years old. Her 4 gold medals came at the Montreal Olympics, when she finished first in the 100-meter freestyle,the 200-meter freestyle, the 100-meter butterfly, and was a member of the winning 4 X 100-meter medley relay team.

Pakistan won only 1 medal at the 1976 Summer Olympics in Montreal. Was it a gold, silver, or bronze medal?

Pakistan won a bronze medal in the team field hockey event at the 1976 Games.

How old was Olympic figure skating champion Sonja Henie when she competed in the Olympics for the first time? Was she 11, 13, or 15 years old?

Sonja Henie of Norway was only 11 years old when she competed in her first Olympics in 1924. She finished last in the competition that year, but later went on to win 3 gold medals (1928, 1932, and 1936).

True or false? A man nicknamed "The Beast of Prague" once won 4 Olympic gold medals.

It's true. "The Beast of Prague" was Emil Zatopek, a Czechoslovakian soldier, who won the 5,000 meters in 1952, the 10,000 meters in 1948 and 1952, and the Olympic marathon in 1952. Zatopek was given that nickname by track experts because he had a terrible running form that was described as totally graceless. Even though he was called a "freak runner," Zatopek became the first Czech to ever win an Olympic championship and 4 gold medals. He is remembered today as one of the greatest distance runners of all time.

True or false? The Olympic Games have never been held in China or Japan.

False. The 1964 Olympics were held at Tokyo, Japan. However, the Games have never been held in China.

Check back on your Olympic memories, sports buffs. Can you remember who Bob Garrett was?

Bob Garrett was a member of the United States team fielded for the first modern Olympic Games at Athens, Greece, in 1896. Garrett won a gold medal in the shot put, a gold medal in the discus throw, a silver medal in the broad jump, and a bronze medal in the high jump.

After the 1952 Winter Games at Oslo, Norway, the International Federation, which makes the rules for Olympic competition, passed legislation for a maximum weight limit in the bobsleigh events. Do you know why?

It was because the German teams that won both bobsleigh events at the 1952 Olympics capitalized on the fact that a heavier sleigh moves faster. By having crewmen who averaged over 260 pounds each, the Germans got this heavier weight and thus, faster bobsleighs. After 1952, the total weight of a two-man team plus the sleigh could not exceed 826.7 pounds and the 4-man sleigh limit was set at 1,388.9 pounds.

When were the Winter Olympics held at Grenoble, France; Sapporo, Japan; and Oslo, Norway?

Grenoble, France, hosted the Winter Olympics in 1968; Sapporo, Japan, in 1972; and Oslo, Norway, in 1952.

Ben Bradshaw, Russell Vis, Shelby Wilson, and Dan Gable all won Olympic gold medals in the same event. Which one was it?

The four were all gold medalists in freestyle wrestling in the lightweight division. Bradshaw won his medal in 1904; Vis, in 1924; Wilson, in 1960; and Gable, in 1972.

Has there ever been a tie for a gold medal in the history of the Olympic pole vaulting competition?

Yes. The one and only first-place tie in an Olympic pole vault event occurred in 1908, when Albert Gilbert and Edward Cooke, Jr., both of the U.S., had identical vaults of 12 feet 2 inches and shared the gold medal.

In 1928, women were allowed to compete in Olympic track and field events for the first time, but they were restricted to only five events. Can you name those five events?

Those five track and field events open to women at the 1928 Olympic Games were the 100 meters, the 800 meters, the 4 X 100-meter relay, the high jump, and the discus throw.

Five former heavyweight boxing champions of the world from the U.S. were former Olympic gold medal winners. Can you name them and the year they won their medals?

The five Olympic gold medalists who later became world champions were Floyd Patterson, middleweight gold medalist in 1952; Cassius Clay (Muhammad Ali), light-heavyweight gold medalist in 1960; Joe Frazier, heavyweight gold medalist in 1964; George Forman, heavyweight gold medalist in 1968; and Leon Spinks light-heavyweight gold medalist in 1976.

True or false? Russia was once absent from Olympic competition for a period of 40 years.

True. Russian athletes did not participate in the Olympics from 1912 to 1952. The World Wars and the Russian Revolution contributed to their absence.

True or false? A husband and wife once won gold medals at the Olympic Games on the very same day.

True. It happened in 1952 at the Olympic Games at Helsinki, Finland. Emil and Dana Zatopek of Czechoslovakia both won gold medals on the same day — Emil, for the 5000-meter race and Dana, for the women's javelin throw.

Bob Seagren of the United States won a gold medal at the 1968 Olympic Games. In which track and field event did he compete?

Bob Seagren's pole vault of 17 feet 18½ inches won him a gold medal at the 1968 Olympics. Although this set an Olympic record, it was later broken in 1972 by Wolfgang Nordwig of East Germany, whose 18-foot ½-inch vault was then tied by Tadeusz Slusarski of Poland in 1976.

True or false? Dick Button was the last American male skater to win a gold medal in figure skating.

False. Dick Button won his last gold medal for the United States in 1952, but was succeeded in 1956 by Hayes Alan Jenkins and in 1960 by David Jenkins, both Americans.

Which was the only country to win 2 gold medals in archery at the 1976 Olympic Games? Was it the United States, Italy, or the U.S.S.R.?

The United States won the 2 gold medals, sparked by Darrell Pace, who set an Olympic record in the men's 90, 70, 50, and 30 meters, and Luann Ryon, who also set an Olympic record in the women's 70, 60, 50, and 30 meters. The Italians won the bronze medal in the men's competition, and the Russians won the silver and bronze medals in the women's competition.

The very first Olympiad consisted of a single foot race. True or false?

True. There is evidence that the very first Olympiad consisted of a 200-yard foot race near the small Greek city of Olympia. Later, the games became demonstrations of national pride and expanded to include other events. Only Greek citizens who were amateurs were permitted to compete in the Olympic Games.

The first time the women's slalom was introduced into the Olympics, it was won by an American skier. Can you name that skier?

At the 1948 Games in St. Moritz, Switzerland, Gretchen Fraser of the United States won the women's slalom race the first time it was held.

According to Olympic rules, can a baton dropped in a relay race be picked up?

Yes. However, if a baton is dropped, it may be picked up only by the athlete who originally dropped it. A team is disqualified only if the baton is picked up by an athlete other than the team member who dropped it.

If a gymnast receives a score of 10 by the judges in Olympic competition, what does that mean?

A score of 10 means that the judges have determined a performance as flawless and perfect. In scoring, all competitors start out with 10 points and during the course of the athlete's routine, the judges subtract points and fractions of points from the initial 10 for various flaws and imperfections.

Why was the site of the 1976 Winter Olympic Games shifted from Denver, Colorado, to Innsbruck, Austria?

The citizens of Denver refused by referendum to act as the host city for the XIIth Winter Olympiad, so the games were moved to Innsbruck.

Can you name the only female American speed skater to win an Olympic gold medal at Innsbruck in 1976?

Sheila Young, who won the women's 500-meter race, was the only American speed skater to win a gold medal at the 1976 Winter Games.

Richard K. Gunn of Great Britain was the oldest man to ever win an Olympic boxing title. Was he 30, 35, or 38 years old when he won it?

Richard Gunn was 38 years old when he won a gold medal in the featherweight division at the 1908 London Olympics.

A young gymnast named Nadia Comaneci from Romania won 3 gold medals at the 1976 Olympics at Montreal, Canada. In what events did she win them?

Nadia Comaneci, the 14-year-old star of the 1976 Olympics, won her 3 gold medals on the balance beam, on the uneven parallel bars and in the all-around individual competition.

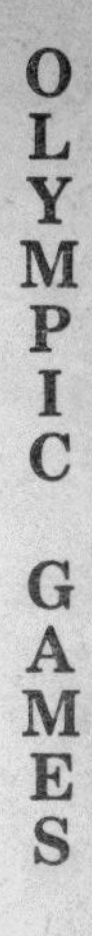

When royalty enters the Olympic stadium, does the bearer of the American flag dip it as a sign of respect?

No. The American flag has never been dipped to royalty at any Olympic celebration. It is an American tradition begun at the 1908 Games when flag bearer Ralph Rose, a shot putter for the U.S., refused to dip America's colors to King Edward VIII. Since then, the tradition of keeping the American flag erect at the Olympic Games in the presence of royalty has never been altered or challenged.

True or false? Adolf Hitler's Nazi Germany was once the host country for the Olympic Games.

True. The XIth Olympiad was held at Berlin, Germany, in 1936. However, the Germans didn't fare too well in the Games, winning only 5 gold medals as compared to the United States' total of 19.

What is the monetary value of an Olympic silver medal? Is it $35, $66, or $84?

An Olympic silver medal is actually worth $66.

Paavo Nurmi was one of the most successful medalists in Olympic history. Was he a boxer, a swimmer, or a runner?

Paavo Nurmi, "The Flying Finn," was a distance runner from Finland. He won 9 gold and 3 silver medals in the 1920, 1924, and 1928 Olympic Games in individual and team regular and cross-country races and in the steeplechase.

At the 1976 Montreal Olympics, Cuba, Mexico, and Trinidad won gold medals. For which of those countries was this a *first* Olympic gold medal?

Cuba, Mexico, and Trinidad *all* won gold medals for the first time at the 1976 Olympic Games. Cuba won 6 gold medals (the men's 400-meter race, the men's 800-meter race, the light flyweight boxing title, the featherweight boxing title, the heavyweight boxing title, and the lightweight judo title). Mexico won the 20-kilometer walk, and Trinidad, the 100-meter race.

At the 1960 Olympic Games in Rome, Italy, the first six runners to cross the finish line in the 1500 meters all broke the previous Olympic record for time. Who won that exciting race?

Australia's Herb Elliott won that gold medal at Rome, with a winning time of 3:35.6, breaking the old Olympic record for that event, 3:41.2 That old time was beaten by Elliott and the next five winners to cross the tape. Elliott's record was later broken in 1968 by Kipchoge Keino of Kenya, with a new Olympic record of 3:34.9.

An interim Olympiad was held in 1906, between the 1904 and 1908 Games. Do you know why?

The 1906 Olympics were held as a tenth anniversary celebration of the renewal of the Games, with the site the same as the 1896 beginning — Athens, Greece.

Which Olympic Games attracted the most competitors? Was it the Munich Games in 1972 or Montreal Olympics in 1976?

The greatest number of athletes to compete in any Summer Games came to Montreal in 1976. That record-setting number of competitors was 7,356.

Dwight Stones of the United States is one of the best high jumpers in the world today. How many Olympic medals has he won?

Dwight Stones has won 2 Olympic bronze medals for his third-place finishes in the high jump at the 1972 and 1976 Olympic Games.

When was basketball first introduced to the Olympic Games? Was it in 1924, 1932, or 1936?

Basketball first became an Olympic event in 1936. The United States won the gold medal that year, with Canada taking the silver medal and Mexico, the bronze.

Martin J. Sheridan and Al Oerter of the United States both competed in the discus throw event at Olympic Games half a century apart. How many gold medals did the two athletes win in all?

Sheridan and Oerter won a total of 7 Olympic gold medals in the discus throw: Sheridan took 3 (1904, 1906, and 1908) and Oerter, 4 (1956, 1960, 1964, and 1968).

Who won the United States' only gold medal at the 1964 Winter Olympic Games at Innsbruck, Austria?

Terry McDermott won the only gold medal for the U.S. at the 1964 Winter Games. He took first place in the 500-meter speed skating race.

True or false? A female swimmer once won the 100-meter freestyle swimming event at three successive Olympic Games.

True. The swimmer was Dawn Fraser of Australia. Fraser won gold medals in the 100-meter freestyle at the Melbourne Olympics in 1956, at the Rome Olympics in 1960, and at the Tokyo Olympics in 1964.

What is the name of the official publication of the International Olympic Committee?

The Olympic Review is the official monthly publication of the International Olympic Committee.

Johnny Weissmuller, who played Tarzan in the movies, won 3 individual and 2 team Olympic gold medals in swimming. At which Olympics did he win those medals?

At the 1924 Olympics at Paris, France, Johnny Weissmuller won 3 gold medals: the 100-meter freestyle, the 400-meter freestyle, and the 4 X 200-meter freestyle relay. At the 1928 Games in Amsterdam, The Netherlands, Weissmuller repeated as the 100-meter freestyle medalist and as a member of the relay team.

Although the Nordic countries (Norway, Finland, Sweden, etc.) are usually the top medal winners in the Winter Olympics, these Winter Games have been held in a Nordic country only once. True or false?

True. The Winter Olympics have been held in a Nordic country only once. That was in 1952, when Oslo, Norway, hosted the competition.

True or false? Speed skater Sheila Young of the United States won a gold, silver, *and* bronze medal at the 1976 Winter Olympics.

True. In 1976, Sheila Young became America's first triple medalist in the Winter Olympic Games by taking a gold medal in the 500-meter speed skating event, a silver medal in the 1500-meter event, and a bronze medal in the 1000-meter event.

Has the United States ever won an Olympic medal in men's or women's volleyball?

No. Ever since the introduction of volleyball as an Olympic event, teams from the U.S.S.R. and Japan have completely dominated the event. The Russians were gold medalists in 1964 (men's), 1968 (men's and women's), and 1972 (women's). Japan had 3 gold medals: 1964 (women's), 1972 (men's), and 1976 (women's).

Grace Kelly, the former American actress and now Princess Grace of Monaco, is the daughter of an Olympic gold medal winner. True or false?

True. John B. Kelly of the U.S., Grace Kelly's father, won 3 Olympic gold medals in rowing. In 1920, he won the single sculls, and in 1920 and 1924, he won the double sculls with his cousin, Paul V. Costello.

Where was the IVth Olympiad (1908) held? Was it in Italy or England?

Originally, the 1908 Olympics were scheduled to take place in Italy, but when Italy resigned its commitment, the Games were moved to London, England. Over 2,000 athletes from 22 nations competed in the IVth Olympiad.

A man once won an Olympic gold medal in the high jump event without even bothering to remove his warm-up suit. True or false?

It's strange, but true. In 1936, the year that the United States swept all of the medals in the high jump competition, Cornelius Johnson won an Olympic gold medal in the high jump without taking off his warm-up suit. Johnson's best leap of 6' 7 15/16" easily won him first-place honors.

In 1976, Jacek Wzsola of Poland won the gold medal in the Olympic high jump. Who was the last American to win a gold medal in that event?

Richard Fosbury was the last American to win the Olympic high jump event when he took the gold medal at the 1968 Games in Mexico City.

No American has ever won an Olympic gold medal in Nordic skiing or ski jumping. True or false?

It's true. No American has ever managed to win a gold medal in either of those events. The Nordic skiing and ski jumping events have been dominated by athletes from Norway, Sweden, and Finland from 1924 to 1976.

Today, athletes who win Olympic events receive gold medals. What did the ancient Greek athletes receive?

Winners in the ancient Greek Olympics received *chaplets* — head garlands of olive leaves, and laurel and palm wreaths.

Who won the women's long horse vault competition at the 1976 Olympics? Was it Nelli Kim, Ludmila Turischeva, or Carola Dombeck?

Young Nelli Kim of the U.S.S.R., with a perfect score of 10, won the 1976 gold medal in the long horse vault, thus becoming the first gymnast ever to do so in this event. Turischeva was second and Dombeck, third.

Who won the decathlon at the 1976 Olympics at Montreal?

Bruce Jenner of the United States became "The World's Greatest Athlete" when he won the gold medal in the 10-event decathlon at the 1976 Olympics. The 26-year-old Californian had finished ninth in the decathlon in the 1972 Games. His point total in 1976, 8,618, shattered the old Olympic record of 8,454, set by Nikolai Avilov of the Soviet Union in 1972. Guido Kratschmer of West Germany was second in 1976, winning the silver medal, and Avilov was third.

Bob Hayes won an Olympic gold medal in track and field before becoming a pro football star. Can you name the event for which he won his medal?

Bob Hayes, who later played professional football for the Dallas Cowboys, won an Olympic gold medal in 1964 in the 100-meter dash.

In Olympic fencing events, do men and women use the same weapons to compete?

No. Men compete with foils, epées, and sabres in the Olympics, while women compete only with foils.

True or false? In the free pistol event at the Olympics, each competitor fires 50 shots at a target.

False. Each competitor gets 60 shots at the target, which is similar to an archery target. The 60 shots are fired in six series from a distance of 164 feet, with a time limit of 2½ hours to complete the event. The contestants are also allowed 15 sighting shots before the competition begins.

Which Olympic track star won more gold medals — Betty Cuthbert of Australia or Wilma Rudolph of the United States?

The answer is Betty Cuthbert, with 4 gold medals. The Australian track star won 3 of those gold medals at the Melbourne Olympics in 1956: in the 100 meters, the 200 meters, and the 4 X 100-meter relay. She won her 4th gold medal in the 400 meters at the 1964 Olympics in Tokyo. Wilma Rudolph's total is 3 gold medals, which she won for the United States at the 1960 Games in Rome. Rudolph won the 100 meters and the 200 meters, and was on the winning 4 X 100-meter relay team.

Springboard diver Marjorie Gestring was the youngest woman to ever win an Olympic gold medal. How old was she when she won it?

Marjorie Gestring of the United States was only 13 years old when she won a gold medal in springboard diving at the 1936 Berlin Olympics.

True or false? A 70-year-old man once won an Olympic gold medal.

True. Sir Eyre Massey Shaw of Great Britain was 70 years old when he won an Olympic gold medal in yachting in 1900. Shaw's record as the oldest man to ever win an Olympic gold medal still stands today.

Which country has won the most gold medals in the Winter Olympics? Is it the United States, the U.S.S.R., or Norway?

The U.S.S.R. is the Winter Olympic record holder, with 51 gold medals. Norway is second with 50, and the United States is third with 30.

In the history of the Olympics, did anyone other than Jim Thorpe of the United States even win the pentathlon *and* the decathlon in the same year?

No one has ever duplicated Jim Thorpe's 1912 monumental feat of winning the pentathlon *and* the decathlon. Although Thorpe's medals were later taken away from him on a technicality, his achievement in the Stockholm, Sweden, Olympics cannot be tarnished: he won 4 out of 5 pentathlon events, scoring twice as many points as the man who finished second, and he scored 700 more points in the decathlon than his closest rival.

Only one woman, an American, has ever won both the springboard and platform diving events at two successive Olympic Games. Can you name her?

The answer is Patricia McCormick. At the 1952 Olympic Games, McCormick took gold medals in springboard and platform diving. Four years later at the 1956 Olympics, she won 2 more gold medals in the same events. No one has duplicated that amazing feat.

True or false? An American skier once lost 2 gold medals — one by 1 second, and the other by 1/10 second.

True. It happened to Penny Pitou of the United States at the 1960 Olympics. Penny lost the downhill event to Heidi Biebl of Germany by 1 second and the giant slalom event to Yvonne Ruegg of Switzerland by a mere 1/10 of a second.

The Olympic marathon run originated in 490 B.C. when a Greek soldier named Pheidippides ran from Marathon to Athens to announce a Greek victory over the Persians. At the end of his 26-mile, 385-yard run, he gasped three now-famous words before dying. What were those words?

Exhausted and bleeding from his run, Pheidippides staggered into Athens and, with his dying breath, cried, "Rejoice, we conquer!" When the Olympic Games were revived in 1896, the historic occasion was commemorated with a marathon race over the original route which Pheidippides had run.

True or false? Bill Toomey won his gold medal in the high jump at the 1968 Olympics in Mexico City.

False. Bill Toomey, the 29-year-old junior high school teacher from California, won his gold medal in the decathlon. His 8,193 points set a record in 1968, but that record has since been broken: first by Nikolai Avilov of the U.S.S.R. in 1972 with 8,454 points, and then by Bruce Jenner of the United States in 1976 with 8,618 points. Jenner is the current record holder.

Alvin C. Kraenzlein, a student at the University of Pennsylvania, did something at the 1900 Olympic Games that no other track star has ever equaled. Do you know what that was?

Alvin Kraenzlein won 4 individual gold medals in a single Olympiad — the 1900 Games. No other track and field Olympian has ever equaled Kraenzlein's feat. He won the 60-meter sprint, the 110-meter high hurdles, the 200-meter low hurdles, and the running broad jump.

Clarence "Buster" Crabbe and Johnny Weissmuller, later famous for their movie roles as Tarzan, were both Olympic gold medalists in swimming. Which one of them won more gold medals?

The answer is Johnny Weissmuller. He won a total of 5 Olympic gold medals: the 100-meter freestyle in 1924 and 1928; the 400-meter freestyle in 1924; and as a member of the winning 4 X 200-meter freestyle relay teams in 1924 and 1928. Buster Crabbe won his only gold medal at the 1932 Olympics in the 400-meter freestyle event.

How many times has the U.S. basketball team been beaten in Olympic competition?

The U.S. basketball team has lost only one game in Olympic competition. From 1936 to 1968, American squads were victorious in 64 consecutive games, earning seven consecutive Olympic titles. But in 1972, the Russian team beat the U.S., 51 to 50, to win the gold medal. In 1976, the American team went undefeated in Olympic competition and again won the gold medal.

At the Winter Olympics, what three events make up the Alpine skiing competition?

The three Alpine skiing events are the downhill, the slalom, and the giant slalom. Each of these Alpine events has a men's and women's division.

True or false? Floyd Patterson won an Olympic gold medal in boxing.

True. Floyd Patterson was a gold medalist in the middleweight division at the 1952 Olympic Games at Helsinki, Finland. Four years later, as a professional, Patterson took the world heavyweight title.

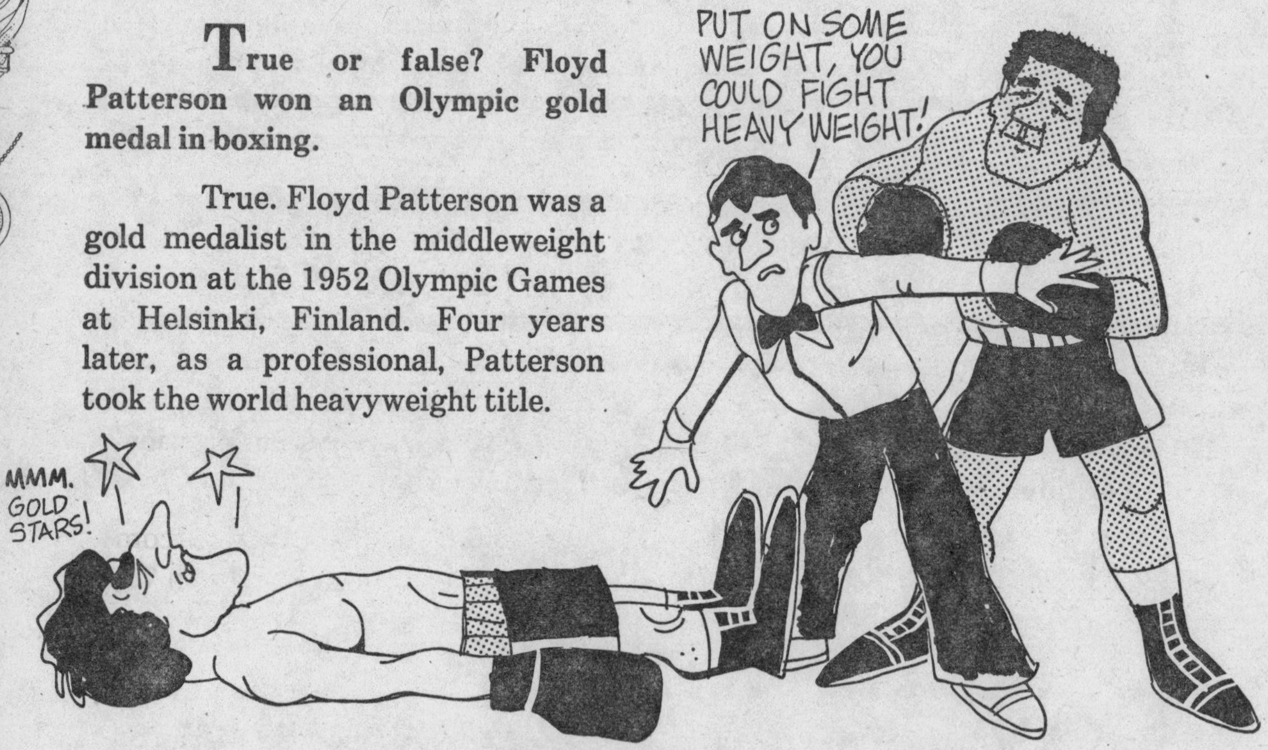

In 1976, who won the Olympic gold medal in women's basketball? Was it the U.S.S.R., the United States, or Bulgaria?

The U.S.S.R. won the gold medal in women's basketball at the 1976 Olympics. The United States took second place, and Bulgaria finished third.

Which country holds the record for winning the Olympic 4-man bobsled title the most times? Is it the United States, Italy, or Switzerland?

The Swiss hold the record, having won the 4-man bobsled event at the Olympics four times (1924, 1936, 1956, 1972).

Check your knowledge about the history of the Olympics. Who was Coroibos of Olis?

Coroibos of Olis, a cook, was the Greek athlete who became the first Olympic champion by winning the lone event — 200-yard dash — at the first Olympics in 776 B.C.

Who is considered to be the strongest man in Olympic history? Here's a clue. He's a Russian weightlifter.

Vassily Alexeev, a Russian super heavyweight, is considered to be the strongest man in Olympic history. In 1972, he lifted 1,411 pounds to win the gold medal in super heavyweight class.

Which country has won the most medals in Olympic competition? Is it the United States, the U.S.S.R., or Great Britain?

The United States has won the most Olympic medals, with a combined gold, silver, and bronze total of 1,472. The U.S.S.R. is second, with 715 medals, and Great Britain is third, with a total of 508.

True or false? Over 1,000 atheltes competed in Oympiad III at St. Louis, Missouri, in 1904.

False. Only 496 athletes (all males) competed in the 1904 Olympics. Now, however, over 5,000 athletes usually compete in the Games.

An American won the gold medal in trap shooting at the 1976 Olympic Games. Was it Don Haldeman or Lanny Bassham?

Don Haldeman was the gold medalist in trap shooting at the 1976 Olympics. Lanny Bassham won his gold medal in the miniature rifle 3-positions event.

True or false? The major reason that the United States does so poorly in the Winter Olympics is because of the limited training facilities for potential Winter Olympians.

Absolutely true. In fact, there are more skating rinks for Winter Olympians to practice on in the tiny country of Japan than there are in the entire United States. America has no luge runs at all and only one bobsled run, which is at Lake Placid, New York.

In 1968, a boxer from the United States won an Olympic gold medal in the heavyweight division. He later turned pro and became the heavyweight champion of the world. Can you name him?

George Foreman was that winner. After taking a gold medal at Mexico City in 1968, Foreman turned pro and became the heavyweight champion of the world in 1973.

Has Great Britain won more gold or more silver medals in Olympic competition?

Olympic athletes from Great Britain have won more silver medals than gold. British Olympians have won a total of 147 gold medals, 199 silver medals, and 162 bronze medals.

Which country has won the most medals in the Winter Olympics Games? Is it Norway, Austria, or Sweden?

Norway, with a grand total of 145 gold, silver, and bronze medals, has won more medals in the Winter Olympics than any other country. Austria is 5th on the list with a total of 80 medals, and Sweden is 6th, with 74.

TV sports commentator Don Schollander won 3 gold medals at the XVIIIth Olympic Games at Tokyo. Can you name the events in which Schollander competed?

Swimmer Don Schollander won gold medals in the 100-meter freestyle, the 400-meter freestyle, and the 4 X 200-meter freestyle relay.

The XIIth and XIIIth Olympic Games were not held because of World War II. But can you name the countries where the Games were scheduled to be held?

Originally, the XIIth Olympic Games were to be held at Tokyo, Japan, in 1940. But when Japan became involved in the war, the Games were shifted to Helsinki, Finland, and later canceled altogether. The XIIIth Olympics were supposed to be held in London, England, in 1944, but again the war canceled them. However, London and Helsinki did host the next scheduled games: London, in 1948 and Helsinki, in 1952.

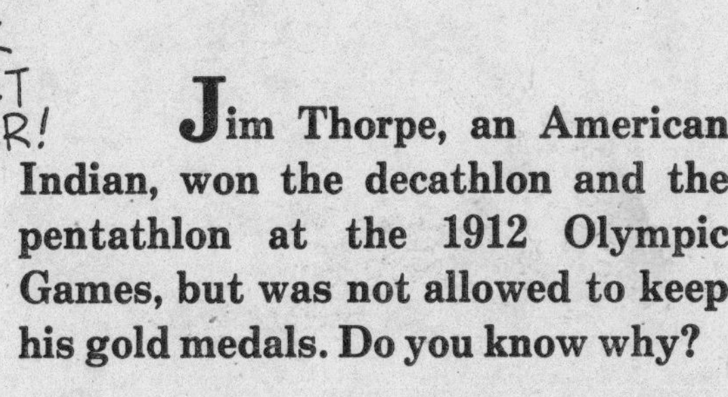

Jim Thorpe, an American Indian, won the decathlon and the pentathlon at the 1912 Olympic Games, but was not allowed to keep his gold medals. Do you know why?

After Thorpe won his Olympic events, the Amateur Athletic Union discovered that he had once accepted payment for playing minor league baseball — a violation of their amateur rules. So Thorpe's name was removed from the roll of champions, and his medals were re-awarded to his runners-up. However, in 1973, twenty years after Jim Thorpe's death, he was reinstated as an amateur by the A.A.U.

Only one man has ever won 7 individual gold medals in Olympic gymnastic competition. Is that gymnast a Russian, a Japanese, or an American?

He's a Russian named Boris Shakhlin. Shakhlin won 2 gold medals in 1956 (side horse and all-around individual), 4 gold medals in 1960 (side horse, long horse vault, parallel bars, and all-around individual), and 1 gold medal in 1964 (horizontal bar). In addition to these 7 individual gold medals, Shakhlin won an 8th in 1956 in the six-event team exercise. Shakhlin also took home 2 silver medals: in 1964 (all-around individual) and in 1960 (the rings). He won a bronze in 1964, also on the rings.

The coveted Sullivan Memorial Trophy is awarded annually to America's top amateur athlete. Which of these Olympic gold medalists have also won the Sullivan Award — Wilma Rudolph, Rafer Johnson, Bill Toomey, or Mark Spitz?

All four Olympic winners were also Sullivan Memorial Trophy winners: Wilma Rudolph, in 1961; Rafer Johnson, in 1960; Bill Toomey, in 1969; and Mark Spitz in 1971. The Trophy has been awarded annually since 1930 by the AAU for the year's outstanding amateur athlete who also exemplifies the amateur creed. It was named for James E. Sullivan, one of the organizers of the AAU.

HORSE & HARNESS RACING

Which jockey holds the record for the most lifetime wins?

Willie Shoemaker, racing's 98-pound, 4' 11" top jockey, holds the record. From April, 1949, to the end of 1977, Shoemaker has ridden 7,331 winners. Johnny Longden is second, with 6,032 wins through 1977.

True or false? A race horse was once unbeaten in 54 races.

True. During the 1870s, the Hungarian horse *Kincsem* won 54 races in Austria, Great Britain, France, and Germany.

In what year did *Bold Forbes* win the Kentucky Derby?

Bold Forbes won the Derby in 1976, upsetting the favorite, *Honest Pleasure*, and winning by a length.

A special breed of horse is used for horse racing. What is the name of that breed?

The tall, slender *thoroughbred* is the horse used for racing. All thoroughbreds are descended from one of three stallions that lived during the 1700s: *Byerly's Turk, Darley's Arabian,* or *Godolphin's Arabian*.

Has a Triple Crown winner ever sired another Triple Crown winner?

It happened, but only once. *Gallant Fox*, who won racing's Triple Crown in 1930, sired *Omaha*, the 1935 Triple Crown winner.

The record payoff for a $2 pari-mutuel win bet is $1,000. True or false?

False. The record, and an old one, is $1,885.20. It was paid on a $2 win bet on a horse called *Wishing Ring* at Latonia Raceway on June 17, 1912.

Which Triple Crown winner was once purchased at public auction?

Seattle Slew, racing's Triple Crown winner in 1977, was purchased at public auction for $17,500 in 1975 by Karen and Mickey Taylor and Jim and Sally Hill, who never dreamed that their unbroken yearling would become a world champion only two years later. A half share in *Slew* was sold for $6,000,000 in 1978.

Can you name the three famous races that make up Great Britain's Triple Crown?

The 2,000 Guineas, the Derby, and the St. Leger form Great Britain's Triple Crown.

How many winners did jockey Eddie Arcaro ride during his career? Was it 3,779, 4,779, or 5,779?

The great Eddie Arcaro rode 4,779 horses to victory, including five Kentucky Derby winners and two Triple Crown champions. Arcaro's 4,779 wins place him third on the all-time win list behind Willie Shoemaker and Johnny Longden.

Race tracks try to make competition keen between the horses in each class by *handicapping* them. What does handicap mean?

Track officials add to or remove the amount of weight a horse must carry. This gives all of the horses in the race an equal chance to win, since the fastest horses carry the most weight.

Organized horse racing in the United States began in 1665. Do you know where the first race track was laid out?

The first American race track was a 2-mile course called New Market. It was laid out on Hempstead Plains, Long Island, New York, by Colonel Richard Nicolls, the royal governor of the colony.

Can you name the thoroughbred that won the Kentucky Derby in 1977?

Seattle Slew, with jockey Jean Cruguet aboard, outdistanced *Run Dusty Run* and *Sanhedrin* by two lengths to win the 1977 Kentucky Derby.

Which thoroughbred won the most money in his racing career? Was it *Secretariat, Kelso*, or *Forego*?

Kelso, a thoroughbred foaled the United States, is the top money winner in the history of horse racing. Between 1959 and 1963, *Kelso* won $1,977,896 in prize money. *Forego* is second, with $1,923,957. *Secretariat* ranks seventh, with a total of $1,316,808.

Who was named Jockey of the Year and Apprentice Jockey of the Year in 1977?

Rookie Steve Cauthen, a 16-year-old, 5' 1", 95-pound jockey, won both Awards in 1977 as a result of his record 487 wins, for a total of $6,151,750. It was the first time in the history of American racing that a single rider won both honors.

A thoroughbred can run up to 40 mph. True or false?

True. In racing trim and on tracks ranging from 5/8 to 1½ miles, a thoroughbred can run at a speed of about 35 to 40 miles per hour.

Which famous race horse was the first to win more than $1,000,000 in prize money? Was it *Seabiscuit*, *Citation*, or *Whirlaway?*

Citation was the first thoroughbred to earn more than a million dollars in prize money. *Citation* won a total of 45 races from 1947 to 1951, including the Triple Crown in 1948.

In which country did organized mounted horse racing begin?

Organized mounted horse racing began in England in 1174 when a public race course was opened at Smithfield, London. The course was a four-mile route, the same distance as ancient chariot races.

True or false? The richest horse race in the world is *not* for thoroughbreds; it's for quarterhorses.

True. Surprised as you might be, the world's richest race, the All-American Futurity, is a race for quarterhorses run at Ruidoso Downs, Ruidoso, New Mexico. The first prize at Ruidoso in 1976, the $330,000 won by *Real Wind*, was the richest in the history of the All-American Futurity.

True or false? *Omar Khayyam, Macbeth,* and *Behave Yourself* were all Kentucky Derby winners.

True. *Omar Khayyam* was the winner of the Derby in 1917; *Macbeth*, in 1888; and *Behave Yourself*, in 1921.

In 1971, *Canonero II* won two of the three races for America's Triple Crown. Can you name those two races?

Canonero II took the Kentucky Derby and the Preakness in 1971, but lost the Belmont Stakes to *Pass Catcher*.

***War Admiral, Count Fleet,* and *Assault* are three Triple Crown winners. True or false?**

True. *War Admiral* won the Kentucky Derby, the Preakness, and the Belmont Stakes to take the Triple Crown in 1937. *Count Fleet* captured the title in 1943, and *Assault* was the 1946 winner.

True or false? Only a jockey is allowed to touch his equipment before a race.

True. This is to make certain that no outsiders tamper with the amount of weight a horse is assigned to carry in a race. Immediately after a race, a jockey must personally unsaddle his horse and be weighed again. Anything more than a one pound deviation in weight may cause the horse to be disqualified and the jockey fined or suspended.

On which horse did Ronnie Franklin win the 1979 Kentucky Derby?

Nineteen-year-old Ronnie Franklin rode *Spectacular Bid* to victory in the 1979 Derby, with *General Assembly* coming in second.

Which horse holds the record for winning the most money in a single year? Is it *Secretariat* or *Seattle Slew*?

In 1973, *Secretariat* won $860,404, which is the most money ever won by a race horse in one year. *Seattle Slew*'s total of $641,370 led all 1977 money winners.

Can you name the horse that won the Preakness in 1978?

Affirmed, ridden by jockey Steve Cauthen, beat *Alydar*, with Jorge Velasquez in the saddle, by a neck to win the 1978 Preakness at Pimlico.

Levi Barlingame holds the record as the oldest jockey to ride in a race. How old was he when he rode in his last race?

Levi Barlingame was 80 years old in 1932 when he rode in his last race at Stafford, Kansas.

Eddie Arcaro's record of five Derby winners was tied in 1969. Can you name the jockey who now shares Arcaro's record?

Eddie Arcaro and Bill Hartack are the only jockeys to ever ride five Derby winners. Arcaro's Derby wins came in 1938 on *Lawrin*; in 1941, on *Whirlaway*; in 1945, on *Hoop Junior*; in 1948, on *Citation*; and in 1952, on *Hail Gail*. Hartack took the Derby in 1957 on *Iron Liege*; in 1960, on *Venetian Way*; in 1962, on *Decidedly*; in 1964, on *Northern Dancer*; and in 1969, on *Majestic Prince*.

In Triple Crown races, all the horses must carry the same weight. What is that weight?

All Triple Crown entries must carry 126 pounds of weight.

How is the distance of a horse race measured?

A horse race is measured in *furlongs*, with each furlong equal to 1/8 of a mile. Most races cover 2 to 16 furlongs.

What do you call a horse that has never won a race?

A horse who has never won a race is called a *maiden*.

Has an undefeated horse ever won the Triple Crown?

Yes. In 1977, *Seattle Slew* won 9 out of 9 races, including America's Triple Crown. It was the first time in the history of racing that a thoroughbred accomplished that amazing feat.

Can you name the horse that won the first Kentucky Derby in 1875?

Aristides, known as "the little red horse," won the first Kentucky Derby in 1875.

True or false? Anyone, regardless of his or her size and weight, can be a jockey.

False. Jockeys are always short, slender people. Carrying a tall, heavy rider would slow down a race horse.

Which thoroughbred earned more money during his racing career — *Buckpasser* or *Native Dancer*?

Buckpasser is the answer, with a career total of $1,462,014. *Native Dancer* never topped the $1 million mark and won $785,240 in prize money.

What does it mean when a race horse is described as *syndicated*?

Syndication means that instead of a horse being owned by a single owner, several parties have invested in the purchase and upkeep of the horse.

The first English Derby was run at Epsom Downs in 1780. Was that first Derby winner *Diomed* or *Eclipse*?

Diomed was the first English Derby winner in 1780 and was later imported to the United States for breeding purposes. *Eclipse*, England's most famous thoroughbred, raced earlier than *Diomed*, in the mid-1700s, and was never beaten.

True or false? To avoid confusion regarding the age class to which a horse is assigned in racing contests, all thoroughbreds have an official birthday other than the day they were born.

True. Throughout most of the racing world, every thoroughbred horse is always one year older on January first.

Can you name the three events that make up the Triple Crown of Horse Racing?

The Belmont Stakes at Elmont, New York, the Preakness Stakes at Pimlico, Maryland, and the Kentucky Derby at Louisville, Kentucky, make up the Triple Crown of Horse Racing.

How far is a *sprint race*?

A *sprint race* covers distances of a mile or less.

How old must thoroughbreds be before they can begin to race?

Thoroughbreds begin to race when they are two years old, and usually continue until the age of eight.

The first time any horse won the Triple Crown was in 1919. Was that first Triple Crown winner *Sir Barton, Gallant Fox,* or *Omaha*?

The answer is *Sir Barton*, who was ridden by Johnny Loftus in 1919.

Man o' War, probably the most famous American thoroughbred, ran in 21 races from 1919 to 1920. How many of those races did he win?

Man o' War won 20 out of his 21 races. The only race he did not win was the Sanford Memorial Stakes at Sarasota, Florida, on August 13, 1919, in which *Man o' War* finished second.

True or false? A horse once lost the Kentucky Derby because the jockey misjudged his position on the track and stood up in the saddle at the sixteenth pole, thinking it was the finish line.

It's nutty, but true. It happened on May 4, 1957. Willie Shoemaker, on *Gallant Man*, was neck and neck with Bill Hartack, on *Iron Liege*, as they raced toward the finish line of the Kentucky Derby. When *Gallant Man* passed the sixteenth pole, Shoemaker stood up in his saddle, thinking he had crossed the finish line. He quickly realized his mistake, but it was too late. *Gallant Man*'s rhythm was interrupted, and *Iron Liege* went on to win the Derby.

The Gold Cup at Hollywood Park, California, was won by the same horse for three consecutive years. Can you name that horse?

Native Diver was the winner of the Gold Cup in 1966, 1967, and 1968 — a feat that has never been duplicated since.

Which horse holds the track record for winning the Kentucky Derby in the fastest time? Is it *Secretariat, Whirlaway,* or *Riva Ridge*?

Secretariat holds the Derby speed record. The swift thoroughbred set that record in 1973 by covering the 1¼-mile track at Churchill Downs in 1 minute and 59 2/5 seconds.

Why is horse racing referred to as the "*Sport of Kings*"?

Horse racing became known as the "*Sport of Kings*" because for many generations, English kings and nobles imported and bred Arabian and Moroccan stallions and mares.

February 22, 1969 marked a revolution in the history of racing. Do you know what occurred on that date?

Charles Town, West Virginia, Race Track was the scene of a great "first" in horse racing when the first female jockey made it to the winner's circle. She was Barbara Jo Rubin, who won her race on *Cohesian*. Earlier that month, Diane Crump had become the first female jockey to race at a major track when she rode at Hialeah in Florida.

What is the largest track bet ever placed in the history of the Kentucky Derby?

Although *Sir Barton* hadn't won a race in six previous starts in 1919, his owner, J.K.L. Ross, bet $250,000 that the thoroughbred would win the Derby against the favorite, *Eternal*. Not only did *Sir Barton* win at Churchill Downs, but he went on to become America's first Triple Crown winner. Ross' $250,000 bet is the largest ever made in the history of the Kentucky Derby.

True or false? Woman jockey Mary Bacon was once voted "The Most Courageous Athlete of the Year" by the Philadelphia Sportswriters Association.

True. Mary Bacon won that Award in 1973 for making an amazing comeback after sustaining a broken back in a racing accident.

Greyhound, one of the greatest trotters in racing history, lost only one race from 1935 to 1940. Of the 64 heats in which *Greyhound* competed, how many did the gelding win? Was it 53 out of 64, 59 out of 64, or 60 out of 64?

Greyhound, who was foaled in 1932 and was the Hambletonian winner in 1935, won an amazing 59 out of 64 heats!

True or false? A pacer named *Bret Hanover* finished in the money in every one of his 68 starts.

True. *Bret Hanover,* the Harness Horse of the Year in 1964, 1965, and 1966, earned $922,616 by winning 62 of 68 starts and finishing 2nd or 3rd in the rest.

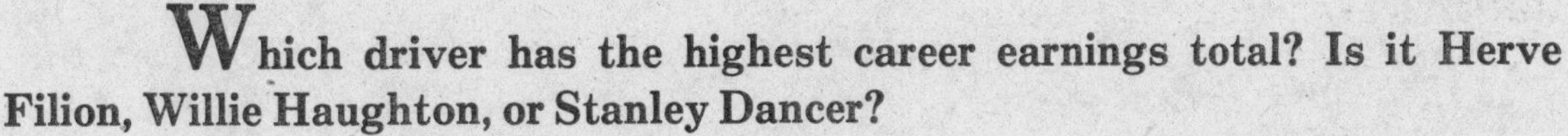

Which driver has the highest career earnings total? Is it Herve Filion, Willie Haughton, or Stanley Dancer?

Willie Haughton, who earned $25,335,453 as of January 1, 1978, holds the record. Herve Filion is second, with $22,591,940, and Stanley Dancer is third, with a total of $20,044,373.

Can you name the three races of Pacing's Triple Crown?

The William H.Cane Futurity at Yonkers, New York, the Messenger Stakes at Westbury, Long Island, New York, and the Little Brown Jug at Delaware, Ohio, make up Pacing's Triple Crown.

Which standardbred pacer had the most two-minute-or-faster races during his career? Was it *Bret Hanover* or *Dan Patch*?

The answer is *Bret Hanover.* From 1964 to 1966, *Bret Hanover* paced a mile in two minutes or faster 31 different times, breaking *Dan Patch*'s record of 30, set between 1900 and 1909.

Can you name the standardbred that won Pacing's Triple Crown in 1970? Was it *Most Happy Fella* or *Rum Customer*?

Most Happy Fella was Pacing's Triple Crown winner in 1970. *Rum Customer* won the Crown two years earlier, in 1968.

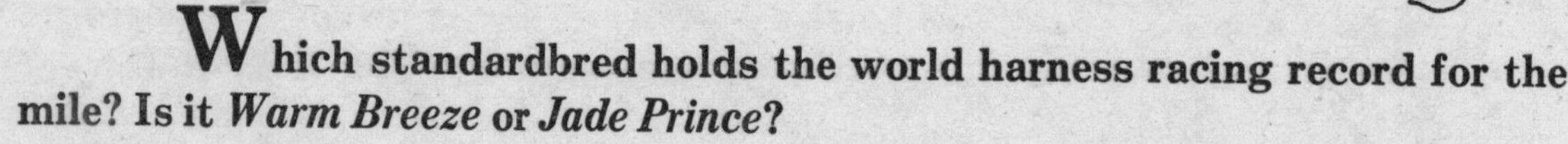

Which standardbred holds the world harness racing record for the mile? Is it *Warm Breeze* or *Jade Prince*?

In June, 1977, at Golden Bear Raceway in Sacramento, California, *Warm Breeze*, the son of *Bret Hanover*, broke the 1976 record of *Jade Prince* by a full second when the swift pacer was clocked at 1:53.2 for the mile.

Which horse holds the world record for pacing geldings? Is it *Shadyside Trixie* or *Young Quinn*?

In 1977, *Shadyside Trixie* broke the world record for pacing geldings at Meadowlands Raceway. With Ken McNutt in the sulky, *Trixie* raced the mile in 1:54 and 3/5.

How old must a harness horse driver be in order to obtain a provisional license to race? Is it 16, 18, or 19 years old?

In order to obtain a provisional license, a harness horse driver must be 18 years old.

In 1962, *Su Mac Lad* was the Harness Horse of the Year. Was *Su Mac Lad* a pacer or a trotter?

Su Mac Lad was a trotter and the leading money winner in 1960 and 1962. When *Su Mac Lad* was retired in 1965, the trotter was seventh on the all-time money-winning list, with a total of $885,095.

Which three races make up Trotting's Triple Crown?

The Triple Crown for trotters consists of the Hambletonian Stakes, a 2-out-of-3 heat race held at DuQuoin, Illinois; the Kentucky Futurity, a single-dash event staged at Lexington, Kentucky; and the Yonkers Futurity, a single-dash race of 1 and 1/16 miles at Yonkers, New York.

True or false? Although thoroughbreds trace their lineage back to *three* founding sires, harness racing's standardbreds trace theirs only to *one*.

True. The founding sire of all standardbreds is an English thoroughbred stallion named *Messenger*. The stallion, foaled in 1780, has a lineage dating back to *Darley Arabian*. After racing successfully in England for many years, *Messenger* was brought to the United States for breeding purposes in 1788.

True or false? A harness driver who races pacers never races trotters and vice versa.

False. Most harness drivers race pacers and trotters.

Which trotter holds the record for winning the most money in a racing career? Is it *Savoir, Bellino II,* or *Une de Mai*?

Bellino II tops the list of all-time money-winning trotters, with a record $1,960,945. *Une de Mai* is second, with $1,660,627, and *Savoir* is third, with $1,307,595.

Did the great *Nevele Pride* ever win the Triple Crown of Trotting?

Yes. *Nevele Pride*, the great trotter who won 57 of 67 races in three years and was the Harness Horse of the Year in 1967, 1968, and 1969, won the Triple Crown in 1968, with Stanley Dancer in the sulky.

True or false? In 1969, *Lindy's Pride* won two of the three races that make up Trotting's Triple Crown.

False. *Lindy's Pride*, with Howard Beissinger driving, won all three races in 1969, thus becoming a Triple Crown winner.

Which driver led *Governor Skipper* to his major 1977 pacing victories? Was it George Sholty, Lucien Fontaine, or John Chapman?

John Chapman was in the sulky for *Governor Skipper*'s 1977 wins in the Little Brown Jug, the Messenger, the Adios, the L.K. Shapiro, and the Monticello-OTB Classic.

If a harness horse *breaks* during a race, what does that mean?

A *break* means that the horse has suddenly gone from a trotting or pacing gait into a gallop, and the driver must try to pull him back immediately into his proper gait.

Do harness drivers have to be short and slim like thoroughbred jockeys?

No. There are no set weights or heights for harness drivers. Usually they weigh between 120 and 200 pounds, and are average height.

Which standardbred holds the world record for trotters of all ages on a 5/8-mile track? Is it *Nevele Pride* or *In Control*?

The answer is *In Control*, who, as a 4-year-old colt in 1976, bettered *Nevele Pride*'s 1969 record of 1:58 by trotting the 5/8-mile track at Brandywine Raceway in Delaware in 1:57 4/5.

Which horse holds the world trotting speed record racing against time? Is it *Nevele Pride, Noble Victory,* or *Matastar*?

Racing against time, *Nevele Pride* set the world record of 1:54.8 on August 31, 1969.

Who selects the Harness Horse of the Year Awards?

The U.S. Trotting Association and the U.S. Harness Writers Association cast ballots to select the Harness Horse of the Year, the Trotter of the Year, the Pacer of the Year, and individual age pacers and trotters.

By looking at the gait of the harness horse pictured below, you should be able to tell whether it is a *pacer* or a *trotter*. Which is it?

The horse is a *trotter*. In a trotting gait, the diagonally opposite legs of the horse strike the ground at the same time. That means that the right front leg and the left back leg lift and strike the track at the same time.

Which pacer holds the record as the all-time career money winner? Is it *Rum Customer, Albatross,* or *Rambling Willie*?

Albatross, who was retired in 1972, holds the record for pacers, with earnings totaling $1,201,470. *Rambling Willie* is second, with $1,066,437, and *Rum Customer* is third, with $1,001,548.

Who is the most successful sulky driver in North America in terms of races won?

Herve Filion of Canada is the answer. By the end of the 1977 season, Filion's total was 6,282 wins — a total he's still adding to. In 1974, Filion set a single-season record, with 637 wins.

In what year did the trotter *Super Bowl* win Harness Racing's Triple Crown? Was it in 1970, 1972, or 1974?

Super Bowl, driven by Stanley Dancer, was the Triple Crown winner in 1972.

Which of these trotters was the winner of the 1977 Hambletonian — *Green Speed, Texas,* or *Native Starlight*?

Green Speed, driven by William Haughton, won the 1977 Hambletonian in straight heats, twice trotting the mile course in 1:55 3/5, to set a new Hambletonian record and to claim $284,131 in prize money. *Green Speed*'s other 1977 victories include the Yonkers Trot, the Colonial, and the Beacon Course Trot.

True or false? A trotter was once sold for $3,000,000.

It's true. The Stoner Creek Stud Farm of Lexington, Kentucky, paid $3 million for *Nevele Pride* in 1969 — the highest price ever paid for a trotter. The most money ever paid for a pacer is $3,600,000 — the selling price of *Nero* in 1976.

Which horse is considered to be the patriarch of the modern standardbred? Is it *Hambletonian, Electioneer,* or *Abbedale*?

The answer is *Hambletonian*. Foaled in 1849, *Hambletonian* was the great-grandson of *Messenger*. The great standardbred went on to sire about 1,330 foals, including *Electioneer* and, in later generations, *Abbedale*.

When was the Hambletonian, a one-mile race for three-year-old trotters, first held? Was it in 1926, 1930, or 1936?

The first Hambletonian was held at Syracuse, New York, in 1926. The winner was *Guy McKinney*, driven by Nat Ray, with a fastest heat of 2:04¾.

Can you name the first pacer to ever win more than one million dollars in prize money?

Cardigan Bay, foaled in New Zealand in 1956 and brought to the United States in 1964, was the first pacer to win more than a million dollars. When the 12-year-old was retired in 1968, he had won 66 races in 134 starts, and was fourth on the list of all-time money-winning horses.

Which major 1977 pacing race had the largest purse — the Cane Pace, the Meadowlands Pace, or the Messenger?

The Meadowlands Pace for 3-year-olds offered the largest purse in 1977 — $425,000.

Can you name the pacer who was foaled in 1896, never lost a race during his career, broke two minutes thirty different times, and was the holder of nine world records when retired in 1909?

That pacer is *Dan Patch*, one of the greatest pacers of all time.

True or false? In harness racing, horses start from a stationary starting gate.

False. Standardbreds always get a running start because they break from a *mobile* starting gate. The starting gate for harness horses is made up of two folding wings that are mounted on an automobile and extend across the width of the track. The mobile starting gate, which was invented in 1946, moves down the track with the horses lined up behind it. When the horses pass the starting pole, the wings fold up, and the car pulls off the track.

In which state will you find the Museum and Hall of Fame of the Trotter? Is it in New York, Kentucky, or Virginia?

The Museum and Hall of Fame of the Trotter is in Goshen, New York. Established there in 1951, it is a repository for the records of famous events in harness racing history.

What is a steeplechase?

A steeplechase is a horse race over a set course covering 2 to 4 miles. The course is obstructed by brush fences, stone walls, or timber rails that are 4' to 5' 2" high. If the course is set in open country, it sometimes also includes a water jump.

True or false? Steeplechasing began as part of hunting matches.

True. As mounted hunters chased stags or foxes, they and their hounds leaped over natural obstacles in the wild. Later, the chases became solely races, usually to "yonder steeple" in a town, and so got their name.

The most famous and prestigious steeplechase of all is the Grand National Steeplechase. In what country is the Grand National held?

The Grand National Steeplechase takes place every spring, as it has since 1839, at Aintree, England. The dangerous and difficult 4½-mile course includes approximately thirty jumps over bushes, fences, rails, and water.

True or false? It is impossible for a horse to jump over 8' high.

False. The official Federation Equestre Internationale high jump record is 8' 1½". It was set by *Huaso*, ridden by Capt. A. Larraguibel Morales of Chile, on February 5, 1949 at Santiago, Chile.

WATER SPORTS

The Hundred-Guineas Cup is a treasured yachting prize now known by a different name. What is that name?

The Hundred-Guineas Cup is the original name of the trophy now known as the America's Cup. In 1851 at the London Exhibition, a 58-mile yacht race was held around the Isle of Wight. The winner of that race was a 100-foot schooner from the United States named the *America,* which was sponsored by the New York Yacht Club. As its prize, the *America* was awarded a trophy called the Hundred-Guineas Cup. Even though the *America* was sold in England, the trophy was brought back to the U.S. and presented to the New York Yacht Club. Here, it ultimately became known as the America's Cup, and is now used as a trophy for international yacht racing.

Which country was the first to organize regular boating competitions? Was it Italy, England, or the United States?

The gondoliers of Venice, Italy, were the first to organize regular boating competitions, probably during the 15th century.

Who captained the United States' yacht *Courageous* in the America's Cup Challenge in 1977?

Ted Turner was the skipper of *Courageous*, the yacht that represented the United States in the America's Cup Challenge in 1977. *Courageous* defeated the foreign challenger, *Australia,* in four straight races to give the U.S. its 23rd title in 23 challenges. Turner is the Georgia millionaire owner of the Atlanta Hawks pro basketball team and former owner of baseball's Atlanta Braves. Because of his flamboyant style and his inclination to be garrulous at times, Turner has been nicknamed "The Mouth of the South."

What is the world sailing-speed record? Is it 21.60 mph, 31.60 mph, or 41.60 mph?

The official world sailing-speed record is 31.60 mph. It was set by the 73½-foot *Crossbow II* off Portland, Dorset, England, on September 30, 1976.

One of the most famous boat races open to oarsmen from all over the world takes place annually on the Thames River. What is the name of that world-famous rowing competition?

That race is the week-long Henley Royal Regatta — an event which since 1839 has been attracting oarsmen from all parts of the world. They compete in many different races, using a wide variety of boats.

The first time an American college boat racing crew went abroad was in 1869, when Harvard University challenged Oxford University. Who won that race?

Oxford defeated Harvard in that historic Thames River race.

The Harvard-Yale Regatta is one of the oldest rowing competitions in the United States. Was it first held in 1851, 1864, or 1885?

The Harvard-Yale Regatta was held for the first time on August 3, 1852, on Lake Winnepesaukee, New Hampshire.

What is the length of the longest regularly contested yacht race in the world? Is it 1,571 miles, 2,571 miles, or 3,571 miles long?

The longest yacht race in the world is the Biennial Los Angeles-Tahiti Trans-Pacific Event, which is slightly over 3,571 miles long. The fastest time ever recorded in this race was 8 days, 13 hours, and 9 minutes. It was established in 1969 by Eric Taberley's *Pen Duck IV* of France.

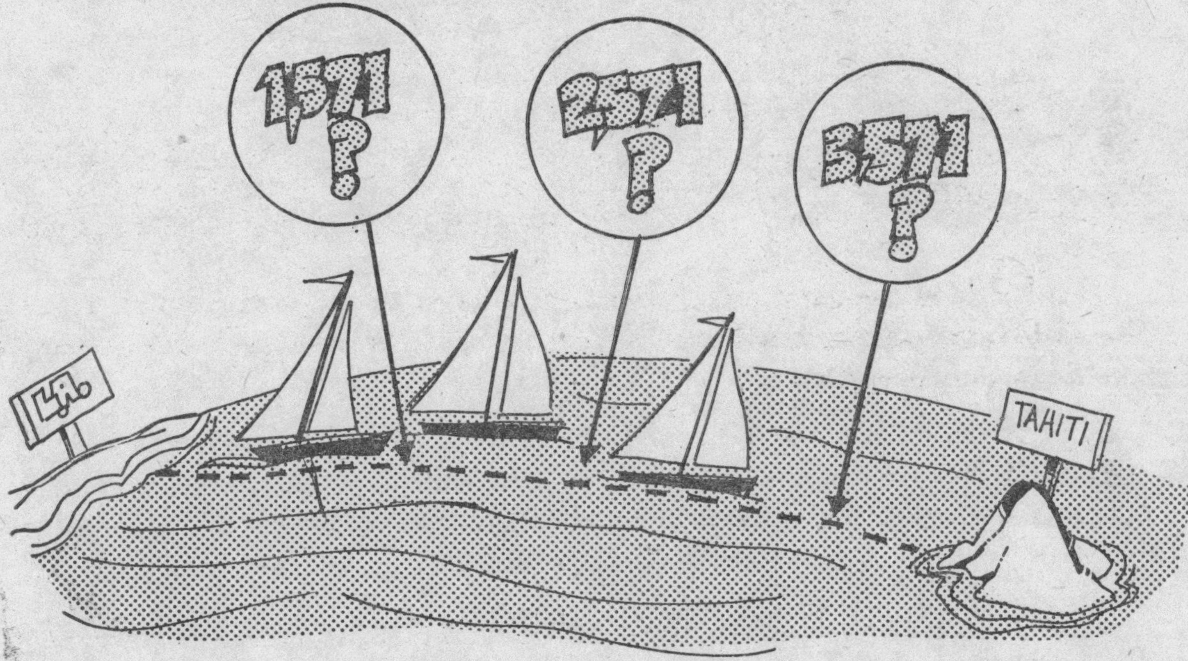

When did the first international challenge for the America's Cup take place? Was it in 1865, 1870, or 1875?

The first international challenge race for the America's Cup took place in 1870, and set a pattern that is still followed today. In 1870, *Cambria*, a yacht owned by James Ashbury of England, raced against *Magic*, a yacht owned by Franklin Osgood of the United States. In that first challenge race, the U.S. successfully defended the America's Cup, as it has done ever since.

Which trophies are awarded to the winners of the North American Yacht Racing Union's yearly championship races?

The winner in the men's division of the North American Championship Race is presented with the Mallory Cup, and the winner in the women's division is presented with the Adams Cup.

The word *canoe* is derived from the Cherokee Indian word *kanu*, which means "water horse." True or false?

Absolutely false. The word *canoe* is derived from the French word *canot*, which means "hollow log."

Stephan Z. Bezuk holds the record for canoeing down the Amazon River in 136 days. Is Bezuk from the United States, Great Britain, or Brazil?

Stephan Bezuk is from the United States. He traveled 3,400 miles down the Amazon in a kayak to set the record in 1970.

True or false? The longest regularly held canoe race in the world is in Texas.

True. The name of the race is the Texas Water Safari. Instituted in 1963, the race, covers 419 miles from San Marcos to Seadrift, and takes place in the San Marcos and Guadalupe rivers.

Where were the canoeing and kayaking World Whitewater Championships held in 1977? Was it in Canada, Austria, or the United States?

In July of 1977, the World Championships for canoes and kayaks were held at Klagenfurt, Austria. The competition was dominated by West German athletes, who won 5 gold, 5 silver, and 2 bronze medals.

Take a bow if you know the answer to this one. Who was John Macgregor?

John Macgregor was the man who pioneered canoeing as a sport in 1865. Macgregor, an English lawyer and writer, instituted competitive canoeing and was instrumental in the sport's advancement through a series of books he had written describing his journeys through Europe and the Middle East in his home-built canoe.

How long was the longest canoe journey ever made? Was it 4,000, 5,797, or 7,516 miles long?

Randy Bauer and Jerry Mimbach of Coon Rapids, Minnesota, traveled 7,516 miles by canoe and portage from Minnesota around the Eastern Coast of the U.S. via New Orleans, New York, and Lake Ontario from September 8, 1974 to August 30, 1976, to set that record.

What is *whitewater canoeing*?

Whitewater canoeing is canoeing over swiftly flowing rapids.

What are the basic differences between a *kayak* and a *canoe?*

A *canoe* is built to hold more than one person. A *kayak* is usually built to hold a single person. A canoe is usually from 10 to 20 feet long and is made of canvas over a wooden framework of light metal alloys of aluminum, magnesium, or fiberglass. A kayak is about 10 feet long and is a narrow, skin-covered craft with a hole in the center into which the paddler inserts himself. A kayak oar has paddles on both ends, while a canoe oar has a paddle on one end.

A powerboat once made a jump of over 100 feet. True or false?

True. For a sequence in the eighth James Bond film, *Live and Let Die*, Jerry Comeaux, in a Glastron GT-150, with a 135hp Evinrude Starflite engine, sped up a greased ramp on an isolated Louisiana waterway at 56 mph and jumped his craft 110 feet through the air, to set the record for the longest jump ever achieved by a powerboat.

Who was the first man to pioneer powerboat racing?

Ole Evinrude, an engine manufacturer of Milwaukee, Wisconsin, is credited with popularizing the outboard motor and starting the motorboating craze in the United States.

True or false? The first offshore boat race took place in 1903.

True. The first offshore race, held in 1903, was from Calais, France, to Dover, England. The winner, in a boat named *Napier*, attained a speed of 18 knots, and was awarded a championship cup presented by Sir Alfred Harmsworth of England.

The American Power Boat Association sanctions all regattas in the U.S. and Canada. True or false?

True. The APBA governs over 600 major powerboat races in North America for over 5,000 racing boats on its register.

What is the length of major powerboat races?

Major powerboat races are conducted on one-mile straightaway runs, with speeds up to 100 miles per hour.

In which country was the first powerboat tested? Was it in England, France, or Holland?

The earliest application of a gasoline engine to a boat was Gottlieb Daimler's experimental powerboat, which he tested on the Seine River in Paris, France, in 1887. Daimler was the inventor of the internal combustion engine.

The Harmsworth Cup Races were held 25 times between 1903 and 1961. One country dominated those races with 16 wins. Can you name that country?

The United States won the Harmsworth Cup 16 times from 1903 to 1961. Garfield A. Wood of the U.S. holds the record for the most individual wins, with 8, between 1920 and 1933.

What is the highest speed ever attained by a powerboat? Is it 120.33 mph, 130.33 mph, or 140.33 mph?

The answer is 130.33 mph. Tony Fahey of Great Britain, in his 22-foot hydroplane, *Vladivar II*, attained that speed on Lake Windermere, England, on May 23, 1977.

How many times has Bill Muncey won the Gold Cup?

Powerboat driver Bill Muncey won the Gold Cup five times: first in 1956, then in 1957, 1961, 1962, and 1972.

True or false? A fish weighing 1/16 of an ounce once won a fishing contest.

True. The fish was a smelt and it was the smallest full-grown fish ever to win a competition. It was caught by Peter Christian, who beat out 107 other competitors at Buckenhain Ferry, Norfolk, England, on January 9, 1977.

What was the weight of the largest fish ever caught on a rod? Was it 1,664 pounds, 2,332 pounds, or 2,664 pounds?

The largest fish ever caught on a rod was a 16'10", 2664-pound man-eating white shark. It was caught by Alf Dean at Denial Bay, South Australia, on April 21, 1959.

Was the biggest freshwater fish ever caught a white sturgeon, a walleye, or a lake trout?

The largest freshwater fish ever caught was a 111-inch-long white sturgeon, weighing 360 pounds. It was caught in 1956 by Willard Cravens at Snake River, Idaho. The largest walleye ever caught weighed 25 pounds and was 41 inches long. It was hooked by Mabry Harper at Old Hickory Lake in Tennessee. Larry Daunis caught the largest lake trout at Great Bear Lake, N.W.T., Canada, in 1970. It weighed 65 pounds and was 52 inches long.

True or false? The largest shark ever landed weighed over 4,000 pounds.

True. Captain Frank Mundus harpooned a 17-foot, 4500-pound white shark off Montauk Point, Long Island, New York, on June 6, 1964. It took five men five hours to land the shark, which was the biggest one ever caught.

Where are the world's highest waves which surfers can ride? Are they in Australia, California, or Hawaii?

The answer is Makaha Beach, Hawaii. The waves here are consistently high, often reaching the rideable limit of 30 to 35 feet. Higher waves are too dangerous to ride.

The winners of the men's and women's 1977 United States Surfing Championships were both Hawaiians. True or false?

False. Although the men's winner, Duane Wong, is from Hawaii, the winner in the women's division, Karen McKay, is from Texas.

In surfing, what is the term used to describe stunt riding or a surfer who performs fancy tricks while riding a wave?

Stunt riding in surfing is called *hot-dogging*, and a surfer who performs fancy tricks is a *hot-dog*.

What is a *howler* or *zipper?*

Howlers or *zippers* are big waves that only experts can ride.

How does a surfer control, or steer, his board?

A surfer controls his board by shifting his weight and position on the board. For example, to turn the board, he moves his rear foot to either side while keeping his forward, or balance, foot in place in the center of the board.

When and where was the first World Surfing Championship held?

The first World Surfing Championship was held in Sydney, Australia, in 1964.

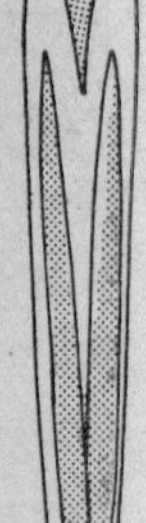

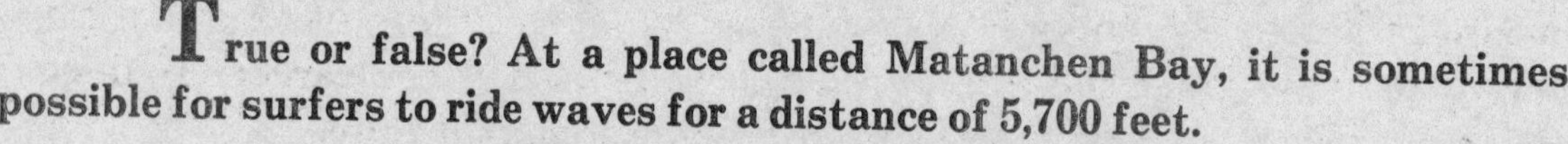

True or false? At a place called Matanchen Bay, it is sometimes possible for surfers to ride waves for a distance of 5,700 feet.

It is true. The longest possible surfing ride in the world can be taken at Matachen Bay on the Pacific Coast of Mexico. But waves break for this ride only four to six times a year.

Was the first surfer to win two World Surfing Championships a male or a female?

Joyce Hoffman of the United States, a woman, was the first surfer to win two World Surfing Championships. She won her titles in 1965 and 1966.

To get the most out of riding a wave, does a surfer travel directly towards shore in a straight line?

No, never. A skilled surfer travels at an angle to the shore rather than directly toward it so he can enjoy a longer ride.

What is a *wipe out?*

When a rider is bumped from his surfboard by a wave, that is called a *wipe out*.

From 1969 to 1972, the NCAA Swimming Championships in the 100-yard butterfly event were won by the same swimmer. Can you name that swimmer who went on to much greater fame?

While attending the University of Indiana, Mark Spitz was the National Collegiate Athletic Association's Champion in the 100-yard butterfly in 1969, 1970, 1971, and 1972.

In 1930, a seventeen-year-old American swimmer held 26 world freestyle records in distances from 50 yards to 1 mile *all at the same time*. Who was this amazing swimmer?

Helene Madison was the swimmer who held those 26 world freestyle records in 1930. According to the Amateur Athletic Union, Madison's amazing accomplishment was a feat never equaled by any other swimmer, male or female, under the AAU's jurisdiction. During her career, Madison captured 12 World and 30 American Swimming Championships.

What is the current record time for swimming the English Channel?

In 1964, Britisher Barry Watson set the current record of 9 hours and 35 minutes for the swim from France to England. In 1976, Wendy Brook, also of Great Britain, set the England-to-France record with a time of 8 hours and 56 minutes.

On August 6, 1926, a woman swam across the English Channel for the first time in history. Can you name that woman?

Nineteen-year-old Gertrude "Trudy" Ederle, the daughter of a New York City butcher, was the first woman to swim across the Channel from France to England. She crossed the twenty-two miles of ocean in 14 hours and 39 minutes.

William E. "Ned" Barnie is the oldest man to ever swim across the English Channel. How old was he when he made his Channel crossing?

When Ned Barnie swam from England to France on August 16, 1951, he was 55 years old. It took him 15 hours and 1 minute to swim across the 21 miles of ocean.

Where is the largest swimming pool in the world? Is it in Morocco, Japan, or Sweden?

The world's largest swimming pool is the salt water Orthlieb Pool in Casablanca, Morocco. It is 1,547 feet long and 246 feet wide, and covers an area of 8.9 acres.

Is the world record holder for the men's 100-meter freestyle event a swimmer from the United States, Great Britain, or South Africa?

The swimmer who holds the world record for the 100-meter freestyle event is Jonty Skinner from South Africa. Skinner set the record time of 49.44 at Philadelphia, Pennsylvania, on August 14, 1976.

What is the highest speed ever attained by a swimmer? Is it 3.19 mph, 4.52 mph, or 5.19 mph?

The correct answer is 5.19 mph. It was attained by Joe Bottom of the U.S., who recorded 19.70 seconds for 50 yards in a 25-yard pool at Cleveland, Ohio, on March 25, 1977.

True or false? The first drawings of swimming for recreation and sport have led experts to believe that swimming didn't become popular until the early 1600s.

Absolutely false. Swimming is probably one of the world's oldest sports. Cave drawings made in the Libyan Desert more than 11,000 years ago show people swimming. An Egyptian nobleman recorded that his children took swimming lessons about 2160 B.C. And about 880 B.C., Assyrian warriors used a crawl-type stroke to swim across streams.

True or false? The first person to swim the English Channel from England to France and back again was Jon Erikson of the United States.

False. The first double crossing of the English Channel was achieved by Antonio Abertondo of Argentina on September 20-21, 1961. Abertondo, who was 45 years old when he made his historical double crossing, completed the feat in 43 hours and 10 minutes. Jon Erikson, however, set a time record for the nonstop double Channel swim, 30 hours, on August 14-15, 1975.

Which swimming stroke is faster — the American crawl or the side stroke?

The American crawl, or freestyle, is not only the faster stroke, but it is the *fastest* of all swimming strokes.

The youngest person to ever swim the English Channel was David Morgan of Scarborough, England, who did it on July 26, 1977. How old was David when he swam the Channel?

David Morgan was only 13 years old in 1977 when he swam the English Channel from Dover to Wissant, France, in 11 hours and 5 minutes.

Florence Chadwick did something on September 11, 1951, that no other woman distance swimmer had ever done. Do you know what that was?

Fighting tides and winds, Florence Chadwick became the first woman to swim the English Channel from England to France. She repeated her 1951 Channel swim again in 1953 and 1955.

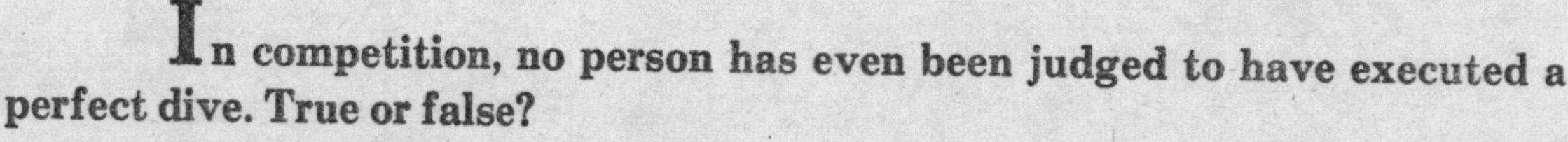

In competition, no person has even been judged to have executed a perfect dive. True or false?

False. According to the record books, a perfect dive has been executed, but only once. At the 1972 Olympic trials in Chicago, Michael Finneran was awarded a perfect score of 10 by all seven judges for a backward 1½ somersault 2½ twist free dive from the 70-meter board. This is an individual achievement without precedent.

Who holds the record for swimming around Manhattan Island? Here's a hint. The record holder is a woman.

Diana Nyad holds the record. On October 5, 1975, Nyad swam around Manhattan Island in 7 hours and 57 minutes to set the record. Nyad was also the first swimmer, male or female, to swim the 32 miles across Lake Ontario.

A swimmer turned actor set more than 50 American and world swimming records during his career. Who is that swimming star?

Johnny Weissmuller is the swimmer who set more than 50 swimming records before retiring from competition to star as Tarzan in motion pictures in the 1930s. Included in those records is the 100-yard freestyle record, which Weissmuller broke five times between 1922 and 1927.

True or false? The only NCAA swimming title Mark Spitz ever won was in the butterfly.

False. In 1969, Mark Spitz of the University of Indiana won National Collegiate Athletic Association swimming titles in the 200-yard freestyle with a time of 1:39.53 and the 500-yard freestyle with a time of 4:33.48, in addition to the butterfly.

The backstroke is one of the five basic swimming strokes. Can you name the other four basic strokes?

The other four basic swimming strokes are the American crawl, or freestyle, the breaststroke, the butterfly, and the sidestroke.

Bruce Furniss, Brian Goodell, and Bobby Hackett hold world records for freestyle swimming. Where do those three swimmers come from?

Furniss, Goodell, and Hackett are all from the United States. Bruce Furniss holds the world record for the 200 meters, with a time of 1:50.29. Brian Goodell is the record holder for the 400 meters and the 1,500 meters, with times of 3:51.93 and 15:02.40. Bobby Hackett's time of 8:01.54 is a world record for the 800 meters.

True or false? The ancient Romans had heated indoor pools.

True. Most Roman cities had indoor public "baths," or pools, which were heated by wood-burning furnaces under the floor. Swimming pools, both indoor and outdoor, were common throughout the Roman Empire.

From January to February 1978, the women's world record in the 800-meter freestyle event was broken three times. The first woman to break the record was Michelle Ford of Australia, with record time of 8:34.86 in early January. Can you name the other two swimmers who broke the world record after Ford?

Michelle Ford broke her own world record two weeks after setting it, by swimming the 800-meter freestyle event in 8:31.30. Less than a month later, Tracy Wickham, a 15-year-old Australian, broke Ford's record with a 8:30.53. Wickham's time is the current women's world record.

In 1967, *Tass* — the official Soviet News Agency, named a young American swimmer as their "Sportswoman of the Year." Who was the swimmer that *Tass* honored?

In 1967, *Tass* named Debbie Meyer of the United States as their "Sportswoman of the Year." The Sacramento, California, swimmer held world records at the time in the 400-, 800-, and 1500-meter freestyle, as well as the 880-yard event.

In April of 1978, Tracy Caulkins, a 15-year-old swimmer from Nashville, Tennessee, became an overnight sensation with record-breaking performances in several events at the AAU National Short Course Championships held at the Olympic Swimming Center in Austin, Texas. How many U.S. records did Tracy set at that meet? Was it 3, 5, or 10 records?

Tracy Caulkins set 5 individual U.S. records. Her time of 1:59.33 in the 200-yard individual medley made her the first woman to ever swim that event in less than two minutes. She also set U.S. records in the 100- and 200-yard breaststroke, the 400-yard individual medley, and the 100-yard freestyle.

Duke Kahanamoku was one of the greatest crawl swimmers in the United States. True or false?

True. Duke Kahanamoku, a native of Honolulu, Hawaii, held the U.S. record for the 100-yard freestyle event from 1913 to 1921. Kahanamoku also helped to develop the crawl, which was introduced to organized swimming competitions in 1902 by Richard Cavill of Australia.

The world records for the men's 100- and 200-meter back stroke events are held by the same U.S. swimmer. Is it John Naber or Rod Strachan?

It's John Naber. In 1976, Naber set world records for both events at Montreal, Canada. Naber's record times are 55.49 for the 100 meters and 1:59.19 for the 200 meters. Rod Strachan holds the world record for the individual medley, with a time of 4:23.68, which he also set at the Montreal Olympics.

Has anyone ever swum the English Channel underwater?

Yes. Fred Baldasare of the U.S. swam from France to England on July 10-11, 1962, using scuba gear. On July 28, 1962, Simon Paterson, an English frogman, swam from France to England underwater, using an air hose attached to his pilot boat.

The one major difference between early and modern water skiing is the location of the tow rope. True or false?

True. When water skis were first invented in 1922, the tow rope was attached to the skis. Therefore, the boat pulled the skis and not the skier. It wasn't until the 1930s that the tow rope was taken off the skis and held by the skier himself.

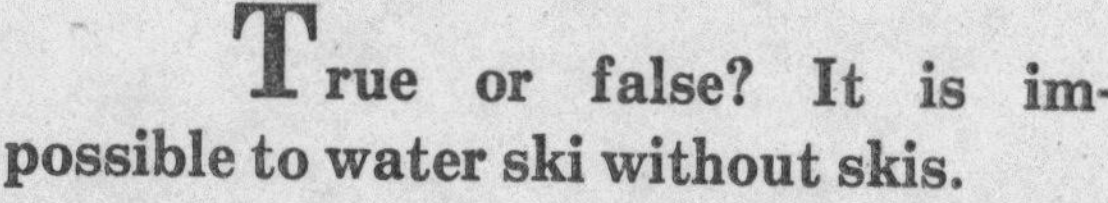

True or false? It is impossible to water ski without skis.

False. It is possible to water ski barefoot and many people do. Paul McMannis of Australia once skied 2 hours and 37 minutes barefoot to establish a world duration record. John Guthrie of New Zealand set a world record by jumping 50 feet, 6 inches barefoot, and John Taylor of the United States holds the barefoot speed record with a mark of 103.68 mph.

Is the longest jump ever made by a person on water skis 150 feet, 165 feet, or 180 feet?

The world record for the longest water ski jump is 180 feet. It was set by Wayne Grimditch of the United States at Callaway Gardens, Pine Mountain, Georgia, on July 13, 1975.

Who is considered to be the pioneer of water skiing?

Ralph Samuelson of Lake Pepin, Minnesota, is generally credited with pioneering water skiing as a sport. He is believed to be the first man to ski on two curved pine boards during the summer of 1922. Samuelson is also the first man to make a jump on water skis, which he did off a greased ramp at Lake Pepin in 1925.

What is the size of a standard water ski?

Although there are many types of skis, the standard water ski for everyone from beginners to experts is 5'4" long by 6¾" wide.

Before water skis became popular, people used *aquaplanes*. What is an aquaplane?

An *aquaplane* is a wide board pulled by a boat.

How many players on a water polo team are allowed in the pool at one time?

Of the 11 men on a water polo team, 7 are allowed in the pool at one time: the goalkeeper; left and right backs; a halfback; and left, center, and right forwards. The 4 extra players remain out of the water at poolside and can be used as substitutes anytime during the game.

How much playing time is there in a water polo game? Is it 20 minutes, 28 minutes, or 36 minutes?

A water polo game consists of 20 minutes of playing time. This is divided into four 5-minute quarters, with a 2-minute rest between each quarter.

The longest water polo game on record lasted 48 hours and 8 minutes. True or false?

True. It was played between two teams from Abraham Lincoln High School in Des Moines, Iowa, in March of 1976. The game was staged to set a water polo marathon record.

If a player pushes a floating ball across the goal line using his head, does it count as a goal?

Yes. Goals can be scored by throwing, pushing, or tipping the ball into the opponent's goal. Like soccer, water polo players can use their head to move the ball.

All water polo players are required to wear colored caps. What colors are they?

The members of one water polo team wear white caps and the members of the other team wear blue caps. Goalkeepers wear a red cap trimmed with the color worn by their teammates.

What kinds of fouls are called in water polo?

The two kinds of fouls that can be called in water polo are *technical fouls* and *major fouls*. Some technical fouls are: starting before the whistle, touching the ball on a throw-in before it hits the water, and leaving the field of play without permission. Some major fouls are: kicking or hitting an opponent, interfering with a player making a free throw, and committing a technical foul to prevent a goal from being scored.

In water polo, is it legal to deliberately splash water in your opponent's face?

No. Deliberately splashing water in an opponent's face is a major foul, and the opposition receives a free throw. If the person fouled is on the attacking team and the foul takes place within 13 feet of the defender's goal, a penalty shot is awarded.

No one on a water polo team is allowed to touch the ball with two hands at the same time. True or false?

False. One person on a water polo team can legally touch the ball with two hands at the same time — the goalkeeper. He is also allowed to punch the ball, but no other players are allowed to use those tactics.

Can a water polo player be thrown out of a game for committing too many major fouls?

Yes. If a player commits three major fouls, he is automatically ejected from the game.

In water polo, what is the difference between a *free throw* and a *penalty throw*?

In a *free-throw*, a player is allowed to put the ball into play unmolested by passing it, but he is not allowed to throw the ball directly into the goal before it is touched by a teammate. In a *penalty throw*, a player can throw the ball directly at the goal from anywhere along the 13-foot line.

WINTER
SPORTS

The *snowplough* and the *christiana* are two skiing techniques. When do skiers use them?

The *snowplough* and the *christiana* are used when skiers want to stop and turn. In the snowplough method, the skier swings out the tails of skis and keeps the tips together, forming an arrowhead shape before turning. In the christiana method, the skier makes his turn by keeping his skis parallel and leaning his body weight in the direction of the turn.

Who were the 1978 United States Figure Skating Champions?

The 1978 U.S. Figure Skating Champions were Linda Fratianne and Charlie Tickner. For both skaters, this was their second consecutive title.

Which college won the 1978 NCAA Skiing Championship?

The University of Colorado won the NCAA Skiing Championship in 1978 — the seventh consecutive year they took the title.

Where did the sport of speed skating originate?

Speed skating began on the frozen canals of Holland in the 1200s.

Anne Marie Proell Moser of Austria won the Women's Downhill event at the World Cup Championships at Laaz, Switzerland, in 1978. Including that victory, how many World Cup races has she won in eight years? Is it 20, 30, or 50?

When Anne Marie Proell Moser won the Downhill at the 1978 World Cup Championships, it marked her 50th World Cup victory in eight years.

In 1978, a team from the U.S. won the World 4-Man Bobsled Championship held at Lake Placid, New York. True or false?

False. A team from East Germany won the World 4-Man Bobsled Championship in 1978.

Who was the first U.S. Freestyle Skiing Champion?

The answer is Suzy Chaffee, who won the first U.S. Freestyle Skiing Championship in 1971 and held the title up to 1973.

The Grand Prix of Snowmobile Races is the St. Paul Winter Carnival International Snowmobile Race. How long is that race?

The St. Paul Winter Carnival International Snowmobile Race is a 576-mile race from St. Paul, Minnesota, to Winnipeg, Manitoba, Canada.

Why is the front of a ski turned up?

The front of a ski is turned up to keep it from driving into the snow.

Which of the following American figure skaters was *not* a World *and* National Figure Skating Champion — Janet Lynn, Peggy Fleming, or Carol Heiss?

The answer is Janet Lynn. Lynn was the U.S. National Figure Skating Champion from 1969 to 1973, but has never won the World Figure Skating title. Fleming and Heiss, however, have held both titles. Peggy Fleming was the U.S. National Champion from 1966 to 1968 and the World Champion from 1966 to 1968. Carol Heiss was the National Champion from 1957 to 1960, and the World Champion from 1956 to 1960.

Beatrix Schuba and Gabriele Seyfert both won the Women's World Figure Skating Championship two times each. Where are these championship skaters from?

Beatrix Schuba, who won the Women's World Figure Skating Championship in 1971 and 1972, is from Austria. Gabriele Seyfert, the World Champion in 1969 and 1970, is from East Germany.

Walter Steiner of Switzerland made the longest ski jump ever measured. Did he jump 570 feet, 587 feet, or 591 feet?

Walter Steiner's jump of 587 feet 3 inches at Oberstdorf, West Germany, on March 10, 1973 was the longest ski jump ever measured. But Steiner fell upon landing, and the jump could not be counted as an official record.

The word *toboggan* comes from a Swedish word. True or false?

False. The word *toboggan* comes from the Micmac American Indian word *tobaakan.* Although not much is known about the origin of the toboggan, American Indians are thought to have been one of the first people to use them.

What is *skijoring*?

Skijoring is a high-speed winter sport in which a skier is towed across the snow by a low-flying aircraft. The record speed for skijoring is 109.23 mph, set by Reto Pitsch at St. Moritz, Switzerland, in 1956.

True or false? The first World Luge Championships were held in East Germany in 1953.

False. The first World Luge Championships were at Oslo, Norway, in 1953. Reichenberg, East Germany, was the site of the first European Luge Championships in 1914.

How long did the longest non-stop skiing marathon last? Was it 24, 36, or 48 hours?

The longest non-stop skiing marathon on record lasted 48 hours and covered 190.1 miles. It was achieved by Onni Savi of Finland, who began the marathon at noon on April 19, 1966 and finished skiing at noon on April 21.

Mike Woods, Jack Walters, and Ed Rudolph are all former U.S. National Skating Champions. Are they figure skaters or speed skaters?

Woods, Walters, and Rudolph are all speed skaters. Woods was the U.S. Champion in 1973; Walters, in 1971; and Rudolph, in 1961.

Which of these famous figure skaters won the U.S. Women's National Figure Skating Title the most times? Is it Janet Lynn, Peggy Fleming, or Tenley Albright?

Lynn, Fleming, and Albright all won the U.S. Women's Figure Skating title five times each. Janet Lynn won it in 1969, 1970, 1971, 1972, and 1973. Peggy Fleming was the U.S. Champion in 1964, 1965, 1966, 1967, and 1968. Tenley Albright won the title in 1952, 1953, 1954, 1955, and 1956.

As of 1978, how many consecutive World Cup Downhill titles has Franz Klammer of Austria won?

In 1978, at Laaz, Switzerland, Franz Klammer won his fourth consecutive World Cup Downhill title.

Who won the Men's Singles World Figure Skating title in 1978?

Charlie Tickner, the 1978 U.S. Champion, also won the Men's Singles World Figure Skating title in 1978. He was the first American to take the world title since Tim Wood won it in 1970.

When were metal skate blades first used for ice skating? Was it in the 1400s, the 1500s, or the 1600s?

Wide metal runners replaced bone blades in ice skates in the 1600s. Thin-edged metal skates came into use in the 1700s, and steel blades were introduced in the mid-1800s.

How long should ski sticks be? Should they reach the skier's waist, elbows, or armpits?

Ski sticks should reach a skier's arm pits.

In The Netherlands, there is an ice skating race that covers more than 124 miles. True or false?

It's true. The 124-mile, 483-yard race regularly held in The Netherlands is called the *Elfstedentocht*, which means "tour of the eleven towns."

Which college has won the most NCAA Team Skiing Championships? Is it the University of Colorado, Denver University, or Dartmouth University?

Denver University has won the NCAA Team Skiing Championship a total of 14 times to top Colorado's total of 9 and Dartmouth's 1. Colorado has been the title holder since 1972.

***Curling* is an extremely popular winter sport in Canada and Scotland. What is curling?**

Curling is an ancient sport, much like a variation of shuffleboard, but on ice. Players use a stick to shove huge, smooth, circular stones with handles on the top along the ice toward the center of a large circle — a *tee* — marked on the ice. The team whose stone stops nearest the tee scores a point. Players also carry regular brooms, which they use to sweep the ice in front of the sliding stones to make them go faster and farther.

Who holds the official world record for the longest ski jump?

The official record of 577 feet 5 inches is held by Toni Innauer of Austria, who made his record jump at Oberstdorf, West Germany, on March 6, 1976.

What is a *ski-bob*?

A *ski-bob* is a unique top-of-snow vehicle that looks like a bicycle frame fitted with skis. In ski-bobbing, the rider wears very short skis and sits on the ski-bob. He heads down the slopes, attempting to keep his balance — a tricky business. Ski-bobbing is a popular form of Alpine competition, and world championships are held in this event.

Karen Magnussen, the 1973 Women's Figure Skating Champion, is from what country?

Karen Magnussen is from Canada and was the Canadian National Figure Skating Champion in 1968 and from 1970 to 1973.

Snowmobiles cannot go faster than 100 mph. True or false?

False. The record speed for a snowmobile is 135.93 mph, and it was set by Don Pitzen of the United States on February 27, 1977 at Union Lake, Michigan.

In figure skating, the most difficult jump in the world is a triple axel. Only one skater has ever performed a triple axel. Is that skater from Japan, the United States, or Norway?

Gordon McKellen, a skater from the United States who was the U.S. Figure Skating Champion in 1973 and 1974, is the only man to ever perform a triple axel.

How many times was Dick Button the U.S. National Figure Skating Champion?

Dick Button was the U.S. National Figure Skating Champion for seven consecutive years, from 1946 to 1952. He was also the World Figure Skating Champion from 1948 to 1952.

In which year were the World Alpine Skiing Championships inaugurated? Was it 1929, 1931, or 1935?

The World Alpine Skiing Championships were inaugurated in 1931 at Murren, Switzerland.

In 1978, a U.S. speed skater from Madison, Wisconsin, won his sixth straight World Championship and his second straight World All-Around title at Goteborg, Sweden. Can you name that skater?

The answer is Eric Heiden. At the World Speed Skating Championships, Heiden skated the 500 meters in 39.01, the 5,000 meters in 7:20.80, and the 1,500 meters in 2:00.22, to earn his titles.

Where was skiing invented? Was it in the Scandinavian countries, in France, or in Siberia?

Skiing was invented in the Scandinavian countries. A rock carving of a skier dating back to 2000 B.C. has been found in northern Norway, and early skis dating back to 2500 B.C. have been found in Scandinavian bogs. The word *ski*, itself, comes from the Norwegian language.

In what country did the sport of curling originate?

In the 1890s, a drained pond near Dunblane, Scotland, uncovered a two-handled curling stone bearing the date 1551 — the earliest evidence of curling in any country.

In what country was the world's first artificial ice rink built?

The first artificial ice rink in the world was the Glaciarium, built in Chelsea, London, England, in 1876.

The largest indoor and outdoor artificial ice rinks in the world are in the United States. True or false?

False. The largest indoor artificial ice rink, with an ice area of 68,000 square feet, is in Canada. It's the Quadruple Rink at Burnaby, British Columbia, which was built in 1972. The largest outdoor artificial rink is the Fujikyu Highland Promenade Rink in Japan. Built in 1967, it has an ice area of 165,750 square feet, which is equal to 3.8 acres of ice.

True or false? A man once skied at the rate of 120.849 mph.

True. Tom Simons of the U.S. set the world speed record on skis at Cervinia, Italy, on July 11, 1976. No man or woman has ever gone faster than Simons' speed of 120.849 mph on skis.

FIELD SPORTS

Field hockey was played for the first time in England in 1277. True or false?

False. Field hockey is a very old game played by the ancient Persians and Egyptians. A drawing of two men playing field hockey was found in an Egyptian tomb dating back to around 2050 B.C. However, modern field hockey has its origins in England, with the game played there as early as 1277.

In which country was the first organized field hockey club formed? Was it in England, Scotland, or the United States?

The Blackheath Club, the first organized field hockey club, was formed in 1842 in England.

How wide and high is a field hockey goal?

A field hockey goal is 12 feet wide and 7 feet high.

How many time-outs is a team allowed in field hockey?

The answer is none. In field hockey, there are no time-outs and no substitutions.

In field hockey, are any of the players allowed to kick the ball?

Yes. Only one of the 11 players on a field hockey team, the goalkeeper, is allowed to kick the ball, and then only when it is in the striking circle.

Where did lacrosse originate? Was it in England, North America, or France?

The game of lacrosse originated in North America among the Iroquois Indians in the St. Lawrence Valley. Their version, *baggataway,* which means "the little brother of war," was played very violently. The game was later renamed by a French Canadian priest, Pierre de Charlevoix, because the Indians' stick reminded him of a bishop's *crozier,* or cross.

When lacrosse was played by the American Indians, as many as 1,000 young men participated in the game at one time. True or false?

It's astounding, but true. The Indian players, as many as a thousand, would gather out in the open prairie early in the morning. Their game of *baggataway* would begin at approximately 9 A.M. and continue nonstop, without any rest periods, until one team scored 100 goals, or until the sun went down.

Mike French is the NCAA's all-time leading scorer in lacrosse and the winner of the Lt. Raymond Enners Award as the Outstanding Player of the Year in 1976. Did French play for Johns Hopkins, Navy, or Cornell?

Mike French played for Cornell from 1973 to 1976, and totaled 191 goals and 296 points, topping the nation from 1974 to 1976.

How are points scored by teams in lacrosse?

Points are scored by firing the ball past the opposing goalkeeper into the goal or net. Scores count as 1 point each.

Which university had the first lacrosse team? Was it Princeton or Harvard?

Harvard formed a lacrosse team in 1881, and was followed the next year by Princeton. With the establishment of the United States Intercollegiate Lacrosse Association in 1882, lacrosse became more popular, until today the ILA has more than 50 member colleges.

How big is a lacrosse ball in circumference?

The solid white India rubber lacrosse ball is 8 inches around and weighs 5 ounces.

When was the first World Lacrosse Championship held? Was it in 1953, 1960, or 1967?

The first World Lacrosse Championship tournament was held in 1967. Toronto, Canada, hosted the games in which England, Canada, Australia, and the United States participated. The U.S. won all 3 of its games; Australia took 2; Canada, 1; and England, none. The second World Championship was held at Melbourne, Australia, in 1974 and was also won by the U.S. The 26-15 score in the 1974 tournament was the highest of any international match in history.

One of the greatest college lacrosse games of all time was played in 1976, when two undefeated teams — the University of Maryland and Cornell University — met for the National Collegiate Athletic Association's Lacrosse Championship. Which team won the 1976 lacrosse title?

With the score tied, 12 to 12, at the end of regulation time, Maryland and Cornell went into an overtime period — two mandatory 4-minute periods followed by sudden death, if necessary. In overtime, Cornell defeated Maryland, 16 to 13, to win the NCAA Lacrosse crown.

How many players are on a lacrosse team? Is the answer 8, 10, or 12 players?

There are 10 players on a lacrosse team, picked from a squad of no more than 19 players. The team is made up of 3 attack players, 3 midfield players, 3 defense players, and a goalkeeper.

True or false? Men and women both play lacrosse.

True. A modified version of lacrosse is played by women. In women's lacrosse, the field is 120 yards long and 80 yards wide. The goals are 100 yards apart. There are 12 players on each side and the game is made up of two 25-minute halves. There is no body checking and no substituting allowed.

In lacrosse, can all of the players touch the ball with their hands?

No. Only the goalkeeper is allowed to play the ball with his hands. The other players may kick the ball, but are penalized if they touch it with their hands.

True or false? Cornell University's lacrosse team did not lose a single game from 1976 to 1978.

True. Cornell put together three consecutive undefeated seasons between 1976 and 1978. In 1976, they beat the University of Maryland to win the lacrosse title, and in 1977 and 1978, they defeated Johns Hopkins University, giving them the National Collegiate Athletic Association lacrosse crown three years in a row.

How are lacrosse players penalized for serious rule infractions?

Lacrosse players who are penalized for unsportsmanlike behavior such as fighting, tripping, or illegal body checks are sent off the field for periods ranging from 30 seconds to 3 minutes.

Where was the modern game of polo first played? Was it in India, England, or Italy?

The modern game of polo was first played in India. In the middle 1800s, British planters joined the native Indians in playing their ancient game. Soon, polo was picked up by army officers stationed in India and subsequently brought back to England by them. The first real polo match was held near London in July of 1871.

Malcolm Stevenson, Cecil Smith, and Harry Payne Whitney have all made their marks in international polo. Did these polo stars play for the United States or Great Britain?

Stevenson, Smith, and Whitney all played polo in international competition for the United States.

True or false? The largest field used for any ball game is a polo field.

True. A polo field is made up of 12.4 acres, or a length of 300 yards and a width, without side-boards, of 200 yards — an area much longer and wider than a football field (360 feet by 160 feet).

If an unmounted player scores a goal in polo, does the point count?

No. According to the rules of the game, an unmounted player cannot score a goal.

The United States and Argentina scored a record number of goals in an international polo game in September, 1936. How many goals were scored in that game? Was it 30, 35, or 40 goals?

The most total goals ever scored in an international polo game is 30. They were scored during a game at Meadowbrook, Long Island, New York, in which Argentina beat the U.S. by the score of 21 to 9.

True or false? Teams that play against very good polo players are awarded free goals, or points, at the start of the game as a handicap.

True. Handicapping good players is polo's way of keeping the game competitive. The highest handicap ever awarded is 10 goals, with 38 players currently in that 10-goal handicap class. The latest players to be awarded a 10-goal handicap are A. Heguy and A. Harriot of Argentina.

How many periods are there in major polo tournaments?

There are usually six or eight periods, or *chukkers*, in major polo tournaments. Each chukker is 7 minutes long, with a 4-minute time-out between them for players to change ponies. A half-time break lasts 10 minutes.

True or false? In India, a game of polo was once played using elephants instead of polo ponies.

It's wacky, but true. It happened in 1976 at Jaipur, India. Men played a game of polo riding elephants instead of ponies, with a record crowd of 40,000 people turning out to watch the madcap match.

A well-known softball pitcher who played for the famous championship women's team, the Brakettes, won 735 games in her career. Can you name that pitcher?

The most famous of all women pitchers was fast pitch champion Bertha Reagan Tickey. Not only did Tickey win 735 games in her career, but she also threw 161 no-hitters to help her team to many world and national softball titles.

Has any player ever pitched a perfect game in softball?

Yes. It has been done twice. Richard Daris of the Monarchs pitched a perfect softball game on May 6, 1976 at Springfield, Massachusetts, and Michael DeMeo of Spindrift duplicated that feat on June 16, 1977 at Newport, Rhode Island.

Originally, the game of softball had several different names before it was officially dubbed *softball*. Do you know any of those names?

When the game was first invented in 1887, it was called *indoor baseball* since it was played indoors. The name was changed to *kitten ball* in 1895, and to *indoor-outdoor baseball*, or *playgound ball*, in 1908. Finally, in 1933, the name *softball* was officially adopted.

How many World Championships has the United States won in softball's men's division?

The U.S. took the World Championship of Softball in 1966 at Mexico City, in 1968 at Oklahoma City, and shared as co-winner with Canada in 1976 at Lower Hutt, New Zealand.

How long was the longest softball game ever played? Was it 50 hours, 60 hours, or 72 hours long?

The longest slow pitch softball game was 72 hours 3 seconds long. It was played in Singapore on December 28-30, 1977, by two U.S. Navy teams of 10 players each. The longest fast pitch softball game ever played was 54 hours long. It was played by two teams of 9 players from New Zealand's North Otago Softball Association on February 4-6, 1978.

The following runners all competed in the 1977 New York Marathon: Frank Shorter of the U.S. — an Olympic runner; Jerome Drayton of Canada, who won the Boston Marathon in 1977; and Bill Rodgers of the U.S., who won the New York Marathon in 1976. Which one of them won the race?

Bill Rodgers won the 1977 New York Marathon for the second year in a row. Drayton finished second, and Shorter dropped out when he pulled a hamstring muscle.

True or false? Jim Ryun was the first high school runner to run the mile in less than 4 minutes.

True. As a teen-ager in 1964, Jim Ryun of Wichita, Kansas, ran the mile in less than 4 minutes, to become the first schoolboy in the history of track to accomplish that feat. The following year, he set the National Interscholastic Track and Field record for the mile with a time of 3:58.3. Later, at the University of Kansas, Ryun bettered that time, with a 3:51.3 in 1966 and a 3:51.1 in 1967.

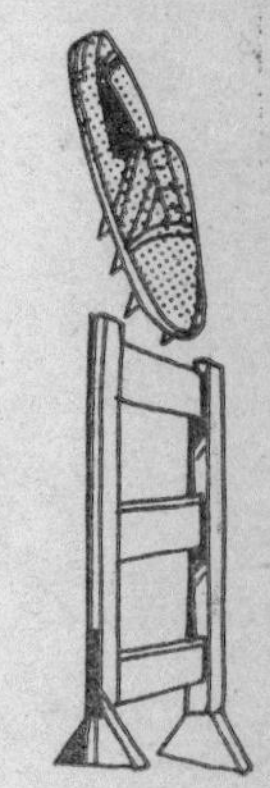

When Yuri Stepanov of Russia set a world record of 7'1" for the high jump in 1957, his record was called into question by the IAAF. Can you remember why?

Stepanov had worn a special shoe with a one-inch thick built-up sole at the Moscow competition. This "catapult shoe" was questioned by the International Amateur Athletic Federation, which debated its use for a year. Finally, Stepanov's record was accepted as valid . . . but the shoe was banned from further use.

Richard Wohlhunter of the United States is the holder of which two individual world records?

Richard Wohlhunter holds individual world records for 880 yards and for 1,000 meters. On June 8, 1974, Wohlhunter set one record for the 880 yards with a time of 1:44.1. Then on July 30, 1974, his time of 2:13.9 for 1,000 meters established another world record.

Who was the first man in history to run the mile in less than 4 minutes? Was it Roger Bannister, Jim Ryun, or Emil Zatopek?

Roger Bannister, an English medical student at Oxford University, was the first man to break the 4-minute barrier. He did it on May 6, 1954 at the Iffley Road track at Oxford. Racing against the clock, Bannister ran the mile in 3:59.4.

Dana Zatopkova is the oldest person to break a standard world track and field record. What event did she participate in and how old was she when she broke the record?

On June 1, 1958, Dana Zatopkova of Czechoslovakia broke the women's javelin record with a throw of 182 feet 10 inches at Prague, Czechoslovakia. When she established the new record, Dana was 35 years and 255 days old.

In 1978, Franklin Jacobs set an indoor track and field world record at the Millrose Games at Madison Square Garden in New York City. What record did Jacobs set?

Franklin Jacobs, the 5'8" star from Fairleigh Dickinson University in Rutherford, New Jersey, set a world indoor record for the high jump by clearing the bar at 7 feet 7¼ inches.

Who was the first man to run 100 yards in 9.1 seconds? Here's a hint. He later became a pro football star with the Dallas Cowboys.

The answer is Bob Hayes. In 1963, Hayes, then a student at Florida A & M Univeristy, ran 100 yards in 9.1 seconds at the first U.S. Championships held on rubberized asphalt.

True or false? Participants in track meets must wear shoes.

False. Mandatory attire includes only shorts and a jersey, or shirt, on which an identifying number can be affixed. Participants are *not* required to wear shoes. Athletes can compete in a track meet *with* shoes, *without* shoes, or wearing only *one* shoe.

Maren Seidler and Earlene Brown are well-known women athletes in track and field. Which event did they both compete in?

Maren Seidler and Earlene Brown are shot putters. Brown won the National Championship of the U.S. eight times, and Seidler set an American record for women in the shot put in 1974, with a toss of 56 feet 7 inches.

What is the field event pictured?

This is a *discus* — a round hardwood or plastic disc with a metal rim. It is used in a field event called the *discus throw*. The discus thrower stands in a ring 8' 2½" in diameter, with the discus held in one hand beneath his extended arm. He spins around to gain momentum, then stops and releases the discus, throwing, or sailing, it as far as he can.

Who holds the women's world indoor track record for the 3,000 meters? Is it Francie Larrieu or Jan Merrill?

Francie Larrieu's old record of 9:02.4 was shattered by Jan Merrill at the 1978 Canadian Championships at Montreal, when she ran the 3,000 meters in 8:57.6.

How many miles does a marathon race usually cover?

A marathon race usually covers 25 miles or more.

Bob Seagren is a famous long jumper. True or false?

False. Bob Seagren of the United States is the world class pole vaulter who has cleared over 18 feet.

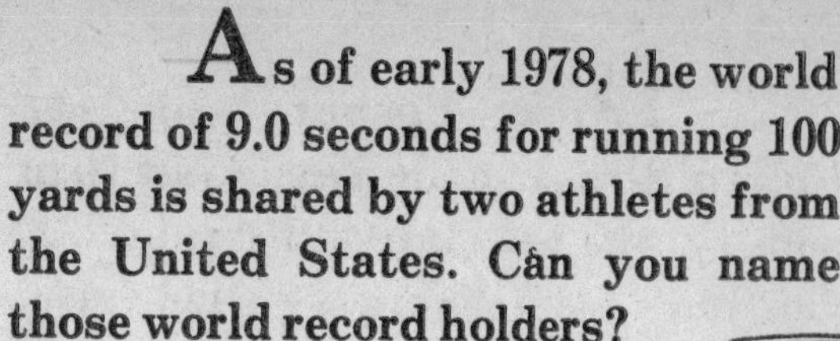

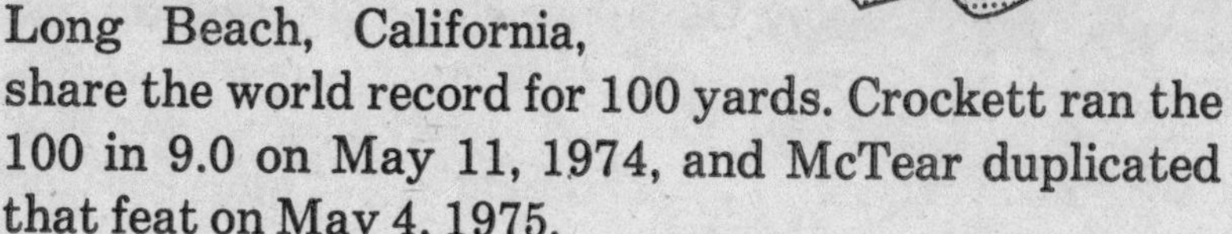

As of early 1978, the world record of 9.0 seconds for running 100 yards is shared by two athletes from the United States. Can you name those world record holders?

Ivory Crockett of Knoxville, Tennessee, and Houston McTear of Long Beach, California, share the world record for 100 yards. Crockett ran the 100 in 9.0 on May 11, 1974, and McTear duplicated that feat on May 4, 1975.

In track, there is an event where the athletes must run 3,000 meters and jump over 35 barriers, of which 7 are water jumps. What is that event?

The event is the steeplechase and it is probably the most physically demanding of all track and field events.

The world record of 29 feet 2½ inches for the long jump is held by an athlete from the United States. Can you name him?

Bob Beamon of the United States set the world record for the long jump at Mexico City, Mexico, on October 18, 1968.

How many indoor track world records did Houston McTear of the United States establish in 1978? Was it two, three, or five world records?

McTear, a sprinter, established three world indoor track records in 1978: the 60 meters in 6.54, the 60 yards in 6.11, and the 50 yards in 5.25.

True or false? A famous sprinter used to finish races by jumping through the tape at the finish line.

It sounds silly, but it's true. Charles W. Paddock of Los Angeles, celebrated as "the fastest human" in 1920, was famous for his jump finish, which was a flying leap through the tape at the finish line.

Dick Fosbury of the United States made track and field history in the late 1960s by inventing something called the *Fosbury Flop*. What is the Fosbury Flop?

The *Fosbury Flop* is an unorthodox style of high jumping invented by high jumper Dick Fosbury. In it, the jumper throws himself over the bar headfirst and literally backwards, landing on his back on the inflated cushion in the landing pit.

Can you name the woman athlete who holds the world record for the 100-yard dash?

Chi Cheng of Taiwan is the record holder. As of 1978, her record of 10.0 seconds for 100 yards, established on June 13, 1970, was still unbroken.

Who holds the record for the Boston Marathon?

Bill Rogers, a 31-year-old sporting goods shopkeeper, set the Boston Marathon speed record in 1979, with his time of 2 hours, 9 minutes, 27 seconds. Rogers became the first runner to win two consecutive Marathons since Aurele Vandendriessche of Belgium did it in 1963-64. Rogers' time in 1979 broke his own record of 2:9.55, set in 1975.

The runner who holds the National Interscholastic Track and Field record for the 2 miles won the NCAA University Division Cross Country Championship in 1970, 1971, and 1973. Can you name him?

The answer is Steve Prefontaine. At Corvallis, Oregon, in 1969, Prefontaine ran the 2 miles in 8:41.5, to set the high school record for that event. He later won the Cross Country Championship as a student at Villanova and the University of Oregon.

Jessie Owens of the United States once set a record for breaking the most world records in a single day. How many did he break to set that record?

On May 25, 1935, Jessie Owens became the only athlete to ever have his name entered in the record book six times in one day. He set records for 100 yards, the 220, the long jump, the 220 low hurdles, the 200-meter run, and the 200 low hurdles.

Henry Rono and Filbert Bayi are well-known names in track and field. Are Rono and Bayi sprinters or distance runners?

Henry Rono and Filbert Bayi are both distance runners. Rono ran the 5,000 meters in 13:08.4 to set a world record in 1978, and Bayi holds the world record of 3:32.2 for 1,500 meters, which he set in 1974.

When Roger Bannister ran the mile in less than four minutes for the first time in history, whose record did he break?

Roger Bannister broke the record of 4:01.4, set by Gunder Hagg of Sweden in 1945.

In 1977, at the 89th Annual AAU Championships in Los Angeles, Edwin Corley Moses of the United States set a new world record in the 400-meter hurdles. Can you name the man whose record Moses broke?

When Edwin Moses turned in a time of 47.45 in the 400-meter hurdles in 1977, he bettered his *own* world record of 47.64, set in 1976.

Dwight Stones is a well-known athlete in track and field. Which event does he compete in?

Dwight Stones is a high jumper and was the first man to clear a height of 7 feet 7 inches, doing it at the 1976 NCAA Track Championships at the University of Pennsylvania.

As a collegian, Marty Liquori was one of the best milers in the United States. Did Liquori go to school at Rutgers, Villanova, or Penn State?

Marty Liquori, the Cedar Grove, New Jersey, miler attended Villanova University and came into national prominence as a distance runner in 1969 when he defeated Jim Ryun of the University of Kansas (at that time the world record holder for the mile) at both the NCAA and AAU National Outdoor Track and Field Championships.

In 1976, a discus thrower threw the discus three times and set three world records. True or false?

True. It happened at the 1976 San Jose Invitational Track Meet. Mac Wilkins of the United States set a world record the first three times he threw the discus. His first toss traveled 229 feet, which was two feet farther than the world record he'd set in an track meet earlier that year. His second throw went 230 feet 5 inches, and his final effort sailed an unbelievable 232 feet 6 inches. Wilkins' distance is the current world record.

True or false? A woman athlete won the United States Championship in the 100-meter dash one year and won it again eighteen years later.

True. The woman was Stella Walsh, a Polish immigrant who was one of the world's first great female athletes. In 1930, at age 19, Walsh won her first U.S. Championship in the 100-meter dash. In 1948, she repeated as the U.S. Champion in that very same event. In addition to four U.S. Championships in the 100 meters, Walsh also won eleven 200-meter crowns, ten broad jump titles, six indoor 200 yards and two 50 yards.

Where is the world's longest annual walking event held? Is it in Canada, France, or Australia?

The world's longest annual walking event is held in France. It's the Strasbourg-Paris race, which was instituted in 1926. The race covers between 313 and 344 miles, depending on the course layout used for a year.

What is the world record for walking across the United States?

The record is exactly 53 days, 12 hours and 15 minutes, and it's held by John Lees of England, who left City Hall in New York City on April 11, 1972 and arrived at City Hall in Los Angeles, California, on June 3. Lees averaged 53.746 miles per day during his record-setting journey.

Plennie L. Wingo of Abilene, Texas, was a well-known long-distance walker with an odd habit. Do you remember what that habit was?

Plennie L. Wingo walked *backwards*. On April, 15, 1931, Wingo set out on a transcontinental backwards walk, leaving Santa Monica, California, and walking 8,000 miles to Istanbul, Turkey, where he arrived on October 24, 1932. At the spry age of 81 in 1976, Wingo celebrated the 45th anniversary of his marathon walk by tackling the 452 miles between Santa Monica and San Francisco in 85 days, also backwards. In all his reverse walks, Wingo used special mirrored glasses to see where he was going.

Ron Laird of the U.S. won more major walking titles than any other person. Did he win 52, 69, or 74 titles?

Ronald Owen Laird of the New York Athletic Club won a total of 65 U.S. National and 4 Canadian Championships from 1958 to 1976.

MORE SPORTS

Who won the 1978 United States Indoor Target Archery Championship? Was it Mike King or Rich McKinney?

Mike King of Kentwood, Michigan, scored 1,158 points to win the 1978 U.S. Men's Indoor Championship. Rich McKinney of Muncie, Indiana, was the 1977 Champion.

The gold bullseye (worth 9 points) on an archery target is encircled by four colored rings. Moving from the bullseye outwards, can you name the colors of those rings in the correct order?

Moving outwards, the colors of the rings on a target are: red (worth 7 points), blue (worth 5 points), black (worth 3 points), and white (worth 1 point).

True or false? Luann Ryon, one of the best women archers in the world, has never won the U.S. Indoor Championship.

False. Luann Ryon is not only the current U.S. Indoor Archery Champion, but is the current World Archery Champion in the women's division as well. These Championships followed on the heels of her National Archery Championships in 1976 and 1977.

Darrell Pace is one of the best-known male archers in the world. Is he from the United States, Great Britain, or Australia?

Darrell Pace is a citizen of the United States, a native of Reading, Ohio. In addition to an Olympic Gold Medal in archery in 1976, Pace was also the U.S. National Men's Champion and the men's title holder at the Championship of the Americas that same year.

Is it possible to shoot an arrow from a bow for a distance of more than a mile?

It can and has been done, but only with a footbow. The world record for the longest flight of an arrow using a footbow is 1 mile, 268 yards. That record was established by Harry Drake on October 24, 1971 at Ivanpah Dry Lake, California. The longest distance ever achieved with a hand bow, 1,077 yards, 3 inches, was set by Bruce Odle at Wendover, Utah, on September 11, 1976.

Which country has won the Men's International Badminton Championship the most times? Is it Indonesia, Japan, or Malaysia?

Indonesia has won the Thomas Cup, which is presented to the Men's International Championship team, six times. This is more than any other country. Malaysia is second, with four wins.

Rudy Hartono of Indonesia is probably the best living male badminton player in the world. How many times has Hartono won the men's singles event at the All-England Championships?

Rudy Hartono has won the All-England Singles Championship eight times, which is a record. He held the title from 1968 to 1974, and won it again in 1976.

Which country has won the Women's International Badminton Championship the most times? Is it Indonesia, the United States, or Japan?

The United States and Japan are tied, with three wins apiece. The Americans took the Uber Cup for their wins in 1956-57, 1959-60, and 1962-63. Japan took the Cup for the next three Championships: in 1965-66, 1968-69, and 1971-72.

Which tournament is universally regarded as the World Championship of Badminton?

The All-England Championship, instituted in 1899, is accepted as the World Championship Tournament of Badminton.

What is the highest speed ever reached on a bicycle? Is it 55.5 mph, 77.5 mph, or 140.5 mph?

Dr. Allan V. Abbot reached a speed of 140.5 mph on a specially modified racing bicycle at the Bonneville Salt Flats, Utah, on August 25, 1973, thereby setting a world record for the highest speed ever reached on a bicycle.

Teuvo Luohivuori of Finland holds the world record for cycling the farthest in a 24-hour period. How far did he ride to set the record? Was it 350.9 miles, 467.6 miles, or 515.8 miles?

Teuvo Luohivuori rode 515.8 miles on September 10, 1974, to set the world record for distance in a 24-hour period.

True or false? Bicycle racing is an event in the Olympic Games.

It's true. Cycling has been on the Olympic program since the revival of the Games in 1896. To date, the record for the most gold medals won by an individual in cycling is 3, and is shared by three men: Paul Masson of France, who won 3 gold medals in 1896; Francisco Verri of Italy, who duplicated that feat in 1906; and Robert Charpentier of France, who took 3 gold medals in cycling in 1936.

In which country was the first bicycle race held? Was it Great Britain, Germany, or France?

The earliest bicycle race on record took place in Paris, France, on May 31, 1868. It was a 2-kilometer (1.24-mile) race, won by James Moore of Great Britain.

One of the most famous bicycle races in the world is held annually in France. What is the name of that race?

That famous race is the Tour de France, a 3000-mile (4100-kilometer) race across the French countryside that lasts almost a month. The Tour de France Race has been held annually since 1903.

True or false? The first bicycles had no pedals.

True. Even though man knew how to use wheels and axles for thousands of years, the first bicycle was not invented until after 1800. It was a crude bike consisting of a seat on a frame between two wheels. It didn't have pedals or brakes, and the rider used his feet to push himself along. It wasn't until the 1870s that cycling became more popular, as rubber tires, metal spokes, and front wheel pedals were added to bicycles.

A man on a bicycle once rode over 100 miles in one hour. True or false?

False. The greatest distance ever covered in one hour by a man on a bicycle is 76 miles, 604 yards. It was accomplished by Leon Vanderstuyft of Belgium on September 30, 1928, on the Montlhery Motor Circuit in France.

Who won the 1977 Tour de France Bicycle Race? Was it Bernard Thevenet of France, Hennie Kuiper of Holland, or Eddy Merckx of Belgium?

Bernard Thevenet won the Tour de France Bicycle Race in 1977, finishing the 4100-kilometer race 48 seconds in front of Hennie Kuiper, who took second place honors. Eddy Merckx, the famous cyclist from Belgium, finished in sixth place.

Eddy Merckx of Belgium and Jacques Anquetil of France are cyclists who share the record for winning the Tour de France Bicycle Race the most times. How many times did they both win that famous race?

Eddy Merckx and Jacques Anquetil both won the Tour de France five times each: Merckx, in 1969, 1970, 1971, 1972, and 1974, and Anquetil, in 1957, 1961, 1962, 1963, and 1964.

Can you name the great billiard player who was known worldwide first as "The Boy Wonder of Billiards" and later as "Mr. Billiards"?

The answer is Willie Hoppe of the United States. At age 18, Hoppe won the World Billiard Championship from previously undefeated Maurice Vigneaux of France. Hoppe then went on to win hundreds of other billiard titles, reigning as the World Billiard Champion for over forty years.

In pocket billiards, what is a *scratch*?

A *scratch* is when the cue ball goes into a pocket. The player who sinks the cue ball forfeits his turn and may forfeit points.

Which of the following men held a U.S. Open *and* a World Pocket Billiards Championship — Joe Balsis, Luther Lassiter, or Steve Mizarek?

Balsis and Lassiter have held both U.S. and World Championships. Joe Balsis was the U.S. Open Champ in 1968 and 1974, and the World Champion in 1966. Luther Lassiter held the U.S. title in 1969 and was the world title holder in 1963, 1964, and 1967. Steve Mizarek was the U.S. Open Champion from 1970 to 1973, but never won the world title.

Who was the first pocket billiard player to *run*, or shoot into the pockets, 310 consecutive balls without a miss?

The answer is Willie Mosconi, the fabulous pool player and 13-time World Pocket Billiards Champion. Mosconi continued to boost his record, and in March, 1954, he set a new record by increasing his consecutive balls without a miss to 525.

Paul Newman and Jackie Gleason starred in a 1961 movie about expert pool players. What was the name of that movie?

The movie was *The Hustler.* The Gleason character was based on the real-life Rudolph "Minnesota Fats" Wanderone, the expert *hustler* — one who plays for money.

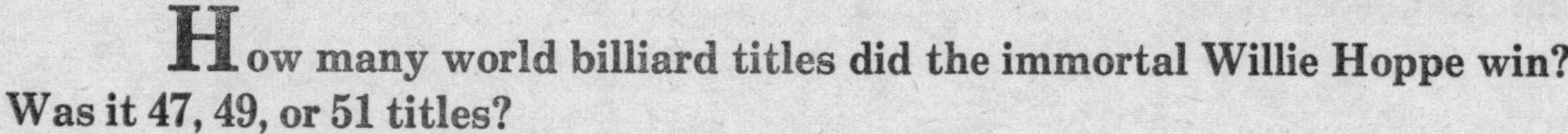

How many world billiard titles did the immortal Willie Hoppe win? Was it 47, 49, or 51 titles?

Willie Hoppe won a grand total of 51 world billiard titles from 1906 to 1952 — more than anyone in the history of billiards.

Which of the following men won more World Pocket Billiards Championships — Luther Lassiter or Irving Crane?

The answer is Irving Crane, who won the title six times (1942, 1946, 1955, 1968, 1970, and 1972). Lassiter was World Champion three times (1963, 1964, and 1967).

Jean Balukas is a famous billiard player. Has she ever won the U.S. Women's Open Pocket Billiards Championship?

Yes. As of 1977, 18-year-old Jean Balukas of Brooklyn, New York, had won the U.S. Women's Open six consecutive times, to set a new record in women's pocket billiards.

True or false? George Washington was a billiard player.

True. The game of billiards was brought to America in 1565 by Spaniards who settled in St. Augustine, Florida. The game quickly became popular in the New World. George Washington, Thomas Jefferson, and Alexander Hamilton were all fond of billiards, and played the game often.

What is the basic difference between a *billiard* and a *pool table*?

A *billiard table* does not have pockets while a *pool table* has pockets, or holes, in it. There are six pockets on a pool table: one pocket at each corner and one each in the middle of the longest sides.

What color are the following pool balls: the #1, the #2, and the #5?

The #1 ball is yellow, the #2 ball is blue, and the #5 ball is orange.

True or false? There is a billiard game called *snooker*.

True. *Snooker* is similar to pool, but more difficult. It is played on a larger table with 15 red balls and 6 variously colored balls. The red balls are worth 1 point and the colored balls range in value from 1 point to 6 points. A player must sink a red ball before he can shoot at a colored ball.

How many balls are used in three-cushion billiards?

Three balls are used in the game of three-cushion billiards. Two of them are white and one is red. One white ball has a small black mark on it to distinguish it from the other.

The earliest recorded mention of the modern game of billiards was from which country — France, Spain, or England?

The earliest recorded mention of the modern game comes from France in 1429. Although many people attribute the game's origin to England, the first recorded mention of billiards in England dates back to 1588 — more than a century later than the French. Historians also believe that the ancient Greeks and Egyptians might have played a crude form of billiards.

In pocket billiards, what is the white ball called?

The white ball is called the *cue ball*, since it is the ball hit with the cue stick as a player attempts to knock the numbered colored balls, called *object balls*, into the pockets.

Is there a billiard game called *balk line*?

Yes. *Balk line* is probably the most difficult of all billiard games. It is played on a pocketless table and is similar to 3-cushion billiards. Lines called balk lines are drawn on the table a specific distance from and parallel to the rails to form 8 spaces called *balk spaces*. A player can score only when both object balls come to rest in the same balk space.

True or false? In pocket billiards, the eight ball is colored dark blue.

False. The eight ball is always black.

If a billiard, or pool, player leans over the table and lifts both of his feet off the floor to take a shot, is that shot legal?

No! In all billiard games, shots must be made with at least one foot on the floor to be legal.

True or false? The ancient Egyptians bowled.

True. Nine pieces of stone used as pins and a stone ball to knock them over were found in the tomb of an Egyptian child who lived about 5200 B.C.

Can you name the pro bowler who won the most professional bowling titles during his career?

Earl Anthony of Tacoma, Washington, holds the récord with 30 PBA career titles. Anthony's 7 wins in 1975 and 7 in 1976 tied Billy Hardwick's single-season record.

Who won the men's and women's divisions of the World Cup of Bowling in 1977?

Arne Stroem of Norway, with a 609, and Rea Rennox of Toronto, Canada, with a 570, won the 1977 World Cup of Bowling.

Which bowlers hold the men's and women's records for the highest pinfall in *FIQ* competition?

In 1971, Ed Luther of the United States set the *FIQ* record for men with a score of 5,963 for 28 games. In the women's event, the record was set in 1975 by Annedore Haefker of West Germany, with a pinfall of 4,615 in 24 games.

Which bowler has the greatest lifetime earnings on the Professional Bowlers Association circuit — Earl Anthony or Dick Weber?

The answer is Earl Anthony. When Anthony won the $100,000 AMF Magic Score Open at Kissimmee, Florida, in February, 1978, he moved ahead of Dick Weber as the PBA's career leader in prize money. Anthony has earned a total of $556,936, while Weber has made $519,943 as a professional bowler.

What is the richest tournament on the Professional Bowlers Association circuit?

The $100,000 Firestone Tournament of Champions is professional bowling's richest tournament, with $25,000 going to the first-place winner. This tournament has been held annually at Akron, Ohio, the home of the PBA since its inception in 1965.

Which woman bowler has been called the "Queen of the Bowling World"?

Marion Ladewig, a former World Bowling Champion and winner of nine PBA Bowler of the Year Awards, has been nicknamed "Queen of the Bowing World." Her first five Awards came consecutively, from 1950 to 1954, then three more from 1957 to 1959. In 1963, when Ladewig was past 48 years old, she received her ninth Bowler of the Year Award.

Who won the Professional Bowlers Association Tournament in 1978 — Fred Jaskie, Marshall Holman, or Earl Anthony?

Fred Jaskie of Milwaukee, Wisconsin, won the 1978 PBA Tournament, defeating Marshall Holman of Medford, Oregon, by the score of 208 to 158.

Who bowled the most 300-point games during his career? Was it Elvin Mesger, George Billick, or Dick Weber?

The answer is Elvin Mesger of Sullivan, Missouri, who bowled twenty-six 300-point games. Second on the all-time list is George Billick of Old Forge, Pennsylvania, with a total of seventeen 300 games. Dick Weber is third, with sixteen.

Who was the winner of the first Firestone Tournament of Champions when it was inaugurated in 1965?

Billy Hardwick, the 1964 Bowler of the Year, was the Firestone Tournament winner in 1965.

In 1961, Dick Weber became the first bowler to ever win three professional tournaments in a row. Can you name the two men who duplicated Weber's feat?

Johnny Petraglia won three consecutive tournaments in 1971, and Mark Roth did it in 1977.

What is the world record for the highest number of consecutive strikes in sanctioned match play? Is it 25, 33, or 39 consecutive strikes?

On March 4, 1976, at Toledo, Ohio, John Pezzin made 33 consecutive strikes, to set a world record that isn't likely to be broken for quite some time.

True or false? Bull fighting began in sixteenth-century Spain as a way for men to demonstrate their courage to their fiancées.

Absolutely false. Bull fighting already existed in Spain as pure sport when the Romans arrived in Baetica (Andalusia) in the third century B.C.

At the end of a bull fight, the matador plunges his sword into the heart of the bull. What is this final act called?

The slaying of the bull is known as "the moment of truth."

In addition to the matadors, two other groups of men go into the ring with the bull. Do you know the names of those groups?

The *banderilleros* and *picadors* are in the ring as well. The *picadors*, armed with long lances and mounted on horses, wound the bull's goring muscle about his shoulder. The *banderilleros*, armed with long darts, go into the ring on foot after the *picadors* leave and stick their darts in the bull's neck. In this way, they anger the bull for the matador who enters the ring after they leave.

A man once became a millionaire by fighting bulls. True or false?

True. Manuel Perez, known as *El Cordobes*, became a multimillionaire as a bull fighter. In 1966, he had 111 fights, with his earnings averaging over $15,000 for every half hour he spent in the ring. Perez topped the $1 million mark in 1970, when he earned about $1,800,000 for 121 bull fights.

When is the word *touché* used in fencing?

The French word *touché* is used in informal fencing contests to acknowledge "hits" or "touchés" made on a fencer. The person hit says "*touché*" when touched by his opponent's blade. In competition, *touchés* are judged by five officials. In major foil and epée events, an official uses an electrical device that records touches by a bell and a light to keep score.

The world record for winning the most individual World Fencing Championships belongs to a fencer from Italy. True or false?

False. Christian d'Oriola of France holds the world record for winning the most individual World Fencing Championships. He won four individual titles in the men's foil division: in 1947, 1949, 1953, and 1954.

True or false? The earliest known practice of fencing as a sport was in Great Britain in the 1500s.

False. Fencing was practiced as a sport as early as 1360 B.C. in Egypt. It became a popular sport in England in the 1500s, when King Henry VIII founded the Corporation of Masters of Defense — the first governing organization for the sport.

Can you name the three types of weapons used in fencing?

The three weapons used in fencing are the *foil*, the *epée*, and the *saber*.

True or false? The University of Pennsylvania defeated the University of Notre Dame to capture the 1978 NCAA Fencing title.

False. In 1978, Notre Dame won its second straight National Collegiate Athletic Association Fencing Championship by defeating the University of Pennsylvania.

The English have won the most World Individual Gliding Championships. True or false?

False. Since the gliding title was established in 1948, West Germany has won more World Individual Championships in gliding than any other country — a total of five championships.

Hans-Werner Grosse of West Germany holds the world record for traveling the farthest distance in a glider. How far did he travel?

On April 25, 1972, Hans-Werner Grosse traveled 907.7 miles in his ASW-12 glider to set the world gliding distance record.

True or false? A man once used a hang-glider to descend 31,600 feet.

True. It was done by Bob McCaffrey of the United States. McCaffrey used a hang-glider to descend 31,600 feet from a hot air balloon over the Mojave Desert in California on November 21, 1976.

What is the farthest distance ever covered by a man on a hang-glider in free flight? Is it 47.81 miles, 61.68 miles, or 82.28 miles?

On June 14, 1977, Robert Pruitt of the United States went 61.68 miles on a hang-glider in free flight to set the distance record.

The first man to ever try to fly with a hang-glider was a monk in the 11th century. True or false?

True. An 11th century monk is reported to have flown from a 60-foot tower in Malmesbury Abby, Wiltshire, England, using a crude form of hang-glider.

True or false? No gymnast has ever chinned a bar one-handed more than ten times.

False. The record for one-handed chin-ups is 27! It was set in Hermann's Gym in Philadelphia in 1918 by a woman, Lillian Leitzel. The record for two-arm chins, 106, is held by William D. Reed, who established the mark on June 23, 1969.

Cathy Rigby, Nadia Comaneci, and Olga Korbut are three world-famous female gymnasts. Which countries do they come from?

Cathy Rigby is from the United States, Nadia Comaneci is from Romania, and Olga Korbut is from the Soviet Union.

True or false? Three gymnasts in the world have achieved a running triple back somersault on the ground.

False. Only one gymnast has ever successfully executed a running triple back somersault on the ground. Vadim Bindler of the U.S.S.R., a 16-year-old gymnast, accomplished that amazing feat in Kiev, in March of 1974.

What is the greatest number of sit-ups ever done by a person in two minutes?

On November 20, 1975, David G. Jones of Maryland did 123 sit-ups in two minutes, to set a world record that averages out to just a fraction more than 1 sit-up a second!

How high is the vaulting horse? Is it 3.3 feet, 4.4 feet, or 5.5 feet high?

The vaulting horse, which is a smooth, leather-covered mount, is 4.4 feet high, with a length of 5.25 feet and a width of 14 to 14.5 inches.

Where is the world's largest gymnasium found? Is it in the United States, the U.S.S.R., or South America?

The world's largest gymnasium is in the United States. It's Yale University's Payne Whitney Gymnasium in New Haven, Connecticut. The gym is equipped with 4 basketball courts, 3 rowing tanks, 28 squash courts, 12 handball courts, a roof jogging track, a 25-yard by 14-yard swimming pool, and an additional 55-yard long pool.

Gymnasts Boris Shakhlin and Larissa Semyonovna Latynina hold the men's and women's records respectively for winning the most individual world championships. Which one holds more individual world titles?

Boris Shakhlin and Larissa Semyonovna Latynina, both of the U.S.S.R., are tied, with 10 individual world championships apiece. Shakhlin won his 10 between 1954 and 1964, and Latynina won her 10 between 1956 and 1964.

The Associated Press selected a gymnast as the 1972 Female Athlete of the Year. Can you name her?

In 1972, the Associated Press named Russian gymnast Olga Korbut as the Female Athlete of the Year.

When performing a routine on the pommel, or side, horse, is the gymnast allowed to touch the apparatus with his feet or legs?

No. When performing on the pommel horse, only the gymnast's hands are allowed to touch the horse, and only on the handles. Points are subtracted from his score any time any other part of his body touches the horse.

Can you guess the world record for the most consecutive push-ups? Is it 6,026, 7,026, or 8,026 push-ups?

Thirteen-year-old Robert Louis Knecht of Minneapolis, Minnesota, set the world record when he did 7,026 consecutive push-ups in 3 hours and 56 minutes on February 5, 1976.

In 1974, Steve Hug became the first gymnast to win three straight All-Round NCAA titles since Joe Giallombardo of the University of Illinois did it in 1938-39-40. Which school was Hug attending when he won these three straight NCAA crowns? Was it Penn State, Stanford, or Duke?

Steve Hug was a student at the University of Stanford in 1972, 1973, and 1974 when he captured the All-Round Championship in Gymnastics of the National Collegiate Athletic Association.

What is the name of the pictured gymnastics apparatus?

If you said that apparatus is the uneven parallel bars, you're absolutely right. The uneven parallel bars are a special piece of equipment used by female gymnasts only. The higher bar is 7.5 feet from the floor, and the lower one, 4.9 feet.

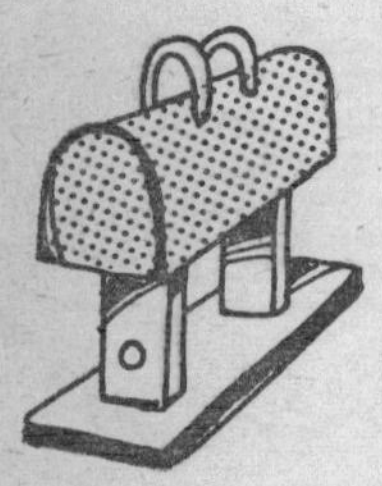

True or false? In 1978, the University of Cal State-Fullerton won the AIAW National Team Championship in Gymnastics.

False. The National Team Championship in Gymnastics of the Association for Intercollegiate Athletics for Women was won by Penn State in 1978. Cal State-Fullerton finished second in the competition.

Which of the following are *not* included in gymnastic floor exercises: somersaults, rhythmical body movements, tumbling vaults over a stationary horse, or handstands and other balance positions?

Vaults over a stationary horse are not included in floor exercises. Vaulting is a separate event.

True or false? In competition, male and female gymnasts perform on all the apparatus.

False. The rings -are used only by male gymnasts, and the balance beam is limited to female gymnasts.

What is the world record for the greatest recorded number of consecutive sit-ups? Is it 2,522, 12,522, or 25,222?

The world record for the greatest recorded number of sit-ups is 25,222. It was established at Idaho Falls High School's gymnasium on December 23, 1972 by Richard John Knecht, who was *8 years old* at the time. Richard did the 25,222 sit-ups in 11 hours and 14 minutes without having his feet pinned or knees bent.

After the collapse of ancient Greek society, gymnastics became a forgotten sport for hundreds of years until three countries rekindled the world's interest in the sport. Can you name those three countries?

Sweden, Germany, and Denmark all played a vital role in the development of modern gymnastics. In the early 1800s, all three countries began various types of gymnastics programs, which soon spread to other parts of the globe.

Who won the 1978 NCAA Gymnastics Championship — the University of Oklahoma or Arizona State University?

Oklahoma was the Gymnastics Champion of the NCAA in 1978. They edged Arizona State by the score of 439.350 to 437.075, to win the title.

Gymnasts often talk about keeping their bodies in a *pike position* while performing certain feats. What is a pike position?

A *pike position* is like a jackknife position in diving. The body is bent at the waist, the legs are straight, and the fingers touch or reach for the ankles.

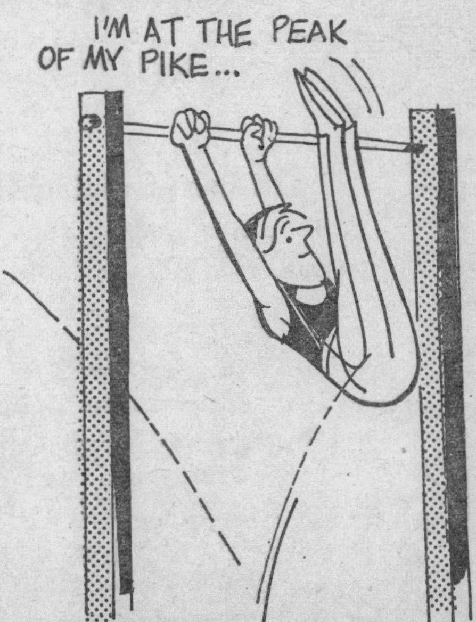

True or false? Male and female gymnasts do floor exercises to music.

False. Only female gymnasts do floor exercises to music, since they are expected to show grace rather than strength.

Which country has been a leading power in the World Cup of Field Handball?

Romania has dominated the World Championships in field handball, winning the men's title in the World Cup four times and the women's title, three times.

One-wall handball originated in a major Northeastern city and is seldom played outside that area. Can you name that city?

The American game of one-wall handball originated in and is most popular in New York City, where more than 1,800 one-wall courts can be found in parks and playgrounds.

Is it legal to play handball without gloves?

No. The rules state that gloves must be worn at all times. However, the gloves may be padded or unpadded.

How many games win a match in court handball?

If a player wins 2 out of 3 games in court handball, he wins the match.

Is an official handball hollow or solid?

The official black rubber handball is a hollow 2-ounce ball.

James Jacobs of the United States has been the most successful player in the United States Handball Association's Four-Wall Championships. How many singles titles has he won?

Between 1955 and 1965, James Jacobs won six USHA Singles Championships. In addition, he shared six doubles titles with Martin Decatur from 1960 to 1968.

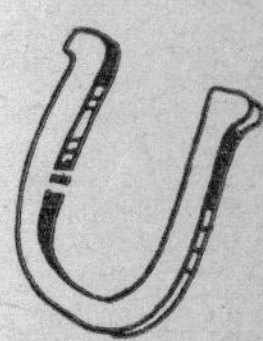

Between 1965 and 1977, how many times did Elmer Hohl win the World Horseshoe Pitching Championship?

Elmer Hohl of Wellesley, Ontario, was the World Horseshoe Pitching Champion six times. He won the coveted title in 1965, 1968, 1972, 1973, 1975, and 1977.

Who has won the most World and National Horseshoe Pitching Championships in the women's division? Is it Vicki Chapelle Winston or Ruth Hangen?

The answer is Vicki Chapelle Winston of Lamonte, Missouri. Between 1956 and 1975, Winston won a record total of nine world and national titles. Ruth Hangen of Getzville, New York, has a total of five. But she also holds the women's record for throwing consecutive ringers — 42 — set in 1974.

Was the 1977 World and National Women's Horseshoe Pitching Champion Ruth Hangen or Debby Michaud?

Debby Michaud took the World and National titles in 1977. Her record of 75.0% ringers gained her the World title over Ruth Hangen.

The record for winning the most World Championships in horseshoe pitching is held by Ted Allen. True or false?

True. Between 1933 and 1959, Ted Allen was the World Champion of Horseshoe Pitching ten times. He also holds the record for the most consecutive ringers — 72 — which he set in 1951. As an amusing sideline in the 1930s and 1940s, Allen toured the country performing a horseshoe-pitching act in which he pitched ringers from horseback, lit matches, and knocked cigars out of people's mouths with his horseshoes.

Where did the modern game of jai alai originate?

Most experts agree that modern jai alai originated during the 17th century with the Basque people who lived in the Pyrenees Mountains between Spain and France. However, a similar game, called *longue paume*, is said to have been played in 13th century Italy.

True or false? Jai alai is one sport where spectators and fans are openly encouraged to bet on the games.

True. In Spain, France, Italy, Cuba, Mexico, South America, The Philippines, and more recently the United States, spectators and fans are able to bet on which players they think will win.

Can a jai alai *cesta* be worn on a player's left hand?

No. According to the rules of the game, the *cesta* must be worn on a player's right hand and the ball can be thrown only with the right forearm.

Who was Chiquito de Cambo?

Chiquito de Cambo (Joseph Apesteguy), whose career spanned 38 years from 1900 to 1938, was one of the best jai alai players who ever lived.

Jai alai is the fastest and most dangerous ball game in the world. True or false?

True. Jai alai balls, or *pelotas*, are made of rubber or leather, and travel across the court at speeds of over 150 mph. They strike with the force of a bullet. Many jai alai players have been seriously injured when struck by the ball and some have actually been killed.

Is the world's largest jai alai building, or *fronton,* located in France, Spain, or the United States?

The largest *fronton* in the world is in Bridgeport, Connecticut. Built at a cost of $16,000,000, it seats 12,000 people.

In 1977, Jose Ramon Areitio made the world's fastest throw of a jai alai ball. Was that throw 158 mph, 166 mph, or 174 mph?

On June 1, 1977, at the Newport, Rhode Island, Jai Alai Fronton, Areitio threw a ball which was electronically timed at the speed of 174 mph.

The *Shihan*, or white belt, which is the highest award in judo, has never been bestowed on any man. True or false?

True. The highest award that judo has ever bestowed has been the extremely rare red belt, or *Judan*, which has been given only to seven men. There are also awards of a *Juichidan* — another red belt, a *Junidan* — a white belt twice as wide as an ordinary belt, and the *Shihan* — the highest award of all, but none of these titles has even been awarded.

True or false? The man who holds the world record for winning the most world judo titles is an Oriental.

False. A Dutchman, Willem Ruska, has won the most world judo titles, including the 1967 and 1971 heavyweight world titles and the 1972 Olympic heavyweight and open titles.

In judo and most martial arts, an important part of training is *kata*. What is *kata?*

Kata is a series of technical movements or sets of exercises. In these exercises, each move is arranged in much the same way that a dancer's or a gymnast's routine is planned.

Which Oriental unarmed combat technique was developed first — ju-jitsu, judo, or karate?

Ju-jitsu was one of the very first forms of unarmed combat. It is thought to be of pre-Christian Chinese origin and was practiced by the Japanese Samurai (knights). Ju-jitsu was a violent practice with tricks intended to maim or kill enemies. Judo was developed from ju-jitsu and other Japanese fighting arts by Dr. Jigoro Kano in 1882. Karate was developed by the unarmed populace of Okinawa as a method of attack and defense against armed Japanese aggressors. It was based on techniques devised from the sixth century Chinese art of *Chuan-Fa*.

Can you name the countries where *Tae-Kwan-Do* and *Kung Fu* were developed?

Tae-Kwan-Do is a military form of karate and was developed in Korea. *Kung-Fu* is believed to have originated in Nepal or Tibet, and was adopted within Chinese temples via India.

What does the word *karate* mean?

The word *karate* means "empty hands" or "empty-handed." In karate, feet, fists, hands, and elbows are used as weapons.

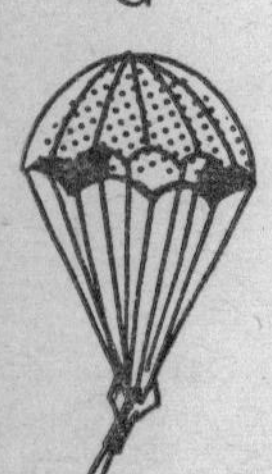

Bob Broadbere is the oldest man to ever make a parachute jump. How old was he when he made his record jump at Honiton, Devon, England, on July 10, 1977?

Broadbere of Great Britain was 85 years old when he set the record as the oldest man to make a parachute jump. The oldest woman to make a jump was Ann Howard Cassell, who was 69 years and 9 months, when she parachuted over Medford, New Jersey, on May 23, 1977.

Lt. Col. Ivan Savkin of the U.S.S.R. has made more parachute jumps than any other person. How many jumps has he made?

Savkin has made over 5,000 jumps during his career. The women's record is held by Patty Wilson of the U.S., who has made over 1,000.

Was Georgina "Tiny" Broadwick the first woman to parachute from an aircraft or the first woman to make a free fall?

Tiny Broadwick did both. In 1913, Broadwick became the first woman to parachute from an aircraft, and in 1914 she made the first free fall.

Which country was the overall winner at the Parchuting World Championships in 1977 — West Germany, Canada, or the United States?

Canada took top honors with 111 points. Although the United States took 42 points in the 8-man team event, the Americans placed third behind Canada and West Germany.

When was the first parachute jump from an airplane made? Was it in 1912, 1916, or 1920?

The first parachute jump from an airplane was made on March 1, 1912 by Captain Albert Berry of the United States Army.

Racquetball combines the elements of which two sports?

The basic elements of tennis and handball are combined in racquetball. The racquet, though smaller, is similar to a tennis racquet. Racquetball is played on a standard four-wall handball court, using all the walls, the ceiling, and the floor. However, the ball used in racquetball is livelier than the balls used in either tennis or handball.

Since the International Racquet Association was founded in 1969, who has won the most Masters Championships?

Bud Buehleisen of San Diego, California, holds the record with three Masters Singles Championships. He earned those titles in 1972, 1973, and 1977.

Two Texans held back-to-back Women's Singles Championships of the International Racquet Association from 1971 to 1975. Can you name them?

Jan Pasternak of Houston and Peggy Steding of Odessa brought the IRA's Women's Singles Championships to Texas between 1971 and 1975. Pasternak held the crown in 1971 and 1972, and Steding, from 1973 to 1975.

Can you name the 1977 winners of the International Racquetball Association's Open Singles Championships?

Jerry Zuckerman of St. Louis, Missouri, took the 1977 Men's Open, and Karin Walton of San Clemente, California, took the Women's.

Rodeos began in Texas when Mexican cowboys and American cowboys competed in contests to see who were the best all-around cowboys. True or false?

False. Rodeos originally began as celebrations held by cattle ranchers at the end of their annual round-ups. At those celebrations, various cowboys would demonstrate their skill at shooting, roping, riding, and bulldogging. Early rodeos were held all over the western frontier. The earliest recorded reference to a rodeo tells of one held in Santa Fe, New Mexico, in 1847.

How long must a cowboy stay on the back of a bull or bronco in order to meet the standard required riding time?

The required time for staying on the animal in bareback bronco riding, saddle bronco riding, and bull riding is 8 seconds.

Where is the largest rodeo in the world held? Is it in the United States, Mexico, or Canada?

The largest rodeo in the world is the Calgary Exhibition and Stampede, held annually at Alberta, Canada. In 1977, 1,069,830 people watched the Calgary Stampede, setting an all-time record for rodeo attendance.

During the years that he was the Rodeo Cowboy Association's All-Around Champion, Larry Mahan earned over $300,000. True or false?

True. Mahan earned some $308,149 during the six years in which he was the RCA's All-Around Champion. Of his 1966-1970 and 1973 Championships, his best year was in 1973, when he won $64,447 enroute to winning the All-Around title.

Which well-known cowboy holds the record for winning the most prize money in a single rodeo season? Is it Tom Ferguson of Miami, Oklahoma, or Larry Mahan of Brooks, Oregon?

The answer is Tom Ferguson. The Oklahoman won a record total of $114,000 in 1976 — the same year he was named the Rodeo Cowboy Association's All-Around Champion.

A normal regulation rodeo program includes six major events. How many of them can you name?

The six major events in a normal regulation rodeo program are: bareback bronco riding, calf roping, saddle bronco riding, bull or steer riding, steer wrestling, and steer roping. Some rodeos also include additional special features such as trick riding, chuck wagon races, barrel racing, team roping, quarterhorse cutting, and greased pig chasing.

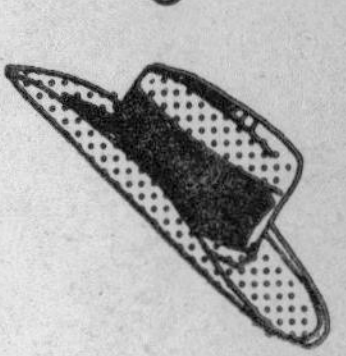

Where is America's biggest and most prestigeous outdoor rodeo held? Is it in Wyoming, Arizona, or Texas?

America's biggest and most prestigeous rodeo — Cheyenne's Frontier Days Rodeo — is held annually in Cheyenne, Wyoming. In 1977, the event drew more than 150,000 spectators and handed out $215,260 in prize money to the winners of the various competitions.

True or false? No cowboy in the world was ever able to ride a bucking bronco named *Midnight*.

True. The bronco *Midnight*, owned by Jim McNab of Alberta, Canada, made twelve appearances at the Calgary Stampede. During that time, not a single cowboy remained on *Midnight*'s back for the required 8 seconds.

Roller hockey began on the streets of New York. True or false?

False. Roller hockey, which is played just like ice hockey except that roller skates are used instead of ice skates, was introduced in London in the 1870s. The game also became popular as a street game in Canada at that time, and youngsters used branches as hockey sticks and frozen horse manure as pucks. It wasn't until the beginning of the 20th century that roller hockey found a new home with teen-agers on the streets of New York.

Who holds the world record for roller skating the greatest distance on a track in one hour? Is it an American, an Italian, or a German?

Alberto Civolani of Italy roller skated 23.133 miles in one hour on a track at Inzell, West Germany, on September 28, 1968, to set the record.

Are there World Championships in roller hockey?

Yes. The Roller Hockey Association has been sponsoring World Championships since 1936. Great Britain won the first title, but between 1947 and 1973, Portugal had the most wins of any country, with 11.

Who won the U.S. Women's Figure Roller Skating Championship in 1978? Was it Natalie Dunn or Joanne Young?

In 1978, Natalie Dunn of Bakersfield, California, won the U.S. Figure Roller Skating title. Joanne Young won the U.S. Championship in 1977, upsetting Dunn, the 1976 title holder. Dunn also held the 1977 World Artistic Championship.

What is the fastest speed ever reached by a person on roller skates? Is it 25.78 mph, 29.87 mph, or 30.12 mph?

The fastest speed ever reached on roller skates is 25.78 mph. Giuseppe Cantarella of Italy set that official world record on a road at Catania, Italy, on September 28, 1963.

Tom Smith of the U.S. holds a world shooting record in what event? Is it the center-fire pistol event or the skeet shooting event?

It's the center-fire pistol event. Smith set the record at Sao Paulo, Brazil, in 1963 by scoring 597 points out of a possible 600.

True or false? Rod Fitz-Randolph won the Individual Championship in the smallbore three-position competition sponsored by the NRA in 1977.

False. Lanny Bassham, an Olympic gold medal winner for the U.S. at the 1976 Games, beat Fitz-Randolph by 12 points to successfully defend his smallbore three-position title at the NRA's Rifle and Pistol Championships at Phoenix, Arizona, in 1977.

There is an annual International B.B. Gun Shooting Championship. True or false?

True. Sponsored by the Daisy B.B. Gun Company and the U.S. Jaycees, the annual Daisy/U.S. Jaycees International B.B. Gun Championship matches were held for the first time in 1965. The competition allows 10 shots from 15 feet in four shooting positions (prone, sitting, kneeling, and standing).

What kind of targets are used in skeet shooting and trap shooting?

The targets used in skeet and trap shooting are saucer-shaped clay targets which are commonly referred to as *clay pigeons*. When hit correctly, they are reduced to dust.

Bob Munden of Kansas City, Missouri, is reputed to be the fastest quick-draw expert in the world. How fast can he draw and hit a man-sized silhouette at 21 feet?

Munden can draw and hit a man-sized silhouette at 21 feet in a record 0.0175 seconds, making him the "World's Fastest Gun."

True or false? The famous Annie Oakley could split a playing card at 30 paces.

True. Annie Oakley, one of the best shots of all time, could split playing cards, hit dimes in mid-air, and shoot cigarettes out of her husband's mouth, all at 30 paces. For 35 years, she consistently demonstrated her ability to hit 100 out of a possible 100 targets in trap shooting.

In 1977, Joseph Clemmons won the United States Skeet Shooting Championship. How many points did Clemmons score out of a possible 300 to win his title?

During the three-day competition at Pacific, Missouri, Clemmons scored 295 out of a possible 300 to win the U.S. Skeet Shooting Championship in 1977. At that same competition, Ira Hill successfully defended her women's title with a score of 277 out of 300.

Angelo Scalzone and Michel Carrega share the world record for trap shooting. Is that record 190, 199, or 200 hits out of a possible 200?

The world record is 199 hits out of a possible 200. Scalzone of Italy set the record at Munich, Germany, in 1972, and Carrega of France equaled it at Thun, Switzerland, in 1974.

A marksman once hit 32,860 consecutive pine cubes tossed into the air. True or false?

True. Using two auto-loading 22-caliber guns, marksman Tom Frye of the United States hit 32,860 consecutive 2½" pine cubes tossed into the air, then went on to hit 100,004 out of 100,010.

When was the pistol invented?

The pistol was invented in 1540 in Pistoia, Italy, and got its name from the town.

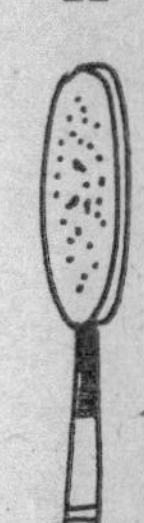

Between 1968 and 1978, how many North American Singles Squash Championships has Sharif Khan won?

Sharif Khan of Toronto, Canada, has won the North American Singles title in squash nine times in that ten-year period. Khan had six consecutive wins from 1969 to 1974, then three more between 1976 and 1978.

Vic Niederhoffer has won four United States National Singles Championships in squash, but he has never won the North American title. True or false?

False. Vic Niederhoffer of New York, the 1972-75 United States National Singles Champion, took the 1975 North American title, breaking Sharif Khan's six-year winning streak.

Between 1968 and 1977, which school has won the most U.S. National Intercollegiate Championships in squash — Harvard or the University of Pennsylvania?

Harvard took six National Championships in that ten-year period to Pennsylvania's one.

Since the introduction of International World Championships in squash, which country has taken the most titles?

Australia has taken four International Championships in squash — the most of any country since the title was introduced in 1967.

True or false? It has been estimated that table tennis balls can travel at speeds of over 100 miles per hour.

True. Tests made by German researchers have measured smashed balls at speeds up to 105.6 mph.

In the 1977 world rankings, China had four women table tennis stars in the top ten. True or false?

True. Although the number-1-ranked player was a Korean, China captured 2nd, 3rd (two in a tie), and 5th places.

G. Viktor Barna has won more World Championships in table tennis than any other man. Is Barna from Romania, Hungary, or Sweden?

G. Viktor Barna, the five-time Men's Singles Table Tennis Champion of the World, is from Hungary. Barna took the title in 1930, 1932-33-34-35. In addition, Barna, playing with two different partners, won the world title in the men's doubles division 8 times: from 1929 to 1935, and again in 1939.

Which country has won the most World Championships in table tennis? Is it Japan, Romania, or Hungary?

Since the World Championships were first instituted in 1926-27, Hungary has by far dominated the sport of table tennis by winning 34 titles: 5 men's singles, 8 men's doubles, 4 men's mixed doubles, 6 women's mixed doubles, and 11 team titles.

In official table tennis games, players are required to wear black shirts. Do you know why?

Players are required to wear black shirts so they'll form a background against which the fast traveling ball may be seen.

True or false? A man once bounced on a trampoline for 179 hours to set a record.

True. Geoffrey Morton of Australia bounced on a trampoline for 179 hours from March 7 to March 14, 1977, to set a record for trampoline bouncing. During the marathon, Morton was allowed one 5-minute break per hour.

Men and women compete as a team in the synchronized trampoline event at the U.S. Trampoline Association National Open Championships. True or false?

False. Separate events are held for two-man and two-woman teams in synchronized trampoline events.

In what year was the sport of trampolining first developed?

Although trampolines were used in circuses as early as the Middle Ages, trampolining did not become a sport until 1936 when the prototype "T" model trampoline was developed and patented by George Nissen of the United States.

How many times did Judy Wills of the United States win the Women's World Trampolining title?

Judy Wills won the Women's World Championship five times, which is a feat no other trampolinist, male or female, has ever duplicated. She took the title every year from 1964 to 1968.

A **former basketball superstar played professional volleyball for the Orange County (Florida) Stars in 1977. Can you guess who that ex-NBA star is? Here's a hint. He still holds most of the individual scoring records in the National Basketball Association.**

Wilt "The Stilt" Chamberlain, the NBA's leading scorer in career points, made his debut as a professional volleyball player for the Stars in 1977. That same year, he was named President of the International Volleyball Association.

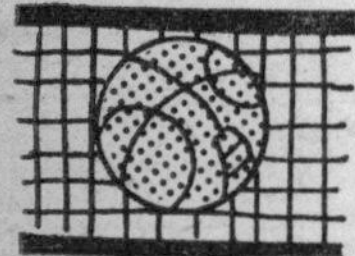

How high above the ground is an international volleyball net?

An international volleyball net is 7' 11½" above the ground. The net itself is 3 feet wide and slightly more than 30 feet long.

True or false? Professional volleyball is now played in the United States.

True. The International Volleyball Association, a professional league, began operation in the United States in 1974. As of 1977, there were seven teams in the IVA: The Tucson (Arizona) Sky, the Denver (Colorado) Comets, the Santa Barbara (California) Spikers, the El Paso/Juarez (Texas) Sol, the Phoenix (Arizona) Heat, the Orange County (Florida) Stars, and the San Diego (California) Breakers.

How many players are on a volleyball team?

There are six players on a volleyball team. They usually line up in three rows on the court: three players in the first row near the net, one in the middle of the second row, and two in the last row. The ball is served by a player in the last row standing at the base line at the right-hand corner. Players *rotate*, or alternate positions, so that each player gets a chance to play a different position.

Which team was the IVA Champion in 1977?

The Orange County Stars took the 1977 Volleyball Championship.

Which country has won the most World Championships in volleyball? Is it the U.S.S.R., Japan, or the United States?

Since the World Championships were instituted in 1949, the U.S.S.R. has won more men's and women's volleyball titles than any other country, taking the men's title 5 times: 1949, 1952, 1960, 1962, and 1968, and the women's title 6 times: 1952, 1956, 1960, 1968, 1970, and 1973.

True or false? There is no such thing as a one-man volleyball team.

False. Bob L. Schaffer of Suffern, New York, is a one-man volleyball team. Schaffer specializes in playing against 6-man volleyball teams singlehandedly and has a very impressive record. Since 1963, he has played 2,105 volleyball games against 6-man teams and has *lost only three times*!

In which country was the game of volleyball invented — the United States, Great Britain, or France?

Volleyball was invented in the United States in 1895 by William G. Morgan at the Y.M.C.A. gymnasium at Holyoke, Massachusetts. Originally the game was called *Minnonette*, but was changed later to "Volleyball" because of the type of play involved in vollying, or continually hitting the ball back and forth over the net.

A volleyball player can pass the ball to himself, hitting it twice in succession. True or false?

False. A player is not allowed to touch the ball two consecutive times. However, he can pass the ball to another player who can pass it back to him. Each team is allowed to pass the ball three times before hitting it back over the net.

A famous weightlifting movie called *Pumping Iron* starred a well-known weightlifter and body builder. Can you name him?

The star of the movie *Pumping Iron* (which is a popular new slang term for lifting weights) was Arnold Schwarzenegger, who won five straight Mr. Universe titles and held the top title in body building — Mr. Olympia. Schwarzenegger is 6' 2" tall and weighs 240 pounds. He has a 57-inch chest, 22-inch biceps, and a 31-inch waist.

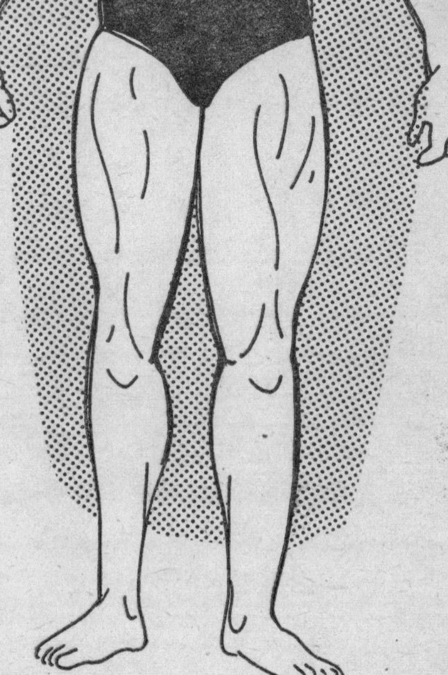

All International Powerlifting Federation records in the super heavyweight division (over 242½ lbs.) were held by one man up to 1978. Do you know who he is?

That super heavyweight is Don Reinhoudt of the United States. In 1975, Reinhoudt set the bench press record of 606¼ pounds and the dead lift record of 885½ pounds. The following year, he set the squat record of 934 pounds. Reinhoudt's bench press record was broken in 1978 by Doug Young, who pressed 611½ pounds.

Who was the first man to lift over 400 pounds?

Charles Rigoulot, a French professional weightlifter, was the first man to lift over 400 pounds. He lifted 402½ lbs. on February 1, 1929.

True or false? A woman weightlifter once lifted 4,232 pounds.

False. The record lift by a woman is held by Mrs. Josephine Schauer Blatt of the United States, who lifted 3,564 pounds at the Bijou Theatre in Hoboken, New Jersey, on April 15, 1895.

What is the difference between a *dumbbell* and a *barbell*?

A *dumbbell* is a short bar, about a foot long, with weights on it. It is held in one hand. A *barbell* is a longer bar, usually about five feet or longer, with weights on it. It is held in two hands.

At the 1977 World Weightlifting Championship in Stuttgart, West Germany, the top three winners were East Germany, the U.S.S.R., and Hungary. Can you place them in their order of finish?

The U.S.S.R. took first place at the World Weightlifting Championship, sweeping all the points in the flyweight, featherweight, middleweight, light heavyweight, and super heavyweight divisions. East Germany was second and Hungary, third.

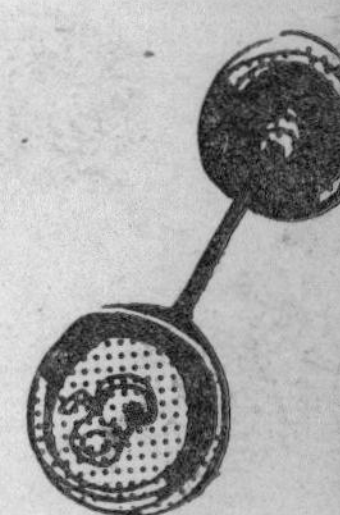

In powerlifting competitions, entrants have to perform three different lifts. Can you name them?

The three lifts performed in competitive powerlifting are the *deep knee bend*, or *squat*; the *two hands bench press*; and the *two hands dead lift*. In none of those lifts does the competitor have to raise the weight above his head.

As of 1978, which weightlifter holds the official world record for lifting the most total weight? Is it Khristo Plachkov of Bularia or Vasili Alexeev of the U.S.S.R.?

The answer is Vasili Alexeev, who lifted a total weight accumulation of 981 pounds on September 1, 1977.

The 1927 welterweight champion pressed 160 pounds overhead with one arm. Can you name him?

That 146-pound weightlifter was Siegmund Klein, who also two-arm pressed 233½ pounds over his head to arm's length. At age 76, Klein still practices weightlifting today.

True or false? A man once lifted 6,270 pounds.

True. Paul Anderson of the United States, a 5' 10", 364-pound Olympic weightlifter, raised 6,270 pounds off tresses in a back lift at Toccoa, Georgia, on June 12, 1957. Anderson's feat set a non-competition record for the heaviest weight ever lifted by a human being.

All of the official world weightlifting records in the flyweight division are held by one man. Is that weightlifter from the U.S.S.R., from the United States, or from West Germany?

All of the records in the flyweight division are held by Aleksandr Voronin of the U.S.S.R. Veronin set the snatch record in 1977, with a lift of 240¼ pounds and the jerk record in 1976, by lifting 310¾ pounds. In 1977, he set the record for lifting the most total weight — 540 pounds.

William J. Cobb holds the record as the heaviest wrestler in history. Can you remember the name he fought under?

If you said "Happy" Humphrey, you're correct. The 802-pound Georgian was known in the early 1960s for his suffocating powers.

True or false? Wrestling bouts are 12 minutes long.

False. Wrestling bouts last 9 minutes and are made up of three 3-minute rounds.

Dan Gable of the United States is the winningest amateur wrestler of all time. Out of 299 bouts, how many did he win?

Between college bouts and the Olympics, Dan Gable won 293 out of 299 wrestling bouts from 1963 to 1973 in the 150-pound class. During that time, Gable was an NCAA wrestling champion, was named the National Collegiate Athletic Associations's Outstanding Wrestler in 1969, and won a gold medal at the 1972 Olympics in the lightweight division.

From 1928 to 1971, one school dominated the NCAA Wrestling Championships by winning the team title thirty times. Was that college the University of Oklahoma, Oklahoma State University, or Penn State?

Oklahoma State University was that wrestling powerhouse, with thirty NCAA Team Championships in the 43-year period from 1928 to 1971. In that same period, the University of Oklahoma took NCAA wrestling titles six times, while Penn State took only one.

True or false? Aleksandr Medred of the U.S.S.R. holds the record for the most World Wrestling Championships.

True. Medred, a free-styler, won ten world titles from 1964 to 1972, including light-heavyweight, heavyweight, and super-heavyweight Olympic titles.

Ed "Strangler" Lewis held world wrestling titles in 1920, 1922, and 1928, but he is best known for his amazingly successful career record. Do you know what that record is?

During "Strangler's" 44-year wrestling career, he fought 6,200 bouts and lost only 33!

Which school won the NCAA Wrestling Championship in 1978? Was it the University of Iowa or Iowa State University?

The University of Iowa, coached by Dan Gable — the winningest wrestler in history, won the 1978 NCAA wrestling title by beating its biggest rival, Iowa State, by the slim margin of 94½ to 94.

What is the name of the traditional Japanese wrestling sport that pits enormous wrestlers against each other in a circular ring?

The answer is *Sumo* wrestling — a sport which has been practiced in Japan since 23 B.C. In *Sumo,* wrestlers weighing 300 pounds and more square off against each other in a small ring. The object is to force the opponent out of the ring any way possible. The wrestler forced out is the loser.

True or false? The highest paid professional wrestler in the world is Andre "The Giant" Roussimoff.

True. As a professional wrestler, Andre "The Giant" Roussimoff earned $400,000 in 1975.

Which country won the World Cup for wrestling in 1978? Was it the United States or the U.S.S.R.?

The U.S.S.R. won the 1978 World Cup in wrestling — their sixth in a row. The Russians won the Cup with 12 points, finishing 4 points ahead of the second-place U.S. team.

When is a wrestler awarded a *fall*?

A wrestler is awarded a *fall* if he is able to pin his opponent's shoulders to the mat for 1 second in college competition and ½ second in international competition.